Emergency Response Guidebook

All inquiries should be addressed to Skyhorse Publishing, 307 West 36th Street, 11th Floor, New York, NY 10018.

Skyhorse Publishing books may be purchased in bulk at special discounts for sales promotion, corporate gifts, fund-raising, or educational purposes. Special editions can also be created to specifications. For details, contact the Special Sales Department, Skyhorse Publishing, 307 West 36th Street, 11th Floor, New York, NY 10018 or info@ skyhorsepublishing.com.

Skyhorse® and Skyhorse Publishing® are registered trademarks of Skyhorse Publishing, Inc.®, a Delaware corporation.

Visit our website at www.skyhorsepublishing.com.

10 9 8 7 6 5 4 3 2 1

Library of Congress Cataloging-in-Publication Data is available on file.

ISBN: 978-1-62087-802-6

Printed in China

Emergency Response Guidebook

A Guidebook for First Responders during the Initial Phase of a Dangerous Goods/Hazardous Materials Transportation Incident

U.S. Department of Transportation

Skyhorse Publishing

SHIPPING DOCUMENTS (PAPERS)

Shipping Documents (Papers) are synonymous and can be found as follows:
- Road – kept in the cab of a motor vehicle
- Rail – kept in possession of a crew member
- Aviation – kept in possession of the aircraft pilot
- Marine – kept in a holder on the bridge of a vessel

Shipping Documents (Papers) provide vital information regarding the hazardous materials/dangerous goods to initiate protective actions*

Information provided:
- 4-Digit Identification Number, UN or NA (go to Yellow Pages) **
- Proper Shipping name (go to Blue Pages)
- Hazard Class or Division number of material
- Packing Group
- Emergency Response Telephone Number
- Information describing the hazards of the material (entered on or attached to shipping document)

EXAMPLE OF PLACARD AND PANEL WITH ID NUMBER

The 4-digit ID Number may be shown on the diamond-shaped placard or on an adjacent orange panel displayed on the ends and sides of a cargo tank, vehicle or rail car.

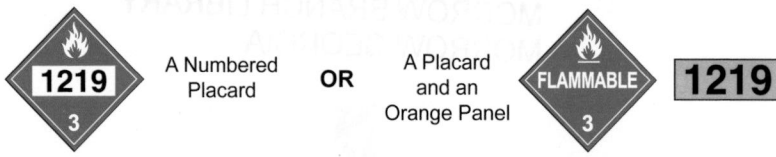

* For the purposes of this guidebook, the terms hazardous materials/dangerous goods are synonymous.
** After January 1, 2013 in the United States, the identification number **must** appear first in the basic description. For example, "UN2744, Cyclobutyl chloroformate, 6.1, (3, 8), PG II". This is currently optional in Canada.

HOW TO USE THIS GUIDEBOOK
RESIST RUSHING IN !
APPROACH INCIDENT FROM UPWIND, UPHILL OR UPSTREAM
STAY CLEAR OF ALL SPILLS, VAPORS, FUMES, SMOKE AND SUSPICIOUS SOURCES

STEP ONE: IDENTIFY THE MATERIAL AND USE ANY OF THE FOLLOWING:

- **IDENTIFICATION NUMBER** (4-DIGIT ID AFTER UN/NA) FROM A:
  - PLACARD
  - ORANGE PANEL
  - SHIPPING PAPER OR PACKAGE

- **NAME OF THE MATERIAL** FROM A:
  - SHIPPING DOCUMENT OR PACKAGE

STEP TWO: IDENTIFY 3-DIGIT GUIDE NUMBER, USE:

- ID NUMBER INDEX in yellow-bordered pages or
- NAME OF MATERIAL INDEX in blue-bordered pages

  Guide number supplemented with the letter **(P)** indicates that the material may undergo violent polymerization if subjected to heat or contamination.

  INDEX ENTRIES HIGHLIGHTED IN GREEN are a TIH (Toxic Inhalation Hazard) material, a chemical warfare agent or a Dangerous Water Reactive Material (produces toxic gas upon contact with water).

  IDENTIFY ID NUMBER AND NAME OF MATERIAL IN TABLE 1 – INITIAL ISOLATION AND PROTECTIVE ACTION DISTANCES (the green-bordered pages).

  IF NECESSARY, BEGIN PROTECTIVE ACTIONS IMMEDIATELY (see Protective Actions page 288). If no protective action required, use the information jointly with the 3-digit guide.

  IF A REFERENCE TO A GUIDE CANNOT BE FOUND AND THIS INCIDENT IS BELIEVED TO INVOLVE DANGEROUS GOODS:
  - Use GUIDE 111, UNTIL ADDITIONAL INFORMATION BECOMES AVAILABLE
  - Use GUIDE 112, EXPLOSIVES (other than 1.4 and 1.6)
  - Use GUIDE 114, EXPLOSIVES (1.4 and 1.6)

STEP THREE: TURN TO THE NUMBERED GUIDE (the orange-bordered pages) READ CAREFULLY.

IF A PLACARD IS THE ONLY SOURCE OF INFORMATION, turn to pages 6-7 and **use the 3-digit guide next to the placard and Proceed to Numbered Guide in orange-bordered pages.**

AS A LAST RESORT: IF ONLY THE CONTAINER CAN BE IDENTIFIED, CONSULT THE TABLE OF RAIL CAR AND ROAD TRAILER IDENTIFICATION CHART (pages 8-9). INFORMATION ASSOCIATED WITH THESE CONTAINERS IS FOR WORST-CASE SCENARIOS.

CALL THE EMERGENCY RESPONSE TELEPHONE NUMBER:

- Listed on the shipping paper, if available.
- If shipping paper is not available, IMMEDIATELY CALL the **appropriate emergency response agency telephone number listed on the inside back cover of this guidebook.**
- Provide as much information as possible, such as the name of the carrier (trucking company or railroad) and vehicle number.

BEFORE AN EMERGENCY – BECOME FAMILIAR WITH THIS GUIDEBOOK!
First responders must be trained in the use of this guidebook.

SAFETY PRECAUTIONS

RESIST RUSHING IN!

APPROACH CAUTIOUSLY FROM *UPWIND, UPHILL* OR *UPSTREAM*:
- Stay clear of *Vapor, Fumes, Smoke* and *Spills*
- Keep vehicle at a safe distance from the scene

SECURE THE SCENE:
- Isolate the area and protect yourself and others

IDENTIFY THE HAZARDS USING ANY OF THE FOLLOWING:
- Placards
- Container labels
- Shipping documents
- Rail Car and Road Trailer Identification Chart
- Material Safety Data Sheets (MSDS)
- Knowledge of persons on scene
- Consult applicable guide page

ASSESS THE SITUATION:
- Is there a fire, a spill or a leak?
- What are the weather conditions?
- What is the terrain like?
- Who/what is at risk: people, property or the environment?
- What actions should be taken – evacuation, shelter in-place or dike?
- What resources (human and equipment) are required?
- What can be done immediately?

OBTAIN HELP:
- Advise your headquarters to notify responsible agencies and call for assistance from qualified personnel

RESPOND:
- Enter only when wearing appropriate protective gear
- Rescue attempts and protecting property must be weighed against you becoming part of the problem
- Establish a command post and lines of communication
- Continually reassess the situation and modify response accordingly
- Consider safety of people in the immediate area first, including your own safety

ABOVE ALL: Do not assume that gases or vapors are harmless because of lack of a smell—odorless gases or vapors may be harmful. Use **CAUTION** when handling empty containers because they may still present hazards until they are cleaned and purged of all residues.

NOTIFICATION AND REQUEST FOR TECHNICAL INFORMATION

Follow the steps outlined in your organization's standard operating procedures and/or local emergency response plan for obtaining qualified assistance. Generally, the notification sequence and requests for technical information beyond what is available in this guidebook should occur in the following order:

1. **NOTIFY YOUR ORGANIZATION/AGENCY**
   - Based on information provided, this will set in motion a series of events
   - Actions may range from dispatching additional trained personnel to the scene, to activating the local emergency response plan
   - Ensure that local fire and police departments have been notified

2. **CALL THE EMERGENCY RESPONSE TELEPHONE NUMBER ON THE SHIPPING DOCUMENT**
   - If shipping paper is not available, use guidance under next section **"NATIONAL ASSISTANCE"**

3. **NATIONAL ASSISTANCE**
   - Contact the appropriate emergency response agency listed on the inside back cover of this guidebook
   - Provide as much information about the hazardous material and the nature of the incident
   - The agency will provide immediate advice on handling the early stages of the incident
   - The agency will also contact the shipper or manufacturer of the material for more detailed information if necessary
   - The agency will request on-scene assistance when necessary

4. **PROVIDE AS MUCH OF THE FOLLOWING INFORMATION AS POSSIBLE**:
   - Your name, call-back telephone number, FAX number
   - Location and nature of problem (spill, fire, etc.)
   - Name and identification number of material(s) involved
   - Shipper/consignee/point-of-origin
   - Carrier name, rail car or truck number
   - Container type and size
   - Quantity of material transported/released
   - Local conditions (weather, terrain)
   - Proximity to schools, hospitals, waterways, etc.
   - Injuries and exposures
   - Local emergency services that have been notified

HAZARD CLASSIFICATION SYSTEM

The hazard class of dangerous goods is indicated either by its class (or division) number or name. Placards are used to identify the class or division of a material. The hazard class or division number must be displayed in the lower corner of a placard and is required for both primary and subsidiary hazard classes and divisions, if applicable. For other than Class 7 or the OXYGEN placard, text indicating a hazard (for example, "CORROSIVE") is not required. Text is shown only in the U.S. The hazard class or division number and subsidiary hazard classes or division numbers placed in parentheses (when applicable), must appear on the shipping document after each proper shipping name.

Class 1 - **Explosives**

Division 1.1	Explosives with a mass explosion hazard
Division 1.2	Explosives with a projection hazard
Division 1.3	Explosives with predominantly a fire hazard
Division 1.4	Explosives with no significant blast hazard
Division 1.5	Very insensitive explosives with a mass explosion hazard
Division 1.6	Extremely insensitive articles

Class 2 - **Gases**

Division 2.1	Flammable gases
Division 2.2	Non-flammable, non-toxic* gases
Division 2.3	Toxic* gases

Class 3 - **Flammable liquids (and Combustible liquids [U.S.])**

Class 4 - **Flammable solids; Spontaneously combustible materials; and Dangerous when wet materials/Water-reactive substances**

Division 4.1	Flammable solids
Division 4.2	Spontaneously combustible materials
Division 4.3	Water-reactive substances/Dangerous when wet materials

Class 5 - **Oxidizing substances and Organic peroxides**

Division 5.1	Oxidizing substances
Division 5.2	Organic peroxides

Class 6 - **Toxic* substances and Infectious substances**

Division 6.1	Toxic*substances
Division 6.2	Infectious substances

Class 7 - **Radioactive materials**

Class 8 - **Corrosive substances**

Class 9 - **Miscellaneous hazardous materials/Products, Substances or Organisms**

* The words "poison" or "poisonous" are synonymous with the word "toxic".

INTRODUCTION TO THE TABLE OF PLACARDS

USE THE TABLE OF PLACARDS ONLY WHEN THE ID NUMBER OR PROPER SHIPPING NAME IS NOT AVAILABLE.

The next two pages display the placards used on transport vehicles carrying dangerous goods with the applicable reference GUIDE circled. Follow these steps:

1. **Approach scene from upwind, uphill or upstream at a safe distance to safely identify and/or read the placard or orange panel. Use binoculars if available.**

2. **Match the vehicle placard(s) with one of the placards displayed on the next two pages.**

3. **Consult the circled guide number associated with the placard. Use that guide information for now. For example:**

   - Use GUIDE (127) for a FLAMMABLE (Class 3) placard

   - Use GUIDE (153) for a CORROSIVE (Class 8) placard

   - Use GUIDE (111) when the DANGER/DANGEROUS placard is displayed or the nature of the spilled, leaking or burning material is not known. Also use this GUIDE when the presence of dangerous goods is suspected but no placards can be seen.

   If multiple placards point to more than one guide, initially use the most conservative guide (i.e., the guide requiring the greatest degree of protective actions).

4. **Guides associated with the placards provide the most significant risk and/or hazard information.**

5. **When specific information, such as ID number or proper shipping name, becomes available, the more specific Guide recommended for that material must be consulted.**

6. **Asterisks (*) on orange placards represent explosives "Compatibility Group" letters; refer to the Glossary (page 375).**

7. **Double asterisks (**) on orange placards represent the division of the explosive.**

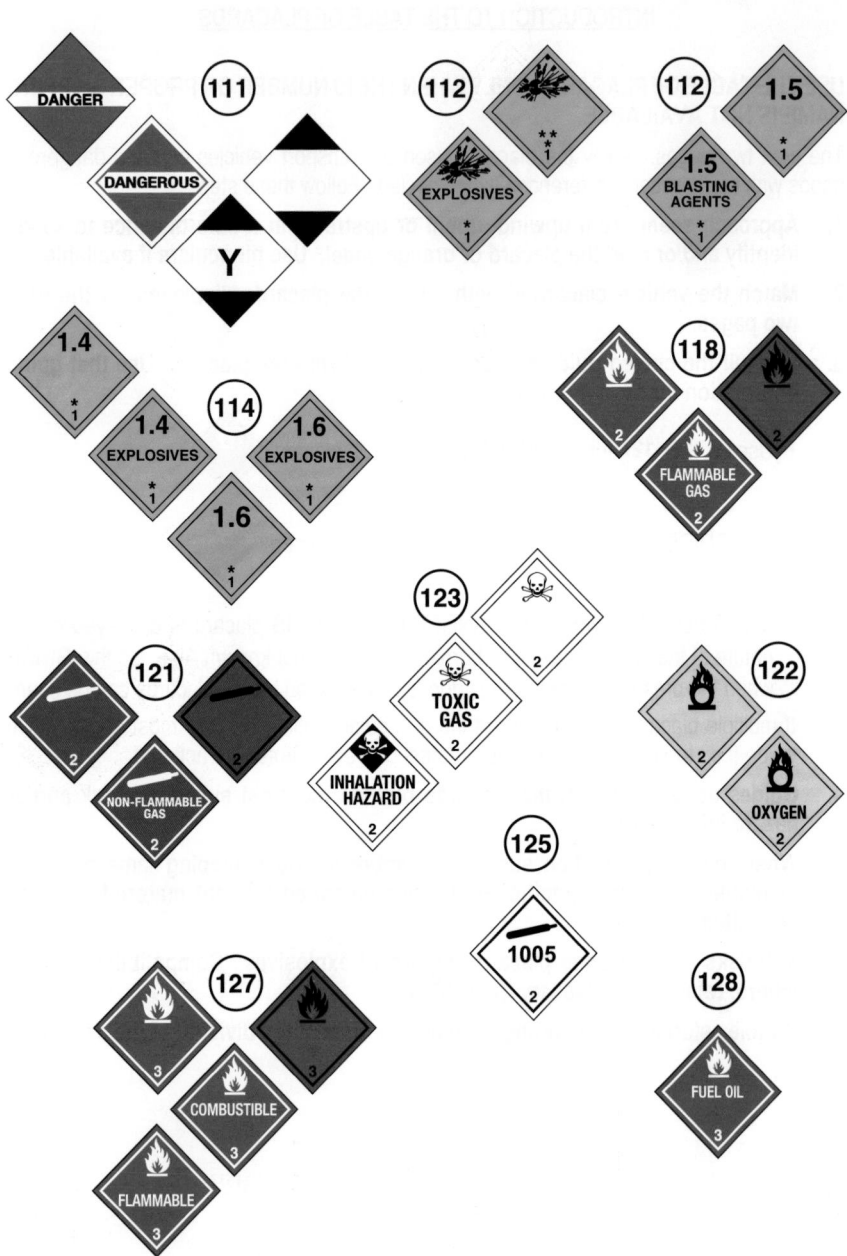

RESPONSE GUIDE TO USE ON-SCENE
USING THE SHIPPING DOCUMENT, NUMBERED PLACARD, OR ORANGE PANEL NUMBER

(134) FLAMMABLE SOLID

(136) SPONTANEOUSLY COMBUSTIBLE

(139) DANGEROUS WHEN WET

(143) OXIDIZER 5.1

(148) ORGANIC PEROXIDE 5.2

(153) TOXIC POISON INHALATION HAZARD 6

(158) INFECTIOUS SUBSTANCE INFECTIOUS INFECTIEUX UN3373

(163) RADIOACTIVE RADIOACTIVE I RADIOACTIVE II RADIOACTIVE III 7

(153) CORROSIVE 8

(171) 9

DANGER

THIS UNIT IS UNDER FUMIGATION WITH
_____ APPLIED ON
Date _____ Time_____

DO NOT ENTER

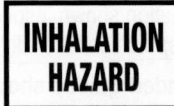

DANGER

This unit is under fumigation with | Cette unité est sous fumigation au
(Name of fumigant) | (Nom du fumigant)
Applied on | Depuis le
Date | Date
Time | Heure
DO NOT ENTER | DÉFENSE D'ENTRER

INHALATION HAZARD

MARINE POLLUTANT

RAIL CAR IDENTIFICATION CHART*

Hopper Car Dry Bulk (140)

Box Car Mixed Cargo (111)

Pressure Tank Car Compressed Liquefied Gases (117)
(Closed Dome Only on top)

Low Pressure Tank Car Liquids (131)
(Closed Dome and Outlets on top)

REPORTING MARKS & CAR NUMBER
LOAD LIMIT (POUNDS OR KG)
EMPTY WEIGHT OF CAR
PLACARD HOLDER
TANK TEST & SAFETY VALVE TEST INFORMATION
CAR SPECIFICATION
COMMODITY NAME
TC PERMIT NUMBER

UNION TANK CAR CO
UTLX 00000
LD LMT 000000
LT WT 00000

SR 0000
00000
DOT 111A100 W-1
SAFETY VALVE /S LB
TESTED 00 00
TEST DUE 00 00

REPORTING MARKS & CAR NUMBER
CAPACITY IN GALLONS OR LITERS
PLACARD HOLDER

UTLX 00000
CAPY 00000 GALS US

CAUTION: Emergency response personnel must be aware that rail tank cars vary widely in construction, fittings and purpose. Tank cars could transport products that may be solids, liquids or gases. The products may be under pressure. It is essential that products be identified by consulting shipping documents or train consist or contacting dispatch centers before emergency response is initiated.

The information stenciled on the sides or ends of tank cars, as illustrated above, may be used to identify the product utilizing:

a. the commodity name shown; or

b. the other information shown, especially reporting marks and car number which, when supplied to a dispatch center, will facilitate the identification of the product.

* **The recommended guides should be considered as last resort if the material cannot be identified by any other means.**

ROAD TRAILER IDENTIFICATION CHART*

DOT406, TC406, SCT-306
Non-pressure Liquid Tank
(MC306, TC306) (131)

MC338, TC338, SCT-338
Cryogenic Liquid Tank
(TC341, CGA341) (117)

DOT407, TC407, SCT-307
Low Pressure Chemical Tank
(MC307, TC307) (137)

Compressed Gas/
Tube Trailer (117)

DOT412, TC412, SCT-312
Corrosive Liquid Tank
(MC312, TC312) (137)

Dry Bulk Cargo
Trailer (134)

MC331, TC331, SCT-331
High Pressure Tank (117)

Mixed Cargo (111)

DOT407, TC407, DOT412, TC412
Vacuum Loaded Tank
(TC350) (137)

Intermodal Tank (117)

CAUTION: This chart depicts only the most general shapes of road trailers. Emergency response personnel must be aware that there are many variations of road trailers, not illustrated above, that are used for shipping chemical products. The suggested guides are for the most hazardous products that may be transported in these trailer types.

* **The recommended guides should be considered as last resort if the material cannot be identified by any other means.**

HAZARD IDENTIFICATION NUMBERS
DISPLAYED ON SOME INTERMODAL CONTAINERS

Hazard identification numbers utilized under European and some South American regulations, may be found in the top half of an orange panel on some intermodal bulk containers. The United Nations 4-digit identification number is in the bottom half of the orange panel.

The hazard identification number in the top half of the orange panel consists of two or three digits. In general, the digits indicate the following hazards:

2 - Emission of gas due to pressure or chemical reaction

3 - Flammability of liquids (vapors) and gases or self-heating liquid

4 - Flammability of solids or self-heating solid

5 - Oxidizing (fire-intensifying) effect

6 - Toxicity or risk of infection

7 - Radioactivity

8 - Corrosivity

9 - Risk of spontaneous violent reaction

NOTE: The risk of spontaneous violent reaction within the meaning of digit 9 include the possibility, due to the nature of a substance, of a risk of explosion, disintegration and polymerization reaction followed by the release of considerable heat or flammable and/or toxic gases.

- Doubling of a digit indicates an intensification of that particular hazard (i.e., 33, 66, 88).

- Where the hazard associated with a substance can be adequately indicated by a single digit, the digit is followed by a zero (i.e., 30, 40, 50).

- A hazard identification number prefixed by the letter "X" indicates that the substance will react dangerously with water (i.e., X88).

HAZARD IDENTIFICATION NUMBERS
DISPLAYED ON SOME INTERMODAL CONTAINERS

The hazard identification numbers listed below have the following meanings:

20	Asphyxiant gas
22	Refrigerated liquefied gas, asphyxiant
223	Refrigerated liquefied gas, flammable
225	Refrigerated liquefied gas, oxidizing (fire-intensifying)
23	Flammable gas
239	Flammable gas which can spontaneously lead to violent reaction
25	Oxidizing (fire-intensifying) gas
26	Toxic gas
263	Toxic gas, flammable
265	Toxic gas, oxidizing (fire-intensifying)
268	Toxic gas, corrosive

30	Flammable liquid, or flammable liquid or solid in the molten state with a flash point above 60°C, heated to a temperature equal to or above its flash point, or self-heating liquid
323	Flammable liquid which reacts with water, emitting flammable gas
X323	Flammable liquid which reacts dangerously with water, emitting flammable gas
33	Highly flammable liquid
333	Pyrophoric liquid
X333	Pyrophoric liquid which reacts dangerously with water
336	Highly flammable liquid, toxic
338	Highly flammable liquid, corrosive
X338	Highly flammable liquid, corrosive, which reacts dangerously with water
339	Highly flammable liquid which can spontaneously lead to violent reaction
36	Flammable liquid, toxic, or self-heating liquid, toxic
362	Flammable liquid, toxic, which reacts with water, emitting flammable gas
X362	Flammable liquid, toxic, which reacts dangerously with water, emitting flammable gas
368	Flammable liquid, toxic, corrosive
38	Flammable liquid, corrosive or self-heating liquid, corrosive
382	Flammable liquid, corrosive, which reacts with water, emitting flammable gas
X382	Flammable liquid, corrosive, which reacts dangerously with water, emitting flammable gas
39	Flammable liquid which can spontaneously lead to violent reaction

40	Flammable solid, or self-reactive substance, or self-heating substance
423	Solid which reacts with water, emitting flammable gas, or flammable solid which reacts with water, emitting flammable gas, or self-heating solid which reacts with water, emitting flammable gas

HAZARD IDENTIFICATION NUMBERS
DISPLAYED ON SOME INTERMODAL CONTAINERS

X423	Solid which reacts dangerously with water, emitting flammable gas, or flammable solid which reacts dangerously with water, emitting flammable gas, or self-heating solid which reacts dangerously with water, emitting flammable gas
43	Spontaneously flammable (pyrophoric) solid
X432	Spontaneously flammable (pyrophoric) solid which reacts dangerously with water, emitting flammable gas
44	Flammable solid, in the molten state at an elevated temperature
446	Flammable solid, toxic, in the molten state at an elevated temperature
46	Flammable solid, toxic, or self-heating solid, toxic
462	Toxic solid which reacts with water, emitting flammable gas
X462	Solid which reacts dangerously with water, emitting toxic gas
48	Flammable or self-heating solid, corrosive
482	Corrosive solid which reacts with water, emitting flammable gas
X482	Solid which reacts dangerously with water, emitting corrosive gas
50	Oxidizing (fire-intensifying) substance
539	Flammable organic peroxide
55	Strongly oxidizing (fire-intensifying) substance
556	Strongly oxidizing (fire-intensifying) substance, toxic
558	Strongly oxidizing (fire-intensifying) substance, corrosive
559	Strongly oxidizing (fire-intensifying) substance which can spontaneously lead to violent reaction
56	Oxidizing (fire-intensifying) substance, toxic
568	Oxidizing (fire-intensifying) substance, toxic, corrosive
58	Oxidizing (fire-intensifying) substance, corrosive
59	Oxidizing (fire intensifying) substance which can spontaneously lead to violent reaction
60	Toxic substance
606	Infectious substance
623	Toxic liquid which reacts with water, emitting flammable gas
63	Toxic substance, flammable
638	Toxic substance, flammable, corrosive
639	Toxic substance, flammable, which can spontaneously lead to violent reaction
64	Toxic solid, flammable or self-heating
642	Toxic solid which reacts with water, emitting flammable gas
65	Toxic substance, oxidizing (fire-intensifying)
66	Highly toxic substance
663	Highly toxic substance, flammable
664	Highly toxic solid, flammable or self-heating

HAZARD IDENTIFICATION NUMBERS
DISPLAYED ON SOME INTERMODAL CONTAINERS

665	Highly toxic substance, oxidizing (fire-intensifying)
668	Highly toxic substance, corrosive
X668	Highly toxic substance, corrosive, which reacts dangerously with water
669	Highly toxic substance which can spontaneously lead to violent reaction
68	Toxic substance, corrosive
69	Toxic substance which can spontaneously lead to violent reaction
70	Radioactive material
78	Radioactive material, corrosive
80	Corrosive substance
X80	Corrosive substance which reacts dangerously with water
823	Corrosive liquid which reacts with water, emitting flammable gas
83	Corrosive substance, flammable
X83	Corrosive substance, flammable, which reacts dangerously with water
839	Corrosive substance, flammable, which can spontaneously lead to violent reaction
X839	Corrosive substance, flammable, which can spontaneously lead to violent reaction and which reacts dangerously with water
84	Corrosive solid, flammable or self-heating
842	Corrosive solid which reacts with water, emitting flammable gas
85	Corrosive substance, oxidizing (fire-intensifying)
856	Corrosive substance, oxidizing (fire-intensifying) and toxic
86	Corrosive substance, toxic
88	Highly corrosive substance
X88	Highly corrosive substance which reacts dangerously with water
883	Highly corrosive substance, flammable
884	Highly corrosive solid, flammable or self-heating
885	Highly corrosive substance, oxidizing (fire-intensifying)
886	Highly corrosive substance, toxic
X886	Highly corrosive substance, toxic, which reacts dangerously with water
89	Corrosive substance which can spontaneously lead to violent reaction
90	Miscellaneous dangerous substance; environmentally hazardous substance
99	Miscellaneous dangerous substance transported at an elevated temperature

PIPELINE TRANSPORTATION

In North America, hazardous materials are transported through millions of miles of underground pipelines and related structures that can contain natural gas, natural gas liquids, crude oil, gasoline, diesel fuel, anhydrous ammonia, carbon dioxide, jet fuel and other commodities. Although pipelines are buried, there are above-ground structures and signs indicating the presence of underground transmission pipelines (see page 19 for U.S. pipeline location information). Natural gas also is transported via underground distribution pipelines.

Gas Pipelines

Natural Gas Transmission Pipelines

Large-diameter, steel pipelines transporting flammable, toxic and non-toxic natural gas at very high pressure.

Structures: Compressor Station Buildings, Valves, Metering Stations, and Aerial Patrol Markers.

Markers: "Warning, Caution, or Danger" appear at road, railroad, and water crossings, or may be posted at property boundaries and include operator's emergency Point-of-Contact (POC) and product transported.

Natural Gas Distribution Pipelines

Natural gas is delivered directly to customers via distribution pipelines--typically smaller-diameter, lower-pressure pipelines, and can be steel, plastic, or cast iron.

Structures: Regulator stations, customer meters and regulators, and valve box covers are the only above-ground indicators of gas distribution pipelines.

Gas Gathering and Gas Well Production Pipelines

Gas gathering/gas well production pipelines collect "raw" natural gas from wellheads and transport product to gas-processing and/or gas-treating plants. These gathering pipelines carry natural gas mixed with some level of gas liquids, water and, in some areas, contaminants such as hydrogen sulfide (H_2S).

Structures – Compressor Station Buildings, Valves, Metering Stations, and Aerial Patrol Markers.

Markers – Often appear at road, railroad, and water crossings. Signs may be posted at property boundaries. Signs include operator's POC and product transported. Warning, Caution, or Danger will appear on signs.

Note: Pipelines transporting natural gas containing dangerous levels of H_2S may have signs that say: "Sour Gas" or "Poison Gas".

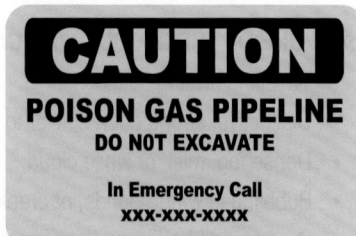

For Natural Gas Pipeline Incidents

Two important things to remember:

- Never attempt to extinguish a gas fire; this could prolong/worsen incident/cause another leak in the pipeline.
- Never attempt to operate pipeline valves; this could prolong/worsen incident/cause another leak in the pipeline.

SIGNS OF GAS PIPELINE RUPTURE:

- Loud roaring or explosive sound; OR
- Large flames and loud roaring noise.

Follow these steps:

- Immediately evacuate area;
- Move upwind, away from flames; prevent individuals from entering;
- If no flames present, do not start/turn off vehicles/electrical equipment (ex: cell phones, pagers, two-way radios, or lights) as this could cause spark/ignition;
- Abandon equipment used in/near area;
- If flames present, driving away from area is acceptable;
- Move far enough from noise to allow normal conversation;
- From safe location, call **911** or contact the local fire/law enforcement; and
- Notify pipeline operator.

ANY ONE OF THESE COULD INDICATE A SUSPECTED GAS PIPELINE LEAK:
- Whistling/hissing sound;
- Distinctive, strong odor, similar to rotten eggs;
- Dense fog, mist, or white cloud;
- Bubbling in water, ponds, or creeks;
- Dust or dirt blowing up from ground; OR
- Discolored/dead vegetation above pipeline right-of-way.

Follow these steps:
- Evacuate area to where you can no longer hear, see, or smell gas;
- Do not start/turn off vehicles/electrical equipment (ex: cell phones, pagers, two-way radios or lights) as this could cause spark/ignition;
- Abandon equipment used in/near the area;
- Avoid open flames;
- Prevent individuals from entering area;
- Call **911** or contact the local fire/law enforcement from a safe location; and
- Notify pipeline operator.

Considerations for Establishing Protective Action Distance:
- Type of product (eg. sour vs sweet);
- Pressure and diameter of pipe;
- Timing of valve closure by utility (quickly for automated valves/longer for manually operated valves);
- Dissipation time of gas in pipe once valves are closed;
- Heat factor of natural gas;
- Local variables such as climate/weather, wind direction, topography, population density, demographics, and fire suppression methods available;
- Nearby building construction material/density;
- Wild land/urban interface; and
- Natural and manmade barriers (highway).

If you know the material involved, identify the three-digit guide number by looking up the name in the alphabetical list (blue-bordered pages), then using the three-digit guide number, consult the recommendations in the assigned guide.

Liquids Pipelines

Petroleum and Hazardous Liquids Pipelines

Crude oil, refined petroleum products, and hazardous liquids often are transported by pipelines and include gasoline, jet fuels, diesel fuel, home heating oils, carbon dioxide and anhydrous ammonia. Sometimes liquids pipelines transport natural gas liquids, which, like carbon dioxide and anhydrous ammonia, rapidly change from liquid to gaseous state when released from a pressurized pipeline.

Structures – Storage Tanks, Valves, Pump Stations, Aerial Patrol Markers

Markers – Often appear at road, railroad and water crossings, and may be posted at property boundaries. Signs include operator emergency POCs and product transported. Warning, Caution, or Danger appear on signs.

For Petroleum and Hazardous Liquids Pipeline Incidents

Two important things to remember:

- Never attempt to extinguish flame before shutting off supply, as this can cause formation of explosive mixtures, and
- Never attempt to operate pipeline valves. This could prolong/worsen incident–or cause another pipeline leak.

SIGNS OF LIQUIDS PIPELINE RUPTURE:

- Loud roaring, hissing, or explosive sound; OR
- Very large flames and loud roaring noise.

Follow these steps:

- Immediately evacuate area;
- Move upwind, far from flames, prevent individuals from entering area;
- If no flames present, do not start/turn off vehicles/electrical equipment (ex: cell phones, pagers, two-way radios, or lights) as this could cause spark/ignition;
- Abandon equipment used in/near the area;
- Keep traffic away; secure the area;

- If flames present, driving away from area is acceptable;
- Move far enough away from noise to allow normal conversation;
- From safe location, call **911** or contact the local fire/law enforcement; and
- From a safe area, call toll-free emergency number on right-of-way marker to notify pipeline operator.

ANY ONE OF THESE COULD INDICATE SUSPECTED LIQUIDS PIPELINE LEAK:
- Liquids bubbling up from ground;
- "Oil slick" on flowing/standing water;
- Flames appearing from ground;
- Vapor clouds;
- Discolored vegetation or snow; and
- Unusual petroleum, skunk or rotten-egg odor.

Follow these steps:
- Do not drive into vapor cloud;
- Carefully evacuate the immediate area so you can no longer hear, see, smell odor;
- Avoid introducing sources of ignition--do not start/turn off vehicles/electrical equipment (ex: cell phones, pagers, two-way radios, or lights); as this could cause spark/ignition;
- Abandon equipment being used in/near area;
- Avoid open flames;
- Prevent individuals from entering area;
- Call **911** or contact the local fire/law enforcement from a safe location; and
- Notify pipeline operator.

Considerations For Establishing Protective Action Distance:
- Type of product (eg. sour vs sweet);
- Pressure/diameter of pipe;
- Timing of valve closure by utility (quickly for automated valves/longer for manually operated valves);
- Dissipation time of material in pipe once valves closed;
- Heat factor of product;
- Local variables such as climate/weather, wind direction, topography, population density, demographics and fire suppression methods available for use;

- Nearby building construction material/density;
- Wild land/urban interface; and
- Natural and man-made barriers (highway).

If you know the material involved, identify the three-digit guide number by looking up the name in the alphabetical list (blue-bordered pages), then using the three-digit guide number, consult the recommendations in the assigned guide.

U.S. Pipeline Resources

U.S. Pipeline Location Source: The National Pipeline Mapping System (NPMS) < *http://www.npms.phmsa.dot.gov* > indicates the locations of hazardous liquids and natural gas transmission pipelines found within the U.S.

U.S. Pipeline Training: Where appropriate, reference Pipeline Emergencies training materials, produced by PHMSA and the National Association of State Fire Marshals (NASFM). This training guide is available at < *http://www.pipelineemergencies.com* > and offers a thorough overview of U.S. pipeline operations and emergency response considerations.

GREEN HIGHLIGHTED ENTRIES IN YELLOW PAGES

For entries highlighted in green follow these steps:

- **IF THERE IS NO FIRE**:
    - Go directly to **Table 1** (green bordered pages)
    - Look up the ID number and name of material
    - Identify initial isolation and protective action distances

- **IF THERE IS A FIRE or A FIRE IS INVOLVED**:
    - Also consult the assigned orange guide
    - If applicable, apply the evacuation information shown under PUBLIC SAFETY

Note: If the name in **Table 1** is shown with "***When Spilled In Water***", these materials produce large amounts of Toxic Inhalation Hazard (TIH) gases when spilled in water. Some Water Reactive materials are also TIH materials themselves (e.g., Bromine trifluoride (1746), Thionyl chloride (1836), etc.). In these instances, two entries are provided in **Table 1** for land-based and water-based spills. If the Water Reactive material **is NOT** a TIH and this material **is NOT** spilled in water, **Table 1** and **Table 2** do not apply and safety distances will be found within the appropriate orange guide.

ID No.	Guide No.	Name of Material	ID No.	Guide No.	Name of Material
——	112	Ammonium nitrate-fuel oil mixtures	1014	122	Oxygen and Carbon dioxide mixture, compressed
——	158	Biological agents	1015	126	Carbon dioxide and Nitrous oxide mixture
——	112	Blasting agent, n.o.s.	1015	126	Nitrous oxide and Carbon dioxide mixture
——	112	Explosives, division 1.1, 1.2, 1.3 or 1.5	1016	119	Carbon monoxide
——	114	Explosives, division 1.4 or 1.6	1016	119	Carbon monoxide, compressed
——	153	Toxins	1017	124	Chlorine
1001	116	Acetylene	1018	126	Chlorodifluoromethane
1001	116	Acetylene, dissolved	1018	126	Refrigerant gas R-22
1002	122	Air, compressed	1020	126	Chloropentafluoroethane
1003	122	Air, refrigerated liquid (cryogenic liquid)	1020	126	Refrigerant gas R-115
1003	122	Air, refrigerated liquid (cryogenic liquid), non-pressurized	1021	126	1-Chloro-1,2,2,2-tetrafluoroethane
			1021	126	Chlorotetrafluoroethane
1005	125	Ammonia, anhydrous	1021	126	Refrigerant gas R-124
1005	125	Anhydrous ammonia	1022	126	Chlorotrifluoromethane
1006	121	Argon	1022	126	Refrigerant gas R-13
1006	121	Argon, compressed	1023	119	Coal gas
1008	125	Boron trifluoride	1023	119	Coal gas, compressed
1008	125	Boron trifluoride, compressed	1026	119	Cyanogen
1009	126	Bromotrifluoromethane	1026	119	Cyanogen gas
1009	126	Refrigerant gas R-13B1	1027	115	Cyclopropane
1010	116P	Butadienes, stabilized	1028	126	Dichlorodifluoromethane
1010	116P	Butadienes and hydrocarbon mixture, stabilized	1028	126	Refrigerant gas R-12
1011	115	Butane	1029	126	Dichlorofluoromethane
1011	115	Butane mixture	1029	126	Refrigerant gas R-21
1012	115	Butylene	1030	115	1,1-Difluoroethane
1013	120	Carbon dioxide	1030	115	Difluoroethane
1013	120	Carbon dioxide, compressed	1030	115	Refrigerant gas R-152a
1014	122	Carbon dioxide and Oxygen mixture, compressed	1032	118	Dimethylamine, anhydrous
			1033	115	Dimethyl ether

ID No.	Guide No.	Name of Material
1035	115	Ethane
1035	115	Ethane, compressed
1036	118	Ethylamine
1037	115	Ethyl chloride
1038	115	Ethylene, refrigerated liquid (cryogenic liquid)
1039	115	Ethyl methyl ether
1039	115	Methyl ethyl ether
1040	119P	Ethylene oxide
1040	119P	Ethylene oxide with Nitrogen
1041	115	Carbon dioxide and Ethylene oxide mixture, with more than 9% but not more than 87% Ethylene oxide
1041	115	Carbon dioxide and Ethylene oxide mixtures, with more than 6% Ethylene oxide
1041	115	Ethylene oxide and Carbon dioxide mixture, with more than 9% but not more than 87% Ethylene oxide
1041	115	Ethylene oxide and Carbon dioxide mixtures, with more than 6 % Ethylene oxide
1043	125	Fertilizer, ammoniating solution, with free Ammonia
1044	126	Fire extinguishers with compressed gas
1044	126	Fire extinguishers with liquefied gas
1045	124	Fluorine
1045	124	Fluorine, compressed
1046	121	Helium
1046	121	Helium, compressed
1048	125	Hydrogen bromide, anhydrous
1049	115	Hydrogen
1049	115	Hydrogen, compressed
1050	125	Hydrogen chloride, anhydrous
1051	117	AC
1051	117	Hydrocyanic acid, aqueous solutions, with more than 20% Hydrogen cyanide
1051	117	Hydrogen cyanide, anhydrous, stabilized
1051	117	Hydrogen cyanide, stabilized
1052	125	Hydrogen fluoride, anhydrous
1053	117P	Hydrogen sulfide
1053	117	Hydrogen sulphide
1055	115	Isobutylene
1056	121	Krypton
1056	121	Krypton, compressed
1057	115	Lighter refills (cigarettes) (flammable gas)
1057	115	Lighters (cigarettes) (flammable gas)
1058	120	Liquefied gases, non-flammable, charged with Nitrogen, Carbon dioxide or Air
1060	116P	Methylacetylene and Propadiene mixture, stabilized
1060	116P	Propadiene and Methylacetylene mixture, stabilized
1061	118	Methylamine, anhydrous
1062	123	Methyl bromide
1063	115	Methyl chloride
1063	115	Refrigerant gas R-40
1064	117	Methyl mercaptan
1065	121	Neon
1065	121	Neon, compressed
1066	121	Nitrogen

ID No.	Guide No.	Name of Material	ID No.	Guide No.	Name of Material
1066	121	Nitrogen, compressed	1079	125	Sulfur dioxide
1067	124	Dinitrogen tetroxide	1079	125	Sulphur dioxide
1067	124	Nitrogen dioxide	1080	126	Sulfur hexafluoride
1069	125	Nitrosyl chloride	1080	126	Sulphur hexafluoride
1070	122	Nitrous oxide	1081	116P	Tetrafluoroethylene, stabilized
1070	122	Nitrous oxide, compressed	1082	119P	Trifluorochloroethylene, stabilized
1071	119	Oil gas	1083	118	Trimethylamine, anhydrous
1071	119	Oil gas, compressed	1085	116P	Vinyl bromide, stabilized
1072	122	Oxygen	1086	116P	Vinyl chloride, stabilized
1072	122	Oxygen, compressed	1087	116P	Vinyl methyl ether, stabilized
1073	122	Oxygen, refrigerated liquid (cryogenic liquid)	1088	127	Acetal
1075	115	Butane	1089	129	Acetaldehyde
1075	115	Butane mixture	1090	127	Acetone
1075	115	Butylene	1091	127	Acetone oils
1075	115	Isobutane	1092	131P	Acrolein, stabilized
1075	115	Isobutane mixture	1093	131P	Acrylonitrile, stabilized
1075	115	Isobutylene	1098	131	Allyl alcohol
1075	115	Liquefied petroleum gas	1099	131	Allyl bromide
1075	115	LPG	1100	131	Allyl chloride
1075	115	Petroleum gases, liquefied	1104	129	Amyl acetates
1075	115	Propane	1105	129	Amyl alcohols
1075	115	Propane mixture	1105	129	Pentanols
1075	115	Propylene	1106	132	Amylamines
1076	125	CG	1107	129	Amyl chloride
1076	125	Diphosgene	1108	128	n-Amylene
1076	125	DP	1108	128	1-Pentene
1076	125	Phosgene	1109	129	Amyl formates
1077	115	Propylene	1110	127	n-Amyl methyl ketone
1078	126	Dispersant gas, n.o.s.	1110	127	Amyl methyl ketone
1078	126	Refrigerant gas, n.o.s.	1110	127	Methyl amyl ketone

ID No.	Guide No.	Name of Material	ID No.	Guide No.	Name of Material
1111	130	Amyl mercaptan	1149	128	Dibutyl ethers
1112	140	Amyl nitrate	1150	130P	1,2-Dichloroethylene
1113	129	Amyl nitrite	1150	130P	Dichloroethylene
1114	130	Benzene	1152	130	Dichloropentanes
1120	129	Butanols	1153	127	Ethylene glycol diethyl ether
1123	129	Butyl acetates	1154	132	Diethylamine
1125	132	n-Butylamine	1155	127	Diethyl ether
1126	130	1-Bromobutane	1155	127	Ethyl ether
1126	130	n-Butyl bromide	1156	127	Diethyl ketone
1127	130	Butyl chloride	1157	128	Diisobutyl ketone
1127	130	Chlorobutanes	1158	132	Diisopropylamine
1128	129	n-Butyl formate	1159	127	Diisopropyl ether
1129	129	Butyraldehyde	1160	132	Dimethylamine, aqueous solution
1130	128	Camphor oil	1160	132	Dimethylamine, solution
1131	131	Carbon bisulfide	1161	129	Dimethyl carbonate
1131	131	Carbon bisulphide	1162	155	Dimethyldichlorosilane
1131	131	Carbon disulfide	1163	131	1,1-Dimethylhydrazine
1131	131	Carbon disulphide	1163	131	Dimethylhydrazine, unsymmetrical
1133	128	Adhesives (flammable)	1164	130	Dimethyl sulfide
1134	130	Chlorobenzene	1164	130	Dimethyl sulphide
1135	131	Ethylene chlorohydrin	1165	127	Dioxane
1136	128	Coal tar distillates, flammable	1166	127	Dioxolane
1139	127	Coating solution	1167	128P	Divinyl ether, stabilized
1143	131P	Crotonaldehyde	1169	127	Extracts, aromatic, liquid
1143	131P	Crotonaldehyde, stabilized	1170	127	Ethanol
1144	128	Crotonylene	1170	127	Ethanol, solution
1145	128	Cyclohexane	1170	127	Ethyl alcohol
1146	128	Cyclopentane	1170	127	Ethyl alcohol, solution
1147	130	Decahydronaphthalene	1171	127	Ethylene glycol monoethyl ether
1148	129	Diacetone alcohol	1172	129	Ethylene glycol monoethyl ether acetate
1149	128	Butyl ethers			

ID No.	Guide No.	Name of Material	ID No.	Guide No.	Name of Material
1173	129	Ethyl acetate	1199	132P	Furfural
1175	130	Ethylbenzene	1199	132P	Furfuraldehydes
1176	129	Ethyl borate	1201	127	Fusel oil
1177	130	2-Ethylbutyl acetate	1202	128	Diesel fuel
1177	130	Ethylbutyl acetate	1202	128	Fuel oil
1178	130	2-Ethylbutyraldehyde	1202	128	Fuel oil, no. 1,2,4,5,6
1179	127	Ethyl butyl ether	1202	128	Gas oil
1180	130	Ethyl butyrate	1202	128	Heating oil, light
1181	155	Ethyl chloroacetate	1203	128	Gasohol
1182	155	Ethyl chloroformate	1203	128	Gasoline
1183	139	Ethyldichlorosilane	1203	128	Motor spirit
1184	131	Ethylene dichloride	1203	128	Petrol
1185	131P	Ethyleneimine, stabilized	1204	127	Nitroglycerin, solution in alcohol, with not more than 1% Nitroglycerin
1188	127	Ethylene glycol monomethyl ether	1206	128	Heptanes
1189	129	Ethylene glycol monomethyl ether acetate	1207	130	Hexaldehyde
1190	129	Ethyl formate	1208	128	Hexanes
1191	129	Ethylhexaldehydes	1208	128	Neohexane
1191	129	Octyl aldehydes	1210	129	Ink, printer's, flammable
1192	129	Ethyl lactate	1210	129	Printing ink, flammable
1193	127	Ethyl methyl ketone	1210	129	Printing ink related material
1193	127	Methyl ethyl ketone	1212	129	Isobutanol
1194	131	Ethyl nitrite, solution	1212	129	Isobutyl alcohol
1195	129	Ethyl propionate	1213	129	Isobutyl acetate
1196	155	Ethyltrichlorosilane	1214	132	Isobutylamine
1197	127	Extracts, flavoring, liquid	1216	128	Isooctenes
1197	127	Extracts, flavouring, liquid	1218	130P	Isoprene, stabilized
1198	132	Formaldehyde, solution, flammable	1219	129	Isopropanol
1198	132	Formaldehyde, solutions (Formalin)	1219	129	Isopropyl alcohol
1199	132P	Furaldehydes	1220	129	Isopropyl acetate
			1221	132	Isopropylamine
			1222	130	Isopropyl nitrate

ID No.	Guide No.	Name of Material	ID No.	Guide No.	Name of Material
1223	128	Kerosene	1262	128	Isooctane
1224	127	Ketones, liquid, n.o.s.	1262	128	Octanes
1228	131	Mercaptan mixture, liquid, flammable, poisonous, n.o.s.	1263	128	Paint (flammable)
			1263	128	Paint related material (flammable)
1228	131	Mercaptan mixture, liquid, flammable, toxic, n.o.s.	1264	129	Paraldehyde
1228	131	Mercaptans, liquid, flammable, poisonous, n.o.s.	1265	128	Isopentane
			1265	128	n-Pentane
1228	131	Mercaptans, liquid, flammable, toxic, n.o.s.	1265	128	Pentanes
1229	129	Mesityl oxide	1266	127	Perfumery products, with flammable solvents
1230	131	Methanol	1267	128	Petroleum crude oil
1230	131	Methyl alcohol	1268	128	Petroleum distillates, n.o.s.
1231	129	Methyl acetate	1268	128	Petroleum products, n.o.s.
1233	130	Methylamyl acetate	1270	128	Oil, petroleum
1234	127	Methylal	1270	128	Petroleum oil
1235	132	Methylamine, aqueous solution	1272	129	Pine oil
1237	129	Methyl butyrate	1274	129	n-Propanol
1238	155	Methyl chloroformate	1274	129	normal Propyl alcohol
1239	131	Methyl chloromethyl ether	1274	129	Propyl alcohol, normal
1242	139	Methyldichlorosilane	1275	129	Propionaldehyde
1243	129	Methyl formate	1276	129	n-Propyl acetate
1244	131	Methylhydrazine	1277	132	Monopropylamine
1245	127	Methyl isobutyl ketone	1277	132	Propylamine
1246	127P	Methyl isopropenyl ketone, stabilized	1278	129	1-Chloropropane
1247	129P	Methyl methacrylate monomer, stabilized	1278	129	Propyl chloride
			1279	130	1,2-Dichloropropane
1248	129	Methyl propionate	1279	130	Dichloropropane
1249	127	Methyl propyl ketone	1279	130	Propylene dichloride
1250	155	Methyltrichlorosilane	1280	127P	Propylene oxide
1251	131P	Methyl vinyl ketone, stabilized	1281	129	Propyl formates
1259	131	Nickel carbonyl	1282	129	Pyridine
1261	129	Nitromethane	1286	127	Rosin oil

ID No.	Guide No.	Name of Material	ID No.	Guide No.	Name of Material
1287	127	Rubber solution	1314	133	Calcium resinate, fused
1288	128	Shale oil	1318	133	Cobalt resinate, precipitated
1289	132	Sodium methylate, solution in alcohol	1320	113	Dinitrophenol, wetted with not less than 15% water
1292	129	Ethyl silicate	1321	113	Dinitrophenolates, wetted with not less than 15% water
1292	129	Tetraethyl silicate	1322	113	Dinitroresorcinol, wetted with not less than 15% water
1293	127	Tinctures, medicinal			
1294	130	Toluene	1323	170	Ferrocerium
1295	139	Trichlorosilane	1324	133	Films, nitrocellulose base
1296	132	Triethylamine	1325	133	Flammable solid, n.o.s.
1297	132	Trimethylamine, aqueous solution	1325	133	Flammable solid, organic, n.o.s.
			1325	133	Fusee (rail or highway)
1298	155	Trimethylchlorosilane	1326	170	Hafnium powder, wetted with not less than 25% water
1299	128	Turpentine			
1300	128	Turpentine substitute	1327	133	Bhusa, wet, damp or contaminated with oil
1301	129P	Vinyl acetate, stabilized			
1302	127P	Vinyl ethyl ether, stabilized	1327	133	Hay, wet, damp or contaminated with oil
1303	130P	Vinylidene chloride, stabilized	1327	133	Straw, wet, damp or contaminated with oil
1304	127P	Vinyl isobutyl ether, stabilized			
1305	155P	Vinyltrichlorosilane	1328	133	Hexamethylenetetramine
1305	155P	Vinyltrichlorosilane, stabilized	1328	133	Hexamine
1306	129	Wood preservatives, liquid	1330	133	Manganese resinate
1307	130	Xylenes	1331	133	Matches, "strike anywhere"
1308	170	Zirconium metal, liquid suspension	1332	133	Metaldehyde
			1333	170	Cerium, slabs, ingots or rods
1308	170	Zirconium suspended in a flammable liquid	1334	133	Naphthalene, crude
1308	170	Zirconium suspended in a liquid (flammable)	1334	133	Naphthalene, refined
			1336	113	Nitroguanidine (Picrite), wetted with not less than 20% water
1309	170	Aluminum powder, coated			
1310	113	Ammonium picrate, wetted with not less than 10% water	1336	113	Nitroguanidine, wetted with not less than 20% water
			1336	113	Picrite, wetted
1312	133	Borneol	1337	113	Nitrostarch, wetted with not less than 20% water
1313	133	Calcium resinate			

ID No.	Guide No.	Name of Material
1337	113	Nitrostarch, wetted with not less than 30% solvent
1338	133	Phosphorus, amorphous
1338	133	Phosphorus, amorphous, red
1338	133	Red phosphorus
1338	133	Red phosphorus, amorphous
1339	139	Phosphorus heptasulfide, free from yellow and white Phosphorus
1339	139	Phosphorus heptasulphide, free from yellow and white Phosphorus
1340	139	Phosphorus pentasulfide, free from yellow and white Phosphorus
1340	139	Phosphorus pentasulphide, free from yellow and white Phosphorus
1341	139	Phosphorus sesquisulfide, free from yellow and white Phosphorus
1341	139	Phosphorus sesquisulphide, free from yellow and white Phosphorus
1343	139	Phosphorus trisulfide, free from yellow and white Phosphorus
1343	139	Phosphorus trisulphide, free from yellow and white Phosphorus
1344	113	Picric acid, wetted with not less than 30% water
1344	113	Trinitrophenol, wetted with not less than 30% water
1345	133	Rubber scrap, powdered or granulated
1345	133	Rubber shoddy, powdered or granulated
1346	170	Silicon powder, amorphous
1347	113	Silver picrate, wetted with not less than 30% water
1348	113	Sodium dinitro-o-cresolate, wetted with not less than 15% water
1348	113	Sodium dinitro-ortho-cresolate, wetted
1349	113	Sodium picramate, wetted with not less than 20% water
1350	133	Sulfur
1350	133	Sulphur
1352	170	Titanium powder, wetted with not less than 25% water
1353	133	Fabrics impregnated with weakly nitrated Nitrocellulose, n.o.s.
1353	133	Fibers impregnated with weakly nitrated Nitrocellulose, n.o.s.
1353	133	Fibres impregnated with weakly nitrated Nitrocellulose, n.o.s.
1353	133	Toe puffs, nitrocellulose base
1354	113	Trinitrobenzene, wetted with not less than 30% water
1355	113	Trinitrobenzoic acid, wetted with not less than 30% water
1356	113	TNT, wetted with not less than 30% water
1356	113	Trinitrotoluene, wetted with not less than 30% water
1357	113	Urea nitrate, wetted with not less than 20% water
1358	170	Zirconium metal, powder, wet
1358	170	Zirconium powder, wetted with not less than 25% water
1360	139	Calcium phosphide
1361	133	Carbon, animal or vegetable origin
1361	133	Charcoal
1362	133	Carbon, activated
1363	135	Copra

ID No.	Guide No.	Name of Material	ID No.	Guide No.	Name of Material
1364	133	Cotton waste, oily	1382	135	Potassium sulfide, anhydrous
1365	133	Cotton	1382	135	Potassium sulfide, with less than 30% water of crystallization
1365	133	Cotton, wet			
1366	135	Diethylzinc			
1369	135	p-Nitrosodimethylaniline	1382	135	Potassium sulfide, with less than 30% water of hydration
1370	135	Dimethylzinc			
1372	133	Fiber, animal or vegetable, n.o.s., burnt, wet or damp	1382	135	Potassium sulphide, anhydrous
			1382	135	Potassium sulphide, with less than 30% water of crystallization
1372	133	Fibers, animal or vegetable, burnt, wet or damp			
1372	133	Fibres, animal or vegetable, burnt, wet or damp	1382	135	Potassium sulphide, with less than 30% water of hydration
1373	133	Fabrics, animal or vegetable or synthetic, n.o.s. with oil	1383	135	Aluminum powder, pyrophoric
			1383	135	Pyrophoric alloy, n.o.s.
1373	133	Fibers, animal or vegetable or synthetic, n.o.s. with oil	1383	135	Pyrophoric metal, n.o.s.
			1384	135	Sodium dithionite
1373	133	Fibres, animal or vegetable or synthetic, n.o.s. with oil	1384	135	Sodium hydrosulfite
			1384	135	Sodium hydrosulphite
1374	133	Fish meal, unstabilized	1385	135	Sodium sulfide, anhydrous
1374	133	Fish scrap, unstabilized	1385	135	Sodium sulfide, with less than 30% water of crystallization
1376	135	Iron oxide, spent			
1376	135	Iron sponge, spent	1385	135	Sodium sulphide, anhydrous
1378	170	Metal catalyst, wetted	1385	135	Sodium sulphide, with less than 30% water of crystallization
1379	133	Paper, unsaturated oil treated			
1380	135	Pentaborane	1386	135	Seed cake, with more than 1.5% oil and not more than 11% moisture
1381	136	Phosphorus, white, dry or under water or in solution			
			1387	133	Wool waste, wet
1381	136	Phosphorus, yellow, dry or under water or in solution	1389	138	Alkali metal amalgam
			1389	138	Alkali metal amalgam, liquid
1381	136	White phosphorus, dry	1389	138	Alkali metal amalgam, solid
1381	136	White phosphorus, in solution	1390	139	Alkali metal amides
1381	136	White phosphorus, under water	1391	138	Alkali metal dispersion
1381	136	Yellow phosphorus, dry	1391	138	Alkaline earth metal dispersion
1381	136	Yellow phosphorus, in solution	1392	138	Alkaline earth metal amalgam
1381	136	Yellow phosphorus, under water			

ID No.	Guide No.	Name of Material	ID No.	Guide No.	Name of Material
1392	138	Alkaline earth metal amalgam, liquid	1420	138	Potassium, metal alloys, liquid
1393	138	Alkaline earth metal alloy, n.o.s.	1421	138	Alkali metal alloy, liquid, n.o.s.
1394	138	Aluminum carbide	1422	138	Potassium sodium alloys
1395	139	Aluminum ferrosilicon powder	1422	138	Potassium sodium alloys, liquid
1396	138	Aluminum powder, uncoated	1422	138	Sodium potassium alloys
1397	139	Aluminum phosphide	1422	138	Sodium potassium alloys, liquid
1398	138	Aluminum silicon powder, uncoated	1423	138	Rubidium
1400	138	Barium	1423	138	Rubidium metal
1401	138	Calcium	1426	138	Sodium borohydride
1402	138	Calcium carbide	1427	138	Sodium hydride
1403	138	Calcium cyanamide, with more than 0.1% Calcium carbide	1428	138	Sodium
			1431	138	Sodium methylate
1404	138	Calcium hydride	1431	138	Sodium methylate, dry
1405	138	Calcium silicide	1432	139	Sodium phosphide
1407	138	Caesium	1433	139	Stannic phosphides
1407	138	Cesium	1435	138	Zinc ashes
1408	139	Ferrosilicon	1435	138	Zinc dross
1409	138	Hydrides, metal, n.o.s.	1435	138	Zinc residue
1409	138	Metal hydrides, water-reactive, n.o.s.	1435	138	Zinc skimmings
			1436	138	Zinc dust
1410	138	Lithium aluminum hydride	1436	138	Zinc powder
1411	138	Lithium aluminum hydride, ethereal	1437	138	Zirconium hydride
			1438	140	Aluminum nitrate
1413	138	Lithium borohydride	1439	141	Ammonium dichromate
1414	138	Lithium hydride	1442	143	Ammonium perchlorate
1415	138	Lithium	1444	140	Ammonium persulfate
1417	138	Lithium silicon	1444	140	Ammonium persulphate
1418	138	Magnesium alloys powder	1445	141	Barium chlorate
1418	138	Magnesium powder	1445	141	Barium chlorate, solid
1419	139	Magnesium aluminum phosphide	1446	141	Barium nitrate
			1447	141	Barium perchlorate
1420	138	Potassium, metal alloys	1447	141	Barium perchlorate, solid

ID No.	Guide No.	Name of Material	ID No.	Guide No.	Name of Material
1448	141	Barium permanganate	1471	140	Lithium hypochlorite mixtures, dry
1449	141	Barium peroxide			
1450	141	Bromates, inorganic, n.o.s.	1472	143	Lithium peroxide
1451	140	Caesium nitrate	1473	140	Magnesium bromate
1451	140	Cesium nitrate	1474	140	Magnesium nitrate
1452	140	Calcium chlorate	1475	140	Magnesium perchlorate
1453	140	Calcium chlorite	1476	140	Magnesium peroxide
1454	140	Calcium nitrate	1477	140	Nitrates, inorganic, n.o.s.
1455	140	Calcium perchlorate	1479	140	Oxidizing solid, n.o.s.
1456	140	Calcium permanganate	1481	140	Perchlorates, inorganic, n.o.s.
1457	140	Calcium peroxide	1482	140	Permanganates, inorganic, n.o.s.
1458	140	Borate and Chlorate mixtures	1483	140	Peroxides, inorganic, n.o.s.
1458	140	Chlorate and Borate mixtures	1484	140	Potassium bromate
1459	140	Chlorate and Magnesium chloride mixture	1485	140	Potassium chlorate
1459	140	Chlorate and Magnesium chloride mixture, solid	1486	140	Potassium nitrate
1459	140	Magnesium chloride and Chlorate mixture	1487	140	Potassium nitrate and Sodium nitrite mixture
1459	140	Magnesium chloride and Chlorate mixture, solid	1487	140	Sodium nitrite and Potassium nitrate mixture
1461	140	Chlorates, inorganic, n.o.s.	1488	140	Potassium nitrite
1462	143	Chlorites, inorganic, n.o.s.	1489	140	Potassium perchlorate
1463	141	Chromium trioxide, anhydrous	1490	140	Potassium permanganate
1465	140	Didymium nitrate	1491	144	Potassium peroxide
1466	140	Ferric nitrate	1492	140	Potassium persulfate
1467	143	Guanidine nitrate	1492	140	Potassium persulphate
1469	141	Lead nitrate	1493	140	Silver nitrate
1470	141	Lead perchlorate	1494	141	Sodium bromate
1470	141	Lead perchlorate, solid	1495	140	Sodium chlorate
1470	141	Lead perchlorate, solution	1496	143	Sodium chlorite
1471	140	Lithium hypochlorite, dry	1498	140	Sodium nitrate
1471	140	Lithium hypochlorite mixture	1499	140	Potassium nitrate and Sodium nitrate mixture

ID No.	Guide No.	Name of Material	ID No.	Guide No.	Name of Material
1499	140	Sodium nitrate and Potassium nitrate mixture	1549	157	Antimony compound, inorganic, solid, n.o.s.
1500	140	Sodium nitrite	1550	151	Antimony lactate
1502	140	Sodium perchlorate	1551	151	Antimony potassium tartrate
1503	140	Sodium permanganate	1553	154	Arsenic acid, liquid
1504	144	Sodium peroxide	1554	154	Arsenic acid, solid
1505	140	Sodium persulfate	1555	151	Arsenic bromide
1505	140	Sodium persulphate	1556	152	Arsenic compound, liquid, n.o.s.
1506	143	Strontium chlorate	1556	152	Arsenic compound, liquid, n.o.s., inorganic
1506	143	Strontium chlorate, solid			
1506	143	Strontium chlorate, solution	1556	152	MD
1507	140	Strontium nitrate	1556	152	Methyldichloroarsine
1508	140	Strontium perchlorate	1556	152	PD
1509	143	Strontium peroxide	1557	152	Arsenic compound, solid, n.o.s.
1510	143	Tetranitromethane	1557	152	Arsenic compound, solid, n.o.s., inorganic
1511	140	Urea hydrogen peroxide			
1512	140	Zinc ammonium nitrite	1558	152	Arsenic
1513	140	Zinc chlorate	1559	151	Arsenic pentoxide
1514	140	Zinc nitrate	1560	157	Arsenic chloride
1515	140	Zinc permanganate	1560	157	Arsenic trichloride
1516	143	Zinc peroxide	1561	151	Arsenic trioxide
1517	113	Zirconium picramate, wetted with not less than 20% water	1562	152	Arsenical dust
			1564	154	Barium compound, n.o.s.
1541	155	Acetone cyanohydrin, stabilized	1565	157	Barium cyanide
1544	151	Alkaloids, solid, n.o.s. (poisonous)	1566	154	Beryllium compound, n.o.s.
1544	151	Alkaloid salts, solid, n.o.s. (poisonous)	1567	134	Beryllium powder
			1569	131	Bromoacetone
1545	155	Allyl isothiocyanate, stabilized	1570	152	Brucine
1546	151	Ammonium arsenate	1571	113	Barium azide, wetted with not less than 50% water
1547	153	Aniline			
1548	153	Aniline hydrochloride	1572	151	Cacodylic acid
1549	157	Antimony compound, inorganic, n.o.s.	1573	151	Calcium arsenate

ID No.	Guide No.	Name of Material	ID No.	Guide No.	Name of Material
1574	151	Calcium arsenate and Calcium arsenite mixture, solid	1590	153	Dichloroanilines, liquid
			1590	153	Dichloroanilines, solid
1574	151	Calcium arsenite and Calcium arsenate mixture, solid	1591	152	o-Dichlorobenzene
1575	157	Calcium cyanide	1593	160	Dichloromethane
1577	153	Chlorodinitrobenzenes	1593	160	Methylene chloride
1577	153	Chlorodinitrobenzenes, liquid	1594	152	Diethyl sulfate
1577	153	Chlorodinitrobenzenes, solid	1594	152	Diethyl sulphate
1577	153	Dinitrochlorobenzenes	1595	156	Dimethyl sulfate
1578	152	Chloronitrobenzenes	1595	156	Dimethyl sulphate
1578	152	Chloronitrobenzenes, liquid	1596	153	Dinitroanilines
1578	152	Chloronitrobenzenes, solid	1597	152	Dinitrobenzenes
1579	153	4-Chloro-o-toluidine hydrochloride	1597	152	Dinitrobenzenes, liquid
			1597	152	Dinitrobenzenes, solid
1579	153	4-Chloro-o-toluidine hydrochloride, solid	1598	153	Dinitro-o-cresol
1580	154	Chloropicrin	1599	153	Dinitrophenol, solution
1581	123	Chloropicrin and Methyl bromide mixture	1600	152	Dinitrotoluenes, molten
			1601	151	Disinfectant, solid, poisonous, n.o.s.
1581	123	Methyl bromide and Chloropicrin mixture	1601	151	Disinfectant, solid, toxic, n.o.s.
1582	119	Chloropicrin and Methyl chloride mixture	1601	151	Disinfectants, solid, n.o.s. (poisonous)
1582	119	Methyl chloride and Chloropicrin mixture	1602	151	Dye, liquid, poisonous, n.o.s.
			1602	151	Dye, liquid, toxic, n.o.s.
1583	154	Chloropicrin mixture, n.o.s.	1602	151	Dye intermediate, liquid, poisonous, n.o.s.
1585	151	Copper acetoarsenite	1602	151	Dye intermediate, liquid, toxic, n.o.s.
1586	151	Copper arsenite			
1587	151	Copper cyanide	1603	155	Ethyl bromoacetate
1588	157	Cyanides, inorganic, n.o.s.	1604	132	Ethylenediamine
1588	157	Cyanides, inorganic, solid, n.o.s.	1605	154	Ethylene dibromide
			1606	151	Ferric arsenate
1589	125	CK	1607	151	Ferric arsenite
1589	125	Cyanogen chloride, stabilized	1608	151	Ferrous arsenate
1590	153	Dichloroanilines			

ID No.	Guide No.	Name of Material	ID No.	Guide No.	Name of Material
1611	151	Hexaethyl tetraphosphate	1636	154	Mercury cyanide
1611	151	Hexaethyl tetraphosphate, liquid	1637	151	Mercury gluconate
			1638	151	Mercury iodide
1611	151	Hexaethyl tetraphosphate, solid	1639	151	Mercury nucleate
1612	123	Hexaethyl tetraphosphate and compressed gas mixture	1640	151	Mercury oleate
			1641	151	Mercury oxide
1613	154	Hydrocyanic acid, aqueous solution, with less than 5% Hydrogen cyanide	1642	151	Mercuric oxycyanide
			1642	151	Mercury oxycyanide, desensitized
1613	154	Hydrocyanic acid, aqueous solution, with not more than 20% Hydrogen cyanide	1643	151	Mercury potassium iodide
			1644	151	Mercury salicylate
1613	154	Hydrogen cyanide, aqueous solution, with not more than 20% Hydrogen cyanide	1645	151	Mercuric sulfate
			1645	151	Mercuric sulphate
1614	152	Hydrogen cyanide, stabilized (absorbed)	1645	151	Mercury sulfate
			1645	151	Mercury sulphate
1616	151	Lead acetate	1646	151	Mercury thiocyanate
1617	151	Lead arsenates	1647	151	Ethylene dibromide and Methyl bromide mixture, liquid
1618	151	Lead arsenites			
1620	151	Lead cyanide	1647	151	Methyl bromide and Ethylene dibromide mixture, liquid
1621	151	London purple			
1622	151	Magnesium arsenate	1648	127	Acetonitrile
1623	151	Mercuric arsenate	1648	127	Methyl cyanide
1624	154	Mercuric chloride	1649	131	Motor fuel anti-knock mixture
1625	141	Mercuric nitrate	1650	153	beta-Naphthylamine
1626	157	Mercuric potassium cyanide	1650	153	beta-Naphthylamine, solid
1627	141	Mercurous nitrate	1650	153	Naphthylamine (beta)
1629	151	Mercury acetate	1650	153	Naphthylamine (beta), solid
1630	151	Mercury ammonium chloride	1651	153	Naphthylthiourea
1631	154	Mercury benzoate	1652	153	Naphthylurea
1634	154	Mercuric bromide	1653	151	Nickel cyanide
1634	154	Mercurous bromide	1654	151	Nicotine
1634	154	Mercury bromides	1655	151	Nicotine compound, solid, n.o.s.
1636	154	Mercuric cyanide			

ID No.	Guide No.	Name of Material	ID No.	Guide No.	Name of Material
1655	151	Nicotine preparation, solid, n.o.s.	1680	157	Potassium cyanide
1656	151	Nicotine hydrochloride	1680	157	Potassium cyanide, solid
1656	151	Nicotine hydrochloride, liquid	1683	151	Silver arsenite
1656	151	Nicotine hydrochloride, solid	1684	151	Silver cyanide
1656	151	Nicotine hydrochloride, solution	1685	151	Sodium arsenate
1657	151	Nicotine salicylate	1686	154	Sodium arsenite, aqueous solution
1658	151	Nicotine sulfate, solid	1687	153	Sodium azide
1658	151	Nicotine sulfate, solution	1688	152	Sodium cacodylate
1658	151	Nicotine sulphate, solid	1689	157	Sodium cyanide
1658	151	Nicotine sulphate, solution	1689	157	Sodium cyanide, solid
1659	151	Nicotine tartrate	1690	154	Sodium fluoride
1660	124	Nitric oxide	1690	154	Sodium fluoride, solid
1660	124	Nitric oxide, compressed	1691	151	Strontium arsenite
1661	153	Nitroanilines	1692	151	Strychnine
1662	152	Nitrobenzene	1692	151	Strychnine salts
1663	153	Nitrophenols	1693	159	Tear gas devices
1664	152	Nitrotoluenes	1693	159	Tear gas substance, liquid, n.o.s.
1664	152	Nitrotoluenes, liquid	1693	159	Tear gas substance, solid, n.o.s.
1664	152	Nitrotoluenes, solid	1694	159	Bromobenzyl cyanides
1665	152	Nitroxylenes	1694	159	Bromobenzyl cyanides, liquid
1665	152	Nitroxylenes, liquid	1694	159	Bromobenzyl cyanides, solid
1665	152	Nitroxylenes, solid	1694	159	CA
1669	151	Pentachloroethane	1695	131	Chloroacetone, stabilized
1670	157	Perchloromethyl mercaptan	1697	153	Chloroacetophenone
1671	153	Phenol, solid	1697	153	Chloroacetophenone, liquid
1672	151	Phenylcarbylamine chloride	1697	153	Chloroacetophenone, solid
1673	153	Phenylenediamines	1697	153	CN
1674	151	Phenylmercuric acetate	1698	154	Adamsite
1677	151	Potassium arsenate	1698	154	Diphenylamine chloroarsine
1678	154	Potassium arsenite			
1679	157	Potassium cuprocyanide			

ID No.	Guide No.	Name of Material
1698	154	DM
1699	151	DA
1699	151	Diphenylchloroarsine
1699	151	Diphenylchloroarsine, liquid
1699	151	Diphenylchloroarsine, solid
1700	159	Tear gas candles
1700	159	Tear gas grenades
1701	152	Xylyl bromide
1701	152	Xylyl bromide, liquid
1702	151	1,1,2,2-Tetrachloroethane
1702	151	Tetrachloroethane
1704	153	Tetraethyl dithiopyrophosphate
1704	153	Tetraethyl dithiopyrophosphate, mixture, dry or liquid
1707	151	Thallium compound, n.o.s.
1708	153	Toluidines
1708	153	Toluidines, liquid
1708	153	Toluidines, solid
1709	151	2,4-Toluenediamine
1709	151	2,4-Toluylenediamine
1709	151	2,4-Toluylenediamine, solid
1710	160	Trichloroethylene
1711	153	Xylidines
1711	153	Xylidines, liquid
1711	153	Xylidines, solid
1712	151	Zinc arsenate
1712	151	Zinc arsenate and Zinc arsenite mixture
1712	151	Zinc arsenite
1712	151	Zinc arsenite and Zinc arsenate mixture
1713	151	Zinc cyanide
1714	139	Zinc phosphide
1715	137	Acetic anhydride
1716	156	Acetyl bromide
1717	155	Acetyl chloride
1718	153	Acid butyl phosphate
1718	153	Butyl acid phosphate
1719	154	Caustic alkali liquid, n.o.s.
1722	155	Allyl chlorocarbonate
1722	155	Allyl chloroformate
1723	132	Allyl iodide
1724	155	Allyltrichlorosilane, stabilized
1725	137	Aluminum bromide, anhydrous
1726	137	Aluminum chloride, anhydrous
1727	154	Ammonium bifluoride, solid
1727	154	Ammonium hydrogendifluoride, solid
1727	154	Ammonium hydrogen fluoride, solid
1728	155	Amyltrichlorosilane
1729	156	Anisoyl chloride
1730	157	Antimony pentachloride, liquid
1731	157	Antimony pentachloride, solution
1732	157	Antimony pentafluoride
1733	157	Antimony trichloride
1733	157	Antimony trichloride, liquid
1733	157	Antimony trichloride, solid
1733	157	Antimony trichloride, solution
1736	137	Benzoyl chloride
1737	156	Benzyl bromide
1738	156	Benzyl chloride
1739	137	Benzyl chloroformate
1740	154	Hydrogendifluorides, n.o.s.

ID No.	Guide No.	Name of Material
1740	154	Hydrogendifluorides, solid, n.o.s.
1741	125	Boron trichloride
1742	157	Boron trifluoride acetic acid complex
1742	157	Boron trifluoride acetic acid complex, liquid
1743	157	Boron trifluoride propionic acid complex
1743	157	Boron trifluoride propionic acid complex, liquid
1744	154	Bromine
1744	154	Bromine, solution
1744	154	Bromine, solution (Inhalation Hazard Zone A)
1744	154	Bromine, solution (Inhalation Hazard Zone B)
1745	144	Bromine pentafluoride
1746	144	Bromine trifluoride
1747	155	Butyltrichlorosilane
1748	140	Calcium hypochlorite, dry
1748	140	Calcium hypochlorite mixture, dry, with more than 39% available Chlorine (8.8% available Oxygen)
1749	124	Chlorine trifluoride
1750	153	Chloroacetic acid, liquid
1750	153	Chloroacetic acid, solution
1751	153	Chloroacetic acid, solid
1752	156	Chloroacetyl chloride
1753	156	Chlorophenyltrichlorosilane
1754	137	Chlorosulfonic acid
1754	137	Chlorosulfonic acid and Sulfur trioxide mixture
1754	137	Chlorosulphonic acid
1754	137	Chlorosulphonic acid and Sulphur trioxide mixture
1754	137	Sulfur trioxide and Chlorosulfonic acid mixture
1754	137	Sulphur trioxide and Chlorosulphonic acid mixture
1755	154	Chromic acid, solution
1756	154	Chromic fluoride, solid
1757	154	Chromic fluoride, solution
1758	137	Chromium oxychloride
1759	154	Corrosive solid, n.o.s.
1759	154	Ferrous chloride, solid
1760	154	Chemical kit
1760	154	Compound, cleaning liquid (corrosive)
1760	154	Compound, tree or weed killing, liquid (corrosive)
1760	154	Corrosive liquid, n.o.s.
1760	154	Ferrous chloride, solution
1761	154	Cupriethylenediamine, solution
1762	156	Cyclohexenyltrichlorosilane
1763	156	Cyclohexyltrichlorosilane
1764	153	Dichloroacetic acid
1765	156	Dichloroacetyl chloride
1766	156	Dichlorophenyltrichlorosilane
1767	155	Diethyldichlorosilane
1768	154	Difluorophosphoric acid, anhydrous
1769	156	Diphenyldichlorosilane
1770	153	Diphenylmethyl bromide
1771	156	Dodecyltrichlorosilane
1773	157	Ferric chloride
1773	157	Ferric chloride, anhydrous

ID No.	Guide No.	Name of Material
1774	154	Fire extinguisher charges, corrosive liquid
1775	154	Fluoboric acid
1775	154	Fluoroboric acid
1776	154	Fluorophosphoric acid, anhydrous
1777	137	Fluorosulfonic acid
1777	137	Fluorosulphonic acid
1778	154	Fluorosilicic acid
1778	154	Fluosilicic acid
1778	154	Hydrofluorosilicic acid
1779	153	Formic acid
1779	153	Formic acid, with more than 85% acid
1780	156	Fumaryl chloride
1781	156	Hexadecyltrichlorosilane
1782	154	Hexafluorophosphoric acid
1783	153	Hexamethylenediamine, solution
1784	156	Hexyltrichlorosilane
1786	157	Hydrofluoric acid and Sulfuric acid mixture
1786	157	Hydrofluoric acid and Sulphuric acid mixture
1786	157	Sulfuric acid and Hydrofluoric acid mixture
1786	157	Sulphuric acid and Hydrofluoric acid mixture
1787	154	Hydriodic acid
1787	154	Hydriodic acid, solution
1788	154	Hydrobromic acid
1788	154	Hydrobromic acid, solution
1789	157	Hydrochloric acid
1789	157	Hydrochloric acid, solution
1789	157	Muriatic acid
1790	157	Hydrofluoric acid
1790	157	Hydrofluoric acid, solution
1791	154	Hypochlorite solution
1791	154	Hypochlorite solution, with more than 5% available Chlorine
1792	157	Iodine monochloride, solid
1793	153	Isopropyl acid phosphate
1794	154	Lead sulfate, with more than 3% free acid
1794	154	Lead sulphate, with more than 3% free acid
1796	157	Nitrating acid mixture with more than 50% nitric acid
1796	157	Nitrating acid mixture with not more than 50% nitric acid
1798	157	Aqua regia
1798	157	Nitrohydrochloric acid
1799	156	Nonyltrichlorosilane
1800	156	Octadecyltrichlorosilane
1801	156	Octyltrichlorosilane
1802	140	Perchloric acid, with not more than 50% acid
1803	153	Phenolsulfonic acid, liquid
1803	153	Phenolsulphonic acid, liquid
1804	156	Phenyltrichlorosilane
1805	154	Phosphoric acid
1805	154	Phosphoric acid, liquid
1805	154	Phosphoric acid, solid
1805	154	Phosphoric acid, solution
1806	137	Phosphorus pentachloride
1807	137	Phosphorus pentoxide
1808	137	Phosphorus tribromide
1809	137	Phosphorus trichloride

ID No.	Guide No.	Name of Material	ID No.	Guide No.	Name of Material
1810	**137**	Phosphorus oxychloride	1826	**157**	Nitrating acid mixture, spent, with more than 50% nitric acid
1811	**154**	Potassium hydrogendifluoride	1826	**157**	Nitrating acid mixture, spent, with not more than 50% nitric acid
1811	**154**	Potassium hydrogen difluoride, solid	1827	**137**	Stannic chloride, anhydrous
1812	**154**	Potassium fluoride	1827	**137**	Tin tetrachloride
1812	**154**	Potassium fluoride, solid	1828	**137**	Sulfur chlorides
1813	**154**	Caustic potash, dry, solid	1828	**137**	Sulphur chlorides
1813	**154**	Potassium hydroxide, dry, solid	1829	**137**	Sulfur trioxide, stabilized
1813	**154**	Potassium hydroxide, flake	1829	**137**	Sulphur trioxide, stabilized
1813	**154**	Potassium hydroxide, solid	1830	**137**	Sulfuric acid
1814	**154**	Caustic potash, liquid	1830	**137**	Sulfuric acid, with more than 51% acid
1814	**154**	Caustic potash, solution	1830	**137**	Sulphuric acid
1814	**154**	Potassium hydroxide, solution	1830	**137**	Sulphuric acid, with more than 51% acid
1815	**132**	Propionyl chloride	1831	**137**	Sulfuric acid, fuming
1816	**155**	Propyltrichlorosilane	1831	**137**	Sulfuric acid, fuming, with less than 30% free Sulfur trioxide
1817	**137**	Pyrosulfuryl chloride	1831	**137**	Sulfuric acid, fuming, with not less than 30% free Sulfur trioxide
1817	**137**	Pyrosulphuryl chloride			
1818	**157**	Silicon tetrachloride	1831	**137**	Sulphuric acid, fuming
1819	**154**	Sodium aluminate, solution	1831	**137**	Sulphuric acid, fuming, with less than 30% free Sulphur trioxide
1823	**154**	Caustic soda, bead			
1823	**154**	Caustic soda, flake	1831	**137**	Sulphuric acid, fuming, with not less than 30% free Sulphur trioxide
1823	**154**	Caustic soda, granular			
1823	**154**	Caustic soda, solid	1832	**137**	Sulfuric acid, spent
1823	**154**	Sodium hydroxide, bead	1832	**137**	Sulphuric acid, spent
1823	**154**	Sodium hydroxide, dry	1833	**154**	Sulfurous acid
1823	**154**	Sodium hydroxide, flake	1833	**154**	Sulphurous acid
1823	**154**	Sodium hydroxide, granular	1834	**137**	Sulfuryl chloride
1823	**154**	Sodium hydroxide, solid	1834	**137**	Sulphuryl chloride
1824	**154**	Caustic soda, solution			
1824	**154**	Sodium hydroxide, solution			
1825	**157**	Sodium monoxide			

ID No.	Guide No.	Name of Material
1835	153	Tetramethylammonium hydroxide
1835	153	Tetramethylammonium hydroxide, solution
1836	137	Thionyl chloride
1837	157	Thiophosphoryl chloride
1838	137	Titanium tetrachloride
1839	153	Trichloroacetic acid
1840	154	Zinc chloride, solution
1841	171	Acetaldehyde ammonia
1843	141	Ammonium dinitro-o-cresolate
1843	141	Ammonium dinitro-o-cresolate, solid
1845	120	Carbon dioxide, solid
1845	120	Dry ice
1846	151	Carbon tetrachloride
1847	153	Potassium sulfide, hydrated, with not less than 30% water of crystallization
1847	153	Potassium sulfide, hydrated, with not less than 30% water of hydration
1847	153	Potassium sulphide, hydrated, with not less than 30% water of crystallization
1847	153	Potassium sulphide, hydrated, with not less than 30% water of hydration
1848	132	Propionic acid
1848	132	Propionic acid, with not less than 10% and less than 90% acid
1849	153	Sodium sulfide, hydrated, with not less than 30% water
1849	153	Sodium sulphide, hydrated, with not less than 30% water
1851	151	Medicine, liquid, poisonous, n.o.s.
1851	151	Medicine, liquid, toxic, n.o.s.
1854	135	Barium alloys, pyrophoric
1855	135	Calcium, metal and alloys, pyrophoric
1855	135	Calcium, pyrophoric
1855	135	Calcium alloys, pyrophoric
1856	133	Rags, oily
1857	133	Textile waste, wet
1858	126	Hexafluoropropylene
1858	126	Hexafluoropropylene, compressed
1858	126	Refrigerant gas R-1216
1859	125	Silicon tetrafluoride
1859	125	Silicon tetrafluoride, compressed
1860	116P	Vinyl fluoride, stabilized
1862	130	Ethyl crotonate
1863	128	Fuel, aviation, turbine engine
1865	131	n-Propyl nitrate
1866	127	Resin solution
1868	134	Decaborane
1869	138	Magnesium
1869	138	Magnesium, in pellets, turnings or ribbons
1869	138	Magnesium alloys, with more than 50% Magnesium, in pellets, turnings or ribbons
1870	138	Potassium borohydride
1871	170	Titanium hydride
1872	141	Lead dioxide
1873	143	Perchloric acid, with more than 50% but not more than 72% acid
1884	157	Barium oxide
1885	153	Benzidine

ID No.	Guide No.	Name of Material
1886	156	Benzylidene chloride
1887	160	Bromochloromethane
1888	151	Chloroform
1889	157	Cyanogen bromide
1891	131	Ethyl bromide
1892	151	ED
1892	151	Ethyldichloroarsine
1894	151	Phenylmercuric hydroxide
1895	151	Phenylmercuric nitrate
1897	160	Perchloroethylene
1897	160	Tetrachloroethylene
1898	156	Acetyl iodide
1902	153	Diisooctyl acid phosphate
1903	153	Disinfectant, liquid, corrosive, n.o.s.
1903	153	Disinfectants, corrosive, liquid, n.o.s.
1905	154	Selenic acid
1906	153	Acid, sludge
1906	153	Sludge acid
1907	154	Soda lime, with more than 4% Sodium hydroxide
1908	154	Chlorite solution
1908	154	Chlorite solution, with more than 5% available Chlorine
1908	154	Sodium chlorite, solution, with more than 5% available Chlorine
1910	157	Calcium oxide
1911	119	Diborane
1911	119	Diborane, compressed
1911	119	Diborane mixtures
1912	115	Methyl chloride and Methylene chloride mixture
1912	115	Methylene chloride and Methyl chloride mixture
1913	120	Neon, refrigerated liquid (cryogenic liquid)
1914	130	Butyl propionates
1915	127	Cyclohexanone
1916	152	2,2'-Dichlorodiethyl ether
1916	152	Dichloroethyl ether
1917	129P	Ethyl acrylate, stabilized
1918	130	Cumene
1918	130	Isopropylbenzene
1919	129P	Methyl acrylate, stabilized
1920	128	Nonanes
1921	131P	Propyleneimine, stabilized
1922	132	Pyrrolidine
1923	135	Calcium dithionite
1923	135	Calcium hydrosulfite
1923	135	Calcium hydrosulphite
1928	135	Methyl magnesium bromide in Ethyl ether
1929	135	Potassium dithionite
1929	135	Potassium hydrosulfite
1929	135	Potassium hydrosulphite
1931	171	Zinc dithionite
1931	171	Zinc hydrosulfite
1931	171	Zinc hydrosulphite
1932	135	Zirconium scrap
1935	157	Cyanide solution, n.o.s.
1938	156	Bromoacetic acid
1938	156	Bromoacetic acid, solution
1939	137	Phosphorus oxybromide
1939	137	Phosphorus oxybromide, solid

ID No.	Guide No.	Name of Material	ID No.	Guide No.	Name of Material
1940	153	Thioglycolic acid	1953	119	Compressed gas, flammable, toxic, n.o.s. (Inhalation Hazard Zone C)
1941	171	Dibromodifluoromethane			
1942	140	Ammonium nitrate, with not more than 0.2% combustible substances	1953	119	Compressed gas, flammable, toxic, n.o.s. (Inhalation Hazard Zone D)
1944	133	Matches, safety	1953	119	Compressed gas, poisonous, flammable, n.o.s.
1945	133	Matches, wax "vesta"			
1950	126	Aerosol dispensers	1953	119	Compressed gas, poisonous, flammable, n.o.s. (Inhalation Hazard Zone A)
1950	126	Aerosols			
1951	120	Argon, refrigerated liquid (cryogenic liquid)	1953	119	Compressed gas, poisonous, flammable, n.o.s. (Inhalation Hazard Zone B)
1952	126	Carbon dioxide and Ethylene oxide mixtures, with not more than 6% Ethylene oxide	1953	119	Compressed gas, poisonous, flammable, n.o.s. (Inhalation Hazard Zone C)
1952	126	Carbon dioxide and Ethylene oxide mixtures, with not more than 9% Ethylene oxide	1953	119	Compressed gas, poisonous, flammable, n.o.s. (Inhalation Hazard Zone D)
1952	126	Ethylene oxide and Carbon dioxide mixtures, with not more than 6% Ethylene oxide	1953	119	Compressed gas, toxic, flammable, n.o.s.
1952	126	Ethylene oxide and Carbon dioxide mixtures, with not more than 9% Ethylene oxide	1953	119	Compressed gas, toxic, flammable, n.o.s. (Inhalation Hazard Zone A)
1953	119	Compressed gas, flammable, poisonous, n.o.s. (Inhalation Hazard Zone A)	1953	119	Compressed gas, toxic, flammable, n.o.s. (Inhalation Hazard Zone B)
1953	119	Compressed gas, flammable, poisonous, n.o.s. (Inhalation Hazard Zone B)	1953	119	Compressed gas, toxic, flammable, n.o.s. (Inhalation Hazard Zone C)
1953	119	Compressed gas, flammable, poisonous, n.o.s. (Inhalation Hazard Zone C)	1953	119	Compressed gas, toxic, flammable, n.o.s. (Inhalation Hazard Zone D)
1953	119	Compressed gas, flammable, poisonous, n.o.s. (Inhalation Hazard Zone D)	1954	115	Compressed gas, flammable, n.o.s.
1953	119	Compressed gas, flammable, toxic, n.o.s. (Inhalation Hazard Zone A)	1954	115	Dispersant gas, n.o.s. (flammable)
1953	119	Compressed gas, flammable, toxic, n.o.s. (Inhalation Hazard Zone B)	1954	115	Refrigerant gas, n.o.s. (flammable)

ID No.	Guide No.	Name of Material
1955	123	Compressed gas, poisonous, n.o.s.
1955	123	Compressed gas, poisonous, n.o.s. (Inhalation Hazard Zone A)
1955	123	Compressed gas, poisonous, n.o.s. (Inhalation Hazard Zone B)
1955	123	Compressed gas, poisonous, n.o.s. (Inhalation Hazard Zone C)
1955	123	Compressed gas, poisonous, n.o.s. (Inhalation Hazard Zone D)
1955	123	Compressed gas, toxic, n.o.s.
1955	123	Compressed gas, toxic, n.o.s. (Inhalation Hazard Zone A)
1955	123	Compressed gas, toxic, n.o.s. (Inhalation Hazard Zone B)
1955	123	Compressed gas, toxic, n.o.s. (Inhalation Hazard Zone C)
1955	123	Compressed gas, toxic, n.o.s. (Inhalation Hazard Zone D)
1955	123	Organic phosphate compound mixed with compressed gas
1955	123	Organic phosphate mixed with compressed gas
1955	123	Organic phosphorus compound mixed with compressed gas
1956	126	Compressed gas, n.o.s.
1957	115	Deuterium
1957	115	Deuterium, compressed
1958	126	1,2-Dichloro-1,1,2,2-tetrafluoroethane
1958	126	Dichlorotetrafluoroethane
1958	126	Refrigerant gas R-114
1959	116P	1,1-Difluoroethylene
1959	116P	Refrigerant gas R-1132a
1961	115	Ethane, refrigerated liquid
1961	115	Ethane-Propane mixture, refrigerated liquid
1961	115	Propane-Ethane mixture, refrigerated liquid
1962	116P	Ethylene
1962	116P	Ethylene, compressed
1963	120	Helium, refrigerated liquid (cryogenic liquid)
1964	115	Hydrocarbon gas, compressed, n.o.s.
1964	115	Hydrocarbon gas mixture, compressed, n.o.s.
1965	115	Hydrocarbon gas, liquefied, n.o.s.
1965	115	Hydrocarbon gas mixture, liquefied, n.o.s.
1966	115	Hydrogen, refrigerated liquid (cryogenic liquid)
1967	123	Insecticide gas, poisonous, n.o.s.
1967	123	Insecticide gas, toxic, n.o.s.
1967	123	Parathion and compressed gas mixture
1968	126	Insecticide gas, n.o.s.
1969	115	Isobutane
1969	115	Isobutane mixture
1970	120	Krypton, refrigerated liquid (cryogenic liquid)
1971	115	Methane
1971	115	Methane, compressed
1971	115	Natural gas, compressed
1972	115	Liquefied natural gas (cryogenic liquid)
1972	115	LNG (cryogenic liquid)
1972	115	Methane, refrigerated liquid (cryogenic liquid)

ID No.	Guide No.	Name of Material	ID No.	Guide No.	Name of Material
1972	115	Natural gas, refrigerated liquid (cryogenic liquid)	1981	121	Rare gases and Nitrogen mixture, compressed
1973	126	Chlorodifluoromethane and Chloropentafluoroethane mixture	1982	126	Refrigerant gas R-14
			1982	126	Refrigerant gas R-14, compressed
1973	126	Chloropentafluoroethane and Chlorodifluoromethane mixture	1982	126	Tetrafluoromethane
			1982	126	Tetrafluoromethane, compressed
1973	126	Refrigerant gas R-502			
1974	126	Bromochlorodifluoromethane	1983	126	1-Chloro-2,2,2-trifluoroethane
1974	126	Chlorodifluorobromomethane	1983	126	Chlorotrifluoroethane
1974	126	Refrigerant gas R-12B1	1983	126	Refrigerant gas R-133a
1975	124	Dinitrogen tetroxide and Nitric oxide mixture	1984	126	Refrigerant gas R-23
			1984	126	Trifluoromethane
1975	124	Nitric oxide and Dinitrogen tetroxide mixture	1986	131	Alcohols, flammable, poisonous, n.o.s.
1975	124	Nitric oxide and Nitrogen dioxide mixture	1986	131	Alcohols, flammable, toxic, n.o.s.
1975	124	Nitric oxide and Nitrogen tetroxide mixture	1986	131	Alcohols, poisonous, n.o.s.
			1986	131	Alcohols, toxic, n.o.s.
1975	124	Nitrogen dioxide and Nitric oxide mixture	1987	127	Alcohols, n.o.s.
1975	124	Nitrogen tetroxide and Nitric oxide mixture	1988	131	Aldehydes, flammable, poisonous, n.o.s.
1976	126	Octafluorocyclobutane	1988	131	Aldehydes, flammable, toxic, n.o.s.
1976	126	Refrigerant gas RC-318	1988	131	Aldehydes, poisonous, n.o.s.
1977	120	Nitrogen, refrigerated liquid (cryogenic liquid)	1988	131	Aldehydes, toxic, n.o.s.
1978	115	Propane	1989	129	Aldehydes, n.o.s.
1978	115	Propane mixture	1990	129	Benzaldehyde
1979	121	Rare gases mixture, compressed	1991	131P	Chloroprene, stabilized
			1992	131	Flammable liquid, poisonous, n.o.s.
1980	121	Oxygen and Rare gases mixture, compressed	1992	131	Flammable liquid, toxic, n.o.s.
1980	121	Rare gases and Oxygen mixture, compressed	1993	128	Combustible liquid, n.o.s.
1981	121	Nitrogen and Rare gases mixture, compressed	1993	128	Compound, cleaning liquid (flammable)

ID No.	Guide No.	Name of Material
1993	**128**	Compound, tree or weed killing, liquid (flammable)
1993	**128**	Diesel fuel
1993	**128**	Flammable liquid, n.o.s.
1993	**128**	Fuel oil
1994	**131**	Iron pentacarbonyl
1999	**130**	Asphalt
1999	**130**	Tars, liquid
2000	**133**	Celluloid, in blocks, rods, rolls, sheets, tubes, etc., except scrap
2001	**133**	Cobalt naphthenates, powder
2002	**135**	Celluloid, scrap
2003	**135**	Metal alkyls, water-reactive, n.o.s.
2003	**135**	Metal aryls, water-reactive, n.o.s.
2004	**135**	Magnesium diamide
2005	**135**	Magnesium diphenyl
2006	**135**	Plastic, nitrocellulose-based, spontaneously combustible, n.o.s.
2006	**135**	Plastics, nitrocellulose-based, self-heating, n.o.s.
2008	**135**	Zirconium powder, dry
2009	**135**	Zirconium, dry, finished sheets, strips or coiled wire
2010	**138**	Magnesium hydride
2011	**139**	Magnesium phosphide
2012	**139**	Potassium phosphide
2013	**139**	Strontium phosphide
2014	**140**	Hydrogen peroxide, aqueous solution, with not less than 20% but not more than 60% Hydrogen peroxide (stabilized as necessary)

ID No.	Guide No.	Name of Material
2015	**143**	Hydrogen peroxide, aqueous solution, stabilized, with more than 60% Hydrogen peroxide
2015	**143**	Hydrogen peroxide, stabilized
2016	**151**	Ammunition, poisonous, non-explosive
2016	**151**	Ammunition, toxic, non-explosive
2017	**159**	Ammunition, tear-producing, non-explosive
2018	**152**	Chloroanilines, solid
2019	**152**	Chloroanilines, liquid
2020	**153**	Chlorophenols, solid
2021	**153**	Chlorophenols, liquid
2022	**153**	Cresylic acid
2023	**131P**	1-Chloro-2,3-epoxypropane
2023	**131P**	Epichlorohydrin
2024	**151**	Mercury compound, liquid, n.o.s.
2025	**151**	Mercury compound, solid, n.o.s.
2026	**151**	Phenylmercuric compound, n.o.s.
2027	**151**	Sodium arsenite, solid
2028	**153**	Bombs, smoke, non-explosive, with corrosive liquid, without initiating device
2029	**132**	Hydrazine, anhydrous
2029	**132**	Hydrazine, aqueous solutions, with more than 64% Hydrazine
2030	**153**	Hydrazine, aqueous solution, with more than 37% Hydrazine
2030	**153**	Hydrazine, aqueous solution, with not less than 37% but not more than 64% Hydrazine
2030	**153**	Hydrazine hydrate

ID No.	Guide No.	Name of Material	ID No.	Guide No.	Name of Material
2031	157	Nitric acid, other than red fuming, with more than 70% nitric acid	2053	129	Methylamyl alcohol
			2053	129	Methyl isobutyl carbinol
2031	157	Nitric acid, other than red fuming, with not more than 70% nitric acid	2053	129	M.I.B.C.
			2054	132	Morpholine
2032	157	Nitric acid, fuming	2055	128P	Styrene monomer, stabilized
2032	157	Nitric acid, red fuming	2056	127	Tetrahydrofuran
2033	154	Potassium monoxide	2057	128	Tripropylene
2034	115	Hydrogen and Methane mixture, compressed	2058	129	Valeraldehyde
			2059	127	Nitrocellulose, solution, flammable
2034	115	Methane and Hydrogen mixture, compressed	2059	127	Nitrocellulose, solution, in a flammable liquid
2035	115	Refrigerant gas R-143a	2067	140	Ammonium nitrate fertilizers
2035	115	1,1,1-Trifluoroethane	2068	140	Ammonium nitrate fertilizers, with Calcium carbonate
2035	115	Trifluoroethane, compressed	2069	140	Ammonium nitrate fertilizers, with Ammonium sulfate
2036	121	Xenon			
2036	121	Xenon, compressed	2069	140	Ammonium nitrate fertilizers, with Ammonium sulphate
2037	115	Gas cartridges			
2037	115	Receptacles, small, containing gas	2069	140	Ammonium nitrate mixed fertilizers
2038	152	Dinitrotoluenes	2070	143	Ammonium nitrate fertilizers, with Phosphate or Potash
2038	152	Dinitrotoluenes, liquid	2071	140	Ammonium nitrate fertilizer, with not more than 0.4% combustible material
2038	152	Dinitrotoluenes, solid			
2044	115	2,2-Dimethylpropane	2071	140	Ammonium nitrate fertilizers
2045	130	Isobutyl aldehyde	2072	140	Ammonium nitrate fertilizer, n.o.s.
2045	130	Isobutyraldehyde			
2046	130	Cymenes	2072	140	Ammonium nitrate fertilizers
2047	129	Dichloropropenes	2073	125	Ammonia, solution, with more than 35% but not more than 50% Ammonia
2048	130	Dicyclopentadiene			
2049	130	Diethylbenzene			
2050	128	Diisobutylene, isomeric compounds	2074	153P	Acrylamide
			2074	153P	Acrylamide, solid
2051	132	2-Dimethylaminoethanol	2075	153	Chloral, anhydrous, stabilized
2051	132	Dimethylethanolamine	2076	153	Cresols
2052	128	Dipentene			

ID No.	Guide No.	Name of Material
2076	153	Cresols, liquid
2076	153	Cresols, solid
2077	153	alpha-Naphthylamine
2077	153	Naphthylamine (alpha)
2078	156	Toluene diisocyanate
2079	154	Diethylenetriamine
2186	125	Hydrogen chloride, refrigerated liquid
2187	120	Carbon dioxide, refrigerated liquid
2188	119	Arsine
2188	119	SA
2189	119	Dichlorosilane
2190	124	Oxygen difluoride
2190	124	Oxygen difluoride, compressed
2191	123	Sulfuryl fluoride
2191	123	Sulphuryl fluoride
2192	119	Germane
2193	126	Hexafluoroethane
2193	126	Hexafluoroethane, compressed
2193	126	Refrigerant gas R-116
2193	126	Refrigerant gas R-116, compressed
2194	125	Selenium hexafluoride
2195	125	Tellurium hexafluoride
2196	125	Tungsten hexafluoride
2197	125	Hydrogen iodide, anhydrous
2198	125	Phosphorus pentafluoride
2198	125	Phosphorus pentafluoride, compressed
2199	119	Phosphine
2200	116P	Propadiene, stabilized

ID No.	Guide No.	Name of Material
2201	122	Nitrous oxide, refrigerated liquid
2202	117	Hydrogen selenide, anhydrous
2203	116	Silane
2203	116	Silane, compressed
2204	119	Carbonyl sulfide
2204	119	Carbonyl sulphide
2205	153	Adiponitrile
2206	155	Isocyanate solution, poisonous, n.o.s.
2206	155	Isocyanate solution, toxic, n.o.s.
2206	155	Isocyanate solutions, n.o.s.
2206	155	Isocyanates, n.o.s.
2206	155	Isocyanates, poisonous, n.o.s.
2206	155	Isocyanates, toxic, n.o.s.
2208	140	Bleaching powder
2208	140	Calcium hypochlorite mixture, dry, with more than 10% but not more than 39% available Chlorine
2209	132	Formaldehyde, solutions (Formalin) (corrosive)
2210	135	Maneb
2210	135	Maneb preparation, with not less than 60% Maneb
2211	133	Polymeric beads, expandable
2211	133	Polystyrene beads, expandable
2212	171	Asbestos
2212	171	Asbestos, blue
2212	171	Asbestos, brown
2212	171	Blue asbestos
2212	171	Brown asbestos
2213	133	Paraformaldehyde
2214	156	Phthalic anhydride

ID No.	Guide No.	Name of Material	ID No.	Guide No.	Name of Material
2215	156	Maleic anhydride	2242	128	Cycloheptene
2215	156	Maleic anhydride, molten	2243	130	Cyclohexyl acetate
2216	171	Fish meal, stabilized	2244	129	Cyclopentanol
2216	171	Fish scrap, stabilized	2245	128	Cyclopentanone
2217	135	Seed cake, with not more than 1.5% oil and not more than 11% moisture	2246	128	Cyclopentene
			2247	128	n-Decane
2218	132P	Acrylic acid, stabilized	2248	132	Di-n-butylamine
2219	129	Allyl glycidyl ether	2249	131	Dichlorodimethyl ether, symmetrical
2222	128	Anisole			
2224	152	Benzonitrile	2250	156	Dichlorophenyl isocyanates
2225	156	Benzenesulfonyl chloride	2251	128P	Bicyclo[2.2.1]hepta-2,5-diene, stabilized
2225	156	Benzenesulphonyl chloride			
2226	156	Benzotrichloride	2251	128P	2,5-Norbornadiene, stabilized
2227	130P	n-Butyl methacrylate, stabilized	2252	127	1,2-Dimethoxyethane
2232	153	Chloroacetaldehyde	2253	153	N,N-Dimethylaniline
2232	153	2-Chloroethanal	2254	133	Matches, fusee
2233	152	Chloroanisidines	2256	130	Cyclohexene
2234	130	Chlorobenzotrifluorides	2257	138	Potassium
2235	153	Chlorobenzyl chlorides	2257	138	Potassium, metal
2235	153	Chlorobenzyl chlorides, liquid	2258	132	1,2-Propylenediamine
2236	156	3-Chloro-4-methylphenyl isocyanate	2258	132	1,3-Propylenediamine
			2259	153	Triethylenetetramine
2236	156	3-Chloro-4-methylphenyl isocyanate, liquid	2260	132	Tripropylamine
			2261	153	Xylenols
2237	153	Chloronitroanilines	2261	153	Xylenols, solid
2238	129	Chlorotoluenes	2262	156	Dimethylcarbamoyl chloride
2239	153	Chlorotoluidines	2263	128	Dimethylcyclohexanes
2239	153	Chlorotoluidines, liquid	2264	132	N,N-Dimethylcyclohexylamine
2239	153	Chlorotoluidines, solid	2264	132	Dimethylcyclohexylamine
2240	154	Chromosulfuric acid	2265	129	N,N-Dimethylformamide
2240	154	Chromosulphuric acid	2266	132	Dimethyl-N-propylamine
2241	128	Cycloheptane	2267	156	Dimethyl thiophosphoryl chloride

ID No.	Guide No.	Name of Material
2269	153	3,3'-Iminodipropylamine
2270	132	Ethylamine, aqueous solution, with not less than 50% but not more than 70% Ethylamine
2271	128	Ethyl amyl ketone
2272	153	N-Ethylaniline
2273	153	2-Ethylaniline
2274	153	N-Ethyl-N-benzylaniline
2275	129	2-Ethylbutanol
2276	132	2-Ethylhexylamine
2277	130P	Ethyl methacrylate
2277	130P	Ethyl methacrylate, stabilized
2278	128	n-Heptene
2279	151	Hexachlorobutadiene
2280	153	Hexamethylenediamine, solid
2281	156	Hexamethylene diisocyanate
2282	129	Hexanols
2283	130P	Isobutyl methacrylate, stabilized
2284	131	Isobutyronitrile
2285	156	Isocyanatobenzotrifluorides
2286	128	Pentamethylheptane
2287	128	Isoheptenes
2288	128	Isohexenes
2289	153	Isophoronediamine
2290	156	IPDI
2290	156	Isophorone diisocyanate
2291	151	Lead compound, soluble, n.o.s.
2293	128	4-Methoxy-4-methylpentan-2-one
2294	153	N-Methylaniline
2295	155	Methyl chloroacetate
2296	128	Methylcyclohexane
2297	128	Methylcyclohexanone
2298	128	Methylcyclopentane
2299	155	Methyl dichloroacetate
2300	153	2-Methyl-5-ethylpyridine
2301	128	2-Methylfuran
2302	127	5-Methylhexan-2-one
2303	128	Isopropenylbenzene
2304	133	Naphthalene, molten
2305	153	Nitrobenzenesulfonic acid
2305	153	Nitrobenzenesulphonic acid
2306	152	Nitrobenzotrifluorides
2306	152	Nitrobenzotrifluorides, liquid
2307	152	3-Nitro-4-chlorobenzotrifluoride
2308	157	Nitrosylsulfuric acid
2308	157	Nitrosylsulfuric acid, liquid
2308	157	Nitrosylsulfuric acid, solid
2308	157	Nitrosylsulphuric acid
2308	157	Nitrosylsulphuric acid, liquid
2308	157	Nitrosylsulphuric acid, solid
2309	128P	Octadiene
2310	131	Pentan-2,4-dione
2310	131	2,4-Pentanedione
2310	131	Pentane-2,4-dione
2311	153	Phenetidines
2312	153	Phenol, molten
2313	129	Picolines
2315	171	Articles containing Polychlorinated biphenyls (PCB)
2315	171	PCB
2315	171	Polychlorinated biphenyls
2315	171	Polychlorinated biphenyls, liquid

ID No.	Guide No.	Name of Material
2315	171	Polychlorinated biphenyls, solid
2316	157	Sodium cuprocyanide, solid
2317	157	Sodium cuprocyanide, solution
2318	135	Sodium hydrosulfide, solid, with less than 25% water of crystallization
2318	135	Sodium hydrosulfide, with less than 25% water of crystallization
2318	135	Sodium hydrosulphide, solid, with less than 25% water of crystallization
2318	135	Sodium hydrosulphide, with less than 25% water of crystallization
2319	128	Terpene hydrocarbons, n.o.s.
2320	153	Tetraethylenepentamine
2321	153	Trichlorobenzenes, liquid
2322	152	Trichlorobutene
2323	130	Triethyl phosphite
2324	128	Triisobutylene
2325	129	1,3,5-Trimethylbenzene
2326	153	Trimethylcyclohexylamine
2327	153	Trimethylhexamethylenediamines
2328	156	Trimethylhexamethylene diisocyanate
2329	130	Trimethyl phosphite
2330	128	Undecane
2331	154	Zinc chloride, anhydrous
2332	129	Acetaldehyde oxime
2333	131	Allyl acetate
2334	131	Allylamine
2335	131	Allyl ethyl ether
2336	131	Allyl formate
2337	131	Phenyl mercaptan

ID No.	Guide No.	Name of Material
2338	127	Benzotrifluoride
2339	130	2-Bromobutane
2340	130	2-Bromoethyl ethyl ether
2341	130	1-Bromo-3-methylbutane
2342	130	Bromomethylpropanes
2343	130	2-Bromopentane
2344	129	2-Bromopropane
2344	129	Bromopropanes
2345	130	3-Bromopropyne
2346	127	Butanedione
2346	127	Diacetyl
2347	130	Butyl mercaptan
2348	129P	Butyl acrylates, stabilized
2350	127	Butyl methyl ether
2351	129	Butyl nitrites
2352	127P	Butyl vinyl ether, stabilized
2353	132	Butyryl chloride
2354	131	Chloromethyl ethyl ether
2356	129	2-Chloropropane
2357	132	Cyclohexylamine
2358	128P	Cyclooctatetraene
2359	132	Diallylamine
2360	131P	Diallyl ether
2361	132	Diisobutylamine
2362	130	1,1-Dichloroethane
2363	129	Ethyl mercaptan
2364	128	n-Propyl benzene
2366	128	Diethyl carbonate
2367	130	alpha-Methylvaleraldehyde
2367	130	Methyl valeraldehyde (alpha)
2368	128	alpha-Pinene

ID No.	Guide No.	Name of Material
2368	128	Pinene (alpha)
2370	128	1-Hexene
2371	128	Isopentenes
2372	129	1,2-Di-(dimethylamino)ethane
2373	127	Diethoxymethane
2374	127	3,3-Diethoxypropene
2375	129	Diethyl sulfide
2375	129	Diethyl sulphide
2376	127	2,3-Dihydropyran
2377	127	1,1-Dimethoxyethane
2378	131	2-Dimethylaminoacetonitrile
2379	132	1,3-Dimethylbutylamine
2380	127	Dimethyldiethoxysilane
2381	130	Dimethyl disulfide
2381	130	Dimethyl disulphide
2382	131	1,2-Dimethylhydrazine
2382	131	Dimethylhydrazine, symmetrical
2383	132	Dipropylamine
2384	127	Di-n-propyl ether
2384	127	Dipropyl ether
2385	129	Ethyl isobutyrate
2386	132	1-Ethylpiperidine
2387	130	Fluorobenzene
2388	130	Fluorotoluenes
2389	128	Furan
2390	129	2-Iodobutane
2391	129	Iodomethylpropanes
2392	129	Iodopropanes
2393	129	Isobutyl formate
2394	129	Isobutyl propionate
2395	132	Isobutyryl chloride

ID No.	Guide No.	Name of Material
2396	131P	Methacrylaldehyde, stabilized
2397	127	3-Methylbutan-2-one
2398	127	Methyl tert-butyl ether
2399	132	1-Methylpiperidine
2400	130	Methyl isovalerate
2401	132	Piperidine
2402	130	Propanethiols
2403	129P	Isopropenyl acetate
2404	131	Propionitrile
2405	129	Isopropyl butyrate
2406	127	Isopropyl isobutyrate
2407	155	Isopropyl chloroformate
2409	129	Isopropyl propionate
2410	129	1,2,3,6-Tetrahydropyridine
2410	129	1,2,5,6-Tetrahydropyridine
2411	131	Butyronitrile
2412	130	Tetrahydrothiophene
2413	128	Tetrapropyl orthotitanate
2414	130	Thiophene
2416	129	Trimethyl borate
2417	125	Carbonyl fluoride
2417	125	Carbonyl fluoride, compressed
2418	125	Sulfur tetrafluoride
2418	125	Sulphur tetrafluoride
2419	116	Bromotrifluoroethylene
2420	125	Hexafluoroacetone
2421	124	Nitrogen trioxide
2422	126	Octafluorobut-2-ene
2422	126	Refrigerant gas R-1318
2424	126	Octafluoropropane
2424	126	Refrigerant gas R-218

ID No.	Guide No.	Name of Material	ID No.	Guide No.	Name of Material
2426	140	Ammonium nitrate, liquid (hot concentrated solution)	2445	135	Lithium alkyls
2427	140	Potassium chlorate, aqueous solution	2445	135	Lithium alkyls, liquid
			2446	153	Nitrocresols
2427	140	Potassium chlorate, solution	2446	153	Nitrocresols, solid
2428	140	Sodium chlorate, aqueous solution	2447	136	Phosphorus, white, molten
			2447	136	White phosphorus, molten
2429	140	Calcium chlorate, aqueous solution	2447	136	Yellow phosphorus, molten
			2448	133	Sulfur, molten
2429	140	Calcium chlorate, solution	2448	133	Sulphur, molten
2430	153	Alkyl phenols, solid, n.o.s. (including C2-C12 homologues)	2451	122	Nitrogen trifluoride
			2451	122	Nitrogen trifluoride, compressed
2431	153	Anisidines	2452	116P	Ethylacetylene, stabilized
2431	153	Anisidines, liquid	2453	115	Ethyl fluoride
2431	153	Anisidines, solid	2453	115	Refrigerant gas R-161
2432	153	N,N-Diethylaniline	2454	115	Methyl fluoride
2433	152	Chloronitrotoluenes	2454	115	Refrigerant gas R-41
2433	152	Chloronitrotoluenes, liquid	2455	116	Methyl nitrite
2433	152	Chloronitrotoluenes, solid	2456	130P	2-Chloropropene
2434	156	Dibenzyldichlorosilane	2457	128	2,3-Dimethylbutane
2435	156	Ethylphenyldichlorosilane	2458	130	Hexadiene
2436	129	Thioacetic acid	2459	128	2-Methyl-1-butene
2437	156	Methylphenyldichlorosilane	2460	128	2-Methyl-2-butene
2438	132	Trimethylacetyl chloride	2461	128	Methylpentadiene
2439	154	Sodium hydrogendifluoride	2463	138	Aluminum hydride
2440	154	Stannic chloride, pentahydrate	2464	141	Beryllium nitrate
2440	154	Tin tetrachloride, pentahydrate	2465	140	Dichloroisocyanuric acid, dry
2441	135	Titanium trichloride, pyrophoric	2465	140	Dichloroisocyanuric acid salts
2441	135	Titanium trichloride mixture, pyrophoric	2465	140	Sodium dichloroisocyanurate
2442	156	Trichloroacetyl chloride	2465	140	Sodium dichloro-s-triazinetrione
2443	137	Vanadium oxytrichloride	2466	143	Potassium superoxide
2444	137	Vanadium tetrachloride	2468	140	Trichloroisocyanuric acid, dry

ID No.	Guide No.	Name of Material	ID No.	Guide No.	Name of Material
2469	140	Zinc bromate	2496	156	Propionic anhydride
2470	152	Phenylacetonitrile, liquid	2498	129	1,2,3,6-Tetrahydrobenzaldehyde
2471	154	Osmium tetroxide	2501	152	1-Aziridinyl phosphine oxide (Tris)
2473	154	Sodium arsanilate			
2474	157	Thiophosgene	2501	152	Tri-(1-aziridinyl)phosphine oxide, solution
2475	157	Vanadium trichloride	2501	152	Tris-(1-aziridinyl)phosphine oxide, solution
2477	131	Methyl isothiocyanate			
2478	155	Isocyanate solution, flammable, poisonous, n.o.s.	2502	132	Valeryl chloride
			2503	137	Zirconium tetrachloride
2478	155	Isocyanate solution, flammable, toxic, n.o.s.	2504	159	Acetylene tetrabromide
			2504	159	Tetrabromoethane
2478	155	Isocyanate solutions, n.o.s.	2505	154	Ammonium fluoride
2478	155	Isocyanates, flammable, poisonous, n.o.s.	2506	154	Ammonium hydrogen sulfate
			2506	154	Ammonium hydrogen sulphate
2478	155	Isocyanates, flammable, toxic, n.o.s.	2507	154	Chloroplatinic acid, solid
2478	155	Isocyanates, n.o.s.	2508	156	Molybdenum pentachloride
2480	155	Methyl isocyanate	2509	154	Potassium hydrogen sulfate
2481	155	Ethyl isocyanate	2509	154	Potassium hydrogen sulphate
2482	155	n-Propyl isocyanate	2511	153	2-Chloropropionic acid
2483	155	Isopropyl isocyanate	2511	153	2-Chloropropionic acid, solid
2484	155	tert-Butyl isocyanate	2511	153	2-Chloropropionic acid, solution
2485	155	n-Butyl isocyanate	2512	152	Aminophenols
2486	155	Isobutyl isocyanate	2513	156	Bromoacetyl bromide
2487	155	Phenyl isocyanate	2514	130	Bromobenzene
2488	155	Cyclohexyl isocyanate	2515	159	Bromoform
2490	153	Dichloroisopropyl ether	2516	151	Carbon tetrabromide
2491	153	Ethanolamine	2517	115	1-Chloro-1,1-difluoroethane
2491	153	Ethanolamine, solution	2517	115	Chlorodifluoroethanes
2491	153	Monoethanolamine	2517	115	Difluorochloroethanes
2493	132	Hexamethyleneimine	2517	115	Refrigerant gas R-142b
2495	144	Iodine pentafluoride	2518	153	1,5,9-Cyclododecatriene
			2520	130P	Cyclooctadienes

ID No.	Guide No.	Name of Material	ID No.	Guide No.	Name of Material
2521	131P	Diketene, stabilized	2556	113	Nitrocellulose with not less than 25% alcohol
2522	153P	2-Dimethylaminoethyl methacrylate	2557	133	Nitrocellulose
2522	153P	Dimethylaminoethyl methacrylate	2557	133	Nitrocellulose mixture, without pigment
2524	129	Ethyl orthoformate	2557	133	Nitrocellulose mixture, without plasticizer
2525	156	Ethyl oxalate	2557	133	Nitrocellulose mixture, with pigment
2526	132	Furfurylamine			
2527	129P	Isobutyl acrylate, stabilized	2557	133	Nitrocellulose mixture, with pigment and plasticizer
2528	130	Isobutyl isobutyrate	2557	133	Nitrocellulose mixture, with plasticizer
2529	132	Isobutyric acid			
2531	153P	Methacrylic acid, stabilized	2558	131	Epibromohydrin
2533	156	Methyl trichloroacetate	2560	129	2-Methylpentan-2-ol
2534	119	Methylchlorosilane	2561	128	3-Methyl-1-butene
2535	132	4-Methylmorpholine	2564	153	Trichloroacetic acid, solution
2535	132	N-Methylmorpholine	2565	153	Dicyclohexylamine
2535	132	Methylmorpholine	2567	154	Sodium pentachlorophenate
2536	127	Methyltetrahydrofuran	2570	154	Cadmium compound
2538	133	Nitronaphthalene	2571	156	Alkylsulfuric acids
2541	128	Terpinolene	2571	156	Alkylsulphuric acids
2542	153	Tributylamine	2571	156	Ethylsulfuric acid
2545	135	Hafnium powder, dry	2571	156	Ethylsulphuric acid
2546	135	Titanium powder, dry	2572	153	Phenylhydrazine
2547	143	Sodium superoxide	2573	141	Thallium chlorate
2548	124	Chlorine pentafluoride	2574	151	Tricresyl phosphate
2552	151	Hexafluoroacetone hydrate	2576	137	Phosphorus oxybromide, molten
2552	151	Hexafluoroacetone hydrate, liquid	2577	156	Phenylacetyl chloride
2554	130P	Methylallyl chloride	2578	157	Phosphorus trioxide
2555	113	Nitrocellulose with water, not less than 25% water	2579	153	Piperazine
			2580	154	Aluminum bromide, solution
2556	113	Nitrocellulose with alcohol	2581	154	Aluminum chloride, solution
			2582	154	Ferric chloride, solution

ID No.	Guide No.	Name of Material
2583	153	Alkyl sulfonic acids, solid, with more than 5% free Sulfuric acid
2583	153	Alkyl sulphonic acids, solid, with more than 5% free Sulphuric acid
2583	153	Aryl sulfonic acids, solid, with more than 5% free Sulfuric acid
2583	153	Aryl sulphonic acids, solid, with more than 5% free Sulphuric acid
2584	153	Alkyl sulfonic acids, liquid, with more than 5% free Sulfuric acid
2584	153	Alkyl sulphonic acids, liquid, with more than 5% free Sulphuric acid
2584	153	Aryl sulfonic acids, liquid, with more than 5% free Sulfuric acid
2584	153	Aryl sulphonic acids, liquid, with more than 5% free Sulphuric acid
2585	153	Alkyl sulfonic acids, solid, with not more than 5% free Sulfuric acid
2585	153	Alkyl sulphonic acids, solid, with not more than 5% free Sulphuric acid
2585	153	Aryl sulfonic acids, solid, with not more than 5% free Sulfuric acid
2585	153	Aryl sulphonic acids, solid, with not more than 5% free Sulphuric acid
2586	153	Alkyl sulfonic acids, liquid, with not more than 5% free Sulfuric acid
2586	153	Alkyl sulphonic acids, liquid, with not more than 5% free Sulphuric acid
2586	153	Aryl sulfonic acids, liquid, with not more than 5% free Sulfuric acid
2586	153	Aryl sulphonic acids, liquid, with not more than 5% free Sulphuric acid
2587	153	Benzoquinone
2588	151	Pesticide, solid, poisonous
2588	151	Pesticide, solid, poisonous, n.o.s.
2588	151	Pesticide, solid, toxic, n.o.s.
2589	155	Vinyl chloroacetate
2590	171	Asbestos, white
2590	171	White asbestos
2591	120	Xenon, refrigerated liquid (cryogenic liquid)
2599	126	Chlorotrifluoromethane and Trifluoromethane azeotropic mixture with approximately 60% Chlorotrifluoromethane
2599	126	Refrigerant gas R-13 and Refrigerant gas R-23 azeotropic mixture with 60% Refrigerant gas R-13
2599	126	Refrigerant gas R-23 and Refrigerant gas R-13 azeotropic mixture with 60% Refrigerant gas R-13
2599	126	Refrigerant gas R-503 (azeotropic mixture of Refrigerant gas R-13 and Refrigerant gas R-23 with approximately 60% Refrigerant gas R-13)
2599	126	Trifluoromethane and Chlorotrifluoromethane azeotropic mixture with approximately 60% Chlorotrifluoromethane
2600	119	Carbon monoxide and Hydrogen mixture, compressed

ID No.	Guide No.	Name of Material	ID No.	Guide No.	Name of Material
2600	119	Hydrogen and Carbon monoxide mixture, compressed	2616	129	Triisopropyl borate
			2617	129	Methylcyclohexanols
2601	115	Cyclobutane	2618	130P	Vinyltoluenes, stabilized
2602	126	Dichlorodifluoromethane and Difluoroethane azeotropic mixture with approximately 74% Dichlorodifluoromethane	2619	132	Benzyldimethylamine
			2620	130	Amyl butyrates
			2621	127	Acetyl methyl carbinol
2602	126	Difluoroethane and Dichlorodifluoromethane azeotropic mixture with approximately 74% Dichlorodifluoromethane	2622	131P	Glycidaldehyde
			2623	133	Firelighters, solid, with flammable liquid
			2624	138	Magnesium silicide
2602	126	Refrigerant gas R-12 and Refrigerant gas R-152a azeotropic mixture with 74% Refrigerant gas R-12	2626	140	Chloric acid, aqueous solution, with not more than 10% Chloric acid
			2627	140	Nitrites, inorganic, n.o.s.
2602	126	Refrigerant gas R-152a and Refrigerant gas R-12 azeotropic mixture with 74% Refrigerant gas R-12	2628	151	Potassium fluoroacetate
			2629	151	Sodium fluoroacetate
			2630	151	Selenates
2602	126	Refrigerant gas R-500 (azeotropic mixture of Refrigerant gas R-12 and Refrigerant gas R-152a with approximately 74% Refrigerant gas R-12)	2630	151	Selenites
			2642	154	Fluoroacetic acid
			2643	155	Methyl bromoacetate
			2644	151	Methyl iodide
			2645	153	Phenacyl bromide
2603	131	Cycloheptatriene	2646	151	Hexachlorocyclopentadiene
2604	132	Boron trifluoride diethyl etherate	2647	153	Malononitrile
2605	155	Methoxymethyl isocyanate	2648	154	1,2-Dibromobutan-3-one
2606	155	Methyl orthosilicate	2649	153	1,3-Dichloroacetone
2607	129P	Acrolein dimer, stabilized	2650	153	1,1-Dichloro-1-nitroethane
2608	129	Nitropropanes	2651	153	4,4'-Diaminodiphenylmethane
2609	156	Triallyl borate	2653	156	Benzyl iodide
2610	132	Triallylamine	2655	151	Potassium fluorosilicate
2611	131	Propylene chlorohydrin	2655	151	Potassium silicofluoride
2612	127	Methyl propyl ether	2656	154	Quinoline
2614	129	Methallyl alcohol	2657	153	Selenium disulfide
2615	127	Ethyl propyl ether			

ID No.	Guide No.	Name of Material	ID No.	Guide No.	Name of Material
2657	153	Selenium disulphide	2680	154	Lithium hydroxide, solid
2659	151	Sodium chloroacetate	2681	154	Caesium hydroxide, solution
2660	153	Mononitrotoluidines	2681	154	Cesium hydroxide, solution
2660	153	Nitrotoluidines (mono)	2682	157	Caesium hydroxide
2661	153	Hexachloroacetone	2682	157	Cesium hydroxide
2662	153	Hydroquinone	2683	132	Ammonium sulfide, solution
2662	153	Hydroquinone, solid	2683	132	Ammonium sulphide, solution
2664	160	Dibromomethane	2684	132	3-Diethylaminopropylamine
2667	152	Butyltoluenes	2684	132	Diethylaminopropylamine
2668	131	Chloroacetonitrile	2685	132	N,N-Diethylethylenediamine
2669	152	Chlorocresols	2686	132	2-Diethylaminoethanol
2669	152	Chlorocresols, liquid	2686	132	Diethylaminoethanol
2669	152	Chlorocresols, solid	2687	133	Dicyclohexylammonium nitrite
2669	152	Chlorocresols, solution	2688	159	1-Bromo-3-chloropropane
2670	157	Cyanuric chloride	2688	159	1-Chloro-3-bromopropane
2671	153	Aminopyridines	2689	153	Glycerol alpha-monochlorohydrin
2672	154	Ammonia, solution, with more than 10% but not more than 35% Ammonia	2690	152	N,n-Butylimidazole
2672	154	Ammonium hydroxide	2691	137	Phosphorus pentabromide
2672	154	Ammonium hydroxide, with more than 10% but not more than 35% Ammonia	2692	157	Boron tribromide
			2693	154	Bisulfites, aqueous solution, n.o.s.
2673	151	2-Amino-4-chlorophenol	2693	154	Bisulfites, inorganic, aqueous solution, n.o.s.
2674	154	Sodium fluorosilicate	2693	154	Bisulphites, aqueous solution, n.o.s.
2674	154	Sodium silicofluoride			
2676	119	Stibine	2693	154	Bisulphites, inorganic, aqueous solution, n.o.s.
2677	154	Rubidium hydroxide, solution			
2678	154	Rubidium hydroxide	2698	156	Tetrahydrophthalic anhydrides
2678	154	Rubidium hydroxide, solid	2699	154	Trifluoroacetic acid
2679	154	Lithium hydroxide, solution	2705	153P	1-Pentol
2680	154	Lithium hydroxide	2707	127	Dimethyldioxanes
2680	154	Lithium hydroxide, monohydrate	2709	128	Butylbenzenes
			2710	128	Dipropyl ketone

ID No.	Guide No.	Name of Material	ID No.	Guide No.	Name of Material
2713	153	Acridine	2734	132	Polyamines, liquid, corrosive, flammable, n.o.s.
2714	133	Zinc resinate	2735	153	Alkylamines, n.o.s.
2715	133	Aluminum resinate	2735	153	Amines, liquid, corrosive, n.o.s.
2716	153	1,4-Butynediol	2735	153	Polyalkylamines, n.o.s.
2717	133	Camphor	2735	153	Polyamines, liquid, corrosive, n.o.s.
2717	133	Camphor, synthetic			
2719	141	Barium bromate	2738	153	N-Butylaniline
2720	141	Chromium nitrate	2739	156	Butyric anhydride
2721	141	Copper chlorate	2740	155	n-Propyl chloroformate
2722	140	Lithium nitrate	2741	141	Barium hypochlorite, with more than 22% available Chlorine
2723	140	Magnesium chlorate			
2724	140	Manganese nitrate	2742	155	sec-Butyl chloroformate
2725	140	Nickel nitrate	2742	155	Chloroformates, n.o.s.
2726	140	Nickel nitrite	2742	155	Chloroformates, poisonous, corrosive, flammable, n.o.s.
2727	141	Thallium nitrate	2742	155	Chloroformates, toxic, corrosive, flammable, n.o.s.
2728	140	Zirconium nitrate			
2729	152	Hexachlorobenzene	2742	155	Isobutyl chloroformate
2730	152	Nitroanisoles	2743	155	n-Butyl chloroformate
2730	152	Nitroanisoles, liquid	2744	155	Cyclobutyl chloroformate
2730	152	Nitroanisoles, solid	2745	157	Chloromethyl chloroformate
2732	152	Nitrobromobenzenes	2746	156	Phenyl chloroformate
2732	152	Nitrobromobenzenes, liquid	2747	156	tert-Butylcyclohexyl chloroformate
2732	152	Nitrobromobenzenes, solid	2748	156	2-Ethylhexyl chloroformate
2733	132	Alkylamines, n.o.s.	2749	130	Tetramethylsilane
2733	132	Amines, flammable, corrosive, n.o.s.	2750	153	1,3-Dichloropropanol-2
2733	132	Polyalkylamines, n.o.s.	2751	155	Diethylthiophosphoryl chloride
2733	132	Polyamines, flammable, corrosive, n.o.s.	2752	127	1,2-Epoxy-3-ethoxypropane
2734	132	Alkylamines, n.o.s.	2753	153	N-Ethylbenzyltoluidines
2734	132	Amines, liquid, corrosive, flammable, n.o.s.	2753	153	N-Ethylbenzyltoluidines, liquid
2734	132	Polyalkylamines, n.o.s.	2753	153	N-Ethylbenzyltoluidines, solid
			2754	153	N-Ethyltoluidines

ID No.	Guide No.	Name of Material	ID No.	Guide No.	Name of Material
2757	151	Carbamate pesticide, solid, poisonous	2772	131	Dithiocarbamate pesticide, liquid, flammable, poisonous
2757	151	Carbamate pesticide, solid, toxic	2772	131	Dithiocarbamate pesticide, liquid, flammable, toxic
2758	131	Carbamate pesticide, liquid, flammable, poisonous	2772	131	Thiocarbamate pesticide, liquid, flammable, poisonous
2758	131	Carbamate pesticide, liquid, flammable, toxic	2772	131	Thiocarbamate pesticide, liquid, flammable, toxic
2759	151	Arsenical pesticide, solid, poisonous	2775	151	Copper based pesticide, solid, poisonous
2759	151	Arsenical pesticide, solid, toxic	2775	151	Copper based pesticide, solid, toxic
2760	131	Arsenical pesticide, liquid, flammable, poisonous	2776	131	Copper based pesticide, liquid, flammable, poisonous
2760	131	Arsenical pesticide, liquid, flammable, toxic	2776	131	Copper based pesticide, liquid, flammable, toxic
2761	151	Organochlorine pesticide, solid, poisonous	2777	151	Mercury based pesticide, solid, poisonous
2761	151	Organochlorine pesticide, solid, toxic	2777	151	Mercury based pesticide, solid, toxic
2762	131	Organochlorine pesticide, liquid, flammable, poisonous	2778	131	Mercury based pesticide, liquid, flammable, poisonous
2762	131	Organochlorine pesticide, liquid, flammable, toxic	2778	131	Mercury based pesticide, liquid, flammable, toxic
2763	151	Triazine pesticide, solid, poisonous	2779	153	Substituted nitrophenol pesticide, solid, poisonous
2763	151	Triazine pesticide, solid, toxic	2779	153	Substituted nitrophenol pesticide, solid, toxic
2764	131	Triazine pesticide, liquid, flammable, poisonous	2780	131	Substituted nitrophenol pesticide, liquid, flammable, poisonous
2764	131	Triazine pesticide, liquid, flammable, toxic	2780	131	Substituted nitrophenol pesticide, liquid, flammable, toxic
2771	151	Dithiocarbamate pesticide, solid, poisonous	2781	151	Bipyridilium pesticide, solid, poisonous
2771	151	Dithiocarbamate pesticide, solid, toxic	2781	151	Bipyridilium pesticide, solid, toxic
2771	151	Thiocarbamate pesticide, solid, poisonous	2782	131	Bipyridilium pesticide, liquid, flammable, poisonous
2771	151	Thiocarbamate pesticide, solid, toxic			

ID No.	Guide No.	Name of Material
2782	131	Bipyridilium pesticide, liquid, flammable, toxic
2783	152	Organophosphorus pesticide, solid, poisonous
2783	152	Organophosphorus pesticide, solid, toxic
2784	131	Organophosphorus pesticide, liquid, flammable, poisonous
2784	131	Organophosphorus pesticide, liquid, flammable, toxic
2785	152	4-Thiapentanal
2785	152	Thia-4-pentanal
2786	153	Organotin pesticide, solid, poisonous
2786	153	Organotin pesticide, solid, toxic
2787	131	Organotin pesticide, liquid, flammable, poisonous
2787	131	Organotin pesticide, liquid, flammable, toxic
2788	153	Organotin compound, liquid, n.o.s.
2789	132	Acetic acid, glacial
2789	132	Acetic acid, solution, more than 80% acid
2790	153	Acetic acid, solution, more than 10% but not more than 80% acid
2793	170	Ferrous metal borings, shavings, turnings or cuttings
2794	154	Batteries, wet, filled with acid
2795	154	Batteries, wet, filled with alkali
2796	157	Battery fluid, acid
2796	157	Sulfuric acid, with not more than 51% acid
2796	157	Sulphuric acid, with not more than 51% acid
2797	154	Battery fluid, alkali
2797	154	Battery fluid, alkali, with battery

ID No.	Guide No.	Name of Material
2797	154	Battery fluid, alkali, with electronic equipment or actuating device
2798	137	Benzene phosphorus dichloride
2798	137	Phenylphosphorus dichloride
2799	137	Benzene phosphorus thiodichloride
2799	137	Phenylphosphorus thiodichloride
2800	154	Batteries, wet, non-spillable
2801	154	Dye, liquid, corrosive, n.o.s.
2801	154	Dye intermediate, liquid, corrosive, n.o.s.
2802	154	Copper chloride
2803	172	Gallium
2805	138	Lithium hydride, fused solid
2806	138	Lithium nitride
2807	171	Magnetized material
2809	172	Mercury
2809	172	Mercury metal
2810	153	Buzz
2810	153	BZ
2810	153	Compound, tree or weed killing, liquid (toxic)
2810	153	CS
2810	153	DC
2810	153	GA
2810	153	GB
2810	153	GD
2810	153	GF
2810	153	H
2810	153	HD
2810	153	HL

ID No.	Guide No.	Name of Material	ID No.	Guide No.	Name of Material
2810	153	HN-1	2810	153	VX
2810	153	HN-2	2811	154	CX
2810	153	HN-3	2811	154	Poisonous solid, organic, n.o.s.
2810	153	L (Lewisite)	2811	154	Toxic solid, organic, n.o.s.
2810	153	Lewisite	2812	154	Sodium aluminate, solid
2810	153	Mustard	2813	138	Water-reactive solid, n.o.s.
2810	153	Mustard Lewisite	2814	158	Infectious substance, affecting humans
2810	153	Poisonous liquid, n.o.s.	2815	153	N-Aminoethylpiperazine
2810	153	Poisonous liquid, n.o.s. (Inhalation Hazard Zone A)	2817	154	Ammonium bifluoride, solution
2810	153	Poisonous liquid, n.o.s. (Inhalation Hazard Zone B)	2817	154	Ammonium hydrogendifluoride, solution
2810	153	Poisonous liquid, organic, n.o.s.	2817	154	Ammonium hydrogen fluoride, solution
2810	153	Poisonous liquid, organic, n.o.s. (Inhalation Hazard Zone A)	2818	154	Ammonium polysulfide, solution
2810	153	Poisonous liquid, organic, n.o.s. (Inhalation Hazard Zone B)	2818	154	Ammonium polysulphide, solution
2810	153	Sarin	2819	153	Amyl acid phosphate
2810	153	Soman	2820	153	Butyric acid
2810	153	Tabun	2821	153	Phenol solution
2810	153	Thickened GD	2822	153	2-Chloropyridine
2810	153	Toxic liquid, n.o.s.	2823	153	Crotonic acid
2810	153	Toxic liquid, n.o.s. (Inhalation Hazard Zone A)	2823	153	Crotonic acid, liquid
2810	153	Toxic liquid, n.o.s. (Inhalation Hazard Zone B)	2823	153	Crotonic acid, solid
2810	153	Toxic liquid, organic, n.o.s.	2826	155	Ethyl chlorothioformate
2810	153	Toxic liquid, organic, n.o.s. (Inhalation Hazard Zone A)	2829	153	Caproic acid
2810	153	Toxic liquid, organic, n.o.s. (Inhalation Hazard Zone B)	2829	153	Hexanoic acid
			2830	139	Lithium ferrosilicon
			2831	160	1,1,1-Trichloroethane
			2834	154	Phosphorous acid
			2834	154	Phosphorous acid, ortho
			2835	138	Sodium aluminum hydride
			2837	154	Bisulfates, aqueous solution

ID No.	Guide No.	Name of Material	ID No.	Guide No.	Name of Material
2837	154	Bisulphates, aqueous solution	2856	151	Fluorosilicates, n.o.s.
2837	154	Sodium bisulfate, solution	2856	151	Silicofluorides, n.o.s.
2837	154	Sodium bisulphate, solution	2857	126	Refrigerating machines, containing Ammonia solutions (UN2672)
2837	154	Sodium hydrogen sulfate, solution			
2837	154	Sodium hydrogen sulphate, solution	2857	126	Refrigerating machines, containing non-flammable, non-poisonous gases
2838	129P	Vinyl butyrate, stabilized	2857	126	Refrigerating machines, containing non-flammable, non-toxic gases
2839	153	Aldol			
2840	129	Butyraldoxime	2858	170	Zirconium, dry, coiled wire, finished metal sheets or strips
2841	131	Di-n-amylamine			
2842	129	Nitroethane			
2844	138	Calcium manganese silicon	2859	154	Ammonium metavanadate
2845	135	Ethyl phosphonous dichloride, anhydrous	2861	151	Ammonium polyvanadate
			2862	151	Vanadium pentoxide
2845	135	Methyl phosphonous dichloride	2863	154	Sodium ammonium vanadate
2845	135	Pyrophoric liquid, n.o.s.	2864	151	Potassium metavanadate
2845	135	Pyrophoric liquid, organic, n.o.s.	2865	154	Hydroxylamine sulfate
			2865	154	Hydroxylamine sulphate
2846	135	Pyrophoric solid, n.o.s.	2869	157	Titanium trichloride mixture
2846	135	Pyrophoric solid, organic, n.o.s.	2870	135	Aluminum borohydride
2849	153	3-Chloropropanol-1	2870	135	Aluminum borohydride in devices
2850	128	Propylene tetramer			
2851	157	Boron trifluoride, dihydrate	2871	170	Antimony powder
2852	113	Dipicryl sulfide, wetted with not less than 10% water	2872	159	Dibromochloropropanes
			2873	153	Dibutylaminoethanol
2852	113	Dipicryl sulphide, wetted with not less than 10% water	2874	153	Furfuryl alcohol
			2875	151	Hexachlorophene
2853	151	Magnesium fluorosilicate	2876	153	Resorcinol
2853	151	Magnesium silicofluoride	2878	170	Titanium sponge granules
2854	151	Ammonium fluorosilicate	2878	170	Titanium sponge powders
2854	151	Ammonium silicofluoride	2879	157	Selenium oxychloride
2855	151	Zinc fluorosilicate			
2855	151	Zinc silicofluoride			

ID No.	Guide No.	Name of Material	ID No.	Guide No.	Name of Material
2880	140	Calcium hypochlorite, hydrated, with not less than 5.5% but not more than 16% water	2909	161	Radioactive material, excepted package, articles manufactured from natural Uranium
2880	140	Calcium hypochlorite, hydrated mixture, with not less than 5.5% but not more than 16% water	2910	161	Radioactive material, excepted package, empty packaging
2881	135	Metal catalyst, dry	2910	161	Radioactive material, excepted package, instruments or articles
2881	135	Nickel catalyst, dry	2910	161	Radioactive material, excepted package, limited quantity of material
2900	158	Infectious substance, affecting animals only	2911	161	Radioactive material, excepted package, instruments or articles
2901	124	Bromine chloride	2912	162	Radioactive material, low specific activity (LSA), n.o.s.
2902	151	Pesticide, liquid, poisonous, n.o.s.	2912	162	Radioactive material, low specific activity (LSA-I), non fissile or fissile-excepted
2902	151	Pesticide, liquid, toxic, n.o.s.	2913	162	Radioactive material, surface contaminated objects (SCO)
2903	131	Pesticide, liquid, poisonous, flammable, n.o.s.	2913	162	Radioactive material, surface contaminated objects (SCO-I), non fissile or fissile-excepted
2903	131	Pesticide, liquid, toxic, flammable, n.o.s.			
2904	154	Chlorophenates, liquid	2913	162	Radioactive material, surface contaminated objects (SCO-II), non fissile or fissile-excepted
2904	154	Chlorophenolates, liquid			
2904	154	Phenolates, liquid	2915	163	Radioactive material, Type A package non-special form, non fissile or fissile-excepted
2905	154	Chlorophenates, solid			
2905	154	Chlorophenolates, solid	2916	163	Radioactive material, Type B(U) package, non fissile or fissile-excepted
2905	154	Phenolates, solid			
2907	133	Isosorbide dinitrate mixture	2917	163	Radioactive material, Type B(M) package, non fissile or fissile-excepted
2908	161	Radioactive material, excepted package, empty packaging			
2909	161	Radioactive material, excepted package, articles manufactured from depleted Uranium	2918	165	Radioactive material, fissile, n.o.s.
2909	161	Radioactive material, excepted package, articles manufactured from natural Thorium	2919	163	Radioactive material, transported under special arrangement, non fissile or fissile-excepted

ID No.	Guide No.	Name of Material
2920	132	Corrosive liquid, flammable, n.o.s.
2921	134	Corrosive solid, flammable, n.o.s.
2922	154	Corrosive liquid, poisonous, n.o.s.
2922	154	Corrosive liquid, toxic, n.o.s.
2923	154	Corrosive solid, poisonous, n.o.s.
2923	154	Corrosive solid, toxic, n.o.s.
2924	132	Flammable liquid, corrosive, n.o.s
2925	134	Flammable solid, corrosive, n.o.s.
2925	134	Flammable solid, corrosive, organic, n.o.s.
2926	134	Flammable solid, poisonous, n.o.s.
2926	134	Flammable solid, poisonous, organic, n.o.s.
2926	134	Flammable solid, toxic, organic, n.o.s.
2927	154	Ethyl phosphonothioic dichloride, anhydrous
2927	154	Ethyl phosphorodichloridate
2927	154	Poisonous liquid, corrosive, n.o.s.
2927	154	Poisonous liquid, corrosive, n.o.s. (Inhalation Hazard Zone A)
2927	154	Poisonous liquid, corrosive, n.o.s. (Inhalation Hazard Zone B)
2927	154	Poisonous liquid, corrosive, organic, n.o.s.
2927	154	Poisonous liquid, corrosive, organic, n.o.s. (Inhalation Hazard Zone A)
2927	154	Poisonous liquid, corrosive, organic, n.o.s. (Inhalation Hazard Zone B)
2927	154	Toxic liquid, corrosive, n.o.s.
2927	154	Toxic liquid, corrosive, n.o.s. (Inhalation Hazard Zone A)
2927	154	Toxic liquid, corrosive, n.o.s. (Inhalation Hazard Zone B)
2927	154	Toxic liquid, corrosive, organic, n.o.s.
2927	154	Toxic liquid, corrosive, organic, n.o.s. (Inhalation Hazard Zone A)
2927	154	Toxic liquid, corrosive, organic, n.o.s. (Inhalation Hazard Zone B)
2928	154	Poisonous solid, corrosive, n.o.s.
2928	154	Toxic solid, corrosive, organic, n.o.s.
2929	131	Poisonous liquid, flammable, n.o.s.
2929	131	Poisonous liquid, flammable, n.o.s. (Inhalation Hazard Zone A)
2929	131	Poisonous liquid, flammable, n.o.s. (Inhalation Hazard Zone B)
2929	131	Poisonous liquid, flammable, organic, n.o.s.
2929	131	Poisonous liquid, flammable, organic, n.o.s. (Inhalation Hazard Zone A)
2929	131	Poisonous liquid, flammable, organic, n.o.s. (Inhalation Hazard Zone B)
2929	131	Toxic liquid, flammable, n.o.s.
2929	131	Toxic liquid, flammable, n.o.s. (Inhalation Hazard Zone A)

ID No.	Guide No.	Name of Material
2929	**131**	Toxic liquid, flammable, n.o.s. (Inhalation Hazard Zone B)
2929	**131**	Toxic liquid, flammable, organic, n.o.s.
2929	**131**	Toxic liquid, flammable, organic, n.o.s. (Inhalation Hazard Zone A)
2929	**131**	Toxic liquid, flammable, organic, n.o.s. (Inhalation Hazard Zone B)
2930	**134**	Poisonous solid, flammable, n.o.s.
2930	**134**	Poisonous solid, flammable, organic, n.o.s.
2930	**134**	Toxic solid, flammable, n.o.s.
2930	**134**	Toxic solid, flammable, organic, n.o.s.
2931	**151**	Vanadyl sulfate
2931	**151**	Vanadyl sulphate
2933	**129**	Methyl 2-chloropropionate
2934	**129**	Isopropyl 2-chloropropionate
2935	**129**	Ethyl 2-chloropropionate
2936	**153**	Thiolactic acid
2937	**153**	alpha-Methylbenzyl alcohol
2937	**153**	alpha-Methylbenzyl alcohol, liquid
2937	**153**	Methylbenzyl alcohol (alpha)
2940	**135**	Cyclooctadiene phosphines
2940	**135**	9-Phosphabicyclononanes
2941	**153**	Fluoroanilines
2942	**153**	2-Trifluoromethylaniline
2943	**129**	Tetrahydrofurfurylamine
2945	**132**	N-Methylbutylamine
2946	**153**	2-Amino-5-diethylaminopentane
2947	**155**	Isopropyl chloroacetate
2948	**153**	3-Trifluoromethylaniline
2949	**154**	Sodium hydrosulfide, with not less than 25% water of crystallization
2949	**154**	Sodium hydrosulphide, with not less than 25% water of crystallization
2950	**138**	Magnesium granules, coated
2956	**149**	5-tert-Butyl-2,4,6-trinitro-m-xylene
2956	**149**	Musk xylene
2965	**139**	Boron trifluoride dimethyl etherate
2966	**153**	Thioglycol
2967	**154**	Sulfamic acid
2967	**154**	Sulphamic acid
2968	**135**	Maneb, stabilized
2968	**135**	Maneb preparation, stabilized
2969	**171**	Castor beans, meal, pomace or flake
2974	**164**	Radioactive material, special form, n.o.s.
2975	**162**	Thorium metal, pyrophoric
2976	**162**	Thorium nitrate, solid
2977	**166**	Radioactive material, Uranium hexafluoride, fissile
2977	**166**	Uranium hexafluoride, fissile containing more than 1% Uranium-235
2978	**166**	Radioactive material, Uranium hexafluoride
2978	**166**	Uranium hexafluoride
2978	**166**	Uranium hexafluoride, non fissile or fissile-excepted
2979	**162**	Uranium metal, pyrophoric
2980	**162**	Uranyl nitrate, hexahydrate, solution

ID No.	Guide No.	Name of Material
2981	162	Uranyl nitrate, solid
2982	163	Radioactive material, n.o.s.
2983	129P	Ethylene oxide and Propylene oxide mixture, with not more than 30% Ethylene oxide
2983	129P	Propylene oxide and Ethylene oxide mixture, with not more than 30% Ethylene oxide
2984	140	Hydrogen peroxide, aqueous solution, with not less than 8% but less than 20% Hydrogen peroxide
2985	155	Chlorosilanes, flammable, corrosive, n.o.s.
2985	155	Chlorosilanes, n.o.s.
2986	155	Chlorosilanes, corrosive, flammable, n.o.s.
2986	155	Chlorosilanes, n.o.s.
2987	156	Chlorosilanes, corrosive, n.o.s.
2987	156	Chlorosilanes, n.o.s.
2988	139	Chlorosilanes, n.o.s.
2988	139	Chlorosilanes, water-reactive, flammable, corrosive, n.o.s.
2989	133	Lead phosphite, dibasic
2990	171	Life-saving appliances, self-inflating
2991	131	Carbamate pesticide, liquid, poisonous, flammable
2991	131	Carbamate pesticide, liquid, toxic, flammable
2992	151	Carbamate pesticide, liquid, poisonous
2992	151	Carbamate pesticide, liquid, toxic
2993	131	Arsenical pesticide, liquid, poisonous, flammable
2993	131	Arsenical pesticide, liquid, toxic, flammable
2994	151	Arsenical pesticide, liquid, poisonous
2994	151	Arsenical pesticide, liquid, toxic
2995	131	Organochlorine pesticide, liquid, poisonous, flammable
2995	131	Organochlorine pesticide, liquid, toxic, flammable
2996	151	Organochlorine pesticide, liquid, poisonous
2996	151	Organochlorine pesticide, liquid, toxic
2997	131	Triazine pesticide, liquid, poisonous, flammable
2997	131	Triazine pesticide, liquid, toxic, flammable
2998	151	Triazine pesticide, liquid, poisonous
2998	151	Triazine pesticide, liquid, toxic
3002	151	Phenyl urea pesticide, liquid, poisonous
3002	151	Phenyl urea pesticide, liquid, toxic
3005	131	Dithiocarbamate pesticide, liquid, poisonous, flammable
3005	131	Dithiocarbamate pesticide, liquid, toxic, flammable
3005	131	Thiocarbamate pesticide, liquid, poisonous, flammable
3005	131	Thiocarbamate pesticide, liquid, toxic, flammable
3006	151	Dithiocarbamate pesticide, liquid, poisonous
3006	151	Dithiocarbamate pesticide, liquid, toxic
3006	151	Thiocarbamate pesticide, liquid, poisonous
3006	151	Thiocarbamate pesticide, liquid, toxic

ID No.	Guide No.	Name of Material	ID No.	Guide No.	Name of Material
3009	131	Copper based pesticide, liquid, poisonous, flammable	3018	152	Organophosphorus pesticide, liquid, toxic
3009	131	Copper based pesticide, liquid, toxic, flammable	3019	131	Organotin pesticide, liquid, poisonous, flammable
3010	151	Copper based pesticide, liquid, poisonous	3019	131	Organotin pesticide, liquid, toxic, flammable
3010	151	Copper based pesticide, liquid, toxic	3020	153	Organotin pesticide, liquid, poisonous
3011	131	Mercury based pesticide, liquid, poisonous, flammable	3020	153	Organotin pesticide, liquid, toxic
3011	131	Mercury based pesticide, liquid, toxic, flammable	3021	131	Pesticide, liquid, flammable, poisonous, n.o.s.
3012	151	Mercury based pesticide, liquid, poisonous	3021	131	Pesticide, liquid, flammable, toxic, n.o.s.
3012	151	Mercury based pesticide, liquid, toxic	3022	127P	1,2-Butylene oxide, stabilized
3013	131	Substituted nitrophenol pesticide, liquid, poisonous, flammable	3023	131	2-Methyl-2-heptanethiol
			3023	131	tert-Octyl mercaptan
3013	131	Substituted nitrophenol pesticide, liquid, toxic, flammable	3024	131	Coumarin derivative pesticide, liquid, flammable, poisonous
3014	153	Substituted nitrophenol pesticide, liquid, poisonous	3024	131	Coumarin derivative pesticide, liquid, flammable, toxic
3014	153	Substituted nitrophenol pesticide, liquid, toxic	3025	131	Coumarin derivative pesticide, liquid, poisonous, flammable
3015	131	Bipyridilium pesticide, liquid, poisonous, flammable	3025	131	Coumarin derivative pesticide, liquid, toxic, flammable
3015	131	Bipyridilium pesticide, liquid, toxic, flammable	3026	151	Coumarin derivative pesticide, liquid, poisonous
3016	151	Bipyridilium pesticide, liquid, poisonous	3026	151	Coumarin derivative pesticide, liquid, toxic
3016	151	Bipyridilium pesticide, liquid, toxic	3027	151	Coumarin derivative pesticide, solid, poisonous
3017	131	Organophosphorus pesticide, liquid, poisonous, flammable	3027	151	Coumarin derivative pesticide, solid, toxic
3017	131	Organophosphorus pesticide, liquid, toxic, flammable	3028	154	Batteries, dry, containing Potassium hydroxide solid
3018	152	Organophosphorus pesticide, liquid, poisonous	3048	157	Aluminum phosphide pesticide
			3049	138	Metal alkyl halides, water-reactive, n.o.s.

ID No.	Guide No.	Name of Material
3049	138	Metal aryl halides, water-reactive, n.o.s.
3050	138	Metal alkyl hydrides, water-reactive, n.o.s.
3050	138	Metal aryl hydrides, water-reactive, n.o.s.
3051	135	Aluminum alkyls
3052	135	Aluminum alkyl halides
3052	135	Aluminum alkyl halides, liquid
3052	135	Aluminum alkyl halides, solid
3053	135	Magnesium alkyls
3054	129	Cyclohexanethiol
3054	129	Cyclohexyl mercaptan
3055	154	2-(2-Aminoethoxy)ethanol
3056	129	n-Heptaldehyde
3057	125	Trifluoroacetyl chloride
3064	127	Nitroglycerin, solution in alcohol, with more than 1% but not more than 5% Nitroglycerin
3065	127	Alcoholic beverages
3066	153	Paint (corrosive)
3066	153	Paint related material (corrosive)
3070	126	Dichlorodifluoromethane and Ethylene oxide mixture, with not more than 12.5% Ethylene oxide
3070	126	Dichlorodifluoromethane and Ethylene oxide mixtures, with not more than 12% Ethylene oxide
3070	126	Ethylene oxide and Dichlorodifluoromethane mixture, with not more than 12.5% Ethylene oxide
3070	126	Ethylene oxide and Dichlorodifluoromethane mixtures, with not more than 12% Ethylene oxide
3071	131	Mercaptan mixture, liquid, poisonous, flammable, n.o.s.
3071	131	Mercaptan mixture, liquid, toxic, flammable, n.o.s.
3071	131	Mercaptans, liquid, poisonous, flammable, n.o.s.
3071	131	Mercaptans, liquid, toxic, flammable, n.o.s.
3072	171	Life-saving appliances, not self-inflating
3073	131P	Vinylpyridines, stabilized
3076	138	Aluminum alkyl hydrides
3077	171	Environmentally hazardous substances, solid, n.o.s.
3077	171	Hazardous waste, solid, n.o.s.
3077	171	Other regulated substances, solid, n.o.s.
3078	138	Cerium, turnings or gritty powder
3079	131P	Methacrylonitrile, stabilized
3080	155	Isocyanate solution, poisonous, flammable, n.o.s.
3080	155	Isocyanate solution, toxic, flammable, n.o.s.
3080	155	Isocyanate solutions, n.o.s.
3080	155	Isocyanates, n.o.s.
3080	155	Isocyanates, poisonous, flammable, n.o.s.
3080	155	Isocyanates, toxic, flammable, n.o.s.
3082	171	Environmentally hazardous substances, liquid, n.o.s.
3082	171	Hazardous waste, liquid, n.o.s.

ID No.	Guide No.	Name of Material	ID No.	Guide No.	Name of Material
3082	171	Other regulated substances, liquid, n.o.s.	3094	138	Corrosive liquid, which in contact with water emits flammable gases, n.o.s.
3083	124	Perchloryl fluoride	3095	136	Corrosive solid, self-heating, n.o.s.
3084	140	Corrosive solid, oxidizing, n.o.s.	3096	138	Corrosive solid, water-reactive, n.o.s.
3085	140	Oxidizing solid, corrosive, n.o.s.	3096	138	Corrosive solid, which in contact with water emits flammable gases, n.o.s.
3086	141	Poisonous solid, oxidizing, n.o.s.			
3086	141	Toxic solid, oxidizing, n.o.s.	3097	140	Flammable solid, oxidizing, n.o.s.
3087	141	Oxidizing solid, poisonous, n.o.s.	3098	140	Oxidizing liquid, corrosive, n.o.s.
3087	141	Oxidizing solid, toxic, n.o.s.	3099	142	Oxidizing liquid, poisonous, n.o.s.
3088	135	Self-heating solid, organic, n.o.s.	3099	142	Oxidizing liquid, toxic, n.o.s.
3089	170	Metal powder, flammable, n.o.s.	3100	135	Oxidizing solid, self-heating, n.o.s.
3090	138	Lithium batteries			
3090	138	Lithium batteries, liquid or solid cathode	3101	146	Organic peroxide type B, liquid
3090	138	Lithium metal batteries (including lithium alloy batteries)	3102	146	Organic peroxide type B, solid
			3103	146	Organic peroxide type C, liquid
3091	138	Lithium batteries contained in equipment	3104	146	Organic peroxide type C, solid
3091	138	Lithium batteries packed with equipment	3105	145	Organic peroxide type D, liquid
			3106	145	Organic peroxide type D, solid
3091	138	Lithium metal batteries contained in equipment (including lithium alloy batteries)	3107	145	Organic peroxide type E, liquid
			3108	145	Organic peroxide type E, solid
			3109	145	Organic peroxide type F, liquid
3091	138	Lithium metal batteries packed with equipment (including lithium alloy batteries)	3110	145	Organic peroxide type F, solid
			3111	148	Organic peroxide type B, liquid, temperature controlled
3092	129	1-Methoxy-2-propanol	3112	148	Organic peroxide type B, solid, temperature controlled
3093	140	Corrosive liquid, oxidizing, n.o.s.	3113	148	Organic peroxide type C, liquid, temperature controlled
3094	138	Corrosive liquid, water-reactive, n.o.s.	3114	148	Organic peroxide type C, solid, temperature controlled

ID No.	Guide No.	Name of Material
3115	**148**	Organic peroxide type D, liquid, temperature controlled
3116	**148**	Organic peroxide type D, solid, temperature controlled
3117	**148**	Organic peroxide type E, liquid, temperature controlled
3118	**148**	Organic peroxide type E, solid, temperature controlled
3119	**148**	Organic peroxide type F, liquid, temperature controlled
3120	**148**	Organic peroxide type F, solid, temperature controlled
3121	**144**	Oxidizing solid, water-reactive, n.o.s.
3122	**142**	Poisonous liquid, oxidizing, n.o.s.
3122	**142**	Poisonous liquid, oxidizing, n.o.s. (Inhalation Hazard Zone A)
3122	**142**	Poisonous liquid, oxidizing, n.o.s. (Inhalation Hazard Zone B)
3122	**142**	Toxic liquid, oxidizing, n.o.s.
3122	**142**	Toxic liquid, oxidizing, n.o.s. (Inhalation Hazard Zone A)
3122	**142**	Toxic liquid, oxidizing, n.o.s. (Inhalation Hazard Zone B)
3123	**139**	Poisonous liquid, water-reactive, n.o.s.
3123	**139**	Poisonous liquid, water-reactive, n.o.s. (Inhalation Hazard Zone A)
3123	**139**	Poisonous liquid, water-reactive, n.o.s. (Inhalation Hazard Zone B)
3123	**139**	Poisonous liquid, which in contact with water emits flammable gases, n.o.s.
3123	**139**	Poisonous liquid, which in contact with water emits flammable gases, n.o.s. (Inhalation Hazard Zone A)
3123	**139**	Poisonous liquid, which in contact with water emits flammable gases, n.o.s. (Inhalation Hazard Zone B)
3123	**139**	Toxic liquid, water-reactive, n.o.s.
3123	**139**	Toxic liquid, water-reactive, n.o.s. (Inhalation Hazard Zone A)
3123	**139**	Toxic liquid, water-reactive, n.o.s. (Inhalation Hazard Zone B)
3123	**139**	Toxic liquid, which in contact with water emits flammable gases, n.o.s.
3123	**139**	Toxic liquid, which in contact with water emits flammable gases, n.o.s. (Inhalation Hazard Zone A)
3123	**139**	Toxic liquid, which in contact with water emits flammable gases, n.o.s. (Inhalation Hazard Zone B)
3124	**136**	Poisonous solid, self-heating, n.o.s.
3124	**136**	Toxic solid, self-heating, n.o.s.
3125	**139**	Poisonous solid, water-reactive, n.o.s.
3125	**139**	Poisonous solid, which in contact with water emits flammable gases, n.o.s.
3125	**139**	Toxic solid, water-reactive, n.o.s.
3125	**139**	Toxic solid, which in contact with water emits flammable gases, n.o.s.
3126	**136**	Self-heating solid, corrosive, organic, n.o.s.

ID No.	Guide No.	Name of Material
3127	135	Self-heating solid, oxidizing, n.o.s.
3128	136	Self-heating solid, poisonous, organic, n.o.s.
3128	136	Self-heating solid, toxic, organic, n.o.s.
3129	138	Water-reactive liquid, corrosive, n.o.s.
3130	139	Water-reactive liquid, poisonous, n.o.s.
3130	139	Water-reactive liquid, toxic, n.o.s.
3131	138	Water-reactive solid, corrosive, n.o.s.
3132	138	Water-reactive solid, flammable, n.o.s.
3133	138	Water-reactive solid, oxidizing, n.o.s.
3134	139	Water-reactive solid, poisonous, n.o.s.
3134	139	Water-reactive solid, toxic, n.o.s.
3135	138	Water-reactive solid, self-heating, n.o.s.
3136	120	Trifluoromethane, refrigerated liquid
3137	140	Oxidizing solid, flammable, n.o.s.
3138	115	Acetylene, Ethylene and Propylene in mixture, refrigerated liquid containing at least 71.5% Ethylene with not more than 22.5% Acetylene and not more than 6% Propylene
3138	115	Ethylene, Acetylene and Propylene in mixture, refrigerated liquid containing at least 71.5% Ethylene with not more than 22.5% Acetylene and not more than 6% Propylene

ID No.	Guide No.	Name of Material
3138	115	Propylene, Ethylene and Acetylene in mixture, refrigerated liquid containing at least 71.5% Ethylene with not more than 22.5% Acetylene and not more than 6% Propylene
3139	140	Oxidizing liquid, n.o.s.
3140	151	Alkaloids, liquid, n.o.s. (poisonous)
3140	151	Alkaloid salts, liquid, n.o.s. (poisonous)
3141	157	Antimony compound, inorganic, liquid, n.o.s.
3142	151	Disinfectant, liquid, poisonous, n.o.s.
3142	151	Disinfectant, liquid, toxic, n.o.s.
3142	151	Disinfectants, liquid, n.o.s. (poisonous)
3143	151	Dye, solid, poisonous, n.o.s.
3143	151	Dye, solid, toxic, n.o.s.
3143	151	Dye intermediate, solid, poisonous, n.o.s.
3143	151	Dye intermediate, solid, toxic, n.o.s.
3144	151	Nicotine compound, liquid, n.o.s.
3144	151	Nicotine preparation, liquid, n.o.s.
3145	153	Alkyl phenols, liquid, n.o.s. (including C2-C12 homologues)
3146	153	Organotin compound, solid, n.o.s.
3147	154	Dye, solid, corrosive, n.o.s.
3147	154	Dye intermediate, solid, corrosive, n.o.s.
3148	138	Water-reactive liquid, n.o.s.

ID No.	Guide No.	Name of Material
3149	140	Hydrogen peroxide and Peroxyacetic acid mixture, with acid(s), water and not more than 5% Peroxyacetic acid, stabilized
3150	115	Devices, small, hydrocarbon gas powered, with release device
3150	115	Hydrocarbon gas refills for small devices, with release device
3151	171	Polyhalogenated biphenyls, liquid
3151	171	Polyhalogenated terphenyls, liquid
3152	171	Polyhalogenated biphenyls, solid
3152	171	Polyhalogenated terphenyls, solid
3153	115	Perfluoromethyl vinyl ether
3153	115	Perfluoro(methyl vinyl ether)
3154	115	Perfluoroethyl vinyl ether
3154	115	Perfluoro(ethyl vinyl ether)
3155	154	Pentachlorophenol
3156	122	Compressed gas, oxidizing, n.o.s.
3157	122	Liquefied gas, oxidizing, n.o.s.
3158	120	Gas, refrigerated liquid, n.o.s.
3159	126	Refrigerant gas R-134a
3159	126	1,1,1,2-Tetrafluoroethane
3160	119	Liquefied gas, poisonous, flammable, n.o.s.
3160	119	Liquefied gas, poisonous, flammable, n.o.s. (Inhalation Hazard Zone A)
3160	119	Liquefied gas, poisonous, flammable, n.o.s. (Inhalation Hazard Zone B)

ID No.	Guide No.	Name of Material
3160	119	Liquefied gas, poisonous, flammable, n.o.s. (Inhalation Hazard Zone C)
3160	119	Liquefied gas, poisonous, flammable, n.o.s. (Inhalation Hazard Zone D)
3160	119	Liquefied gas, toxic, flammable, n.o.s.
3160	119	Liquefied gas, toxic, flammable, n.o.s. (Inhalation Hazard Zone A)
3160	119	Liquefied gas, toxic, flammable, n.o.s. (Inhalation Hazard Zone B)
3160	119	Liquefied gas, toxic, flammable, n.o.s. (Inhalation Hazard Zone C)
3160	119	Liquefied gas, toxic, flammable, n.o.s. (Inhalation Hazard Zone D)
3161	115	Liquefied gas, flammable, n.o.s.
3162	123	Liquefied gas, poisonous, n.o.s.
3162	123	Liquefied gas, poisonous, n.o.s. (Inhalation Hazard Zone A)
3162	123	Liquefied gas, poisonous, n.o.s. (Inhalation Hazard Zone B)
3162	123	Liquefied gas, poisonous, n.o.s. (Inhalation Hazard Zone C)
3162	123	Liquefied gas, poisonous, n.o.s. (Inhalation Hazard Zone D)
3162	123	Liquefied gas, toxic, n.o.s.
3162	123	Liquefied gas, toxic, n.o.s. (Inhalation Hazard Zone A)
3162	123	Liquefied gas, toxic, n.o.s. (Inhalation Hazard Zone B)
3162	123	Liquefied gas, toxic, n.o.s. (Inhalation Hazard Zone C)
3162	123	Liquefied gas, toxic, n.o.s. (Inhalation Hazard Zone D)

ID No.	Guide No.	Name of Material	ID No.	Guide No.	Name of Material
3163	126	Liquefied gas, n.o.s.	3170	138	Aluminum dross
3164	126	Articles, pressurized, hydraulic (containing non-flammable gas)	3170	138	Aluminum processing by-products
			3170	138	Aluminum remelting by-products
3164	126	Articles, pressurized, pneumatic (containing non-flammable gas)	3170	138	Aluminum smelting by-products
3165	131	Aircraft hydraulic power unit fuel tank	3171	154	Battery-powered equipment (wet battery)
3166	128	Engine, fuel cell, flammable gas powered	3171	154	Battery-powered vehicle (wet battery)
3166	128	Engine, fuel cell, flammable liquid powered	3171	154	Wheelchair, electric, with batteries
3166	128	Engine, internal combustion	3172	153	Toxins, extracted from living sources, liquid, n.o.s.
3166	128	Engines, internal combustion, flammable gas powered	3172	153	Toxins, extracted from living sources, n.o.s.
3166	128	Engines, internal combustion, flammable liquid powered	3172	153	Toxins, extracted from living sources, solid, n.o.s.
3166	128	Vehicle, flammable gas powered	3174	135	Titanium disulfide
3166	128	Vehicle, flammable liquid powered	3174	135	Titanium disulphide
3166	128	Vehicle, fuel cell, flammable gas powered	3175	133	Solids containing flammable liquid, n.o.s.
3166	128	Vehicle, fuel cell, flammable liquid powered	3176	133	Flammable solid, organic, molten, n.o.s.
3167	115	Gas sample, non-pressurized, flammable, n.o.s., not refrigerated liquid	3178	133	Flammable solid, inorganic, n.o.s.
			3178	133	Smokeless powder for small arms
3168	119	Gas sample, non-pressurized, poisonous, flammable, n.o.s., not refrigerated liquid	3179	134	Flammable solid, poisonous, inorganic, n.o.s.
3168	119	Gas sample, non-pressurized, toxic, flammable, n.o.s., not refrigerated liquid	3179	134	Flammable solid, toxic, inorganic, n.o.s.
			3180	134	Flammable solid, corrosive, inorganic, n.o.s.
3169	123	Gas sample, non-pressurized, poisonous, n.o.s., not refrigerated liquid	3180	134	Flammable solid, inorganic, corrosive, n.o.s.
3169	123	Gas sample, non-pressurized, toxic, n.o.s., not refrigerated liquid	3181	133	Metal salts of organic compounds, flammable, n.o.s.

ID No.	Guide No.	Name of Material	ID No.	Guide No.	Name of Material
3182	170	Metal hydrides, flammable, n.o.s.	3203	135	Pyrophoric organometallic compound, water-reactive, n.o.s.
3183	135	Self-heating liquid, organic, n.o.s.	3205	135	Alkaline earth metal alcoholates, n.o.s.
3184	136	Self-heating liquid, poisonous, organic, n.o.s.	3206	136	Alkali metal alcoholates, self-heating, corrosive, n.o.s.
3184	136	Self-heating liquid, toxic, organic, n.o.s.	3207	138	Organometallic compound, water-reactive, flammable, n.o.s.
3185	136	Self-heating liquid, corrosive, organic, n.o.s.	3207	138	Organometallic compound dispersion, water-reactive, flammable, n.o.s.
3186	135	Self-heating liquid, inorganic, n.o.s.	3207	138	Organometallic compound solution, water-reactive, flammable, n.o.s.
3187	136	Self-heating liquid, poisonous, inorganic, n.o.s.			
3187	136	Self-heating liquid, toxic, inorganic, n.o.s.	3208	138	Metallic substance, water-reactive, n.o.s.
3188	136	Self-heating liquid, corrosive, inorganic, n.o.s.	3209	138	Metallic substance, water-reactive, self-heating, n.o.s.
3189	135	Metal powder, self-heating, n.o.s.	3210	140	Chlorates, inorganic, aqueous solution, n.o.s.
3189	135	Self-heating metal powders, n.o.s.	3211	140	Perchlorates, inorganic, aqueous solution, n.o.s.
3190	135	Self-heating solid, inorganic, n.o.s.	3212	140	Hypochlorites, inorganic, n.o.s.
3191	136	Self-heating solid, inorganic, poisonous, n.o.s.	3213	140	Bromates, inorganic, aqueous solution, n.o.s.
3191	136	Self-heating solid, inorganic, toxic, n.o.s.	3214	140	Permanganates, inorganic, aqueous solution, n.o.s.
3191	136	Self-heating solid, poisonous, inorganic, n.o.s.	3215	140	Persulfates, inorganic, n.o.s.
3191	136	Self-heating solid, toxic, inorganic, n.o.s.	3215	140	Persulphates, inorganic, n.o.s.
3192	136	Self-heating solid, corrosive, inorganic, n.o.s.	3216	140	Persulfates, inorganic, aqueous solution, n.o.s.
3194	135	Pyrophoric liquid, inorganic, n.o.s.	3216	140	Persulphates, inorganic, aqueous solution, n.o.s.
3200	135	Pyrophoric solid, inorganic, n.o.s.	3218	140	Nitrates, inorganic, aqueous solution, n.o.s.
			3219	140	Nitrites, inorganic, aqueous solution, n.o.s.
			3220	126	Pentafluoroethane

ID No.	Guide No.	Name of Material	ID No.	Guide No.	Name of Material
3220	126	Refrigerant gas R-125	3243	151	Solids containing toxic liquid, n.o.s.
3221	149	Self-reactive liquid type B	3244	154	Solids containing corrosive liquid, n.o.s.
3222	149	Self-reactive solid type B			
3223	149	Self-reactive liquid type C	3245	171	Genetically modified micro-organisms
3224	149	Self-reactive solid type C			
3225	149	Self-reactive liquid type D	3245	171	Genetically modified organisms
3226	149	Self-reactive solid type D	3246	156	Methanesulfonyl chloride
3227	149	Self-reactive liquid type E	3246	156	Methanesulphonyl chloride
3228	149	Self-reactive solid type E	3247	140	Sodium peroxoborate, anhydrous
3229	149	Self-reactive liquid type F			
3230	149	Self-reactive solid type F	3248	131	Medicine, liquid, flammable, poisonous, n.o.s.
3231	150	Self-reactive liquid type B, temperature controlled	3248	131	Medicine, liquid, flammable, toxic, n.o.s.
3232	150	Self-reactive solid type B, temperature controlled	3249	151	Medicine, solid, poisonous, n.o.s.
3233	150	Self-reactive liquid type C, temperature controlled	3249	151	Medicine, solid, toxic, n.o.s.
3234	150	Self-reactive solid type C, temperature controlled	3250	153	Chloroacetic acid, molten
3235	150	Self-reactive liquid type D, temperature controlled	3251	133	Isosorbide-5-mononitrate
3236	150	Self-reactive solid type D, temperature controlled	3252	115	Difluoromethane
			3252	115	Refrigerant gas R-32
3237	150	Self-reactive liquid type E, temperature controlled	3253	154	Disodium trioxosilicate
3238	150	Self-reactive solid type E, temperature controlled	3253	154	Disodium trioxosilicate, pentahydrate
3239	150	Self-reactive liquid type F, temperature controlled	3254	135	Tributylphosphane
			3254	135	Tributylphosphine
3240	150	Self-reactive solid type F, temperature controlled	3255	135	tert-Butyl hypochlorite
3241	133	2-Bromo-2-nitropropane-1, 3-diol	3256	128	Elevated temperature liquid, flammable, n.o.s., with flash point above 37.8°C (100°F), at or above its flash point
3242	149	Azodicarbonamide	3256	128	Elevated temperature liquid, flammable, n.o.s., with flash point above 60°C (140°F), at or above its flash point
3243	151	Solids containing poisonous liquid, n.o.s.			

ID No.	Guide No.	Name of Material	ID No.	Guide No.	Name of Material
3257	128	Elevated temperature liquid, n.o.s., at or above 100°C (212°F), and below its flash point	3273	131	Nitriles, flammable, poisonous, n.o.s.
3258	171	Elevated temperature solid, n.o.s., at or above 240°C (464°F)	3273	131	Nitriles, flammable, toxic, n.o.s.
			3274	132	Alcoholates solution, n.o.s., in alcohol
3259	154	Amines, solid, corrosive, n.o.s.	3275	131	Nitriles, poisonous, flammable, n.o.s.
3259	154	Polyamines, solid, corrosive, n.o.s.	3275	131	Nitriles, toxic, flammable, n.o.s.
3260	154	Corrosive solid, acidic, inorganic, n.o.s.	3276	151	Nitriles, liquid, poisonous, n.o.s.
3261	154	Corrosive solid, acidic, organic, n.o.s.	3276	151	Nitriles, liquid, toxic, n.o.s.
3262	154	Corrosive solid, basic, inorganic, n.o.s.	3276	151	Nitriles, poisonous, liquid, n.o.s.
3263	154	Corrosive solid, basic, organic, n.o.s.	3276	151	Nitriles, poisonous, n.o.s.
3264	154	Corrosive liquid, acidic, inorganic, n.o.s.	3276	151	Nitriles, toxic, liquid, n.o.s.
			3276	151	Nitriles, toxic, n.o.s.
3265	153	Corrosive liquid, acidic, organic, n.o.s.	3277	154	Chloroformates, poisonous, corrosive, n.o.s.
3266	154	Corrosive liquid, basic, inorganic, n.o.s.	3277	154	Chloroformates, toxic, corrosive, n.o.s.
3267	153	Corrosive liquid, basic, organic, n.o.s.	3278	151	Organophosphorus compound, liquid, poisonous, n.o.s.
3268	171	Air bag inflators	3278	151	Organophosphorus compound, liquid, toxic, n.o.s.
3268	171	Air bag inflators, pyrotechnic	3278	151	Organophosphorus compound, poisonous, liquid, n.o.s.
3268	171	Air bag modules			
3268	171	Air bag modules, pyrotechnic	3278	151	Organophosphorus compound, poisonous, n.o.s.
3268	171	Seat-belt modules	3278	151	Organophosphorus compound, toxic, liquid, n.o.s.
3268	171	Seat-belt pre-tensioners			
3268	171	Seat-belt pre-tensioners, pyrotechnic	3278	151	Organophosphorus compound, toxic, n.o.s.
3269	128	Polyester resin kit	3279	131	Organophosphorus compound, poisonous, flammable, n.o.s.
3270	133	Nitrocellulose membrane filters			
3271	127	Ethers, n.o.s.	3279	131	Organophosphorus compound, toxic, flammable, n.o.s.
3272	127	Esters, n.o.s.			

ID No.	Guide No.	Name of Material
3280	**151**	Organoarsenic compound, liquid, n.o.s.
3280	**151**	Organoarsenic compound, n.o.s.
3281	**151**	Metal carbonyls, liquid, n.o.s.
3281	**151**	Metal carbonyls, n.o.s.
3282	**151**	Organometallic compound, liquid, poisonous, n.o.s.
3282	**151**	Organometallic compound, liquid, toxic, n.o.s.
3282	**151**	Organometallic compound, poisonous, liquid, n.o.s.
3282	**151**	Organometallic compound, poisonous, n.o.s.
3282	**151**	Organometallic compound, toxic, liquid, n.o.s.
3282	**151**	Organometallic compound, toxic, n.o.s.
3283	**151**	Selenium compound, n.o.s.
3283	**151**	Selenium compound, solid, n.o.s.
3284	**151**	Tellurium compound, n.o.s.
3285	**151**	Vanadium compound, n.o.s.
3286	**131**	Flammable liquid, poisonous, corrosive, n.o.s.
3286	**131**	Flammable liquid, toxic, corrosive, n.o.s.
3287	**151**	Poisonous liquid, inorganic, n.o.s.
3287	**151**	Poisonous liquid, inorganic, n.o.s. (Inhalation Hazard Zone A)
3287	**151**	Poisonous liquid, inorganic, n.o.s. (Inhalation Hazard Zone B)
3287	**151**	Toxic liquid, inorganic, n.o.s.
3287	**151**	Toxic liquid, inorganic, n.o.s. (Inhalation Hazard Zone A)
3287	**151**	Toxic liquid, inorganic, n.o.s. (Inhalation Hazard Zone B)
3288	**151**	Poisonous solid, inorganic, n.o.s.
3288	**151**	Toxic solid, inorganic, n.o.s.
3289	**154**	Poisonous liquid, corrosive, inorganic, n.o.s.
3289	**154**	Poisonous liquid, corrosive, inorganic, n.o.s. (Inhalation Hazard Zone A)
3289	**154**	Poisonous liquid, corrosive, inorganic, n.o.s. (Inhalation Hazard Zone B)
3289	**154**	Toxic liquid, corrosive, inorganic, n.o.s.
3289	**154**	Toxic liquid, corrosive, inorganic, n.o.s. (Inhalation Hazard Zone A)
3289	**154**	Toxic liquid, corrosive, inorganic, n.o.s. (Inhalation Hazard Zone B)
3290	**154**	Poisonous solid, corrosive, inorganic, n.o.s.
3290	**154**	Toxic solid, corrosive, inorganic, n.o.s.
3291	**158**	(Bio)Medical waste, n.o.s.
3291	**158**	Clinical waste, unspecified, n.o.s.
3291	**158**	Medical waste, n.o.s.
3291	**158**	Regulated medical waste, n.o.s.
3292	**138**	Batteries, containing Sodium
3292	**138**	Cells, containing Sodium
3293	**152**	Hydrazine, aqueous solution, with not more than 37% Hydrazine
3294	**131**	Hydrogen cyanide, solution in alcohol, with not more than 45% Hydrogen cyanide
3295	**128**	Hydrocarbons, liquid, n.o.s.

ID No.	Guide No.	Name of Material
3296	126	Heptafluoropropane
3296	126	Refrigerant gas R-227
3297	126	Chlorotetrafluoroethane and Ethylene oxide mixture, with not more than 8.8% Ethylene oxide
3297	126	Ethylene oxide and Chlorotetrafluoroethane mixture, with not more than 8.8% Ethylene oxide
3298	126	Ethylene oxide and Pentafluoroethane mixture, with not more than 7.9% Ethylene oxide
3298	126	Pentafluoroethane and Ethylene oxide mixture, with not more than 7.9% Ethylene oxide
3299	126	Ethylene oxide and Tetrafluoroethane mixture, with not more than 5.6% Ethylene oxide
3299	126	Tetrafluoroethane and Ethylene oxide mixture, with not more than 5.6% Ethylene oxide
3300	119P	Carbon dioxide and Ethylene oxide mixture, with more than 87% Ethylene oxide
3300	119P	Ethylene oxide and Carbon dioxide mixture, with more than 87% Ethylene oxide
3301	136	Corrosive liquid, self-heating, n.o.s.
3302	152	2-Dimethylaminoethyl acrylate
3303	124	Compressed gas, poisonous, oxidizing, n.o.s.
3303	124	Compressed gas, poisonous, oxidizing, n.o.s. (Inhalation Hazard Zone A)
3303	124	Compressed gas, poisonous, oxidizing, n.o.s. (Inhalation Hazard Zone B)

ID No.	Guide No.	Name of Material
3303	124	Compressed gas, poisonous, oxidizing, n.o.s. (Inhalation Hazard Zone C)
3303	124	Compressed gas, poisonous, oxidizing, n.o.s. (Inhalation Hazard Zone D)
3303	124	Compressed gas, toxic, oxidizing, n.o.s.
3303	124	Compressed gas, toxic, oxidizing, n.o.s. (Inhalation Hazard Zone A)
3303	124	Compressed gas, toxic, oxidizing, n.o.s. (Inhalation Hazard Zone B)
3303	124	Compressed gas, toxic, oxidizing, n.o.s. (Inhalation Hazard Zone C)
3303	124	Compressed gas, toxic, oxidizing, n.o.s. (Inhalation Hazard Zone D)
3304	123	Compressed gas, poisonous, corrosive, n.o.s.
3304	123	Compressed gas, poisonous, corrosive, n.o.s. (Inhalation Hazard Zone A)
3304	123	Compressed gas, poisonous, corrosive, n.o.s. (Inhalation Hazard Zone B)
3304	123	Compressed gas, poisonous, corrosive, n.o.s. (Inhalation Hazard Zone C)
3304	123	Compressed gas, poisonous, corrosive, n.o.s. (Inhalation Hazard Zone D)
3304	123	Compressed gas, toxic, corrosive, n.o.s.
3304	123	Compressed gas, toxic, corrosive, n.o.s. (Inhalation Hazard Zone A)

ID No.	Guide No.	Name of Material
3304	**123**	Compressed gas, toxic, corrosive, n.o.s. (Inhalation Hazard Zone B)
3304	**123**	Compressed gas, toxic, corrosive, n.o.s. (Inhalation Hazard Zone C)
3304	**123**	Compressed gas, toxic, corrosive, n.o.s. (Inhalation Hazard Zone D)
3305	**119**	Compressed gas, poisonous, flammable, corrosive, n.o.s.
3305	**119**	Compressed gas, poisonous, flammable, corrosive, n.o.s. (Inhalation Hazard Zone A)
3305	**119**	Compressed gas, poisonous, flammable, corrosive, n.o.s. (Inhalation Hazard Zone B)
3305	**119**	Compressed gas, poisonous, flammable, corrosive, n.o.s. (Inhalation Hazard Zone C)
3305	**119**	Compressed gas, poisonous, flammable, corrosive, n.o.s. (Inhalation Hazard Zone D)
3305	**119**	Compressed gas, toxic, flammable, corrosive, n.o.s.
3305	**119**	Compressed gas, toxic, flammable, corrosive, n.o.s. (Inhalation Hazard Zone A)
3305	**119**	Compressed gas, toxic, flammable, corrosive, n.o.s. (Inhalation Hazard Zone B)
3305	**119**	Compressed gas, toxic, flammable, corrosive, n.o.s. (Inhalation Hazard Zone C)
3305	**119**	Compressed gas, toxic, flammable, corrosive, n.o.s. (Inhalation Hazard Zone D)
3306	**124**	Compressed gas, poisonous, oxidizing, corrosive, n.o.s.
3306	**124**	Compressed gas, poisonous, oxidizing, corrosive, n.o.s. (Inhalation Hazard Zone A)
3306	**124**	Compressed gas, poisonous, oxidizing, corrosive, n.o.s. (Inhalation Hazard Zone B)
3306	**124**	Compressed gas, poisonous, oxidizing, corrosive, n.o.s. (Inhalation Hazard Zone C)
3306	**124**	Compressed gas, poisonous, oxidizing, corrosive, n.o.s. (Inhalation Hazard Zone D)
3306	**124**	Compressed gas, toxic, oxidizing, corrosive, n.o.s.
3306	**124**	Compressed gas, toxic, oxidizing, corrosive, n.o.s. (Inhalation Hazard Zone A)
3306	**124**	Compressed gas, toxic, oxidizing, corrosive, n.o.s. (Inhalation Hazard Zone B)
3306	**124**	Compressed gas, toxic, oxidizing, corrosive, n.o.s. (Inhalation Hazard Zone C)
3306	**124**	Compressed gas, toxic, oxidizing, corrosive, n.o.s. (Inhalation Hazard Zone D)
3307	**124**	Liquefied gas, poisonous, oxidizing, n.o.s.
3307	**124**	Liquefied gas, poisonous, oxidizing, n.o.s. (Inhalation Hazard Zone A)
3307	**124**	Liquefied gas, poisonous, oxidizing, n.o.s. (Inhalation Hazard Zone B)
3307	**124**	Liquefied gas, poisonous, oxidizing, n.o.s. (Inhalation Hazard Zone C)
3307	**124**	Liquefied gas, poisonous, oxidizing, n.o.s. (Inhalation Hazard Zone D)

ID No.	Guide No.	Name of Material
3307	**124**	Liquefied gas, toxic, oxidizing, n.o.s.
3307	**124**	Liquefied gas, toxic, oxidizing, n.o.s. (Inhalation Hazard Zone A)
3307	**124**	Liquefied gas, toxic, oxidizing, n.o.s. (Inhalation Hazard Zone B)
3307	**124**	Liquefied gas, toxic, oxidizing, n.o.s. (Inhalation Hazard Zone C)
3307	**124**	Liquefied gas, toxic, oxidizing, n.o.s. (Inhalation Hazard Zone D)
3308	**123**	Liquefied gas, poisonous, corrosive, n.o.s.
3308	**123**	Liquefied gas, poisonous, corrosive, n.o.s. (Inhalation Hazard Zone A)
3308	**123**	Liquefied gas, poisonous, corrosive, n.o.s. (Inhalation Hazard Zone B)
3308	**123**	Liquefied gas, poisonous, corrosive, n.o.s. (Inhalation Hazard Zone C)
3308	**123**	Liquefied gas, poisonous, corrosive, n.o.s. (Inhalation Hazard Zone D)
3308	**123**	Liquefied gas, toxic, corrosive, n.o.s.
3308	**123**	Liquefied gas, toxic, corrosive, n.o.s. (Inhalation Hazard Zone A)
3308	**123**	Liquefied gas, toxic, corrosive, n.o.s. (Inhalation Hazard Zone B)
3308	**123**	Liquefied gas, toxic, corrosive, n.o.s. (Inhalation Hazard Zone C)
3308	**123**	Liquefied gas, toxic, corrosive, n.o.s. (Inhalation Hazard Zone D)
3309	**119**	Liquefied gas, poisonous, flammable, corrosive, n.o.s.
3309	**119**	Liquefied gas, poisonous, flammable, corrosive, n.o.s. (Inhalation Hazard Zone A)
3309	**119**	Liquefied gas, poisonous, flammable, corrosive, n.o.s. (Inhalation Hazard Zone B)
3309	**119**	Liquefied gas, poisonous, flammable, corrosive, n.o.s. (Inhalation Hazard Zone C)
3309	**119**	Liquefied gas, poisonous, flammable, corrosive, n.o.s. (Inhalation Hazard Zone D)
3309	**119**	Liquefied gas, toxic, flammable, corrosive, n.o.s.
3309	**119**	Liquefied gas, toxic, flammable, corrosive, n.o.s. (Inhalation Hazard Zone A)
3309	**119**	Liquefied gas, toxic, flammable, corrosive, n.o.s. (Inhalation Hazard Zone B)
3309	**119**	Liquefied gas, toxic, flammable, corrosive, n.o.s. (Inhalation Hazard Zone C)
3309	**119**	Liquefied gas, toxic, flammable, corrosive, n.o.s. (Inhalation Hazard Zone D)
3310	**124**	Liquefied gas, poisonous, oxidizing, corrosive, n.o.s.
3310	**124**	Liquefied gas, poisonous, oxidizing, corrosive, n.o.s. (Inhalation Hazard Zone A)
3310	**124**	Liquefied gas, poisonous, oxidizing, corrosive, n.o.s. (Inhalation Hazard Zone B)

ID No.	Guide No.	Name of Material
3310	**124**	Liquefied gas, poisonous, oxidizing, corrosive, n.o.s. (Inhalation Hazard Zone C)
3310	**124**	Liquefied gas, poisonous, oxidizing, corrosive, n.o.s. (Inhalation Hazard Zone D)
3310	**124**	Liquefied gas, toxic, oxidizing, corrosive, n.o.s.
3310	**124**	Liquefied gas, toxic, oxidizing, corrosive, n.o.s. (Inhalation Hazard Zone A)
3310	**124**	Liquefied gas, toxic, oxidizing, corrosive, n.o.s. (Inhalation Hazard Zone B)
3310	**124**	Liquefied gas, toxic, oxidizing, corrosive, n.o.s. (Inhalation Hazard Zone C)
3310	**124**	Liquefied gas, toxic, oxidizing, corrosive, n.o.s. (Inhalation Hazard Zone D)
3311	**122**	Gas, refrigerated liquid, oxidizing, n.o.s.
3312	**115**	Gas, refrigerated liquid, flammable, n.o.s.
3313	**135**	Organic pigments, self-heating
3314	**171**	Plastic molding compound
3314	**171**	Plastics moulding compound
3315	**151**	Chemical sample, poisonous
3315	**151**	Chemical sample, poisonous liquid
3315	**151**	Chemical sample, poisonous solid
3315	**151**	Chemical sample, toxic
3315	**151**	Chemical sample, toxic liquid
3315	**151**	Chemical sample, toxic solid
3316	**171**	Chemical kit
3316	**171**	First aid kit
3317	**113**	2-Amino-4,6-dinitrophenol, wetted with not less than 20% water
3318	**125**	Ammonia solution, with more than 50% Ammonia
3319	**113**	Nitroglycerin mixture, desensitized, solid, n.o.s., with more than 2% but not more than 10% Nitroglycerin
3319	**113**	Nitroglycerin mixture with more than 2% but not more than 10% Nitroglycerin, desensitized
3320	**157**	Sodium borohydride and Sodium hydroxide solution, with not more than 12% Sodium borohydride and not more than 40% Sodium hydroxide
3321	**162**	Radioactive material, low specific activity (LSA-II), non fissile or fissile-excepted
3322	**162**	Radioactive material, low specific activity (LSA-III), non fissile or fissile-excepted
3323	**163**	Radioactive material, Type C package, non-fissile or fissile excepted
3324	**165**	Radioactive material, low specific activity (LSA-II), fissile
3325	**165**	Radioactive material, low specific activity (LSA-III), fissile
3326	**165**	Radioactive material, surface contaminated objects (SCO-I), fissile
3326	**165**	Radioactive material, surface contaminated objects (SCO-II), fissile
3327	**165**	Radioactive material, Type A package, fissile, non-special form

ID No.	Guide No.	Name of Material
3328	165	Radioactive material, Type B(U) package, fissile
3329	165	Radioactive material, Type B(M) package, fissile
3330	165	Radioactive material, Type C package, fissile
3331	165	Radioactive material, transported under special arrangement, fissile
3332	164	Radioactive material, Type A package, special form, non fissile or fissile-excepted
3333	165	Radioactive material, Type A package, special form, fissile
3334	171	Aviation regulated liquid, n.o.s.
3334	171	Self-defense spray, non-pressurized
3335	171	Aviation regulated solid, n.o.s.
3336	130	Mercaptan mixture, liquid, flammable, n.o.s.
3336	130	Mercaptans, liquid, flammable, n.o.s.
3337	126	Refrigerant gas R-404A
3338	126	Refrigerant gas R-407A
3339	126	Refrigerant gas R-407B
3340	126	Refrigerant gas R-407C
3341	135	Thiourea dioxide
3342	135	Xanthates
3343	113	Nitroglycerin mixture, desensitized, liquid, flammable, n.o.s., with not more than 30% Nitroglycerin
3344	113	Pentaerythrite tetranitrate mixture, desensitized, solid, n.o.s., with more than 10% but not more than 20% PETN
3344	113	Pentaerythritol tetranitrate mixture, desensitized, solid, n.o.s., with more than 10% but not more than 20% PETN
3344	113	PETN mixture, desensitized, solid, n.o.s., with more than 10% but not more than 20% PETN
3345	153	Phenoxyacetic acid derivative pesticide, solid, poisonous
3345	153	Phenoxyacetic acid derivative pesticide, solid, toxic
3346	131	Phenoxyacetic acid derivative pesticide, liquid, flammable, poisonous
3346	131	Phenoxyacetic acid derivative pesticide, liquid, flammable, toxic
3347	131	Phenoxyacetic acid derivative pesticide, liquid, poisonous, flammable
3347	131	Phenoxyacetic acid derivative pesticide, liquid, toxic, flammable
3348	153	Phenoxyacetic acid derivative pesticide, liquid, poisonous
3348	153	Phenoxyacetic acid derivative pesticide, liquid, toxic
3349	151	Pyrethroid pesticide, solid, poisonous
3349	151	Pyrethroid pesticide, solid, toxic
3350	131	Pyrethroid pesticide, liquid, flammable, poisonous
3350	131	Pyrethroid pesticide, liquid, flammable, toxic
3351	131	Pyrethroid pesticide, liquid, poisonous, flammable
3351	131	Pyrethroid pesticide, liquid, toxic, flammable
3352	151	Pyrethroid pesticide, liquid, poisonous
3352	151	Pyrethroid pesticide, liquid, toxic

ID	Guide	Name of Material
3353	126	Air bag inflators, compressed gas
3353	126	Air bag modules, compressed gas
3353	126	Seat-belt pre-tensioners, compressed gas
3354	115	Insecticide gas, flammable, n.o.s.
3355	119	Insecticide gas, poisonous, flammable, n.o.s.
3355	119	Insecticide gas, poisonous, flammable, n.o.s. (Inhalation Hazard Zone A)
3355	119	Insecticide gas, poisonous, flammable, n.o.s. (Inhalation Hazard Zone B)
3355	119	Insecticide gas, poisonous, flammable, n.o.s. (Inhalation Hazard Zone C)
3355	119	Insecticide gas, poisonous, flammable, n.o.s. (Inhalation Hazard Zone D)
3355	119	Insecticide gas, toxic, flammable, n.o.s.
3355	119	Insecticide gas, toxic, flammable, n.o.s. (Inhalation Hazard Zone A)
3355	119	Insecticide gas, toxic, flammable, n.o.s. (Inhalation Hazard Zone B)
3355	119	Insecticide gas, toxic, flammable, n.o.s. (Inhalation Hazard Zone C)
3355	119	Insecticide gas, toxic, flammable, n.o.s. (Inhalation Hazard Zone D)
3356	140	Oxygen generator, chemical
3356	140	Oxygen generator, chemical, spent
3357	113	Nitroglycerin mixture, desensitized, liquid, n.o.s., with not more than 30% Nitroglycerin
3358	115	Refrigerating machines, containing flammable, non-poisonous, liquefied gases
3358	115	Refrigerating machines, containing flammable, non-toxic, liquefied gases
3359	171	Fumigated cargo transport unit
3359	171	Fumigated unit
3360	133	Fibers, vegetable, dry
3360	133	Fibres, vegetable, dry
3361	156	Chlorosilanes, poisonous, corrosive, n.o.s.
3361	156	Chlorosilanes, toxic, corrosive, n.o.s.
3362	155	Chlorosilanes, poisonous, corrosive, flammable, n.o.s.
3362	155	Chlorosilanes, toxic, corrosive, flammable, n.o.s.
3363	171	Dangerous goods in apparatus
3363	171	Dangerous goods in machinery
3364	113	Picric acid, wetted with not less than 10% water
3364	113	Trinitrophenol, wetted with not less than 10% water
3365	113	Picryl chloride, wetted with not less than 10% water
3365	113	Trinitrochlorobenzene, wetted with not less than 10% water
3366	113	TNT, wetted with not less than 10% water
3366	113	Trinitrotoluene, wetted with not less than 10% water
3367	113	Trinitrobenzene, wetted with not less than 10% water

ID No.	Guide No.	Name of Material
3368	113	Trinitrobenzoic acid, wetted with not less than 10% water
3369	113	Sodium dinitro-o-cresolate, wetted with not less than 10% water
3370	113	Urea nitrate, wetted with not less than 10% water
3371	129	2-Methylbutanal
3372	138	Organometallic compound, solid, water-reactive, flammable, n.o.s.
3373	158	Biological substance, category B
3373	158	Clinical specimens
3373	158	Diagnostic specimens
3374	116	Acetylene, solvent free
3375	140	Ammonium nitrate emulsion
3375	140	Ammonium nitrate gel
3375	140	Ammonium nitrate suspension
3376	113	4-Nitrophenylhydrazine, with not less than 30% water
3377	140	Sodium perborate monohydrate
3378	140	Sodium carbonate peroxyhydrate
3379	128	Desensitized explosive, liquid, n.o.s.
3380	133	Desensitized explosive, solid, n.o.s.
3381	151	Poisonous by inhalation liquid, n.o.s. (Inhalation Hazard Zone A)
3381	151	Toxic by inhalation liquid, n.o.s. (Inhalation Hazard Zone A)
3382	151	Poisonous by inhalation liquid, n.o.s. (Inhalation Hazard Zone B)
3382	151	Toxic by inhalation liquid, n.o.s. (Inhalation Hazard Zone B)

ID No.	Guide No.	Name of Material
3383	131	Poisonous by inhalation liquid, flammable, n.o.s. (Inhalation Hazard Zone A)
3383	131	Toxic by inhalation liquid, flammable, n.o.s. (Inhalation Hazard Zone A)
3384	131	Poisonous by inhalation liquid, flammable, n.o.s. (Inhalation Hazard Zone B)
3384	131	Toxic by inhalation liquid, flammable, n.o.s. (Inhalation Hazard Zone B)
3385	139	Poisonous by inhalation liquid, water-reactive, n.o.s. (Inhalation Hazard Zone A)
3385	139	Toxic by inhalation liquid, water-reactive, n.o.s. (Inhalation Hazard Zone A)
3386	139	Poisonous by inhalation liquid, water-reactive, n.o.s. (Inhalation Hazard Zone B)
3386	139	Toxic by inhalation liquid, water-reactive, n.o.s. (Inhalation Hazard Zone B)
3387	142	Poisonous by inhalation liquid, oxidizing, n.o.s. (Inhalation Hazard Zone A)
3387	142	Toxic by inhalation liquid, oxidizing, n.o.s. (Inhalation Hazard Zone A)
3388	142	Poisonous by inhalation liquid, oxidizing, n.o.s. (Inhalation Hazard Zone B)
3388	142	Toxic by inhalation liquid, oxidizing, n.o.s. (Inhalation Hazard Zone B)
3389	154	Poisonous by inhalation liquid, corrosive, n.o.s. (Inhalation Hazard Zone A)
3389	154	Toxic by inhalation liquid, corrosive, n.o.s. (Inhalation Hazard Zone A)

ID No.	Guide No.	Name of Material	ID No.	Guide No.	Name of Material
3390	154	Poisonous by inhalation liquid, corrosive, n.o.s. (Inhalation Hazard Zone B)	3407	140	Chlorate and Magnesium chloride mixture, solution
3390	154	Toxic by inhalation liquid, corrosive, n.o.s. (Inhalation Hazard Zone B)	3407	140	Magnesium chloride and Chlorate mixture, solution
3391	135	Organometallic substance, solid, pyrophoric	3408	141	Lead perchlorate, solution
			3409	152	Chloronitrobenzenes, liquid
3392	135	Organometallic substance, liquid, pyrophoric	3410	153	4-Chloro-o-toluidine hydrochloride, solution
3393	135	Organometallic substance, solid, pyrophoric, water-reactive	3411	153	beta-Naphthylamine, solution
3394	135	Organometallic substance, liquid, pyrophoric, water-reactive	3411	153	Naphthylamine (beta), solution
			3412	153	Formic acid, with not less than 5% but less than 10% acid
3395	135	Organometallic substance, solid, water-reactive	3412	153	Formic acid, with not less than 10% but not more than 85% acid
3396	138	Organometallic substance, solid, water-reactive, flammable	3413	157	Potassium cyanide, solution
			3414	157	Sodium cyanide, solution
3397	138	Organometallic substance, solid, water-reactive, self-heating	3415	154	Sodium fluoride, solution
			3416	153	Chloroacetophenone, liquid
			3417	152	Xylyl bromide, solid
3398	135	Organometallic substance, liquid, water-reactive	3418	151	2,4-Toluylenediamine, solution
3399	138	Organometallic substance, liquid, water-reactive, flammable	3419	157	Boron trifluoride acetic acid complex, solid
			3420	157	Boron trifluoride propionic acid complex, solid
3400	138	Organometallic substance, solid, self-heating	3421	154	Potassium hydrogen difluoride, solution
3401	138	Alkali metal amalgam, solid	3422	154	Potassium fluoride, solution
3402	138	Alkaline earth metal amalgam, solid	3423	153	Tetramethylammonium hydroxide, solid
3403	138	Potassium, metal alloys, solid	3424	141	Ammonium dinitro-o-cresolate, solution
3404	138	Potassium sodium alloys, solid	3425	156	Bromoacetic acid, solid
3404	138	Sodium potassium alloys, solid	3426	153P	Acrylamide, solution
3405	141	Barium chlorate, solution	3427	153	Chlorobenzyl chlorides, solid
3406	141	Barium perchlorate, solution	3428	156	3-Chloro-4-methylphenyl isocyanate, solid

ID No.	Guide No.	Name of Material	ID No.	Guide No.	Name of Material
3429	153	Chlorotoluidines, liquid	3454	152	Dinitrotoluenes, solid
3430	153	Xylenols, liquid	3455	153	Cresols, solid
3431	152	Nitrobenzotrifluorides, solid	3456	157	Nitrosylsulfuric acid, solid
3432	171	Polychlorinated biphenyls, solid	3456	157	Nitrosylsulphuric acid, solid
3433	135	Lithium alkyls, solid	3457	152	Chloronitrotoluenes, solid
3434	153	Nitrocresols, liquid	3458	152	Nitroanisoles, solid
3435	153	Hydroquinone, solution	3459	152	Nitrobromobenzenes, solid
3436	151	Hexafluoroacetone hydrate, solid	3460	153	N-Ethylbenzyltoluidines, solid
3437	152	Chlorocresols, solid	3461	135	Aluminum alkyl halides, solid
3438	153	alpha-Methylbenzyl alcohol, solid	3462	153	Toxins, extracted from living sources, solid, n.o.s.
3439	151	Nitriles, poisonous, solid, n.o.s.	3463	132	Propionic acid, with not less than 90% acid
3439	151	Nitriles, solid, poisonous, n.o.s.	3464	151	Organophosphorus compound, poisonous, solid, n.o.s.
3439	151	Nitriles, solid, toxic, n.o.s.	3464	151	Organophosphorus compound, solid, poisonous, n.o.s.
3439	151	Nitriles, toxic, solid, n.o.s.	3464	151	Organophosphorus compound, solid, toxic, n.o.s.
3440	151	Selenium compound, liquid, n.o.s.	3464	151	Organophosphorus compound, toxic, solid, n.o.s.
3441	153	Chlorodinitrobenzenes, solid	3465	151	Organoarsenic compound, solid, n.o.s.
3442	153	Dichloroanilines, solid	3466	151	Metal carbonyls, solid, n.o.s.
3443	152	Dinitrobenzenes, solid	3467	151	Organometallic compound, poisonous, solid, n.o.s.
3444	151	Nicotine hydrochloride, solid			
3445	151	Nicotine sulfate, solid	3467	151	Organometallic compound, solid, poisonous, n.o.s.
3445	151	Nicotine sulphate, solid	3467	151	Organometallic compound, solid, toxic, n.o.s.
3446	152	Nitrotoluenes, solid			
3447	152	Nitroxylenes, solid	3467	151	Organometallic compound, toxic, solid, n.o.s.
3448	159	Tear gas substance, solid, n.o.s.			
3449	159	Bromobenzyl cyanides, solid	3468	115	Hydrogen in a metal hydride storage system
3450	151	Diphenylchloroarsine, solid	3468	115	Hydrogen in a metal hydride storage system contained in equipment
3451	153	Toluidines, solid			
3452	153	Xylidines, solid			
3453	154	Phosphoric acid, solid			

ID No.	Guide No.	Name of Material
3468	115	Hydrogen in a metal hydride storage system packed with equipment
3469	132	Paint, flammable, corrosive
3469	132	Paint related material, flammable, corrosive
3470	132	Paint, corrosive, flammable
3470	132	Paint related material, corrosive, flammable
3471	154	Hydrogendifluorides, solution, n.o.s.
3472	153	Crotonic acid, liquid
3473	128	Fuel cell cartridges contained in equipment, containing flammable liquids
3473	128	Fuel cell cartridges containing flammable liquids
3473	128	Fuel cell cartridges packed with equipment, containing flammable liquids
3474	113	1-Hydroxybenzotriazole, anhydrous, wetted with not less than 20% water
3474	113	1-Hydroxybenzotriazole, monohydrate
3475	127	Ethanol and gasoline mixture, with more than 10% ethanol
3475	127	Ethanol and motor spirit mixture, with more than 10% ethanol
3475	127	Ethanol and petrol mixture, with more than 10% ethanol
3475	127	Gasoline and ethanol mixture, with more than 10% ethanol
3475	127	Motor spirit and ethanol mixture, with more than 10% ethanol
3475	127	Petrol and ethanol mixture, with more than 10% ethanol

ID No.	Guide No.	Name of Material
3476	138	Fuel cell cartridges contained in equipment, containing water-reactive substances
3476	138	Fuel cell cartridges, containing water-reactive substances
3476	138	Fuel cell cartridges packed with equipment, containing water-reactive substances
3477	153	Fuel cell cartridges contained in equipment, containing corrosive substances
3477	153	Fuel cell cartridges, containing corrosive substances
3477	153	Fuel cell cartridges packed with equipment, containing corrosive substances
3478	115	Fuel cell cartridges contained in equipment, containing liquefied flammable gas
3478	115	Fuel cell cartridges, containing liquefied flammable gas
3478	115	Fuel cell cartridges packed with equipment, containing liquefied flammable gas
3479	115	Fuel cell cartridges contained in equipment, containing hydrogen in metal hydride
3479	115	Fuel cell cartridges, containing hydrogen in metal hydride
3479	115	Fuel cell cartridges packed with equipment, containing hydrogen in metal hydride
3480	147	Lithium ion batteries (including lithium ion polymer batteries)
3481	147	Lithium ion batteries contained in equipment (including lithium ion polymer batteries)
3481	147	Lithium ion batteries packed with equipment (including lithium ion polymer batteries)
3482	138	Alkali metal dispersion, flammable

ID No.	Guide No.	Name of Material
3482	138	Alkaline earth metal dispersion, flammable
3483	131	Motor fuel anti-knock mixture, flammable
3484	132	Hydrazine aqueous solution, flammable, with more than 37% hydrazine, by mass
3485	140	Calcium hypochlorite, dry, corrosive, with more than 39% available chlorine (8.8% available oxygen)
3485	140	Calcium hypochlorite mixture, dry, corrosive, with more than 39% available chlorine (8.8% available oxygen)
3486	140	Calcium hypochlorite mixture, dry, corrosive, with more than 10% but not more than 39% available chlorine
3487	140	Calcium hypochlorite, hydrated, corrosive, with not less than 5.5% but not more than 16% water
3487	140	Calcium hypochlorite, hydrated mixture, corrosive, with not less than 5.5% but not more than 16% water
3488	131	Poisonous by inhalation liquid, flammable, corrosive, n.o.s. (Inhalation Hazard Zone A)
3488	131	Toxic by inhalation liquid, flammable, corrosive, n.o.s. (Inhalation Hazard Zone A)
3489	131	Poisonous by inhalation liquid, flammable, corrosive, n.o.s. (Inhalation Hazard Zone B)
3489	131	Toxic by inhalation liquid, flammable, corrosive, n.o.s. (Inhalation Hazard Zone B)
3490	155	Poisonous by inhalation liquid, water-reactive, flammable, n.o.s. (Inhalation Hazard Zone A)
3490	155	Toxic by inhalation liquid, water-reactive, flammable, n.o.s. (Inhalation Hazard Zone A)

ID No.	Guide No.	Name of Material
3491	155	Poisonous by inhalation liquid, water-reactive, flammable, n.o.s. (Inhalation Hazard Zone B)
3491	155	Toxic by inhalation liquid, water-reactive, flammable, n.o.s. (Inhalation Hazard Zone B)
3492	131	Poisonous by inhalation liquid, corrosive, flammable, n.o.s. (Inhalation Hazard Zone A)
3492	131	Toxic by inhalation liquid, corrosive, flammable, n.o.s. (Inhalation Hazard Zone A)
3493	131	Poisonous by inhalation liquid, corrosive, flammable, n.o.s. (Inhalation Hazard Zone B)
3493	131	Toxic by inhalation liquid, corrosive, flammable, n.o.s. (Inhalation Hazard Zone B)
3494	131	Petroleum sour crude oil, flammable, toxic
3495	154	Iodine
3496	171	Batteries, nickel-metal hydride
3497	133	Krill meal
3498	157	Iodine monochloride, liquid
3499	171	Capacitor, electric double layer
3500	126	Chemical under pressure, n.o.s.
3501	115	Chemical under pressure, flammable, n.o.s.
3502	123	Chemical under pressure, poisonous, n.o.s.
3502	123	Chemical under pressure, toxic, n.o.s.
3503	125	Chemical under pressure, corrosive, n.o.s.
3504	119	Chemical under pressure, flammable, poisonous, n.o.s.
3504	119	Chemical under pressure, flammable, toxic, n.o.s.

ID No.	Guide No.	Name of Material
3505	118	Chemical under pressure, flammable, corrosive, n.o.s.
3506	172	Mercury contained in manufactured articles
8000	171	Consumer commodity
9035	123	Gas identification set
9191	143	Chlorine dioxide, hydrate, frozen
9202	168	Carbon monoxide, refrigerated liquid (cryogenic liquid)
9206	137	Methyl phosphonic dichloride
9260	169	Aluminum, molten
9263	156	Chloropivaloyl chloride
9264	151	3,5-Dichloro-2,4,6-trifluoropyridine
9269	132	Trimethoxysilane
9279	115	Hydrogen absorbed in metal hydride

GREEN HIGHLIGHTED ENTRIES IN BLUE PAGES

For entries highlighted in green follow these steps:

- **IF THERE IS NO FIRE**:
    - Go directly to **Table 1** (green bordered pages)
    - Look up the ID number and name of material
    - Identify initial isolation and protective action distances

- **IF THERE IS A FIRE or A FIRE IS INVOLVED**:
    - Also consult the assigned orange guide
    - If applicable, apply the evacuation information shown under PUBLIC SAFETY

Note: If the name in **Table 1** is shown with "**When Spilled In Water**", these materials produce large amounts of Toxic Inhalation Hazard (TIH) gases when spilled in water. Some Water Reactive materials are also TIH materials themselves (e.g., Bromine trifluoride (1746), Thionyl chloride (1836), etc.). In these instances, two entries are provided in **Table 1** for land-based and water-based spills. If the Water Reactive material **is NOT** a TIH and this material **is NOT** spilled in water, **Table 1** and **Table 2** do not apply and safety distances will be found within the appropriate orange guide.

Name of Material	Guide No.	ID No.	Name of Material	Guide No.	ID No.
AC	117	1051	Acrolein dimer, stabilized	129P	2607
Acetal	127	1088	Acrylamide	153P	2074
Acetaldehyde	129	1089	Acrylamide, solid	153P	2074
Acetaldehyde ammonia	171	1841	Acrylamide, solution	153P	3426
Acetaldehyde oxime	129	2332	Acrylic acid, stabilized	132P	2218
Acetic acid, glacial	132	2789	Acrylonitrile, stabilized	131P	1093
Acetic acid, solution, more than 10% but not more than 80% acid	153	2790	Adamsite	154	1698
Acetic acid, solution, more than 80% acid	132	2789	Adhesives (flammable)	128	1133
Acetic anhydride	137	1715	Adiponitrile	153	2205
Acetone	127	1090	Aerosol dispensers	126	1950
Acetone cyanohydrin, stabilized	155	1541	Aerosols	126	1950
			Air, compressed	122	1002
Acetone oils	127	1091	Air, refrigerated liquid (cryogenic liquid)	122	1003
Acetonitrile	127	1648	Air, refrigerated liquid (cryogenic liquid), non-pressurized	122	1003
Acetyl bromide	156	1716			
Acetyl chloride	155	1717	Air bag inflators	171	3268
Acetylene	116	1001	Air bag inflators, compressed gas	126	3353
Acetylene, dissolved	116	1001			
Acetylene, solvent free	116	3374	Air bag inflators, pyrotechnic	171	3268
Acetylene, Ethylene and Propylene in mixture, refrigerated liquid containing at least 71.5% Ethylene with not more than 22.5% Acetylene and not more than 6% Propylene	115	3138	Air bag modules	171	3268
			Air bag modules, compressed gas	126	3353
			Air bag modules, pyrotechnic	171	3268
			Aircraft hydraulic power unit fuel tank	131	3165
Acetylene tetrabromide	159	2504	Alcoholates solution, n.o.s., in alcohol	132	3274
Acetyl iodide	156	1898			
Acetyl methyl carbinol	127	2621	Alcoholic beverages	127	3065
Acid, sludge	153	1906	Alcohols, flammable, poisonous, n.o.s.	131	1986
Acid butyl phosphate	153	1718			
Acridine	153	2713	Alcohols, flammable, toxic, n.o.s.	131	1986
Acrolein, stabilized	131P	1092	Alcohols, n.o.s.	127	1987
			Alcohols, poisonous, n.o.s.	131	1986

Name of Material	Guide No.	ID No.	Name of Material	Guide No.	ID No.
Alcohols, toxic, n.o.s.	131	1986	Alkaloid salts, liquid, n.o.s. (poisonous)	151	3140
Aldehydes, flammable, poisonous, n.o.s.	131	1988	Alkaloid salts, solid, n.o.s. (poisonous)	151	1544
Aldehydes, flammable, toxic, n.o.s.	131	1988	Alkylamines, n.o.s.	132	2733
Aldehydes, n.o.s.	129	1989	Alkylamines, n.o.s.	132	2734
Aldehydes, poisonous, n.o.s.	131	1988	Alkylamines, n.o.s.	153	2735
Aldehydes, toxic, n.o.s.	131	1988	Alkyl phenols, liquid, n.o.s. (including C2-C12 homologues)	153	3145
Aldol	153	2839			
Alkali metal alcoholates, self-heating, corrosive, n.o.s.	136	3206	Alkyl phenols, solid, n.o.s. (including C2-C12 homologues)	153	2430
Alkali metal alloy, liquid, n.o.s.	138	1421	Alkyl sulfonic acids, liquid, with more than 5% free Sulfuric acid	153	2584
Alkali metal amalgam	138	1389			
Alkali metal amalgam, liquid	138	1389	Alkyl sulfonic acids, liquid, with not more than 5% free Sulfuric acid	153	2586
Alkali metal amalgam, solid	138	1389			
Alkali metal amalgam, solid	138	3401	Alkyl sulfonic acids, solid, with more than 5% free Sulfuric acid	153	2583
Alkali metal amides	139	1390			
Alkali metal dispersion	138	1391	Alkyl sulfonic acids, solid, with not more than 5% free Sulfuric acid	153	2585
Alkali metal dispersion, flammable	138	3482			
Alkaline earth metal alcoholates, n.o.s.	135	3205	Alkylsulfuric acids	156	2571
Alkaline earth metal alloy, n.o.s.	138	1393	Alkyl sulphonic acids, liquid, with more than 5% free Sulphuric acid	153	2584
Alkaline earth metal amalgam	138	1392	Alkyl sulphonic acids, liquid, with not more than 5% free Sulphuric acid	153	2586
Alkaline earth metal amalgam, liquid	138	1392			
Alkaline earth metal amalgam, solid	138	3402	Alkyl sulphonic acids, solid, with more than 5% free Sulphuric acid	153	2583
Alkaline earth metal dispersion	138	1391	Alkyl sulphonic acids, solid, with not more than 5% free Sulphuric acid	153	2585
Alkaline earth metal dispersion, flammable	138	3482			
Alkaloids, liquid, n.o.s. (poisonous)	151	3140	Alkylsulphuric acids	156	2571
			Allyl acetate	131	2333
Alkaloids, solid, n.o.s. (poisonous)	151	1544	Allyl alcohol	131	1098
			Allylamine	131	2334

Name of Material	Guide No.	ID No.	Name of Material	Guide No.	ID No.
Allyl bromide	131	1099	Aluminum remelting by-products	138	3170
Allyl chloride	131	1100	Aluminum resinate	133	2715
Allyl chlorocarbonate	155	1722	Aluminum silicon powder, uncoated	138	1398
Allyl chloroformate	155	1722			
Allyl ethyl ether	131	2335	Aluminum smelting by-products	138	3170
Allyl formate	131	2336			
Allyl glycidyl ether	129	2219	Amines, flammable, corrosive, n.o.s.	132	2733
Allyl iodide	132	1723			
Allyl isothiocyanate, stabilized	155	1545	Amines, liquid, corrosive, flammable, n.o.s.	132	2734
Allyltrichlorosilane, stabilized	155	1724	Amines, liquid, corrosive, n.o.s.	153	2735
Aluminum, molten	169	9260			
Aluminum alkyl halides	135	3052	Amines, solid, corrosive, n.o.s.	154	3259
Aluminum alkyl halides, liquid	135	3052			
Aluminum alkyl halides, solid	135	3052	2-Amino-4-chlorophenol	151	2673
Aluminum alkyl halides, solid	135	3461	2-Amino-5-diethylaminopentane	153	2946
Aluminum alkyl hydrides	138	3076	2-Amino-4,6-dinitrophenol, wetted with not less than 20% water	113	3317
Aluminum alkyls	135	3051			
Aluminum borohydride	135	2870			
Aluminum borohydride in devices	135	2870	2-(2-Aminoethoxy)ethanol	154	3055
			N-Aminoethylpiperazine	153	2815
Aluminum bromide, anhydrous	137	1725	Aminophenols	152	2512
Aluminum bromide, solution	154	2580	Aminopyridines	153	2671
Aluminum carbide	138	1394	Ammonia, anhydrous	125	1005
Aluminum chloride, anhydrous	137	1726	Ammonia, solution, with more than 10% but not more than 35% Ammonia	154	2672
Aluminum chloride, solution	154	2581			
Aluminum dross	138	3170	Ammonia, solution, with more than 35% but not more than 50% Ammonia	125	2073
Aluminum ferrosilicon powder	139	1395			
Aluminum hydride	138	2463	Ammonia solution, with more than 50% Ammonia	125	3318
Aluminum nitrate	140	1438			
Aluminum phosphide	139	1397	Ammonium arsenate	151	1546
Aluminum phosphide pesticide	157	3048	Ammonium bifluoride, solid	154	1727
Aluminum powder, coated	170	1309	Ammonium bifluoride, solution	154	2817
Aluminum powder, pyrophoric	135	1383	Ammonium dichromate	141	1439
Aluminum powder, uncoated	138	1396	Ammonium dinitro-o-cresolate	141	1843
Aluminum processing by-products	138	3170			

Name of Material	Guide No.	ID No.	Name of Material	Guide No.	ID No.
Ammonium dinitro-o-cresolate, solid	141	1843	Ammonium nitrate fertilizers, with Calcium carbonate	140	2068
Ammonium dinitro-o-cresolate, solution	141	3424	Ammonium nitrate fertilizers, with Phosphate or Potash	143	2070
Ammonium fluoride	154	2505	Ammonium nitrate-fuel oil mixtures	112	——
Ammonium fluorosilicate	151	2854	Ammonium nitrate gel	140	3375
Ammonium hydrogendifluoride, solid	154	1727	Ammonium nitrate mixed fertilizers	140	2069
Ammonium hydrogendifluoride, solution	154	2817	Ammonium nitrate suspension	140	3375
Ammonium hydrogen fluoride, solid	154	1727	Ammonium perchlorate	143	1442
Ammonium hydrogen fluoride, solution	154	2817	Ammonium persulfate	140	1444
Ammonium hydrogen sulfate	154	2506	Ammonium persulphate	140	1444
Ammonium hydrogen sulphate	154	2506	Ammonium picrate, wetted with not less than 10% water	113	1310
Ammonium hydroxide	154	2672	Ammonium polysulfide, solution	154	2818
Ammonium hydroxide, with more than 10% but not more than 35% Ammonia	154	2672	Ammonium polysulphide, solution	154	2818
Ammonium metavanadate	154	2859	Ammonium polyvanadate	151	2861
Ammonium nitrate, liquid (hot concentrated solution)	140	2426	Ammonium silicofluoride	151	2854
Ammonium nitrate, with not more than 0.2% combustible substances	140	1942	Ammonium sulfide, solution	132	2683
			Ammonium sulphide, solution	132	2683
Ammonium nitrate emulsion	140	3375	Ammunition, poisonous, non-explosive	151	2016
Ammonium nitrate fertilizer, n.o.s.	140	2072	Ammunition, tear-producing, non-explosive	159	2017
Ammonium nitrate fertilizer, with not more than 0.4% combustible material	140	2071	Ammunition, toxic, non-explosive	151	2016
Ammonium nitrate fertilizers	140	2067	Amyl acetates	129	1104
Ammonium nitrate fertilizers	140	2071	Amyl acid phosphate	153	2819
Ammonium nitrate fertilizers	140	2072	Amyl alcohols	129	1105
Ammonium nitrate fertilizers, with Ammonium sulfate	140	2069	Amylamines	132	1106
			Amyl butyrates	130	2620
Ammonium nitrate fertilizers, with Ammonium sulphate	140	2069	Amyl chloride	129	1107
			n-Amylene	128	1108
			Amyl formates	129	1109

Name of Material	Guide No.	ID No.	Name of Material	Guide No.	ID No.
Amyl mercaptan	130	1111	Argon, compressed	121	1006
n-Amyl methyl ketone	127	1110	Argon, refrigerated liquid (cryogenic liquid)	120	1951
Amyl methyl ketone	127	1110	Arsenic	152	1558
Amyl nitrate	140	1112	Arsenic acid, liquid	154	1553
Amyl nitrite	129	1113	Arsenic acid, solid	154	1554
Amyltrichlorosilane	155	1728	Arsenical dust	152	1562
Anhydrous ammonia	125	1005	Arsenical pesticide, liquid, flammable, poisonous	131	2760
Aniline	153	1547			
Aniline hydrochloride	153	1548	Arsenical pesticide, liquid, flammable, toxic	131	2760
Anisidines	153	2431	Arsenical pesticide, liquid, poisonous	151	2994
Anisidines, liquid	153	2431	Arsenical pesticide, liquid, poisonous, flammable	131	2993
Anisidines, solid	153	2431			
Anisole	128	2222	Arsenical pesticide, liquid, toxic	151	2994
Anisoyl chloride	156	1729	Arsenical pesticide, liquid, toxic, flammable	131	2993
Antimony compound, inorganic, liquid, n.o.s.	157	3141			
Antimony compound, inorganic, n.o.s.	157	1549	Arsenical pesticide, solid, poisonous	151	2759
Antimony compound, inorganic, solid, n.o.s.	157	1549	Arsenical pesticide, solid, toxic	151	2759
Antimony lactate	151	1550	Arsenic bromide	151	1555
Antimony pentachloride, liquid	157	1730	Arsenic chloride	157	1560
Antimony pentachloride, solution	157	1731	Arsenic compound, liquid, n.o.s.	152	1556
Antimony pentafluoride	157	1732	Arsenic compound, liquid, n.o.s., inorganic	152	1556
Antimony potassium tartrate	151	1551	Arsenic compound, solid, n.o.s.	152	1557
Antimony powder	170	2871	Arsenic compound, solid, n.o.s., inorganic	152	1557
Antimony trichloride	157	1733			
Antimony trichloride, liquid	157	1733	Arsenic pentoxide	151	1559
Antimony trichloride, solid	157	1733	Arsenic trichloride	157	1560
Antimony trichloride, solution	157	1733	Arsenic trioxide	151	1561
Aqua regia	157	1798	Arsine	119	2188
Argon	121	1006			

Name of Material	Guide No.	ID No.	Name of Material	Guide No.	ID No.
Articles containing Polychlorinated biphenyls (PCB)	171	2315	1-Aziridinyl phosphine oxide (Tris)	152	2501
Articles, pressurized, hydraulic (containing non-flammable gas)	126	3164	Azodicarbonamide	149	3242
			Barium	138	1400
Articles, pressurized, pneumatic (containing non-flammable gas)	126	3164	Barium alloys, pyrophoric	135	1854
			Barium azide, wetted with not less than 50% water	113	1571
Aryl sulfonic acids, liquid, with more than 5% free Sulfuric acid	153	2584	Barium bromate	141	2719
			Barium chlorate	141	1445
Aryl sulfonic acids, liquid, with not more than 5% free Sulfuric acid	153	2586	Barium chlorate, solid	141	1445
			Barium chlorate, solution	141	3405
Aryl sulfonic acids, solid, with more than 5% free Sulfuric acid	153	2583	Barium compound, n.o.s.	154	1564
			Barium cyanide	157	1565
Aryl sulfonic acids, solid, with not more than 5% free Sulfuric acid	153	2585	Barium hypochlorite, with more than 22% available Chlorine	141	2741
			Barium nitrate	141	1446
Aryl sulphonic acids, liquid, with more than 5% free Sulphuric acid	153	2584	Barium oxide	157	1884
			Barium perchlorate	141	1447
Aryl sulphonic acids, liquid, with not more than 5% free Sulphuric acid	153	2586	Barium perchlorate, solid	141	1447
			Barium perchlorate, solution	141	3406
Aryl sulphonic acids, solid, with more than 5% free Sulphuric acid	153	2583	Barium permanganate	141	1448
			Barium peroxide	141	1449
Aryl sulphonic acids, solid, with not more than 5% free Sulphuric acid	153	2585	Batteries, containing Sodium	138	3292
			Batteries, dry, containing Potassium hydroxide solid	154	3028
Asbestos	171	2212	Batteries, nickel-metal hydride	171	3496
Asbestos, blue	171	2212	Batteries, wet, filled with acid	154	2794
Asbestos, brown	171	2212	Batteries, wet, filled with alkali	154	2795
Asbestos, white	171	2590	Batteries, wet, non-spillable	154	2800
Asphalt	130	1999	Battery fluid, acid	157	2796
Aviation regulated liquid, n.o.s.	171	3334	Battery fluid, alkali	154	2797
Aviation regulated solid, n.o.s.	171	3335	Battery fluid, alkali, with battery	154	2797

Name of Material	Guide No.	ID No.
Battery fluid, alkali, with electronic equipment or actuating device	154	2797
Battery-powered equipment (wet battery)	154	3171
Battery-powered vehicle (wet battery)	154	3171
Benzaldehyde	129	1990
Benzene	130	1114
Benzene phosphorus dichloride	137	2798
Benzene phosphorus thiodichloride	137	2799
Benzenesulfonyl chloride	156	2225
Benzenesulphonyl chloride	156	2225
Benzidine	153	1885
Benzonitrile	152	2224
Benzoquinone	153	2587
Benzotrichloride	156	2226
Benzotrifluoride	127	2338
Benzoyl chloride	137	1736
Benzyl bromide	156	1737
Benzyl chloride	156	1738
Benzyl chloroformate	137	1739
Benzyldimethylamine	132	2619
Benzylidene chloride	156	1886
Benzyl iodide	156	2653
Beryllium compound, n.o.s.	154	1566
Beryllium nitrate	141	2464
Beryllium powder	134	1567
Bhusa, wet, damp or contaminated with oil	133	1327
Bicyclo[2.2.1]hepta-2,5-diene, stabilized	128P	2251
Biological agents	158	——

Name of Material	Guide No.	ID No.
Biological substance, category B	158	3373
(Bio)Medical waste, n.o.s.	158	3291
Bipyridilium pesticide, liquid, flammable, poisonous	131	2782
Bipyridilium pesticide, liquid, flammable, toxic	131	2782
Bipyridilium pesticide, liquid, poisonous	151	3016
Bipyridilium pesticide, liquid, poisonous, flammable	131	3015
Bipyridilium pesticide, liquid, toxic	151	3016
Bipyridilium pesticide, liquid, toxic, flammable	131	3015
Bipyridilium pesticide, solid, poisonous	151	2781
Bipyridilium pesticide, solid, toxic	151	2781
Bisulfates, aqueous solution	154	2837
Bisulfites, aqueous solution, n.o.s.	154	2693
Bisulfites, inorganic, aqueous solution, n.o.s.	154	2693
Bisulphates, aqueous solution	154	2837
Bisulphites, aqueous solution, n.o.s.	154	2693
Bisulphites, inorganic, aqueous solution, n.o.s.	154	2693
Blasting agent, n.o.s.	112	——
Bleaching powder	140	2208
Blue asbestos	171	2212
Bombs, smoke, non-explosive, with corrosive liquid, without initiating device	153	2028
Borate and Chlorate mixtures	140	1458
Borneol	133	1312
Boron tribromide	157	2692
Boron trichloride	125	1741

Name of Material	Guide No.	ID No.	Name of Material	Guide No.	ID No.
Boron trifluoride	125	1008	Bromobenzyl cyanides, liquid	159	1694
Boron trifluoride, compressed	125	1008	Bromobenzyl cyanides, solid	159	1694
Boron trifluoride, dihydrate	157	2851	Bromobenzyl cyanides, solid	159	3449
Boron trifluoride acetic acid complex	157	1742	1-Bromobutane	130	1126
			2-Bromobutane	130	2339
Boron trifluoride acetic acid complex, liquid	157	1742	Bromochlorodifluoromethane	126	1974
			Bromochloromethane	160	1887
Boron trifluoride acetic acid complex, solid	157	3419	1-Bromo-3-chloropropane	159	2688
Boron trifluoride diethyl etherate	132	2604	2-Bromoethyl ethyl ether	130	2340
			Bromoform	159	2515
Boron trifluoride dimethyl etherate	139	2965	1-Bromo-3-methylbutane	130	2341
			Bromomethylpropanes	130	2342
Boron trifluoride propionic acid complex	157	1743	2-Bromo-2-nitropropane-1,3-diol	133	3241
			2-Bromopentane	130	2343
Boron trifluoride propionic acid complex, liquid	157	1743	2-Bromopropane	129	2344
			Bromopropanes	129	2344
Boron trifluoride propionic acid complex, solid	157	3420	3-Bromopropyne	130	2345
Bromates, inorganic, aqueous solution, n.o.s.	140	3213	Bromotrifluoroethylene	116	2419
			Bromotrifluoromethane	126	1009
Bromates, inorganic, n.o.s.	141	1450	Brown asbestos	171	2212
Bromine	154	1744	Brucine	152	1570
Bromine, solution	154	1744	Butadienes, stabilized	116P	1010
Bromine, solution (Inhalation Hazard Zone A)	154	1744	Butadienes and hydrocarbon mixture, stabilized	116P	1010
Bromine, solution (Inhalation Hazard Zone B)	154	1744	Butane	115	1011
			Butane	115	1075
Bromine chloride	124	2901	Butanedione	127	2346
Bromine pentafluoride	144	1745	Butane mixture	115	1011
Bromine trifluoride	144	1746	Butane mixture	115	1075
Bromoacetic acid	156	1938	Butanols	129	1120
Bromoacetic acid, solid	156	3425	Butyl acetates	129	1123
Bromoacetic acid, solution	156	1938	Butyl acid phosphate	153	1718
Bromoacetone	131	1569	Butyl acrylates, stabilized	129P	2348
Bromoacetyl bromide	156	2513			
Bromobenzene	130	2514			
Bromobenzyl cyanides	159	1694			

Name of Material	Guide No.	ID No.	Name of Material	Guide No.	ID No.
n-Butylamine	132	1125	Butyric anhydride	156	2739
N-Butylaniline	153	2738	Butyronitrile	131	2411
Butylbenzenes	128	2709	Butyryl chloride	132	2353
n-Butyl bromide	130	1126	Buzz	153	2810
Butyl chloride	130	1127	BZ	153	2810
n-Butyl chloroformate	155	2743	CA	159	1694
sec-Butyl chloroformate	155	2742	Cacodylic acid	151	1572
tert-Butylcyclohexyl chloroformate	156	2747	Cadmium compound	154	2570
Butylene	115	1012	Caesium	138	1407
Butylene	115	1075	Caesium hydroxide	157	2682
1,2-Butylene oxide, stabilized	127P	3022	Caesium hydroxide, solution	154	2681
Butyl ethers	128	1149	Caesium nitrate	140	1451
n-Butyl formate	129	1128	Calcium	138	1401
tert-Butyl hypochlorite	135	3255	Calcium, metal and alloys, pyrophoric	135	1855
N,n-Butylimidazole	152	2690	Calcium, pyrophoric	135	1855
n-Butyl isocyanate	155	2485	Calcium alloys, pyrophoric	135	1855
tert-Butyl isocyanate	155	2484	Calcium arsenate	151	1573
Butyl mercaptan	130	2347	Calcium arsenate and Calcium arsenite mixture, solid	151	1574
n-Butyl methacrylate, stabilized	130P	2227	Calcium arsenite and Calcium arsenate mixture, solid	151	1574
Butyl methyl ether	127	2350	Calcium carbide	138	1402
Butyl nitrites	129	2351	Calcium chlorate	140	1452
Butyl propionates	130	1914	Calcium chlorate, aqueous solution	140	2429
Butyltoluenes	152	2667	Calcium chlorate, solution	140	2429
Butyltrichlorosilane	155	1747	Calcium chlorite	140	1453
5-tert-Butyl-2,4,6-trinitro-m-xylene	149	2956	Calcium cyanamide, with more than 0.1% Calcium carbide	138	1403
Butyl vinyl ether, stabilized	127P	2352	Calcium cyanide	157	1575
1,4-Butynediol	153	2716	Calcium dithionite	135	1923
Butyraldehyde	129	1129	Calcium hydride	138	1404
Butyraldoxime	129	2840	Calcium hydrosulfite	135	1923
Butyric acid	153	2820	Calcium hydrosulphite	135	1923

Name of Material	Guide No.	ID No.	Name of Material	Guide No.	ID No.
Calcium hypochlorite, dry	140	1748	Calcium peroxide	140	1457
Calcium hypochlorite, dry, corrosive, with more than 39% available chlorine (8.8% available oxygen)	140	3485	Calcium phosphide	139	1360
			Calcium resinate	133	1313
			Calcium resinate, fused	133	1314
Calcium hypochlorite, hydrated, corrosive, with not less than 5.5% but not more than 16% water	140	3487	Calcium silicide	138	1405
			Camphor	133	2717
			Camphor, synthetic	133	2717
Calcium hypochlorite, hydrated, with not less than 5.5% but not more than 16% water	140	2880	Camphor oil	128	1130
			Capacitor, electric double layer	171	3499
			Caproic acid	153	2829
Calcium hypochlorite, hydrated mixture, corrosive, with not less than 5.5% but not more than 16% water	140	3487	Carbamate pesticide, liquid, flammable, poisonous	131	2758
			Carbamate pesticide, liquid, flammable, toxic	131	2758
Calcium hypochlorite, hydrated mixture, with not less than 5.5% but not more than 16% water	140	2880	Carbamate pesticide, liquid, poisonous	151	2992
			Carbamate pesticide, liquid, poisonous, flammable	131	2991
Calcium hypochlorite mixture, dry, corrosive, with more than 10% but not more than 39% available chlorine	140	3486	Carbamate pesticide, liquid, toxic	151	2992
			Carbamate pesticide, liquid, toxic, flammable	131	2991
Calcium hypochlorite mixture, dry, corrosive, with more than 39% available chlorine (8.8% available oxygen)	140	3485	Carbamate pesticide, solid, poisonous	151	2757
			Carbamate pesticide, solid, toxic	151	2757
Calcium hypochlorite mixture, dry, with more than 10% but not more than 39% available Chlorine	140	2208	Carbon, activated	133	1362
			Carbon, animal or vegetable origin	133	1361
Calcium hypochlorite mixture, dry, with more than 39% available Chlorine (8.8% available Oxygen)	140	1748	Carbon bisulfide	131	1131
			Carbon bisulphide	131	1131
			Carbon dioxide	120	1013
Calcium manganese silicon	138	2844	Carbon dioxide, compressed	120	1013
Calcium nitrate	140	1454	Carbon dioxide, refrigerated liquid	120	2187
Calcium oxide	157	1910			
Calcium perchlorate	140	1455	Carbon dioxide, solid	120	1845
Calcium permanganate	140	1456			

Name of Material	Guide No.	ID No.	Name of Material	Guide No.	ID No.
Carbon dioxide and Ethylene oxide mixture, with more than 9% but not more than 87% Ethylene oxide	115	1041	Caustic potash, liquid	154	1814
			Caustic potash, solution	154	1814
			Caustic soda, bead	154	1823
Carbon dioxide and Ethylene oxide mixture, with more than 87% Ethylene oxide	119P	3300	Caustic soda, flake	154	1823
			Caustic soda, granular	154	1823
			Caustic soda, solid	154	1823
Carbon dioxide and Ethylene oxide mixtures, with more than 6% Ethylene oxide	115	1041	Caustic soda, solution	154	1824
			Cells, containing Sodium	138	3292
Carbon dioxide and Ethylene oxide mixtures, with not more than 6% Ethylene oxide	126	1952	Celluloid, in blocks, rods, rolls, sheets, tubes, etc., except scrap	133	2000
Carbon dioxide and Ethylene oxide mixtures, with not more than 9% Ethylene oxide	126	1952	Celluloid, scrap	135	2002
			Cerium, slabs, ingots or rods	170	1333
			Cerium, turnings or gritty powder	138	3078
Carbon dioxide and Nitrous oxide mixture	126	1015	Cesium	138	1407
Carbon dioxide and Oxygen mixture, compressed	122	1014	Cesium hydroxide	157	2682
			Cesium hydroxide, solution	154	2681
Carbon disulfide	131	1131	Cesium nitrate	140	1451
Carbon disulphide	131	1131	CG	125	1076
Carbon monoxide	119	1016	Charcoal	133	1361
Carbon monoxide, compressed	119	1016	Chemical kit	154	1760
			Chemical kit	171	3316
Carbon monoxide, refrigerated liquid (cryogenic liquid)	168	9202	Chemical sample, poisonous	151	3315
Carbon monoxide and Hydrogen mixture, compressed	119	2600	Chemical sample, poisonous liquid	151	3315
			Chemical sample, poisonous solid	151	3315
Carbon tetrabromide	151	2516	Chemical sample, toxic	151	3315
Carbon tetrachloride	151	1846	Chemical sample, toxic liquid	151	3315
Carbonyl fluoride	125	2417	Chemical sample, toxic solid	151	3315
Carbonyl fluoride, compressed	125	2417	Chemical under pressure, corrosive, n.o.s.	125	3503
Carbonyl sulfide	119	2204			
Carbonyl sulphide	119	2204	Chemical under pressure, flammable, corrosive, n.o.s.	118	3505
Castor beans, meal, pomace or flake	171	2969			
Caustic alkali liquid, n.o.s.	154	1719			
Caustic potash, dry, solid	154	1813			

Name of Material	Guide No.	ID No.	Name of Material	Guide No.	ID No.
Chemical under pressure, flammable, n.o.s.	115	3501	Chloroacetic acid, solid	153	1751
Chemical under pressure, flammable, poisonous, n.o.s.	119	3504	Chloroacetic acid, solution	153	1750
			Chloroacetone, stabilized	131	1695
Chemical under pressure, flammable, toxic, n.o.s.	119	3504	Chloroacetonitrile	131	2668
Chemical under pressure, n.o.s.	126	3500	Chloroacetophenone	153	1697
Chemical under pressure, poisonous, n.o.s.	123	3502	Chloroacetophenone, liquid	153	1697
			Chloroacetophenone, liquid	153	3416
Chemical under pressure, toxic, n.o.s.	123	3502	Chloroacetophenone, solid	153	1697
Chloral, anhydrous, stabilized	153	2075	Chloroacetyl chloride	156	1752
Chlorate and Borate mixtures	140	1458	Chloroanilines, liquid	152	2019
Chlorate and Magnesium chloride mixture	140	1459	Chloroanilines, solid	152	2018
			Chloroanisidines	152	2233
Chlorate and Magnesium chloride mixture, solid	140	1459	Chlorobenzene	130	1134
Chlorate and Magnesium chloride mixture, solution	140	3407	Chlorobenzotrifluorides	130	2234
			Chlorobenzyl chlorides	153	2235
Chlorates, inorganic, aqueous solution, n.o.s.	140	3210	Chlorobenzyl chlorides, liquid	153	2235
Chlorates, inorganic, n.o.s.	140	1461	Chlorobenzyl chlorides, solid	153	3427
Chloric acid, aqueous solution, with not more than 10% Chloric acid	140	2626	1-Chloro-3-bromopropane	159	2688
			Chlorobutanes	130	1127
Chlorine	124	1017	Chlorocresols	152	2669
Chlorine dioxide, hydrate, frozen	143	9191	Chlorocresols, liquid	152	2669
			Chlorocresols, solid	152	2669
Chlorine pentafluoride	124	2548	Chlorocresols, solid	152	3437
Chlorine trifluoride	124	1749	Chlorocresols, solution	152	2669
Chlorite solution	154	1908	Chlorodifluorobromomethane	126	1974
Chlorite solution, with more than 5% available Chlorine	154	1908	1-Chloro-1,1-difluoroethane	115	2517
			Chlorodifluoroethanes	115	2517
Chlorites, inorganic, n.o.s.	143	1462	Chlorodifluoromethane	126	1018
Chloroacetaldehyde	153	2232	Chlorodifluoromethane and Chloropentafluoroethane mixture	126	1973
Chloroacetic acid, liquid	153	1750			
Chloroacetic acid, molten	153	3250	Chlorodinitrobenzenes	153	1577

Name of Material	Guide No.	ID No.	Name of Material	Guide No.	ID No.
Chlorodinitrobenzenes, liquid	**153**	1577	Chlorophenates, liquid	**154**	2904
Chlorodinitrobenzenes, solid	**153**	1577	Chlorophenates, solid	**154**	2905
Chlorodinitrobenzenes, solid	**153**	3441	Chlorophenolates, liquid	**154**	2904
1-Chloro-2,3-epoxypropane	**131P**	2023	Chlorophenolates, solid	**154**	2905
2-Chloroethanal	**153**	2232	Chlorophenols, liquid	**153**	2021
Chloroform	**151**	1888	Chlorophenols, solid	**153**	2020
Chloroformates, n.o.s.	**155**	2742	Chlorophenyltrichlorosilane	**156**	1753
Chloroformates, poisonous, corrosive, flammable, n.o.s.	**155**	2742	Chloropicrin	**154**	1580
Chloroformates, poisonous, corrosive, n.o.s.	**154**	3277	Chloropicrin and Methyl bromide mixture	**123**	1581
Chloroformates, toxic, corrosive, flammable, n.o.s.	**155**	2742	Chloropicrin and Methyl chloride mixture	**119**	1582
Chloroformates, toxic, corrosive, n.o.s.	**154**	3277	Chloropicrin mixture, n.o.s.	**154**	1583
Chloromethyl chloroformate	**157**	2745	Chloropivaloyl chloride	**156**	9263
Chloromethyl ethyl ether	**131**	2354	Chloroplatinic acid, solid	**154**	2507
3-Chloro-4-methylphenyl isocyanate	**156**	2236	Chloroprene, stabilized	**131P**	1991
3-Chloro-4-methylphenyl isocyanate, liquid	**156**	2236	1-Chloropropane	**129**	1278
3-Chloro-4-methylphenyl isocyanate, solid	**156**	3428	2-Chloropropane	**129**	2356
Chloronitroanilines	**153**	2237	3-Chloropropanol-1	**153**	2849
Chloronitrobenzenes	**152**	1578	2-Chloropropene	**130P**	2456
Chloronitrobenzenes, liquid	**152**	1578	2-Chloropropionic acid	**153**	2511
Chloronitrobenzenes, liquid	**152**	3409	2-Chloropropionic acid, solid	**153**	2511
Chloronitrobenzenes, solid	**152**	1578	2-Chloropropionic acid, solution	**153**	2511
Chloronitrotoluenes	**152**	2433	2-Chloropyridine	**153**	2822
Chloronitrotoluenes, liquid	**152**	2433	Chlorosilanes, corrosive, flammable, n.o.s.	**155**	2986
Chloronitrotoluenes, solid	**152**	2433	Chlorosilanes, corrosive, n.o.s.	**156**	2987
Chloronitrotoluenes, solid	**152**	3457	Chlorosilanes, flammable, corrosive, n.o.s.	**155**	2985
Chloropentafluoroethane	**126**	1020	Chlorosilanes, n.o.s.	**155**	2985
Chloropentafluoroethane and Chlorodifluoromethane mixture	**126**	1973	Chlorosilanes, n.o.s.	**155**	2986
			Chlorosilanes, n.o.s.	**156**	2987

Name of Material	Guide No.	ID No.
Chlorosilanes, n.o.s.	139	2988
Chlorosilanes, poisonous, corrosive, flammable, n.o.s.	155	3362
Chlorosilanes, poisonous, corrosive, n.o.s.	156	3361
Chlorosilanes, toxic, corrosive, flammable, n.o.s.	155	3362
Chlorosilanes, toxic, corrosive, n.o.s.	156	3361
Chlorosilanes, water-reactive, flammable, corrosive, n.o.s.	139	2988
Chlorosulfonic acid	137	1754
Chlorosulfonic acid and Sulfur trioxide mixture	137	1754
Chlorosulphonic acid	137	1754
Chlorosulphonic acid and Sulphur trioxide mixture	137	1754
1-Chloro-1,2,2,2-tetrafluoroethane	126	1021
Chlorotetrafluoroethane	126	1021
Chlorotetrafluoroethane and Ethylene oxide mixture, with not more than 8.8% Ethylene oxide	126	3297
Chlorotoluenes	129	2238
4-Chloro-o-toluidine hydrochloride	153	1579
4-Chloro-o-toluidine hydrochloride, solid	153	1579
4-Chloro-o-toluidine hydrochloride, solution	153	3410
Chlorotoluidines	153	2239
Chlorotoluidines, liquid	153	2239
Chlorotoluidines, liquid	153	3429
Chlorotoluidines, solid	153	2239
1-Chloro-2,2,2-trifluoroethane	126	1983
Chlorotrifluoroethane	126	1983
Chlorotrifluoromethane	126	1022
Chlorotrifluoromethane and Trifluoromethane azeotropic mixture with approximately 60% Chlorotrifluoromethane	126	2599
Chromic acid, solution	154	1755
Chromic fluoride, solid	154	1756
Chromic fluoride, solution	154	1757
Chromium nitrate	141	2720
Chromium oxychloride	137	1758
Chromium trioxide, anhydrous	141	1463
Chromosulfuric acid	154	2240
Chromosulphuric acid	154	2240
CK	125	1589
Clinical specimens	158	3373
Clinical waste, unspecified, n.o.s.	158	3291
CN	153	1697
Coal gas	119	1023
Coal gas, compressed	119	1023
Coal tar distillates, flammable	128	1136
Coating solution	127	1139
Cobalt naphthenates, powder	133	2001
Cobalt resinate, precipitated	133	1318
Combustible liquid, n.o.s.	128	1993
Compound, cleaning liquid (corrosive)	154	1760
Compound, cleaning liquid (flammable)	128	1993
Compound, tree or weed killing, liquid (corrosive)	154	1760
Compound, tree or weed killing, liquid (flammable)	128	1993
Compound, tree or weed killing, liquid (toxic)	153	2810
Compressed gas, flammable, n.o.s.	115	1954

Name of Material	Guide No.	ID No.	Name of Material	Guide No.	ID No.
Compressed gas, flammable, poisonous, n.o.s. (Inhalation Hazard Zone A)	119	1953	Compressed gas, poisonous, flammable, corrosive, n.o.s. (Inhalation Hazard Zone A)	119	3305
Compressed gas, flammable, poisonous, n.o.s. (Inhalation Hazard Zone B)	119	1953	Compressed gas, poisonous, flammable, corrosive, n.o.s. (Inhalation Hazard Zone B)	119	3305
Compressed gas, flammable, poisonous, n.o.s. (Inhalation Hazard Zone C)	119	1953	Compressed gas, poisonous, flammable, corrosive, n.o.s. (Inhalation Hazard Zone C)	119	3305
Compressed gas, flammable, poisonous, n.o.s. (Inhalation Hazard Zone D)	119	1953	Compressed gas, poisonous, flammable, corrosive, n.o.s. (Inhalation Hazard Zone D)	119	3305
Compressed gas, flammable, toxic, n.o.s. (Inhalation Hazard Zone A)	119	1953	Compressed gas, poisonous, flammable, n.o.s.	119	1953
Compressed gas, flammable, toxic, n.o.s. (Inhalation Hazard Zone B)	119	1953	Compressed gas, poisonous, flammable, n.o.s. (Inhalation Hazard Zone A)	119	1953
Compressed gas, flammable, toxic, n.o.s. (Inhalation Hazard Zone C)	119	1953	Compressed gas, poisonous, flammable, n.o.s. (Inhalation Hazard Zone B)	119	1953
Compressed gas, flammable, toxic, n.o.s. (Inhalation Hazard Zone D)	119	1953	Compressed gas, poisonous, flammable, n.o.s. (Inhalation Hazard Zone C)	119	1953
Compressed gas, n.o.s.	126	1956	Compressed gas, poisonous, flammable, n.o.s. (Inhalation Hazard Zone D)	119	1953
Compressed gas, oxidizing, n.o.s.	122	3156	Compressed gas, poisonous, n.o.s.	123	1955
Compressed gas, poisonous, corrosive, n.o.s.	123	3304	Compressed gas, poisonous, n.o.s. (Inhalation Hazard Zone A)	123	1955
Compressed gas, poisonous, corrosive, n.o.s. (Inhalation Hazard Zone A)	123	3304	Compressed gas, poisonous, n.o.s. (Inhalation Hazard Zone B)	123	1955
Compressed gas, poisonous, corrosive, n.o.s. (Inhalation Hazard Zone B)	123	3304	Compressed gas, poisonous, n.o.s. (Inhalation Hazard Zone C)	123	1955
Compressed gas, poisonous, corrosive, n.o.s. (Inhalation Hazard Zone C)	123	3304	Compressed gas, poisonous, n.o.s. (Inhalation Hazard Zone D)	123	1955
Compressed gas, poisonous, corrosive, n.o.s. (Inhalation Hazard Zone D)	123	3304	Compressed gas, poisonous, oxidizing, corrosive, n.o.s.	124	3306
Compressed gas, poisonous, flammable, corrosive, n.o.s.	119	3305	Compressed gas, poisonous, oxidizing, corrosive, n.o.s. (Inhalation Hazard Zone A)	124	3306

Name of Material	Guide No.	ID No.	Name of Material	Guide No.	ID No.
Compressed gas, poisonous, oxidizing, corrosive, n.o.s. (Inhalation Hazard Zone B)	124	3306	Compressed gas, toxic, flammable, corrosive, n.o.s. (Inhalation Hazard Zone C)	119	3305
Compressed gas, poisonous, oxidizing, corrosive, n.o.s. (Inhalation Hazard Zone C)	124	3306	Compressed gas, toxic, flammable, corrosive, n.o.s. (Inhalation Hazard Zone D)	119	3305
Compressed gas, poisonous, oxidizing, corrosive, n.o.s. (Inhalation Hazard Zone D)	124	3306	Compressed gas, toxic, flammable, n.o.s.	119	1953
Compressed gas, poisonous, oxidizing, n.o.s.	124	3303	Compressed gas, toxic, flammable, n.o.s. (Inhalation Hazard Zone A)	119	1953
Compressed gas, poisonous, oxidizing, n.o.s. (Inhalation Hazard Zone A)	124	3303	Compressed gas, toxic, flammable, n.o.s. (Inhalation Hazard Zone B)	119	1953
Compressed gas, poisonous, oxidizing, n.o.s. (Inhalation Hazard Zone B)	124	3303	Compressed gas, toxic, flammable, n.o.s. (Inhalation Hazard Zone C)	119	1953
Compressed gas, poisonous, oxidizing, n.o.s. (Inhalation Hazard Zone C)	124	3303	Compressed gas, toxic, flammable, n.o.s. (Inhalation Hazard Zone D)	119	1953
Compressed gas, poisonous, oxidizing, n.o.s. (Inhalation Hazard Zone D)	124	3303	Compressed gas, toxic, n.o.s.	123	1955
Compressed gas, toxic, corrosive, n.o.s.	123	3304	Compressed gas, toxic, n.o.s. (Inhalation Hazard Zone A)	123	1955
Compressed gas, toxic, corrosive, n.o.s. (Inhalation Hazard Zone A)	123	3304	Compressed gas, toxic, n.o.s. (Inhalation Hazard Zone B)	123	1955
Compressed gas, toxic, corrosive, n.o.s. (Inhalation Hazard Zone B)	123	3304	Compressed gas, toxic, n.o.s. (Inhalation Hazard Zone C)	123	1955
Compressed gas, toxic, corrosive, n.o.s. (Inhalation Hazard Zone C)	123	3304	Compressed gas, toxic, n.o.s. (Inhalation Hazard Zone D)	123	1955
Compressed gas, toxic, corrosive, n.o.s. (Inhalation Hazard Zone D)	123	3304	Compressed gas, toxic, oxidizing, corrosive, n.o.s.	124	3306
Compressed gas, toxic, flammable, corrosive, n.o.s.	119	3305	Compressed gas, toxic, oxidizing, corrosive, n.o.s. (Inhalation Hazard Zone A)	124	3306
Compressed gas, toxic, flammable, corrosive, n.o.s. (Inhalation Hazard Zone A)	119	3305	Compressed gas, toxic, oxidizing, corrosive, n.o.s. (Inhalation Hazard Zone B)	124	3306
Compressed gas, toxic, flammable, corrosive, n.o.s. (Inhalation Hazard Zone B)	119	3305	Compressed gas, toxic, oxidizing, corrosive, n.o.s. (Inhalation Hazard Zone C)	124	3306
			Compressed gas, toxic, oxidizing, corrosive, n.o.s. (Inhalation Hazard Zone D)	124	3306

Name of Material	Guide No.	ID No.
Compressed gas, toxic, oxidizing, n.o.s.	124	3303
Compressed gas, toxic, oxidizing, n.o.s. (Inhalation Hazard Zone A)	124	3303
Compressed gas, toxic, oxidizing, n.o.s. (Inhalation Hazard Zone B)	124	3303
Compressed gas, toxic, oxidizing, n.o.s. (Inhalation Hazard Zone C)	124	3303
Compressed gas, toxic, oxidizing, n.o.s. (Inhalation Hazard Zone D)	124	3303
Consumer commodity	171	8000
Copper acetoarsenite	151	1585
Copper arsenite	151	1586
Copper based pesticide, liquid, flammable, poisonous	131	2776
Copper based pesticide, liquid, flammable, toxic	131	2776
Copper based pesticide, liquid, poisonous	151	3010
Copper based pesticide, liquid, poisonous, flammable	131	3009
Copper based pesticide, liquid, toxic	151	3010
Copper based pesticide, liquid, toxic, flammable	131	3009
Copper based pesticide, solid, poisonous	151	2775
Copper based pesticide, solid, toxic	151	2775
Copper chlorate	141	2721
Copper chloride	154	2802
Copper cyanide	151	1587
Copra	135	1363
Corrosive liquid, acidic, inorganic, n.o.s.	154	3264

Name of Material	Guide No.	ID No.
Corrosive liquid, acidic, organic, n.o.s.	153	3265
Corrosive liquid, basic, inorganic, n.o.s.	154	3266
Corrosive liquid, basic, organic, n.o.s.	153	3267
Corrosive liquid, flammable, n.o.s.	132	2920
Corrosive liquid, n.o.s.	154	1760
Corrosive liquid, oxidizing, n.o.s.	140	3093
Corrosive liquid, poisonous, n.o.s.	154	2922
Corrosive liquid, self-heating, n.o.s.	136	3301
Corrosive liquid, toxic, n.o.s.	154	2922
Corrosive liquid, water-reactive, n.o.s.	138	3094
Corrosive liquid, which in contact with water emits flammable gases, n.o.s.	138	3094
Corrosive solid, acidic, inorganic, n.o.s.	154	3260
Corrosive solid, acidic, organic, n.o.s.	154	3261
Corrosive solid, basic, inorganic, n.o.s.	154	3262
Corrosive solid, basic, organic, n.o.s.	154	3263
Corrosive solid, flammable, n.o.s.	134	2921
Corrosive solid, n.o.s.	154	1759
Corrosive solid, oxidizing, n.o.s.	140	3084
Corrosive solid, poisonous, n.o.s.	154	2923
Corrosive solid, self-heating, n.o.s.	136	3095
Corrosive solid, toxic, n.o.s.	154	2923
Corrosive solid, water-reactive, n.o.s.	138	3096

Name of Material	Guide No.	ID No.
Corrosive solid, which in contact with water emits flammable gases, n.o.s.	138	3096
Cotton	133	1365
Cotton, wet	133	1365
Cotton waste, oily	133	1364
Coumarin derivative pesticide, liquid, flammable, poisonous	131	3024
Coumarin derivative pesticide, liquid, flammable, toxic	131	3024
Coumarin derivative pesticide, liquid, poisonous	151	3026
Coumarin derivative pesticide, liquid, poisonous, flammable	131	3025
Coumarin derivative pesticide, liquid, toxic	151	3026
Coumarin derivative pesticide, liquid, toxic, flammable	131	3025
Coumarin derivative pesticide, solid, poisonous	151	3027
Coumarin derivative pesticide, solid, toxic	151	3027
Cresols	153	2076
Cresols, liquid	153	2076
Cresols, solid	153	2076
Cresols, solid	153	3455
Cresylic acid	153	2022
Crotonaldehyde	131P	1143
Crotonaldehyde, stabilized	131P	1143
Crotonic acid	153	2823
Crotonic acid, liquid	153	2823
Crotonic acid, liquid	153	3472
Crotonic acid, solid	153	2823
Crotonylene	128	1144
CS	153	2810

Name of Material	Guide No.	ID No.
Cumene	130	1918
Cupriethylenediamine, solution	154	1761
CX	154	2811
Cyanide solution, n.o.s.	157	1935
Cyanides, inorganic, n.o.s.	157	1588
Cyanides, inorganic, solid, n.o.s.	157	1588
Cyanogen	119	1026
Cyanogen bromide	157	1889
Cyanogen chloride, stabilized	125	1589
Cyanogen gas	119	1026
Cyanuric chloride	157	2670
Cyclobutane	115	2601
Cyclobutyl chloroformate	155	2744
1,5,9-Cyclododecatriene	153	2518
Cycloheptane	128	2241
Cycloheptatriene	131	2603
Cycloheptene	128	2242
Cyclohexane	128	1145
Cyclohexanethiol	129	3054
Cyclohexanone	127	1915
Cyclohexene	130	2256
Cyclohexenyltrichlorosilane	156	1762
Cyclohexyl acetate	130	2243
Cyclohexylamine	132	2357
Cyclohexyl isocyanate	155	2488
Cyclohexyl mercaptan	129	3054
Cyclohexyltrichlorosilane	156	1763
Cyclooctadiene phosphines	135	2940
Cyclooctadienes	130P	2520
Cyclooctatetraene	128P	2358

Name of Material	Guide No.	ID No.	Name of Material	Guide No.	ID No.
Cyclopentane	128	1146	1,2-Dibromobutan-3-one	154	2648
Cyclopentanol	129	2244	Dibromochloropropanes	159	2872
Cyclopentanone	128	2245	Dibromodifluoromethane	171	1941
Cyclopentene	128	2246	Dibromomethane	160	2664
Cyclopropane	115	1027	Di-n-butylamine	132	2248
Cymenes	130	2046	Dibutylaminoethanol	153	2873
DA	151	1699	Dibutyl ethers	128	1149
Dangerous goods in apparatus	171	3363	Dichloroacetic acid	153	1764
Dangerous goods in machinery	171	3363	1,3-Dichloroacetone	153	2649
DC	153	2810	Dichloroacetyl chloride	156	1765
Decaborane	134	1868	Dichloroanilines	153	1590
Decahydronaphthalene	130	1147	Dichloroanilines, liquid	153	1590
n-Decane	128	2247	Dichloroanilines, solid	153	1590
Desensitized explosive, liquid, n.o.s.	128	3379	Dichloroanilines, solid	153	3442
			o-Dichlorobenzene	152	1591
Desensitized explosive, solid, n.o.s.	133	3380	2,2'-Dichlorodiethyl ether	152	1916
Deuterium	115	1957	Dichlorodifluoromethane	126	1028
Deuterium, compressed	115	1957	Dichlorodifluoromethane and Difluoroethane azeotropic mixture with approximately 74% Dichlorodifluoromethane	126	2602
Devices, small, hydrocarbon gas powered, with release device	115	3150	Dichlorodifluoromethane and Ethylene oxide mixture, with not more than 12.5% Ethylene oxide	126	3070
Diacetone alcohol	129	1148	Dichlorodifluoromethane and Ethylene oxide mixtures, with not more than 12% Ethylene oxide	126	3070
Diacetyl	127	2346			
Diagnostic specimens	158	3373			
Diallylamine	132	2359			
Diallyl ether	131P	2360	Dichlorodimethyl ether, symmetrical	131	2249
4,4'-Diaminodiphenylmethane	153	2651	1,1-Dichloroethane	130	2362
Di-n-amylamine	131	2841	1,2-Dichloroethylene	130P	1150
Dibenzyldichlorosilane	156	2434	Dichloroethylene	130P	1150
Diborane	119	1911	Dichloroethyl ether	152	1916
Diborane, compressed	119	1911			
Diborane mixtures	119	1911			

Name of Material	Guide No.	ID No.	Name of Material	Guide No.	ID No.
Dichlorofluoromethane	126	1029	Diethylaminopropylamine	132	2684
Dichloroisocyanuric acid, dry	140	2465	N,N-Diethylaniline	153	2432
Dichloroisocyanuric acid salts	140	2465	Diethylbenzene	130	2049
Dichloroisopropyl ether	153	2490	Diethyl carbonate	128	2366
Dichloromethane	160	1593	Diethyldichlorosilane	155	1767
1,1-Dichloro-1-nitroethane	153	2650	Diethylenetriamine	154	2079
Dichloropentanes	130	1152	Diethyl ether	127	1155
Dichlorophenyl isocyanates	156	2250	N,N-Diethylethylenediamine	132	2685
Dichlorophenyltrichlorosilane	156	1766	Diethyl ketone	127	1156
1,2-Dichloropropane	130	1279	Diethyl sulfate	152	1594
Dichloropropane	130	1279	Diethyl sulfide	129	2375
1,3-Dichloropropanol-2	153	2750	Diethyl sulphate	152	1594
Dichloropropenes	129	2047	Diethyl sulphide	129	2375
Dichlorosilane	119	2189	Diethylthiophosphoryl chloride	155	2751
1,2-Dichloro-1,1,2,2-tetrafluoroethane	126	1958	Diethylzinc	135	1366
Dichlorotetrafluoroethane	126	1958	Difluorochloroethanes	115	2517
3,5-Dichloro-2,4,6-trifluoropyridine	151	9264	1,1-Difluoroethane	115	1030
			Difluoroethane	115	1030
Dicyclohexylamine	153	2565	Difluoroethane and Dichlorodifluoromethane azeotropic mixture with approximately 74% Dichlorodifluoromethane	126	2602
Dicyclohexylammonium nitrite	133	2687			
Dicyclopentadiene	130	2048			
1,2-Di-(dimethylamino)ethane	129	2372			
Didymium nitrate	140	1465	1,1-Difluoroethylene	116P	1959
Diesel fuel	128	1202	Difluoromethane	115	3252
Diesel fuel	128	1993	Difluorophosphoric acid, anhydrous	154	1768
Diethoxymethane	127	2373	2,3-Dihydropyran	127	2376
3,3-Diethoxypropene	127	2374	Diisobutylamine	132	2361
Diethylamine	132	1154	Diisobutylene, isomeric compounds	128	2050
2-Diethylaminoethanol	132	2686			
Diethylaminoethanol	132	2686	Diisobutyl ketone	128	1157
3-Diethylaminopropylamine	132	2684	Diisooctyl acid phosphate	153	1902
			Diisopropylamine	132	1158

Name of Material	Guide No.	ID No.
Diisopropyl ether	127	1159
Diketene, stabilized	131P	2521
1,1-Dimethoxyethane	127	2377
1,2-Dimethoxyethane	127	2252
Dimethylamine, anhydrous	118	1032
Dimethylamine, aqueous solution	132	1160
Dimethylamine, solution	132	1160
2-Dimethylaminoacetonitrile	131	2378
2-Dimethylaminoethanol	132	2051
2-Dimethylaminoethyl acrylate	152	3302
2-Dimethylaminoethyl methacrylate	153P	2522
Dimethylaminoethyl methacrylate	153P	2522
N,N-Dimethylaniline	153	2253
2,3-Dimethylbutane	128	2457
1,3-Dimethylbutylamine	132	2379
Dimethylcarbamoyl chloride	156	2262
Dimethyl carbonate	129	1161
Dimethylcyclohexanes	128	2263
N,N-Dimethylcyclohexylamine	132	2264
Dimethylcyclohexylamine	132	2264
Dimethyldichlorosilane	155	1162
Dimethyldiethoxysilane	127	2380
Dimethyldioxanes	127	2707
Dimethyl disulfide	130	2381
Dimethyl disulphide	130	2381
Dimethylethanolamine	132	2051
Dimethyl ether	115	1033
N,N-Dimethylformamide	129	2265
1,1-Dimethylhydrazine	131	1163
1,2-Dimethylhydrazine	131	2382
Dimethylhydrazine, symmetrical	131	2382
Dimethylhydrazine, unsymmetrical	131	1163
2,2-Dimethylpropane	115	2044
Dimethyl-N-propylamine	132	2266
Dimethyl sulfate	156	1595
Dimethyl sulfide	130	1164
Dimethyl sulphate	156	1595
Dimethyl sulphide	130	1164
Dimethyl thiophosphoryl chloride	156	2267
Dimethylzinc	135	1370
Dinitroanilines	153	1596
Dinitrobenzenes	152	1597
Dinitrobenzenes, liquid	152	1597
Dinitrobenzenes, solid	152	1597
Dinitrobenzenes, solid	152	3443
Dinitrochlorobenzenes	153	1577
Dinitro-o-cresol	153	1598
Dinitrogen tetroxide	124	1067
Dinitrogen tetroxide and Nitric oxide mixture	124	1975
Dinitrophenol, solution	153	1599
Dinitrophenol, wetted with not less than 15% water	113	1320
Dinitrophenolates, wetted with not less than 15% water	113	1321
Dinitroresorcinol, wetted with not less than 15% water	113	1322
Dinitrotoluenes	152	2038
Dinitrotoluenes, liquid	152	2038
Dinitrotoluenes, molten	152	1600
Dinitrotoluenes, solid	152	2038
Dinitrotoluenes, solid	152	3454

Name of Material	Guide No.	ID No.	Name of Material	Guide No.	ID No.
Dioxane	127	1165	Disodium trioxosilicate, pentahydrate	154	3253
Dioxolane	127	1166	Dispersant gas, n.o.s.	126	1078
Dipentene	128	2052			
Diphenylamine chloroarsine	154	1698	Dispersant gas, n.o.s. (flammable)	115	1954
Diphenylchloroarsine	151	1699	Dithiocarbamate pesticide, liquid, flammable, poisonous	131	2772
Diphenylchloroarsine, liquid	151	1699			
Diphenylchloroarsine, solid	151	1699	Dithiocarbamate pesticide, liquid, flammable, toxic	131	2772
Diphenylchloroarsine, solid	151	3450			
Diphenyldichlorosilane	156	1769	Dithiocarbamate pesticide, liquid, poisonous	151	3006
Diphenylmethyl bromide	153	1770	Dithiocarbamate pesticide, liquid, poisonous, flammable	131	3005
Diphosgene	125	1076			
Dipicryl sulfide, wetted with not less than 10% water	113	2852	Dithiocarbamate pesticide, liquid, toxic	151	3006
Dipicryl sulphide, wetted with not less than 10% water	113	2852	Dithiocarbamate pesticide, liquid, toxic, flammable	131	3005
Dipropylamine	132	2383	Dithiocarbamate pesticide, solid, poisonous	151	2771
Di-n-propyl ether	127	2384			
Dipropyl ether	127	2384	Dithiocarbamate pesticide, solid, toxic	151	2771
Dipropyl ketone	128	2710	Divinyl ether, stabilized	128P	1167
Disinfectant, liquid, corrosive, n.o.s.	153	1903	DM	154	1698
Disinfectant, liquid, poisonous, n.o.s.	151	3142	Dodecyltrichlorosilane	156	1771
Disinfectant, liquid, toxic, n.o.s.	151	3142	DP	125	1076
Disinfectant, solid, poisonous, n.o.s.	151	1601	Dry ice	120	1845
			Dye, liquid, corrosive, n.o.s.	154	2801
Disinfectant, solid, toxic, n.o.s.	151	1601	Dye, liquid, poisonous, n.o.s.	151	1602
Disinfectants, corrosive, liquid, n.o.s.	153	1903	Dye, liquid, toxic, n.o.s.	151	1602
Disinfectants, liquid, n.o.s. (poisonous)	151	3142	Dye, solid, corrosive, n.o.s.	154	3147
			Dye, solid, poisonous, n.o.s.	151	3143
Disinfectants, solid, n.o.s. (poisonous)	151	1601	Dye, solid, toxic, n.o.s.	151	3143
Disodium trioxosilicate	154	3253	Dye intermediate, liquid, corrosive, n.o.s.	154	2801
			Dye intermediate, liquid, poisonous, n.o.s.	151	1602

Name of Material	Guide No.	ID No.
Dye intermediate, liquid, toxic, n.o.s.	151	1602
Dye intermediate, solid, corrosive, n.o.s.	154	3147
Dye intermediate, solid, poisonous, n.o.s.	151	3143
Dye intermediate, solid, toxic, n.o.s.	151	3143
ED	151	1892
Elevated temperature liquid, flammable, n.o.s., with flash point above 37.8°C (100°F), at or above its flash point	128	3256
Elevated temperature liquid, flammable, n.o.s., with flash point above 60°C (140°F), at or above its flash point	128	3256
Elevated temperature liquid, n.o.s., at or above 100°C (212°F), and below its flash point	128	3257
Elevated temperature solid, n.o.s., at or above 240°C (464°F)	171	3258
Engine, fuel cell, flammable gas powered	128	3166
Engine, fuel cell, flammable liquid powered	128	3166
Engine, internal combustion	128	3166
Engines, internal combustion, flammable gas powered	128	3166
Engines, internal combustion, flammable liquid powered	128	3166
Environmentally hazardous substances, liquid, n.o.s.	171	3082
Environmentally hazardous substances, solid, n.o.s.	171	3077
Epibromohydrin	131	2558
Epichlorohydrin	131P	2023
1,2-Epoxy-3-ethoxypropane	127	2752
Esters, n.o.s.	127	3272
Ethane	115	1035

Name of Material	Guide No.	ID No.
Ethane, compressed	115	1035
Ethane, refrigerated liquid	115	1961
Ethane-Propane mixture, refrigerated liquid	115	1961
Ethanol	127	1170
Ethanol and gasoline mixture, with more than 10% ethanol	127	3475
Ethanol and motor spirit mixture, with more than 10% ethanol	127	3475
Ethanol and petrol mixture, with more than 10% ethanol	127	3475
Ethanol, solution	127	1170
Ethanolamine	153	2491
Ethanolamine, solution	153	2491
Ethers, n.o.s.	127	3271
Ethyl acetate	129	1173
Ethylacetylene, stabilized	116P	2452
Ethyl acrylate, stabilized	129P	1917
Ethyl alcohol	127	1170
Ethyl alcohol, solution	127	1170
Ethylamine	118	1036
Ethylamine, aqueous solution, with not less than 50% but not more than 70% Ethylamine	132	2270
Ethyl amyl ketone	128	2271
2-Ethylaniline	153	2273
N-Ethylaniline	153	2272
Ethylbenzene	130	1175
N-Ethyl-N-benzylaniline	153	2274
N-Ethylbenzyltoluidines	153	2753
N-Ethylbenzyltoluidines, liquid	153	2753
N-Ethylbenzyltoluidines, solid	153	2753
N-Ethylbenzyltoluidines, solid	153	3460

Name of Material	Guide No.	ID No.
Ethyl borate	129	1176
Ethyl bromide	131	1891
Ethyl bromoacetate	155	1603
2-Ethylbutanol	129	2275
2-Ethylbutyl acetate	130	1177
Ethylbutyl acetate	130	1177
Ethyl butyl ether	127	1179
2-Ethylbutyraldehyde	130	1178
Ethyl butyrate	130	1180
Ethyl chloride	115	1037
Ethyl chloroacetate	155	1181
Ethyl chloroformate	155	1182
Ethyl 2-chloropropionate	129	2935
Ethyl chlorothioformate	155	2826
Ethyl crotonate	130	1862
Ethyldichloroarsine	151	1892
Ethyldichlorosilane	139	1183
Ethylene	116P	1962
Ethylene, Acetylene and Propylene in mixture, refrigerated liquid containing at least 71.5% Ethylene with not more than 22.5% Acetylene and not more than 6% Propylene	115	3138
Ethylene, compressed	116P	1962
Ethylene, refrigerated liquid (cryogenic liquid)	115	1038
Ethylene chlorohydrin	131	1135
Ethylenediamine	132	1604
Ethylene dibromide	154	1605
Ethylene dibromide and Methyl bromide mixture, liquid	151	1647
Ethylene dichloride	131	1184
Ethylene glycol diethyl ether	127	1153

Name of Material	Guide No.	ID No.
Ethylene glycol monoethyl ether	127	1171
Ethylene glycol monoethyl ether acetate	129	1172
Ethylene glycol monomethyl ether	127	1188
Ethylene glycol monomethyl ether acetate	129	1189
Ethyleneimine, stabilized	131P	1185
Ethylene oxide	119P	1040
Ethylene oxide and Carbon dioxide mixture, with more than 9% but not more than 87% Ethylene oxide	115	1041
Ethylene oxide and Carbon dioxide mixture, with more than 87% Ethylene oxide	119P	3300
Ethylene oxide and Carbon dioxide mixtures, with more than 6 % Ethylene oxide	115	1041
Ethylene oxide and Carbon dioxide mixtures, with not more than 6% Ethylene oxide	126	1952
Ethylene oxide and Carbon dioxide mixtures, with not more than 9% Ethylene oxide	126	1952
Ethylene oxide and Chlorotetrafluoroethane mixture, with not more than 8.8% Ethylene oxide	126	3297
Ethylene oxide and Dichlorodifluoromethane mixture, with not more than 12.5% Ethylene oxide	126	3070
Ethylene oxide and Dichlorodifluoromethane mixtures, with not more than 12% Ethylene oxide	126	3070
Ethylene oxide and Pentafluoroethane mixture, with not more than 7.9% Ethylene oxide	126	3298

Name of Material	Guide No.	ID No.
Ethylene oxide and Propylene oxide mixture, with not more than 30% Ethylene oxide	129P	2983
Ethylene oxide and Tetrafluoroethane mixture, with not more than 5.6% Ethylene oxide	126	3299
Ethylene oxide with Nitrogen	119P	1040
Ethyl ether	127	1155
Ethyl fluoride	115	2453
Ethyl formate	129	1190
Ethylhexaldehydes	129	1191
2-Ethylhexylamine	132	2276
2-Ethylhexyl chloroformate	156	2748
Ethyl isobutyrate	129	2385
Ethyl isocyanate	155	2481
Ethyl lactate	129	1192
Ethyl mercaptan	129	2363
Ethyl methacrylate	130P	2277
Ethyl methacrylate, stabilized	130P	2277
Ethyl methyl ether	115	1039
Ethyl methyl ketone	127	1193
Ethyl nitrite, solution	131	1194
Ethyl orthoformate	129	2524
Ethyl oxalate	156	2525
Ethylphenyldichlorosilane	156	2435
Ethyl phosphonothioic dichloride, anhydrous	154	2927
Ethyl phosphonous dichloride, anhydrous	135	2845
Ethyl phosphorodichloridate	154	2927
1-Ethylpiperidine	132	2386
Ethyl propionate	129	1195
Ethyl propyl ether	127	2615
Ethyl silicate	129	1292

Name of Material	Guide No.	ID No.
Ethylsulfuric acid	156	2571
Ethylsulphuric acid	156	2571
N-Ethyltoluidines	153	2754
Ethyltrichlorosilane	155	1196
Explosives, division 1.1, 1.2, 1.3 or 1.5	112	—
Explosives, division 1.4 or 1.6	114	—
Extracts, aromatic, liquid	127	1169
Extracts, flavoring, liquid	127	1197
Extracts, flavouring, liquid	127	1197
Fabrics, animal or vegetable or synthetic, n.o.s. with oil	133	1373
Fabrics impregnated with weakly nitrated Nitrocellulose, n.o.s.	133	1353
Ferric arsenate	151	1606
Ferric arsenite	151	1607
Ferric chloride	157	1773
Ferric chloride, anhydrous	157	1773
Ferric chloride, solution	154	2582
Ferric nitrate	140	1466
Ferrocerium	170	1323
Ferrosilicon	139	1408
Ferrous arsenate	151	1608
Ferrous chloride, solid	154	1759
Ferrous chloride, solution	154	1760
Ferrous metal borings, shavings, turnings or cuttings	170	2793
Fertilizer, ammoniating solution, with free Ammonia	125	1043
Fiber, animal or vegetable, n.o.s., burnt, wet or damp	133	1372
Fibers, animal or vegetable or synthetic, n.o.s. with oil	133	1373

Name of Material	Guide No.	ID No.
Fibers, animal or vegetable, burnt, wet or damp	133	1372
Fibers, vegetable, dry	133	3360
Fibers impregnated with weakly nitrated Nitrocellulose, n.o.s.	133	1353
Fibres, animal or vegetable, burnt, wet or damp	133	1372
Fibres, animal or vegetable or synthetic, n.o.s. with oil	133	1373
Fibres, vegetable, dry	133	3360
Fibres impregnated with weakly nitrated Nitrocellulose, n.o.s.	133	1353
Films, nitrocellulose base	133	1324
Fire extinguisher charges, corrosive liquid	154	1774
Fire extinguishers with compressed gas	126	1044
Fire extinguishers with liquefied gas	126	1044
Firelighters, solid, with flammable liquid	133	2623
First aid kit	171	3316
Fish meal, stabilized	171	2216
Fish meal, unstabilized	133	1374
Fish scrap, stabilized	171	2216
Fish scrap, unstabilized	133	1374
Flammable liquid, corrosive, n.o.s	132	2924
Flammable liquid, n.o.s.	128	1993
Flammable liquid, poisonous, corrosive, n.o.s.	131	3286
Flammable liquid, poisonous, n.o.s.	131	1992
Flammable liquid, toxic, corrosive, n.o.s.	131	3286
Flammable liquid, toxic, n.o.s.	131	1992
Flammable solid, corrosive, inorganic, n.o.s.	134	3180

Name of Material	Guide No.	ID No.
Flammable solid, corrosive, n.o.s.	134	2925
Flammable solid, corrosive, organic, n.o.s.	134	2925
Flammable solid, inorganic, corrosive, n.o.s.	134	3180
Flammable solid, inorganic, n.o.s.	133	3178
Flammable solid, n.o.s.	133	1325
Flammable solid, organic, molten, n.o.s.	133	3176
Flammable solid, organic, n.o.s.	133	1325
Flammable solid, oxidizing, n.o.s.	140	3097
Flammable solid, poisonous, inorganic, n.o.s.	134	3179
Flammable solid, poisonous, n.o.s.	134	2926
Flammable solid, poisonous, organic, n.o.s.	134	2926
Flammable solid, toxic, inorganic, n.o.s.	134	3179
Flammable solid, toxic, organic, n.o.s.	134	2926
Fluoboric acid	154	1775
Fluorine	124	1045
Fluorine, compressed	124	1045
Fluoroacetic acid	154	2642
Fluoroanilines	153	2941
Fluorobenzene	130	2387
Fluoroboric acid	154	1775
Fluorophosphoric acid, anhydrous	154	1776
Fluorosilicates, n.o.s.	151	2856
Fluorosilicic acid	154	1778
Fluorosulfonic acid	137	1777
Fluorosulphonic acid	137	1777

Name of Material	Guide No.	ID No.	Name of Material	Guide No.	ID No.
Fluorotoluenes	130	2388	Fuel cell cartridges, containing water-reactive substances	138	3476
Fluosilicic acid	154	1778			
Formaldehyde, solution, flammable	132	1198	Fuel cell cartridges packed with equipment, containing corrosive substances	153	3477
Formaldehyde, solutions (Formalin)	132	1198			
Formaldehyde, solutions (Formalin) (corrosive)	132	2209	Fuel cell cartridges packed with equipment, containing flammable liquids	128	3473
Formic acid	153	1779	Fuel cell cartridges packed with equipment, containing hydrogen in metal hydride	115	3479
Formic acid, with more than 85% acid	153	1779			
Formic acid, with not less than 5% but less than 10% acid	153	3412	Fuel cell cartridges packed with equipment, containing liquefied flammable gas	115	3478
Formic acid, with not less than 10% but not more than 85% acid	153	3412	Fuel cell cartridges packed with equipment, containing water-reactive substances	138	3476
Fuel, aviation, turbine engine	128	1863	Fuel oil	128	1202
Fuel cell cartridges contained in equipment, containing corrosive substances	153	3477	Fuel oil	128	1993
			Fuel oil, no. 1,2,4,5,6	128	1202
Fuel cell cartridges contained in equipment, containing flammable liquids	128	3473	Fumaryl chloride	156	1780
			Fumigated cargo transport unit	171	3359
Fuel cell cartridges contained in equipment, containing hydrogen in metal hydride	115	3479	Fumigated unit	171	3359
			Furaldehydes	132P	1199
Fuel cell cartridges contained in equipment, containing liquefied flammable gas	115	3478	Furan	128	2389
			Furfural	132P	1199
Fuel cell cartridges contained in equipment, containing water-reactive substances	138	3476	Furfuraldehydes	132P	1199
			Furfuryl alcohol	153	2874
Fuel cell cartridges, containing corrosive substances	153	3477	Furfurylamine	132	2526
			Fusee (rail or highway)	133	1325
Fuel cell cartridges, containing flammable liquids	128	3473	Fusel oil	127	1201
			GA	153	2810
Fuel cell cartridges, containing hydrogen in metal hydride	115	3479	Gallium	172	2803
			Gas, refrigerated liquid, flammable, n.o.s.	115	3312
Fuel cell cartridges, containing liquefied flammable gas	115	3478	Gas, refrigerated liquid, n.o.s.	120	3158

Name of Material	Guide No.	ID No.	Name of Material	Guide No.	ID No.
Gas, refrigerated liquid, oxidizing, n.o.s.	122	3311	Hafnium powder, wetted with not less than 25% water	170	1326
Gas cartridges	115	2037	Hay, wet, damp or contaminated with oil	133	1327
Gas identification set	123	9035	Hazardous waste, liquid, n.o.s.	171	3082
Gasohol	128	1203	Hazardous waste, solid, n.o.s.	171	3077
Gas oil	128	1202	HD	153	2810
Gasoline	128	1203	Heating oil, light	128	1202
Gasoline and ethanol mixture, with more than 10% ethanol	127	3475	Helium	121	1046
Gas sample, non-pressurized, flammable, n.o.s., not refrigerated liquid	115	3167	Helium, compressed	121	1046
			Helium, refrigerated liquid (cryogenic liquid)	120	1963
Gas sample, non-pressurized, poisonous, flammable, n.o.s., not refrigerated liquid	119	3168	Heptafluoropropane	126	3296
			n-Heptaldehyde	129	3056
Gas sample, non-pressurized, poisonous, n.o.s., not refrigerated liquid	123	3169	Heptanes	128	1206
			n-Heptene	128	2278
Gas sample, non-pressurized, toxic, flammable, n.o.s., not refrigerated liquid	119	3168	Hexachloroacetone	153	2661
			Hexachlorobenzene	152	2729
			Hexachlorobutadiene	151	2279
Gas sample, non-pressurized, toxic, n.o.s., not refrigerated liquid	123	3169	Hexachlorocyclopentadiene	151	2646
			Hexachlorophene	151	2875
GB	153	2810	Hexadecyltrichlorosilane	156	1781
GD	153	2810	Hexadiene	130	2458
Genetically modified micro-organisms	171	3245	Hexaethyl tetraphosphate	151	1611
Genetically modified organisms	171	3245	Hexaethyl tetraphosphate, liquid	151	1611
Germane	119	2192	Hexaethyl tetraphosphate, solid	151	1611
GF	153	2810	Hexaethyl tetraphosphate and compressed gas mixture	123	1612
Glycerol alpha-monochlorohydrin	153	2689	Hexafluoroacetone	125	2420
Glycidaldehyde	131P	2622	Hexafluoroacetone hydrate	151	2552
Guanidine nitrate	143	1467	Hexafluoroacetone hydrate, liquid	151	2552
H	153	2810			
Hafnium powder, dry	135	2545			

Name of Material	Guide No.	ID No.	Name of Material	Guide No.	ID No.
Hexafluoroacetone hydrate, solid	151	3436	Hydrazine, aqueous solution, with not more than 37% Hydrazine	152	3293
Hexafluoroethane	126	2193	Hydrazine, aqueous solutions, with more than 64% Hydrazine	132	2029
Hexafluoroethane, compressed	126	2193	Hydrazine hydrate	153	2030
Hexafluorophosphoric acid	154	1782	Hydrides, metal, n.o.s.	138	1409
Hexafluoropropylene	126	1858	Hydriodic acid	154	1787
Hexafluoropropylene, compressed	126	1858	Hydriodic acid, solution	154	1787
Hexaldehyde	130	1207	Hydrobromic acid	154	1788
Hexamethylenediamine, solid	153	2280	Hydrobromic acid, solution	154	1788
Hexamethylenediamine, solution	153	1783	Hydrocarbon gas, compressed, n.o.s.	115	1964
Hexamethylene diisocyanate	156	2281	Hydrocarbon gas, liquefied, n.o.s.	115	1965
Hexamethyleneimine	132	2493	Hydrocarbon gas mixture, compressed, n.o.s.	115	1964
Hexamethylenetetramine	133	1328	Hydrocarbon gas mixture, liquefied, n.o.s.	115	1965
Hexamine	133	1328	Hydrocarbon gas refills for small devices, with release device	115	3150
Hexanes	128	1208			
Hexanoic acid	153	2829			
Hexanols	129	2282			
1-Hexene	128	2370	Hydrocarbons, liquid, n.o.s.	128	3295
Hexyltrichlorosilane	156	1784	Hydrochloric acid	157	1789
HL	153	2810	Hydrochloric acid, solution	157	1789
HN-1	153	2810	Hydrocyanic acid, aqueous solution, with less than 5% Hydrogen cyanide	154	1613
HN-2	153	2810			
HN-3	153	2810	Hydrocyanic acid, aqueous solution, with not more than 20% Hydrogen cyanide	154	1613
Hydrazine, anhydrous	132	2029			
Hydrazine aqueous solution, flammable, with more than 37% hydrazine, by mass	132	3484	Hydrocyanic acid, aqueous solutions, with more than 20% Hydrogen cyanide	117	1051
Hydrazine, aqueous solution, with more than 37% Hydrazine	153	2030	Hydrofluoric acid	157	1790
			Hydrofluoric acid, solution	157	1790
Hydrazine, aqueous solution, with not less than 37% but not more than 64% Hydrazine	153	2030	Hydrofluoric acid and Sulfuric acid mixture	157	1786

Name of Material	Guide No.	ID No.	Name of Material	Guide No.	ID No.
Hydrofluoric acid and Sulphuric acid mixture	157	1786	Hydrogendifluorides, solution, n.o.s.	154	3471
Hydrofluorosilicic acid	154	1778	Hydrogen fluoride, anhydrous	125	1052
Hydrogen	115	1049	Hydrogen iodide, anhydrous	125	2197
Hydrogen absorbed in metal hydride	115	9279	Hydrogen peroxide, aqueous solution, stabilized, with more than 60% Hydrogen peroxide	143	2015
Hydrogen, compressed	115	1049			
Hydrogen in a metal hydride storage system	115	3468	Hydrogen peroxide, aqueous solution, with not less than 8% but less than 20% Hydrogen peroxide	140	2984
Hydrogen in a metal hydride storage system contained in equipment	115	3468			
Hydrogen in a metal hydride storage system packed with equipment	115	3468	Hydrogen peroxide, aqueous solution, with not less than 20% but not more than 60% Hydrogen peroxide (stabilized as necessary)	140	2014
Hydrogen, refrigerated liquid (cryogenic liquid)	115	1966	Hydrogen peroxide, stabilized	143	2015
Hydrogen and Carbon monoxide mixture, compressed	119	2600	Hydrogen peroxide and Peroxyacetic acid mixture, with acid(s), water and not more than 5% Peroxyacetic acid, stabilized	140	3149
Hydrogen and Methane mixture, compressed	115	2034			
Hydrogen bromide, anhydrous	125	1048	Hydrogen selenide, anhydrous	117	2202
Hydrogen chloride, anhydrous	125	1050	Hydrogen sulfide	117	1053
Hydrogen chloride, refrigerated liquid	125	2186	Hydrogen sulphide	117	1053
Hydrogen cyanide, anhydrous, stabilized	117	1051	Hydroquinone	153	2662
			Hydroquinone, solid	153	2662
Hydrogen cyanide, aqueous solution, with not more than 20% Hydrogen cyanide	154	1613	Hydroquinone, solution	153	3435
Hydrogen cyanide, solution in alcohol, with not more than 45% Hydrogen cyanide	131	3294	1-Hydroxybenzotriazole, anhydrous, wetted with not less than 20% water	113	3474
			1-Hydroxybenzotriazole, monohydrate	113	3474
Hydrogen cyanide, stabilized	117	1051	Hydroxylamine sulfate	154	2865
Hydrogen cyanide, stabilized (absorbed)	152	1614	Hydroxylamine sulphate	154	2865
Hydrogendifluorides, n.o.s.	154	1740	Hypochlorite solution	154	1791
Hydrogendifluorides, solid, n.o.s.	154	1740	Hypochlorite solution, with more than 5% available Chlorine	154	1791

Name of Material	Guide No.	ID No.
Hypochlorites, inorganic, n.o.s.	140	3212
3,3'-Iminodipropylamine	153	2269
Infectious substance, affecting animals only	158	2900
Infectious substance, affecting humans	158	2814
Ink, printer's, flammable	129	1210
Insecticide gas, flammable, n.o.s.	115	3354
Insecticide gas, n.o.s.	126	1968
Insecticide gas, poisonous, flammable, n.o.s.	119	3355
Insecticide gas, poisonous, flammable, n.o.s. (Inhalation Hazard Zone A)	119	3355
Insecticide gas, poisonous, flammable, n.o.s. (Inhalation Hazard Zone B)	119	3355
Insecticide gas, poisonous, flammable, n.o.s. (Inhalation Hazard Zone C)	119	3355
Insecticide gas, poisonous, flammable, n.o.s. (Inhalation Hazard Zone D)	119	3355
Insecticide gas, poisonous, n.o.s.	123	1967
Insecticide gas, toxic, flammable, n.o.s.	119	3355
Insecticide gas, toxic, flammable, n.o.s. (Inhalation Hazard Zone A)	119	3355
Insecticide gas, toxic, flammable, n.o.s. (Inhalation Hazard Zone B)	119	3355
Insecticide gas, toxic, flammable, n.o.s. (Inhalation Hazard Zone C)	119	3355
Insecticide gas, toxic, flammable, n.o.s. (Inhalation Hazard Zone D)	119	3355
Insecticide gas, toxic, n.o.s.	123	1967

Name of Material	Guide No.	ID No.
Iodine	154	3495
Iodine monochloride, liquid	157	3498
Iodine monochloride, solid	157	1792
Iodine pentafluoride	144	2495
2-Iodobutane	129	2390
Iodomethylpropanes	129	2391
Iodopropanes	129	2392
IPDI	156	2290
Iron oxide, spent	135	1376
Iron pentacarbonyl	131	1994
Iron sponge, spent	135	1376
Isobutane	115	1075
Isobutane	115	1969
Isobutane mixture	115	1075
Isobutane mixture	115	1969
Isobutanol	129	1212
Isobutyl acetate	129	1213
Isobutyl acrylate, stabilized	129P	2527
Isobutyl alcohol	129	1212
Isobutyl aldehyde	130	2045
Isobutylamine	132	1214
Isobutyl chloroformate	155	2742
Isobutylene	115	1055
Isobutylene	115	1075
Isobutyl formate	129	2393
Isobutyl isobutyrate	130	2528
Isobutyl isocyanate	155	2486
Isobutyl methacrylate, stabilized	130P	2283
Isobutyl propionate	129	2394
Isobutyraldehyde	130	2045
Isobutyric acid	132	2529

Name of Material	Guide No.	ID No.	Name of Material	Guide No.	ID No.
Isobutyronitrile	131	2284	Isopentenes	128	2371
Isobutyryl chloride	132	2395	Isophoronediamine	153	2289
Isocyanate solution, flammable, poisonous, n.o.s.	155	2478	Isophorone diisocyanate	156	2290
Isocyanate solution, flammable, toxic, n.o.s.	155	2478	Isoprene, stabilized	130P	1218
			Isopropanol	129	1219
Isocyanate solution, poisonous, flammable, n.o.s.	155	3080	Isopropenyl acetate	129P	2403
			Isopropenylbenzene	128	2303
Isocyanate solution, poisonous, n.o.s.	155	2206	Isopropyl acetate	129	1220
Isocyanate solution, toxic, flammable, n.o.s.	155	3080	Isopropyl acid phosphate	153	1793
Isocyanate solution, toxic, n.o.s.	155	2206	Isopropyl alcohol	129	1219
			Isopropylamine	132	1221
Isocyanate solutions, n.o.s.	155	2206	Isopropylbenzene	130	1918
Isocyanate solutions, n.o.s.	155	2478	Isopropyl butyrate	129	2405
Isocyanate solutions, n.o.s.	155	3080	Isopropyl chloroacetate	155	2947
Isocyanates, flammable, poisonous, n.o.s.	155	2478	Isopropyl chloroformate	155	2407
Isocyanates, flammable, toxic, n.o.s.	155	2478	Isopropyl 2-chloropropionate	129	2934
			Isopropyl isobutyrate	127	2406
Isocyanates, n.o.s.	155	2206	Isopropyl isocyanate	155	2483
Isocyanates, n.o.s.	155	2478	Isopropyl nitrate	130	1222
Isocyanates, n.o.s.	155	3080	Isopropyl propionate	129	2409
Isocyanates, poisonous, flammable, n.o.s.	155	3080	Isosorbide dinitrate mixture	133	2907
Isocyanates, poisonous, n.o.s.	155	2206	Isosorbide-5-mononitrate	133	3251
Isocyanates, toxic, flammable, n.o.s.	155	3080	Kerosene	128	1223
			Ketones, liquid, n.o.s.	127	1224
Isocyanates, toxic, n.o.s.	155	2206	Krill meal	133	3497
Isocyanatobenzotrifluorides	156	2285	Krypton	121	1056
Isoheptenes	128	2287	Krypton, compressed	121	1056
Isohexenes	128	2288	Krypton, refrigerated liquid (cryogenic liquid)	120	1970
Isooctane	128	1262	L (Lewisite)	153	2810
Isooctenes	128	1216	Lead acetate	151	1616
Isopentane	128	1265	Lead arsenates	151	1617

Name of Material	Guide No.	ID No.
Lead arsenites	151	1618
Lead compound, soluble, n.o.s.	151	2291
Lead cyanide	151	1620
Lead dioxide	141	1872
Lead nitrate	141	1469
Lead perchlorate	141	1470
Lead perchlorate, solid	141	1470
Lead perchlorate, solution	141	1470
Lead perchlorate, solution	141	3408
Lead phosphite, dibasic	133	2989
Lead sulfate, with more than 3% free acid	154	1794
Lead sulphate, with more than 3% free acid	154	1794
Lewisite	153	2810
Life-saving appliances, not self-inflating	171	3072
Life-saving appliances, self-inflating	171	2990
Lighter refills (cigarettes) (flammable gas)	115	1057
Lighters (cigarettes) (flammable gas)	115	1057
Liquefied gas, flammable, n.o.s.	115	3161
Liquefied gas, n.o.s.	126	3163
Liquefied gas, oxidizing, n.o.s.	122	3157
Liquefied gas, poisonous, corrosive, n.o.s.	123	3308
Liquefied gas, poisonous, corrosive, n.o.s. (Inhalation Hazard Zone A)	123	3308
Liquefied gas, poisonous, corrosive, n.o.s. (Inhalation Hazard Zone B)	123	3308
Liquefied gas, poisonous, corrosive, n.o.s. (Inhalation Hazard Zone C)	123	3308
Liquefied gas, poisonous, corrosive, n.o.s. (Inhalation Hazard Zone D)	123	3308
Liquefied gas, poisonous, flammable, corrosive, n.o.s.	119	3309
Liquefied gas, poisonous, flammable, corrosive, n.o.s. (Inhalation Hazard Zone A)	119	3309
Liquefied gas, poisonous, flammable, corrosive, n.o.s. (Inhalation Hazard Zone B)	119	3309
Liquefied gas, poisonous, flammable, corrosive, n.o.s. (Inhalation Hazard Zone C)	119	3309
Liquefied gas, poisonous, flammable, corrosive, n.o.s. (Inhalation Hazard Zone D)	119	3309
Liquefied gas, poisonous, flammable, n.o.s.	119	3160
Liquefied gas, poisonous, flammable, n.o.s. (Inhalation Hazard Zone A)	119	3160
Liquefied gas, poisonous, flammable, n.o.s. (Inhalation Hazard Zone B)	119	3160
Liquefied gas, poisonous, flammable, n.o.s. (Inhalation Hazard Zone C)	119	3160
Liquefied gas, poisonous, flammable, n.o.s. (Inhalation Hazard Zone D)	119	3160
Liquefied gas, poisonous, n.o.s.	123	3162
Liquefied gas, poisonous, n.o.s. (Inhalation Hazard Zone A)	123	3162
Liquefied gas, poisonous, n.o.s. (Inhalation Hazard Zone B)	123	3162
Liquefied gas, poisonous, n.o.s. (Inhalation Hazard Zone C)	123	3162
Liquefied gas, poisonous, n.o.s. (Inhalation Hazard Zone D)	123	3162

Name of Material	Guide No.	ID No.	Name of Material	Guide No.	ID No.
Liquefied gas, poisonous, oxidizing, corrosive, n.o.s.	124	3310	Liquefied gas, toxic, flammable, corrosive, n.o.s. (Inhalation Hazard Zone A)	119	3309
Liquefied gas, poisonous, oxidizing, corrosive, n.o.s. (Inhalation Hazard Zone A)	124	3310	Liquefied gas, toxic, flammable, corrosive, n.o.s. (Inhalation Hazard Zone B)	119	3309
Liquefied gas, poisonous, oxidizing, corrosive, n.o.s. (Inhalation Hazard Zone B)	124	3310	Liquefied gas, toxic, flammable, corrosive, n.o.s. (Inhalation Hazard Zone C)	119	3309
Liquefied gas, poisonous, oxidizing, corrosive, n.o.s. (Inhalation Hazard Zone C)	124	3310	Liquefied gas, toxic, flammable, corrosive, n.o.s. (Inhalation Hazard Zone D)	119	3309
Liquefied gas, poisonous, oxidizing, corrosive, n.o.s. (Inhalation Hazard Zone D)	124	3310	Liquefied gas, toxic, flammable, n.o.s.	119	3160
Liquefied gas, poisonous, oxidizing, n.o.s.	124	3307	Liquefied gas, toxic, flammable, n.o.s. (Inhalation Hazard Zone A)	119	3160
Liquefied gas, poisonous, oxidizing, n.o.s. (Inhalation Hazard Zone A)	124	3307	Liquefied gas, toxic, flammable, n.o.s. (Inhalation Hazard Zone B)	119	3160
Liquefied gas, poisonous, oxidizing, n.o.s. (Inhalation Hazard Zone B)	124	3307	Liquefied gas, toxic, flammable, n.o.s. (Inhalation Hazard Zone C)	119	3160
Liquefied gas, poisonous, oxidizing, n.o.s. (Inhalation Hazard Zone C)	124	3307	Liquefied gas, toxic, flammable, n.o.s. (Inhalation Hazard Zone D)	119	3160
Liquefied gas, poisonous, oxidizing, n.o.s. (Inhalation Hazard Zone D)	124	3307	Liquefied gas, toxic, n.o.s.	123	3162
Liquefied gas, toxic, corrosive, n.o.s.	123	3308	Liquefied gas, toxic, n.o.s. (Inhalation Hazard Zone A)	123	3162
Liquefied gas, toxic, corrosive, n.o.s. (Inhalation Hazard Zone A)	123	3308	Liquefied gas, toxic, n.o.s. (Inhalation Hazard Zone B)	123	3162
Liquefied gas, toxic, corrosive, n.o.s. (Inhalation Hazard Zone B)	123	3308	Liquefied gas, toxic, n.o.s. (Inhalation Hazard Zone C)	123	3162
Liquefied gas, toxic, corrosive, n.o.s. (Inhalation Hazard Zone C)	123	3308	Liquefied gas, toxic, n.o.s. (Inhalation Hazard Zone D)	123	3162
Liquefied gas, toxic, corrosive, n.o.s. (Inhalation Hazard Zone D)	123	3308	Liquefied gas, toxic, oxidizing, corrosive, n.o.s.	124	3310
Liquefied gas, toxic, flammable, corrosive, n.o.s.	119	3309	Liquefied gas, toxic, oxidizing, corrosive, n.o.s. (Inhalation Hazard Zone A)	124	3310
			Liquefied gas, toxic, oxidizing, corrosive, n.o.s. (Inhalation Hazard Zone B)	124	3310

Name of Material	Guide No.	ID No.
Liquefied gas, toxic, oxidizing, corrosive, n.o.s. (Inhalation Hazard Zone C)	124	3310
Liquefied gas, toxic, oxidizing, corrosive, n.o.s. (Inhalation Hazard Zone D)	124	3310
Liquefied gas, toxic, oxidizing, n.o.s.	124	3307
Liquefied gas, toxic, oxidizing, n.o.s. (Inhalation Hazard Zone A)	124	3307
Liquefied gas, toxic, oxidizing, n.o.s. (Inhalation Hazard Zone B)	124	3307
Liquefied gas, toxic, oxidizing, n.o.s. (Inhalation Hazard Zone C)	124	3307
Liquefied gas, toxic, oxidizing, n.o.s. (Inhalation Hazard Zone D)	124	3307
Liquefied gases, non-flammable, charged with Nitrogen, Carbon dioxide or Air	120	1058
Liquefied natural gas (cryogenic liquid)	115	1972
Liquefied petroleum gas	115	1075
Lithium	138	1415
Lithium alkyls	135	2445
Lithium alkyls, liquid	135	2445
Lithium alkyls, solid	135	3433
Lithium aluminum hydride	138	1410
Lithium aluminum hydride, ethereal	138	1411
Lithium batteries	138	3090
Lithium batteries contained in equipment	138	3091
Lithium batteries, liquid or solid cathode	138	3090
Lithium batteries packed with equipment	138	3091
Lithium borohydride	138	1413
Lithium ferrosilicon	139	2830
Lithium hydride	138	1414
Lithium hydride, fused solid	138	2805
Lithium hydroxide	154	2680
Lithium hydroxide, monohydrate	154	2680
Lithium hydroxide, solid	154	2680
Lithium hydroxide, solution	154	2679
Lithium hypochlorite, dry	140	1471
Lithium hypochlorite mixture	140	1471
Lithium hypochlorite mixtures, dry	140	1471
Lithium ion batteries contained in equipment (including lithium ion polymer batteries)	147	3481
Lithium ion batteries (including lithium ion polymer batteries)	147	3480
Lithium ion batteries packed with equipment (including lithium ion polymer batteries)	147	3481
Lithium metal batteries contained in equipment (including lithium alloy batteries)	138	3091
Lithium metal batteries (including lithium alloy batteries)	138	3090
Lithium metal batteries packed with equipment (including lithium alloy batteries)	138	3091
Lithium nitrate	140	2722
Lithium nitride	138	2806
Lithium peroxide	143	1472
Lithium silicon	138	1417
LNG (cryogenic liquid)	115	1972

Name of Material	Guide No.	ID No.	Name of Material	Guide No.	ID No.
London purple	151	1621	Maleic anhydride, molten	156	2215
LPG	115	1075	Malononitrile	153	2647
Magnesium	138	1869	Maneb	135	2210
Magnesium, in pellets, turnings or ribbons	138	1869	Maneb, stabilized	135	2968
Magnesium alkyls	135	3053	Maneb preparation, stabilized	135	2968
Magnesium alloys, with more than 50% Magnesium, in pellets, turnings or ribbons	138	1869	Maneb preparation, with not less than 60% Maneb	135	2210
Magnesium alloys powder	138	1418	Manganese nitrate	140	2724
Magnesium aluminum phosphide	139	1419	Manganese resinate	133	1330
Magnesium arsenate	151	1622	Matches, fusee	133	2254
Magnesium bromate	140	1473	Matches, safety	133	1944
Magnesium chlorate	140	2723	Matches, "strike anywhere"	133	1331
Magnesium chloride and Chlorate mixture	140	1459	Matches, wax "vesta"	133	1945
Magnesium chloride and Chlorate mixture, solid	140	1459	MD	152	1556
Magnesium chloride and Chlorate mixture, solution	140	3407	Medical waste, n.o.s.	158	3291
Magnesium diamide	135	2004	Medicine, liquid, flammable, poisonous, n.o.s.	131	3248
Magnesium diphenyl	135	2005	Medicine, liquid, flammable, toxic, n.o.s.	131	3248
Magnesium fluorosilicate	151	2853	Medicine, liquid, poisonous, n.o.s.	151	1851
Magnesium granules, coated	138	2950	Medicine, liquid, toxic, n.o.s.	151	1851
Magnesium hydride	138	2010	Medicine, solid, poisonous, n.o.s.	151	3249
Magnesium nitrate	140	1474	Medicine, solid, toxic, n.o.s.	151	3249
Magnesium perchlorate	140	1475	Mercaptan mixture, liquid, flammable, n.o.s.	130	3336
Magnesium peroxide	140	1476	Mercaptan mixture, liquid, flammable, poisonous, n.o.s.	131	1228
Magnesium phosphide	139	2011	Mercaptan mixture, liquid, flammable, toxic, n.o.s.	131	1228
Magnesium powder	138	1418	Mercaptan mixture, liquid, poisonous, flammable, n.o.s.	131	3071
Magnesium silicide	138	2624			
Magnesium silicofluoride	151	2853	Mercaptan mixture, liquid, toxic, flammable, n.o.s.	131	3071
Magnetized material	171	2807			
Maleic anhydride	156	2215			

Name of Material	Guide No.	ID No.
Mercaptans, liquid, flammable, n.o.s.	130	3336
Mercaptans, liquid, flammable, poisonous, n.o.s.	131	1228
Mercaptans, liquid, flammable, toxic, n.o.s.	131	1228
Mercaptans, liquid, poisonous, flammable, n.o.s.	131	3071
Mercaptans, liquid, toxic, flammable, n.o.s.	131	3071
Mercuric arsenate	151	1623
Mercuric bromide	154	1634
Mercuric chloride	154	1624
Mercuric cyanide	154	1636
Mercuric nitrate	141	1625
Mercuric oxycyanide	151	1642
Mercuric potassium cyanide	157	1626
Mercuric sulfate	151	1645
Mercuric sulphate	151	1645
Mercurous bromide	154	1634
Mercurous nitrate	141	1627
Mercury	172	2809
Mercury acetate	151	1629
Mercury ammonium chloride	151	1630
Mercury based pesticide, liquid, flammable, poisonous	131	2778
Mercury based pesticide, liquid, flammable, toxic	131	2778
Mercury based pesticide, liquid, poisonous	151	3012
Mercury based pesticide, liquid, poisonous, flammable	131	3011
Mercury based pesticide, liquid, toxic	151	3012
Mercury based pesticide, liquid, toxic, flammable	131	3011
Mercury based pesticide, solid, poisonous	151	2777
Mercury based pesticide, solid, toxic	151	2777
Mercury benzoate	154	1631
Mercury bromides	154	1634
Mercury compound, liquid, n.o.s.	151	2024
Mercury compound, solid, n.o.s.	151	2025
Mercury contained in manufactured articles	172	3506
Mercury cyanide	154	1636
Mercury gluconate	151	1637
Mercury iodide	151	1638
Mercury metal	172	2809
Mercury nucleate	151	1639
Mercury oleate	151	1640
Mercury oxide	151	1641
Mercury oxycyanide, desensitized	151	1642
Mercury potassium iodide	151	1643
Mercury salicylate	151	1644
Mercury sulfate	151	1645
Mercury sulphate	151	1645
Mercury thiocyanate	151	1646
Mesityl oxide	129	1229
Metal alkyl halides, water-reactive, n.o.s.	138	3049
Metal alkyl hydrides, water-reactive, n.o.s.	138	3050
Metal alkyls, water-reactive, n.o.s.	135	2003
Metal aryl halides, water-reactive, n.o.s.	138	3049
Metal aryl hydrides, water-reactive, n.o.s.	138	3050

Name of Material	Guide No.	ID No.
Metal aryls, water-reactive, n.o.s.	135	2003
Metal carbonyls, liquid, n.o.s.	151	3281
Metal carbonyls, n.o.s.	151	3281
Metal carbonyls, solid, n.o.s.	151	3466
Metal catalyst, dry	135	2881
Metal catalyst, wetted	170	1378
Metaldehyde	133	1332
Metal hydrides, flammable, n.o.s.	170	3182
Metal hydrides, water-reactive, n.o.s.	138	1409
Metallic substance, water-reactive, n.o.s.	138	3208
Metallic substance, water-reactive, self-heating, n.o.s.	138	3209
Metal powder, flammable, n.o.s.	170	3089
Metal powder, self-heating, n.o.s.	135	3189
Metal salts of organic compounds, flammable, n.o.s.	133	3181
Methacrylaldehyde, stabilized	131P	2396
Methacrylic acid, stabilized	153P	2531
Methacrylonitrile, stabilized	131P	3079
Methallyl alcohol	129	2614
Methane	115	1971
Methane, compressed	115	1971
Methane, refrigerated liquid (cryogenic liquid)	115	1972
Methane and Hydrogen mixture, compressed	115	2034
Methanesulfonyl chloride	156	3246
Methanesulphonyl chloride	156	3246
Methanol	131	1230
Methoxymethyl isocyanate	155	2605

Name of Material	Guide No.	ID No.
4-Methoxy-4-methylpentan-2-one	128	2293
1-Methoxy-2-propanol	129	3092
Methyl acetate	129	1231
Methylacetylene and Propadiene mixture, stabilized	116P	1060
Methyl acrylate, stabilized	129P	1919
Methylal	127	1234
Methyl alcohol	131	1230
Methylallyl chloride	130P	2554
Methylamine, anhydrous	118	1061
Methylamine, aqueous solution	132	1235
Methylamyl acetate	130	1233
Methylamyl alcohol	129	2053
Methyl amyl ketone	127	1110
N-Methylaniline	153	2294
alpha-Methylbenzyl alcohol	153	2937
alpha-Methylbenzyl alcohol, liquid	153	2937
alpha-Methylbenzyl alcohol, solid	153	3438
Methylbenzyl alcohol (alpha)	153	2937
Methyl bromide	123	1062
Methyl bromide and Chloropicrin mixture	123	1581
Methyl bromide and Ethylene dibromide mixture, liquid	151	1647
Methyl bromoacetate	155	2643
2-Methylbutanal	129	3371
3-Methylbutan-2-one	127	2397
2-Methyl-1-butene	128	2459
2-Methyl-2-butene	128	2460
3-Methyl-1-butene	128	2561

Name of Material	Guide No.	ID No.
N-Methylbutylamine	132	2945
Methyl tert-butyl ether	127	2398
Methyl butyrate	129	1237
Methyl chloride	115	1063
Methyl chloride and Chloropicrin mixture	119	1582
Methyl chloride and Methylene chloride mixture	115	1912
Methyl chloroacetate	155	2295
Methyl chloroformate	155	1238
Methyl chloromethyl ether	131	1239
Methyl 2-chloropropionate	129	2933
Methylchlorosilane	119	2534
Methyl cyanide	127	1648
Methylcyclohexane	128	2296
Methylcyclohexanols	129	2617
Methylcyclohexanone	128	2297
Methylcyclopentane	128	2298
Methyl dichloroacetate	155	2299
Methyldichloroarsine	152	1556
Methyldichlorosilane	139	1242
Methylene chloride	160	1593
Methylene chloride and Methyl chloride mixture	115	1912
Methyl ethyl ether	115	1039
Methyl ethyl ketone	127	1193
2-Methyl-5-ethylpyridine	153	2300
Methyl fluoride	115	2454
Methyl formate	129	1243
2-Methylfuran	128	2301
2-Methyl-2-heptanethiol	131	3023
5-Methylhexan-2-one	127	2302
Methylhydrazine	131	1244
Methyl iodide	151	2644
Methyl isobutyl carbinol	129	2053
Methyl isobutyl ketone	127	1245
Methyl isocyanate	155	2480
Methyl isopropenyl ketone, stabilized	127P	1246
Methyl isothiocyanate	131	2477
Methyl isovalerate	130	2400
Methyl magnesium bromide in Ethyl ether	135	1928
Methyl mercaptan	117	1064
Methyl methacrylate monomer, stabilized	129P	1247
4-Methylmorpholine	132	2535
N-Methylmorpholine	132	2535
Methylmorpholine	132	2535
Methyl nitrite	116	2455
Methyl orthosilicate	155	2606
Methylpentadiene	128	2461
2-Methylpentan-2-ol	129	2560
Methylphenyldichlorosilane	156	2437
Methyl phosphonic dichloride	137	9206
Methyl phosphonous dichloride	135	2845
1-Methylpiperidine	132	2399
Methyl propionate	129	1248
Methyl propyl ether	127	2612
Methyl propyl ketone	127	1249
Methyltetrahydrofuran	127	2536
Methyl trichloroacetate	156	2533
Methyltrichlorosilane	155	1250
alpha-Methylvaleraldehyde	130	2367
Methyl valeraldehyde (alpha)	130	2367

Name of Material	Guide No.	ID No.
Methyl vinyl ketone, stabilized	131P	1251
M.I.B.C.	129	2053
Molybdenum pentachloride	156	2508
Monoethanolamine	153	2491
Mononitrotoluidines	153	2660
Monopropylamine	132	1277
Morpholine	132	2054
Motor fuel anti-knock mixture	131	1649
Motor fuel anti-knock mixture, flammable	131	3483
Motor spirit	128	1203
Motor spirit and ethanol mixture, with more than 10% ethanol	127	3475
Muriatic acid	157	1789
Musk xylene	149	2956
Mustard	153	2810
Mustard Lewisite	153	2810
Naphthalene, crude	133	1334
Naphthalene, molten	133	2304
Naphthalene, refined	133	1334
alpha-Naphthylamine	153	2077
Naphthylamine (alpha)	153	2077
beta-Naphthylamine	153	1650
beta-Naphthylamine, solid	153	1650
beta-Naphthylamine, solution	153	3411
Naphthylamine (beta)	153	1650
Naphthylamine (beta), solid	153	1650
Naphthylamine (beta), solution	153	3411
Naphthylthiourea	153	1651
Naphthylurea	153	1652
Natural gas, compressed	115	1971

Name of Material	Guide No.	ID No.
Natural gas, refrigerated liquid (cryogenic liquid)	115	1972
Neohexane	128	1208
Neon	121	1065
Neon, compressed	121	1065
Neon, refrigerated liquid (cryogenic liquid)	120	1913
Nickel carbonyl	131	1259
Nickel catalyst, dry	135	2881
Nickel cyanide	151	1653
Nickel nitrate	140	2725
Nickel nitrite	140	2726
Nicotine	151	1654
Nicotine compound, liquid, n.o.s.	151	3144
Nicotine compound, solid, n.o.s.	151	1655
Nicotine hydrochloride	151	1656
Nicotine hydrochloride, liquid	151	1656
Nicotine hydrochloride, solid	151	1656
Nicotine hydrochloride, solid	151	3444
Nicotine hydrochloride, solution	151	1656
Nicotine preparation, liquid, n.o.s.	151	3144
Nicotine preparation, solid, n.o.s.	151	1655
Nicotine salicylate	151	1657
Nicotine sulfate, solid	151	1658
Nicotine sulfate, solid	151	3445
Nicotine sulfate, solution	151	1658
Nicotine sulphate, solid	151	1658
Nicotine sulphate, solid	151	3445
Nicotine sulphate, solution	151	1658
Nicotine tartrate	151	1659

Name of Material	Guide No.	ID No.	Name of Material	Guide No.	ID No.
Nitrates, inorganic, aqueous solution, n.o.s.	140	3218	Nitriles, poisonous, solid, n.o.s.	151	3439
Nitrates, inorganic, n.o.s.	140	1477	Nitriles, solid, poisonous, n.o.s.	151	3439
Nitrating acid mixture with more than 50% nitric acid	157	1796	Nitriles, solid, toxic, n.o.s.	151	3439
Nitrating acid mixture with not more than 50% nitric acid	157	1796	Nitriles, toxic, flammable, n.o.s.	131	3275
Nitrating acid mixture, spent, with more than 50% nitric acid	157	1826	Nitriles, toxic, liquid, n.o.s.	151	3276
			Nitriles, toxic, n.o.s.	151	3276
Nitrating acid mixture, spent, with not more than 50% nitric acid	157	1826	Nitriles, toxic, solid, n.o.s.	151	3439
			Nitrites, inorganic, aqueous solution, n.o.s.	140	3219
Nitric acid, fuming	157	2032	Nitrites, inorganic, n.o.s.	140	2627
Nitric acid, other than red fuming, with more than 70% nitric acid	157	2031	Nitroanilines	153	1661
			Nitroanisoles	152	2730
Nitric acid, other than red fuming, with not more than 70% nitric acid	157	2031	Nitroanisoles, liquid	152	2730
			Nitroanisoles, solid	152	2730
Nitric acid, red fuming	157	2032	Nitroanisoles, solid	152	3458
Nitric oxide	124	1660	Nitrobenzene	152	1662
Nitric oxide, compressed	124	1660	Nitrobenzenesulfonic acid	153	2305
Nitric oxide and Dinitrogen tetroxide mixture	124	1975	Nitrobenzenesulphonic acid	153	2305
			Nitrobenzotrifluorides	152	2306
Nitric oxide and Nitrogen dioxide mixture	124	1975	Nitrobenzotrifluorides, liquid	152	2306
			Nitrobenzotrifluorides, solid	152	3431
Nitric oxide and Nitrogen tetroxide mixture	124	1975	Nitrobromobenzenes	152	2732
			Nitrobromobenzenes, liquid	152	2732
Nitriles, flammable, poisonous, n.o.s.	131	3273	Nitrobromobenzenes, solid	152	2732
Nitriles, flammable, toxic, n.o.s.	131	3273	Nitrobromobenzenes, solid	152	3459
Nitriles, liquid, poisonous, n.o.s.	151	3276	Nitrocellulose	133	2557
Nitriles, liquid, toxic, n.o.s.	151	3276	Nitrocellulose membrane filters	133	3270
Nitriles, poisonous, flammable, n.o.s.	131	3275	Nitrocellulose mixture, without pigment	133	2557
Nitriles, poisonous, liquid, n.o.s.	151	3276	Nitrocellulose mixture, without plasticizer	133	2557
Nitriles, poisonous, n.o.s.	151	3276			

Name of Material	Guide No.	ID No.	Name of Material	Guide No.	ID No.
Nitrocellulose mixture, with pigment	133	2557	Nitroglycerin, solution in alcohol, with not more than 1% Nitroglycerin	127	1204
Nitrocellulose mixture, with pigment and plasticizer	133	2557	Nitroglycerin mixture, desensitized, liquid, flammable, n.o.s., with not more than 30% Nitroglycerin	113	3343
Nitrocellulose mixture, with plasticizer	133	2557			
Nitrocellulose, solution, flammable	127	2059	Nitroglycerin mixture, desensitized, liquid, n.o.s., with not more than 30% Nitroglycerin	113	3357
Nitrocellulose, solution, in a flammable liquid	127	2059			
Nitrocellulose with alcohol	113	2556	Nitroglycerin mixture, desensitized, solid, n.o.s., with more than 2% but not more than 10% Nitroglycerin	113	3319
Nitrocellulose with not less than 25% alcohol	113	2556			
Nitrocellulose with water, not less than 25% water	113	2555	Nitroglycerin mixture with more than 2% but not more than 10% Nitroglycerin, desensitized	113	3319
3-Nitro-4-chlorobenzotrifluoride	152	2307			
Nitrocresols	153	2446	Nitroguanidine (Picrite), wetted with not less than 20% water	113	1336
Nitrocresols, liquid	153	3434			
Nitrocresols, solid	153	2446	Nitroguanidine, wetted with not less than 20% water	113	1336
Nitroethane	129	2842	Nitrohydrochloric acid	157	1798
Nitrogen	121	1066	Nitromethane	129	1261
Nitrogen, compressed	121	1066	Nitronaphthalene	133	2538
Nitrogen, refrigerated liquid (cryogenic liquid)	120	1977	Nitrophenols	153	1663
Nitrogen and Rare gases mixture, compressed	121	1981	4-Nitrophenylhydrazine, with not less than 30% water	113	3376
Nitrogen dioxide	124	1067	Nitropropanes	129	2608
Nitrogen dioxide and Nitric oxide mixture	124	1975	p-Nitrosodimethylaniline	135	1369
Nitrogen tetroxide and Nitric oxide mixture	124	1975	Nitrostarch, wetted with not less than 20% water	113	1337
Nitrogen trifluoride	122	2451	Nitrostarch, wetted with not less than 30% solvent	113	1337
Nitrogen trifluoride, compressed	122	2451	Nitrosyl chloride	125	1069
Nitrogen trioxide	124	2421	Nitrosylsulfuric acid	157	2308
Nitroglycerin, solution in alcohol, with more than 1% but not more than 5% Nitroglycerin	127	3064	Nitrosylsulfuric acid, liquid	157	2308
			Nitrosylsulfuric acid, solid	157	2308
			Nitrosylsulfuric acid, solid	157	3456

Name of Material	Guide No.	ID No.
Nitrosylsulphuric acid	157	2308
Nitrosylsulphuric acid, liquid	157	2308
Nitrosylsulphuric acid, solid	157	2308
Nitrosylsulphuric acid, solid	157	3456
Nitrotoluenes	152	1664
Nitrotoluenes, liquid	152	1664
Nitrotoluenes, solid	152	1664
Nitrotoluenes, solid	152	3446
Nitrotoluidines (mono)	153	2660
Nitrous oxide	122	1070
Nitrous oxide, compressed	122	1070
Nitrous oxide, refrigerated liquid	122	2201
Nitrous oxide and Carbon dioxide mixture	126	1015
Nitroxylenes	152	1665
Nitroxylenes, liquid	152	1665
Nitroxylenes, solid	152	1665
Nitroxylenes, solid	152	3447
Nonanes	128	1920
Nonyltrichlorosilane	156	1799
2,5-Norbornadiene, stabilized	128P	2251
Octadecyltrichlorosilane	156	1800
Octadiene	128P	2309
Octafluorobut-2-ene	126	2422
Octafluorocyclobutane	126	1976
Octafluoropropane	126	2424
Octanes	128	1262
Octyl aldehydes	129	1191
tert-Octyl mercaptan	131	3023
Octyltrichlorosilane	156	1801
Oil, petroleum	128	1270

Name of Material	Guide No.	ID No.
Oil gas	119	1071
Oil gas, compressed	119	1071
Organic peroxide type B, liquid	146	3101
Organic peroxide type B, liquid, temperature controlled	148	3111
Organic peroxide type B, solid	146	3102
Organic peroxide type B, solid, temperature controlled	148	3112
Organic peroxide type C, liquid	146	3103
Organic peroxide type C, liquid, temperature controlled	148	3113
Organic peroxide type C, solid	146	3104
Organic peroxide type C, solid, temperature controlled	148	3114
Organic peroxide type D, liquid	145	3105
Organic peroxide type D, liquid, temperature controlled	148	3115
Organic peroxide type D, solid	145	3106
Organic peroxide type D, solid, temperature controlled	148	3116
Organic peroxide type E, liquid	145	3107
Organic peroxide type E, liquid, temperature controlled	148	3117
Organic peroxide type E, solid	145	3108
Organic peroxide type E, solid, temperature controlled	148	3118
Organic peroxide type F, liquid	145	3109
Organic peroxide type F, liquid, temperature controlled	148	3119
Organic peroxide type F, solid	145	3110
Organic peroxide type F, solid, temperature controlled	148	3120

Name of Material	Guide No.	ID No.
Organic phosphate compound mixed with compressed gas	123	1955
Organic phosphate mixed with compressed gas	123	1955
Organic phosphorus compound mixed with compressed gas	123	1955
Organic pigments, self-heating	135	3313
Organoarsenic compound, liquid, n.o.s.	151	3280
Organoarsenic compound, n.o.s.	151	3280
Organoarsenic compound, solid, n.o.s.	151	3465
Organochlorine pesticide, liquid, flammable, poisonous	131	2762
Organochlorine pesticide, liquid, flammable, toxic	131	2762
Organochlorine pesticide, liquid, poisonous	151	2996
Organochlorine pesticide, liquid, poisonous, flammable	131	2995
Organochlorine pesticide, liquid, toxic	151	2996
Organochlorine pesticide, liquid, toxic, flammable	131	2995
Organochlorine pesticide, solid, poisonous	151	2761
Organochlorine pesticide, solid, toxic	151	2761
Organometallic compound, liquid, poisonous, n.o.s.	151	3282
Organometallic compound, liquid, toxic, n.o.s.	151	3282
Organometallic compound, poisonous, liquid, n.o.s.	151	3282
Organometallic compound, poisonous, n.o.s.	151	3282
Organometallic compound, poisonous, solid, n.o.s.	151	3467

Name of Material	Guide No.	ID No.
Organometallic compound, solid, poisonous, n.o.s.	151	3467
Organometallic compound, solid, toxic, n.o.s.	151	3467
Organometallic compound, solid, water-reactive, flammable, n.o.s.	138	3372
Organometallic compound, toxic, liquid, n.o.s.	151	3282
Organometallic compound, toxic, n.o.s.	151	3282
Organometallic compound, toxic, solid, n.o.s.	151	3467
Organometallic compound, water-reactive, flammable, n.o.s.	138	3207
Organometallic compound dispersion, water-reactive, flammable, n.o.s.	138	3207
Organometallic compound solution, water-reactive, flammable, n.o.s.	138	3207
Organometallic substance, liquid, pyrophoric	135	3392
Organometallic substance, liquid, pyrophoric, water-reactive	135	3394
Organometallic substance, liquid, water-reactive	135	3398
Organometallic substance, liquid, water-reactive, flammable	138	3399
Organometallic substance, solid, pyrophoric	135	3391
Organometallic substance, solid, pyrophoric, water-reactive	135	3393
Organometallic substance, solid, self-heating	138	3400
Organometallic substance, solid, water-reactive	135	3395
Organometallic substance, solid, water-reactive, flammable	138	3396

Name of Material	Guide No.	ID No.	Name of Material	Guide No.	ID No.
Organometallic substance, solid, water-reactive, self-heating	138	3397	Organophosphorus pesticide, solid, toxic	152	2783
Organophosphorus compound, liquid, poisonous, n.o.s.	151	3278	Organotin compound, liquid, n.o.s.	153	2788
Organophosphorus compound, liquid, toxic, n.o.s.	151	3278	Organotin compound, solid, n.o.s.	153	3146
Organophosphorus compound, poisonous, flammable, n.o.s.	131	3279	Organotin pesticide, liquid, flammable, poisonous	131	2787
Organophosphorus compound, poisonous, liquid, n.o.s.	151	3278	Organotin pesticide, liquid, flammable, toxic	131	2787
Organophosphorus compound, poisonous, n.o.s.	151	3278	Organotin pesticide, liquid, poisonous	153	3020
Organophosphorus compound, poisonous, solid, n.o.s.	151	3464	Organotin pesticide, liquid, poisonous, flammable	131	3019
Organophosphorus compound, solid, poisonous, n.o.s.	151	3464	Organotin pesticide, liquid, toxic	153	3020
Organophosphorus compound, solid, toxic, n.o.s.	151	3464	Organotin pesticide, liquid, toxic, flammable	131	3019
Organophosphorus compound, toxic, flammable, n.o.s.	131	3279	Organotin pesticide, solid, poisonous	153	2786
Organophosphorus compound, toxic, liquid, n.o.s.	151	3278	Organotin pesticide, solid, toxic	153	2786
Organophosphorus compound, toxic, n.o.s.	151	3278	Osmium tetroxide	154	2471
Organophosphorus compound, toxic, solid, n.o.s.	151	3464	Other regulated substances, liquid, n.o.s.	171	3082
Organophosphorus pesticide, liquid, flammable, poisonous	131	2784	Other regulated substances, solid, n.o.s.	171	3077
Organophosphorus pesticide, liquid, flammable, toxic	131	2784	Oxidizing liquid, corrosive, n.o.s.	140	3098
Organophosphorus pesticide, liquid, poisonous	152	3018	Oxidizing liquid, n.o.s.	140	3139
Organophosphorus pesticide, liquid, poisonous, flammable	131	3017	Oxidizing liquid, poisonous, n.o.s.	142	3099
Organophosphorus pesticide, liquid, toxic	152	3018	Oxidizing liquid, toxic, n.o.s.	142	3099
Organophosphorus pesticide, liquid, toxic, flammable	131	3017	Oxidizing solid, corrosive, n.o.s.	140	3085
Organophosphorus pesticide, solid, poisonous	152	2783	Oxidizing solid, flammable, n.o.s.	140	3137
			Oxidizing solid, n.o.s.	140	1479
			Oxidizing solid, poisonous, n.o.s.	141	3087
			Oxidizing solid, self-heating, n.o.s.	135	3100

Name of Material	Guide No.	ID No.	Name of Material	Guide No.	ID No.
Oxidizing solid, toxic, n.o.s.	141	3087	Pentachloroethane	151	1669
Oxidizing solid, water-reactive, n.o.s.	144	3121	Pentachlorophenol	154	3155
Oxygen	122	1072	Pentaerythrite tetranitrate mixture, desensitized, solid, n.o.s., with more than 10% but not more than 20% PETN	113	3344
Oxygen, compressed	122	1072			
Oxygen, refrigerated liquid (cryogenic liquid)	122	1073			
Oxygen and Carbon dioxide mixture, compressed	122	1014	Pentaerythritol tetranitrate mixture, desensitized, solid, n.o.s., with more than 10% but not more than 20% PETN	113	3344
Oxygen and Rare gases mixture, compressed	121	1980			
Oxygen difluoride	124	2190	Pentafluoroethane	126	3220
Oxygen difluoride, compressed	124	2190	Pentafluoroethane and Ethylene oxide mixture, with not more than 7.9% Ethylene oxide	126	3298
Oxygen generator, chemical	140	3356			
Oxygen generator, chemical, spent	140	3356	Pentamethylheptane	128	2286
Paint (corrosive)	153	3066	Pentan-2,4-dione	131	2310
Paint, corrosive, flammable	132	3470	n-Pentane	128	1265
Paint (flammable)	128	1263	2,4-Pentanedione	131	2310
Paint, flammable, corrosive	132	3469	Pentane-2,4-dione	131	2310
Paint related material (corrosive)	153	3066	Pentanes	128	1265
Paint related material, corrosive, flammable	132	3470	Pentanols	129	1105
Paint related material (flammable)	128	1263	1-Pentene	128	1108
Paint related material, flammable, corrosive	132	3469	1-Pentol	153P	2705
			Perchlorates, inorganic, aqueous solution, n.o.s.	140	3211
Paper, unsaturated oil treated	133	1379	Perchlorates, inorganic, n.o.s.	140	1481
Paraformaldehyde	133	2213	Perchloric acid, with more than 50% but not more than 72% acid	143	1873
Paraldehyde	129	1264			
Parathion and compressed gas mixture	123	1967	Perchloric acid, with not more than 50% acid	140	1802
PCB	171	2315	Perchloroethylene	160	1897
PD	152	1556	Perchloromethyl mercaptan	157	1670
Pentaborane	135	1380	Perchloryl fluoride	124	3083
			Perfluoroethyl vinyl ether	115	3154

Name of Material	Guide No.	ID No.	Name of Material	Guide No.	ID No.
Perfluoro(ethyl vinyl ether)	115	3154	Petroleum distillates, n.o.s.	128	1268
Perfluoromethyl vinyl ether	115	3153	Petroleum gases, liquefied	115	1075
Perfluoro(methyl vinyl ether)	115	3153	Petroleum oil	128	1270
Perfumery products, with flammable solvents	127	1266	Petroleum products, n.o.s.	128	1268
Permanganates, inorganic, aqueous solution, n.o.s.	140	3214	Petroleum sour crude oil, flammable, toxic	131	3494
Permanganates, inorganic, n.o.s.	140	1482	Phenacyl bromide	153	2645
			Phenetidines	153	2311
Peroxides, inorganic, n.o.s.	140	1483	Phenol, molten	153	2312
Persulfates, inorganic, aqueous solution, n.o.s.	140	3216	Phenol, solid	153	1671
			Phenol solution	153	2821
Persulfates, inorganic, n.o.s.	140	3215	Phenolates, liquid	154	2904
Persulphates, inorganic, aqueous solution, n.o.s.	140	3216	Phenolates, solid	154	2905
			Phenolsulfonic acid, liquid	153	1803
Persulphates, inorganic, n.o.s.	140	3215	Phenolsulphonic acid, liquid	153	1803
Pesticide, liquid, flammable, poisonous, n.o.s.	131	3021	Phenoxyacetic acid derivative pesticide, liquid, flammable, poisonous	131	3346
Pesticide, liquid, flammable, toxic, n.o.s.	131	3021	Phenoxyacetic acid derivative pesticide, liquid, flammable, toxic	131	3346
Pesticide, liquid, poisonous, flammable, n.o.s.	131	2903	Phenoxyacetic acid derivative pesticide, liquid, poisonous	153	3348
Pesticide, liquid, poisonous, n.o.s.	151	2902	Phenoxyacetic acid derivative pesticide, liquid, poisonous, flammable	131	3347
Pesticide, liquid, toxic, flammable, n.o.s.	131	2903	Phenoxyacetic acid derivative pesticide, liquid, toxic	153	3348
Pesticide, liquid, toxic, n.o.s.	151	2902	Phenoxyacetic acid derivative pesticide, liquid, toxic, flammable	131	3347
Pesticide, solid, poisonous	151	2588			
Pesticide, solid, poisonous, n.o.s.	151	2588	Phenoxyacetic acid derivative pesticide, solid, poisonous	153	3345
Pesticide, solid, toxic, n.o.s.	151	2588	Phenoxyacetic acid derivative pesticide, solid, toxic	153	3345
PETN mixture, desensitized, solid, n.o.s., with more than 10% but not more than 20% PETN	113	3344	Phenylacetonitrile, liquid	152	2470
Petrol	128	1203	Phenylacetyl chloride	156	2577
Petrol and ethanol mixture, with more than 10% ethanol	127	3475	Phenylcarbylamine chloride	151	1672
Petroleum crude oil	128	1267			

Name of Material	Guide No.	ID No.	Name of Material	Guide No.	ID No.
Phenyl chloroformate	156	2746	Phosphorus heptasulfide, free from yellow and white Phosphorus	139	1339
Phenylenediamines	153	1673			
Phenylhydrazine	153	2572	Phosphorus heptasulphide, free from yellow and white Phosphorus	139	1339
Phenyl isocyanate	155	2487			
Phenyl mercaptan	131	2337	Phosphorus oxybromide	137	1939
Phenylmercuric acetate	151	1674	Phosphorus oxybromide, molten	137	2576
Phenylmercuric compound, n.o.s.	151	2026	Phosphorus oxybromide, solid	137	1939
Phenylmercuric hydroxide	151	1894	Phosphorus oxychloride	137	1810
Phenylmercuric nitrate	151	1895	Phosphorus pentabromide	137	2691
Phenylphosphorus dichloride	137	2798	Phosphorus pentachloride	137	1806
Phenylphosphorus thiodichloride	137	2799	Phosphorus pentafluoride	125	2198
Phenyltrichlorosilane	156	1804	Phosphorus pentafluoride, compressed	125	2198
Phenyl urea pesticide, liquid, poisonous	151	3002	Phosphorus pentasulfide, free from yellow and white Phosphorus	139	1340
Phenyl urea pesticide, liquid, toxic	151	3002	Phosphorus pentasulphide, free from yellow and white Phosphorus	139	1340
Phosgene	125	1076			
9-Phosphabicyclononanes	135	2940	Phosphorus pentoxide	137	1807
Phosphine	119	2199	Phosphorus sesquisulfide, free from yellow and white Phosphorus	139	1341
Phosphoric acid	154	1805			
Phosphoric acid, liquid	154	1805	Phosphorus sesquisulphide, free from yellow and white Phosphorus	139	1341
Phosphoric acid, solid	154	1805			
Phosphoric acid, solid	154	3453	Phosphorus tribromide	137	1808
Phosphoric acid, solution	154	1805	Phosphorus trichloride	137	1809
Phosphorous acid	154	2834	Phosphorus trioxide	157	2578
Phosphorous acid, ortho	154	2834	Phosphorus trisulfide, free from yellow and white Phosphorus	139	1343
Phosphorus, amorphous	133	1338			
Phosphorus, amorphous, red	133	1338	Phosphorus trisulphide, free from yellow and white Phosphorus	139	1343
Phosphorus, white, dry or under water or in solution	136	1381			
Phosphorus, white, molten	136	2447	Phthalic anhydride	156	2214
Phosphorus, yellow, dry or under water or in solution	136	1381	Picolines	129	2313

Name of Material	Guide No.	ID No.
Picric acid, wetted with not less than 10% water	113	3364
Picric acid, wetted with not less than 30% water	113	1344
Picrite, wetted	113	1336
Picryl chloride, wetted with not less than 10% water	113	3365
alpha-Pinene	128	2368
Pinene (alpha)	128	2368
Pine oil	129	1272
Piperazine	153	2579
Piperidine	132	2401
Plastic molding compound	171	3314
Plastic, nitrocellulose-based, spontaneously combustible, n.o.s.	135	2006
Plastics moulding compound	171	3314
Plastics, nitrocellulose-based, self-heating, n.o.s.	135	2006
Poisonous by inhalation liquid, corrosive, flammable, n.o.s. (Inhalation Hazard Zone A)	131	3492
Poisonous by inhalation liquid, corrosive, flammable, n.o.s. (Inhalation Hazard Zone B)	131	3493
Poisonous by inhalation liquid, corrosive, n.o.s. (Inhalation Hazard Zone A)	154	3389
Poisonous by inhalation liquid, corrosive, n.o.s. (Inhalation Hazard Zone B)	154	3390
Poisonous by inhalation liquid, flammable, corrosive, n.o.s. (Inhalation Hazard Zone A)	131	3488
Poisonous by inhalation liquid, flammable, corrosive, n.o.s. (Inhalation Hazard Zone B)	131	3489
Poisonous by inhalation liquid, flammable, n.o.s. (Inhalation Hazard Zone A)	131	3383
Poisonous by inhalation liquid, flammable, n.o.s. (Inhalation Hazard Zone B)	131	3384
Poisonous by inhalation liquid, n.o.s. (Inhalation Hazard Zone A)	151	3381
Poisonous by inhalation liquid, n.o.s. (Inhalation Hazard Zone B)	151	3382
Poisonous by inhalation liquid, oxidizing, n.o.s. (Inhalation Hazard Zone A)	142	3387
Poisonous by inhalation liquid, oxidizing, n.o.s. (Inhalation Hazard Zone B)	142	3388
Poisonous by inhalation liquid, water-reactive, flammable, n.o.s. (Inhalation Hazard Zone A)	155	3490
Poisonous by inhalation liquid, water-reactive, flammable, n.o.s. (Inhalation Hazard Zone B)	155	3491
Poisonous by inhalation liquid, water-reactive, n.o.s. (Inhalation Hazard Zone A)	139	3385
Poisonous by inhalation liquid, water-reactive, n.o.s. (Inhalation Hazard Zone B)	139	3386
Poisonous liquid, corrosive, inorganic, n.o.s.	154	3289
Poisonous liquid, corrosive, inorganic, n.o.s. (Inhalation Hazard Zone A)	154	3289
Poisonous liquid, corrosive, inorganic, n.o.s. (Inhalation Hazard Zone B)	154	3289
Poisonous liquid, corrosive, n.o.s.	154	2927
Poisonous liquid, corrosive, n.o.s. (Inhalation Hazard Zone A)	154	2927
Poisonous liquid, corrosive, n.o.s. (Inhalation Hazard Zone B)	154	2927

Name of Material	Guide No.	ID No.	Name of Material	Guide No.	ID No.
Poisonous liquid, corrosive, organic, n.o.s.	154	2927	Poisonous liquid, organic, n.o.s. (Inhalation Hazard Zone B)	153	2810
Poisonous liquid, corrosive, organic, n.o.s. (Inhalation Hazard Zone A)	154	2927	Poisonous liquid, oxidizing, n.o.s.	142	3122
Poisonous liquid, corrosive, organic, n.o.s. (Inhalation Hazard Zone B)	154	2927	Poisonous liquid, oxidizing, n.o.s. (Inhalation Hazard Zone A)	142	3122
Poisonous liquid, flammable, n.o.s.	131	2929	Poisonous liquid, oxidizing, n.o.s. (Inhalation Hazard Zone B)	142	3122
Poisonous liquid, flammable, n.o.s. (Inhalation Hazard Zone A)	131	2929	Poisonous liquid, water-reactive, n.o.s.	139	3123
Poisonous liquid, flammable, n.o.s. (Inhalation Hazard Zone B)	131	2929	Poisonous liquid, water-reactive, n.o.s. (Inhalation Hazard Zone A)	139	3123
Poisonous liquid, flammable, organic, n.o.s.	131	2929	Poisonous liquid, water-reactive, n.o.s. (Inhalation Hazard Zone B)	139	3123
Poisonous liquid, flammable, organic, n.o.s. (Inhalation Hazard Zone A)	131	2929	Poisonous liquid, which in contact with water emits flammable gases, n.o.s.	139	3123
Poisonous liquid, flammable, organic, n.o.s. (Inhalation Hazard Zone B)	131	2929	Poisonous liquid, which in contact with water emits flammable gases, n.o.s. (Inhalation Hazard Zone A)	139	3123
Poisonous liquid, inorganic, n.o.s.	151	3287	Poisonous liquid, which in contact with water emits flammable gases, n.o.s. (Inhalation Hazard Zone B)	139	3123
Poisonous liquid, inorganic, n.o.s. (Inhalation Hazard Zone A)	151	3287	Poisonous solid, corrosive, inorganic, n.o.s.	154	3290
Poisonous liquid, inorganic, n.o.s. (Inhalation Hazard Zone B)	151	3287	Poisonous solid, corrosive, n.o.s.	154	2928
Poisonous liquid, n.o.s.	153	2810	Poisonous solid, flammable, n.o.s.	134	2930
Poisonous liquid, n.o.s. (Inhalation Hazard Zone A)	153	2810	Poisonous solid, flammable, organic, n.o.s.	134	2930
Poisonous liquid, n.o.s. (Inhalation Hazard Zone B)	153	2810	Poisonous solid, inorganic, n.o.s.	151	3288
Poisonous liquid, organic, n.o.s.	153	2810	Poisonous solid, organic, n.o.s.	154	2811
Poisonous liquid, organic, n.o.s. (Inhalation Hazard Zone A)	153	2810	Poisonous solid, oxidizing, n.o.s.	141	3086

Name of Material	Guide No.	ID No.
Poisonous solid, self-heating, n.o.s.	136	3124
Poisonous solid, water-reactive, n.o.s.	139	3125
Poisonous solid, which in contact with water emits flammable gases, n.o.s.	139	3125
Polyalkylamines, n.o.s.	132	2733
Polyalkylamines, n.o.s.	132	2734
Polyalkylamines, n.o.s.	153	2735
Polyamines, flammable, corrosive, n.o.s.	132	2733
Polyamines, liquid, corrosive, flammable, n.o.s.	132	2734
Polyamines, liquid, corrosive, n.o.s.	153	2735
Polyamines, solid, corrosive, n.o.s.	154	3259
Polychlorinated biphenyls	171	2315
Polychlorinated biphenyls, liquid	171	2315
Polychlorinated biphenyls, solid	171	2315
Polychlorinated biphenyls, solid	171	3432
Polyester resin kit	128	3269
Polyhalogenated biphenyls, liquid	171	3151
Polyhalogenated biphenyls, solid	171	3152
Polyhalogenated terphenyls, liquid	171	3151
Polyhalogenated terphenyls, solid	171	3152
Polymeric beads, expandable	133	2211
Polystyrene beads, expandable	133	2211
Potassium	138	2257
Potassium, metal	138	2257
Potassium, metal alloys	138	1420

Name of Material	Guide No.	ID No.
Potassium, metal alloys, liquid	138	1420
Potassium, metal alloys, solid	138	3403
Potassium arsenate	151	1677
Potassium arsenite	154	1678
Potassium borohydride	138	1870
Potassium bromate	140	1484
Potassium chlorate	140	1485
Potassium chlorate, aqueous solution	140	2427
Potassium chlorate, solution	140	2427
Potassium cuprocyanide	157	1679
Potassium cyanide	157	1680
Potassium cyanide, solid	157	1680
Potassium cyanide, solution	157	3413
Potassium dithionite	135	1929
Potassium fluoride	154	1812
Potassium fluoride, solid	154	1812
Potassium fluoride, solution	154	3422
Potassium fluoroacetate	151	2628
Potassium fluorosilicate	151	2655
Potassium hydrogendifluoride	154	1811
Potassium hydrogen difluoride, solid	154	1811
Potassium hydrogen difluoride, solution	154	3421
Potassium hydrogen sulfate	154	2509
Potassium hydrogen sulphate	154	2509
Potassium hydrosulfite	135	1929
Potassium hydrosulphite	135	1929
Potassium hydroxide, dry, solid	154	1813
Potassium hydroxide, flake	154	1813
Potassium hydroxide, solid	154	1813

Name of Material	Guide No.	ID No.	Name of Material	Guide No.	ID No.
Potassium hydroxide, solution	154	1814	Potassium sulphide, hydrated, with not less than 30% water of hydration	153	1847
Potassium metavanadate	151	2864			
Potassium monoxide	154	2033	Potassium sulphide, with less than 30% water of crystallization	135	1382
Potassium nitrate	140	1486			
Potassium nitrate and Sodium nitrate mixture	140	1499	Potassium sulphide, with less than 30% water of hydration	135	1382
Potassium nitrate and Sodium nitrite mixture	140	1487	Potassium superoxide	143	2466
Potassium nitrite	140	1488	Printing ink, flammable	129	1210
Potassium perchlorate	140	1489	Printing ink related material	129	1210
Potassium permanganate	140	1490	Propadiene, stabilized	116P	2200
Potassium peroxide	144	1491	Propadiene and Methylacetylene mixture, stabilized	116P	1060
Potassium persulfate	140	1492			
Potassium persulphate	140	1492	Propane	115	1075
Potassium phosphide	139	2012	Propane	115	1978
Potassium silicofluoride	151	2655	Propane-Ethane mixture, refrigerated liquid	115	1961
Potassium sodium alloys	138	1422			
Potassium sodium alloys, liquid	138	1422	Propane mixture	115	1075
			Propane mixture	115	1978
Potassium sodium alloys, solid	138	3404	Propanethiols	130	2402
Potassium sulfide, anhydrous	135	1382	n-Propanol	129	1274
Potassium sulfide, hydrated, with not less than 30% water of crystallization	153	1847	Propionaldehyde	129	1275
			Propionic acid	132	1848
Potassium sulfide, hydrated, with not less than 30% water of hydration	153	1847	Propionic acid, with not less than 10% and less than 90% acid	132	1848
Potassium sulfide, with less than 30% water of crystallization	135	1382	Propionic acid, with not less than 90% acid	132	3463
			Propionic anhydride	156	2496
Potassium sulfide, with less than 30% water of hydration	135	1382	Propionitrile	131	2404
Potassium sulphide, anhydrous	135	1382	Propionyl chloride	132	1815
			n-Propyl acetate	129	1276
Potassium sulphide, hydrated, with not less than 30% water of crystallization	153	1847	normal Propyl alcohol	129	1274
			Propyl alcohol, normal	129	1274
			Propylamine	132	1277

Name of Material	Guide No.	ID No.	Name of Material	Guide No.	ID No.
n-Propyl benzene	128	2364	Pyrethroid pesticide, solid, poisonous	151	3349
Propyl chloride	129	1278	Pyrethroid pesticide, solid, toxic	151	3349
n-Propyl chloroformate	155	2740			
Propylene	115	1075	Pyridine	129	1282
Propylene	115	1077	Pyrophoric alloy, n.o.s.	135	1383
Propylene, Ethylene and Acetylene in mixture, refrigerated liquid containing at least 71.5% Ethylene with not more than 22.5% Acetylene and not more than 6% Propylene	115	3138	Pyrophoric liquid, inorganic, n.o.s.	135	3194
			Pyrophoric liquid, n.o.s.	135	2845
			Pyrophoric liquid, organic, n.o.s.	135	2845
			Pyrophoric metal, n.o.s.	135	1383
Propylene chlorohydrin	131	2611	Pyrophoric organometallic compound, water-reactive, n.o.s.	135	3203
1,2-Propylenediamine	132	2258			
1,3-Propylenediamine	132	2258			
Propylene dichloride	130	1279	Pyrophoric solid, inorganic, n.o.s.	135	3200
Propyleneimine, stabilized	131P	1921	Pyrophoric solid, n.o.s.	135	2846
Propylene oxide	127P	1280	Pyrophoric solid, organic, n.o.s.	135	2846
Propylene oxide and Ethylene oxide mixture, with not more than 30% Ethylene oxide	129P	2983	Pyrosulfuryl chloride	137	1817
			Pyrosulphuryl chloride	137	1817
Propylene tetramer	128	2850	Pyrrolidine	132	1922
Propyl formates	129	1281	Quinoline	154	2656
n-Propyl isocyanate	155	2482	Radioactive material, excepted package, articles manufactured from depleted Uranium	161	2909
n-Propyl nitrate	131	1865			
Propyltrichlorosilane	155	1816			
Pyrethroid pesticide, liquid, flammable, poisonous	131	3350	Radioactive material, excepted package, articles manufactured from natural Thorium	161	2909
Pyrethroid pesticide, liquid, flammable, toxic	131	3350			
Pyrethroid pesticide, liquid, poisonous	151	3352	Radioactive material, excepted package, articles manufactured from natural Uranium	161	2909
Pyrethroid pesticide, liquid, poisonous, flammable	131	3351			
Pyrethroid pesticide, liquid, toxic	151	3352	Radioactive material, excepted package, empty packaging	161	2908
Pyrethroid pesticide, liquid, toxic, flammable	131	3351	Radioactive material, excepted package, empty packaging	161	2910

Name of Material	Guide No.	ID No.	Name of Material	Guide No.	ID No.
Radioactive material, excepted package, instruments or articles	161	2910	Radioactive material, surface contaminated objects (SCO-II), non fissile or fissile-excepted	162	2913
Radioactive material, excepted package, instruments or articles	161	2911	Radioactive material, transported under special arrangement, fissile	165	3331
Radioactive material, excepted package, limited quantity of material	161	2910	Radioactive material, transported under special arrangement, non fissile or fissile-excepted	163	2919
Radioactive material, fissile, n.o.s.	165	2918	Radioactive material, Type A package, fissile, non-special form	165	3327
Radioactive material, low specific activity (LSA), n.o.s.	162	2912	Radioactive material, Type A package non-special form, non fissile or fissile-excepted	163	2915
Radioactive material, low specific activity (LSA-I), non fissile or fissile-excepted	162	2912	Radioactive material, Type A package, special form, fissile	165	3333
Radioactive material, low specific activity (LSA-II), fissile	165	3324	Radioactive material, Type A package, special form, non fissile or fissile-excepted	164	3332
Radioactive material, low specific activity (LSA-II), non fissile or fissile-excepted	162	3321	Radioactive material, Type B(M) package, fissile	165	3329
Radioactive material, low specific activity (LSA-III), fissile	165	3325	Radioactive material, Type B(M) package, non fissile or fissile-excepted	163	2917
Radioactive material, low specific activity (LSA-III), non fissile or fissile-excepted	162	3322	Radioactive material, Type B(U) package, fissile	165	3328
Radioactive material, n.o.s.	163	2982	Radioactive material, Type B(U) package, non fissile or fissile-excepted	163	2916
Radioactive material, special form, n.o.s.	164	2974	Radioactive material, Type C package, non fissile or fissile excepted	163	3323
Radioactive material, surface contaminated objects (SCO)	162	2913	Radioactive material, Type C package, fissile	165	3330
Radioactive material, surface contaminated objects (SCO-I), fissile	165	3326	Radioactive material, Uranium hexafluoride	166	2978
Radioactive material, surface contaminated objects (SCO-I), non fissile or fissile-excepted	162	2913	Radioactive material, Uranium hexafluoride, fissile	166	2977
Radioactive material, surface contaminated objects (SCO-II), fissile	165	3326	Rags, oily	133	1856

Name of Material	Guide No.	ID No.	Name of Material	Guide No.	ID No.
Rare gases and Nitrogen mixture, compressed	121	1981	Refrigerant gas R-115	126	1020
Rare gases and Oxygen mixture, compressed	121	1980	Refrigerant gas R-116	126	2193
			Refrigerant gas R-116, compressed	126	2193
Rare gases mixture, compressed	121	1979	Refrigerant gas R-124	126	1021
Receptacles, small, containing gas	115	2037	Refrigerant gas R-125	126	3220
			Refrigerant gas R-133a	126	1983
Red phosphorus	133	1338	Refrigerant gas R-134a	126	3159
Red phosphorus, amorphous	133	1338	Refrigerant gas R-142b	115	2517
Refrigerant gas, n.o.s.	126	1078	Refrigerant gas R-143a	115	2035
Refrigerant gas, n.o.s. (flammable)	115	1954	Refrigerant gas R-152a	115	1030
Refrigerant gas R-12	126	1028	Refrigerant gas R-152a and Refrigerant gas R-12 azeotropic mixture with 74% Refrigerant gas R-12	126	2602
Refrigerant gas R-12 and Refrigerant gas R-152a azeotropic mixture with 74% Refrigerant gas R-12	126	2602			
			Refrigerant gas R-161	115	2453
Refrigerant gas R-12B1	126	1974	Refrigerant gas R-218	126	2424
Refrigerant gas R-13	126	1022	Refrigerant gas R-227	126	3296
Refrigerant gas R-13 and Refrigerant gas R-23 azeotropic mixture with 60% Refrigerant gas R-13	126	2599	Refrigerant gas R-404A	126	3337
			Refrigerant gas R-407A	126	3338
			Refrigerant gas R-407B	126	3339
Refrigerant gas R-13B1	126	1009	Refrigerant gas R-407C	126	3340
Refrigerant gas R-14	126	1982	Refrigerant gas R-500 (azeotropic mixture of Refrigerant gas R-12 and Refrigerant gas R-152a with approximately 74% Refrigerant gas R-12)	126	2602
Refrigerant gas R-14, compressed	126	1982			
Refrigerant gas R-21	126	1029			
Refrigerant gas R-22	126	1018			
Refrigerant gas R-23	126	1984	Refrigerant gas R-502	126	1973
Refrigerant gas R-23 and Refrigerant gas R-13 azeotropic mixture with 60% Refrigerant gas R-13	126	2599	Refrigerant gas R-503 (azeotropic mixture of Refrigerant gas R-13 and Refrigerant gas R-23 with approximately 60% Refrigerant gas R-13)	126	2599
Refrigerant gas R-32	115	3252			
Refrigerant gas R-40	115	1063			
Refrigerant gas R-41	115	2454	Refrigerant gas R-1132a	116P	1959
Refrigerant gas R-114	126	1958	Refrigerant gas R-1216	126	1858
			Refrigerant gas R-1318	126	2422

Name of Material	Guide No.	ID No.
Refrigerant gas RC-318	126	1976
Refrigerating machines, containing Ammonia solutions (UN2672)	126	2857
Refrigerating machines, containing flammable, non-poisonous, liquefied gases	115	3358
Refrigerating machines, containing flammable, non-toxic, liquefied gases	115	3358
Refrigerating machines, containing non-flammable, non-poisonous gases	126	2857
Refrigerating machines, containing non-flammable, non-toxic gases	126	2857
Regulated medical waste, n.o.s.	158	3291
Resin solution	127	1866
Resorcinol	153	2876
Rosin oil	127	1286
Rubber scrap, powdered or granulated	133	1345
Rubber shoddy, powdered or granulated	133	1345
Rubber solution	127	1287
Rubidium	138	1423
Rubidium hydroxide	154	2678
Rubidium hydroxide, solid	154	2678
Rubidium hydroxide, solution	154	2677
Rubidium metal	138	1423
SA	119	2188
Sarin	153	2810
Seat-belt modules	171	3268
Seat-belt pre-tensioners	171	3268
Seat-belt pre-tensioners, compressed gas	126	3353
Seat-belt pre-tensioners, pyrotechnic	171	3268

Name of Material	Guide No.	ID No.
Seed cake, with more than 1.5% oil and not more than 11% moisture	135	1386
Seed cake, with not more than 1.5% oil and not more than 11% moisture	135	2217
Selenates	151	2630
Selenic acid	154	1905
Selenites	151	2630
Selenium compound, liquid, n.o.s.	151	3440
Selenium compound, n.o.s.	151	3283
Selenium compound, solid, n.o.s.	151	3283
Selenium disulfide	153	2657
Selenium disulphide	153	2657
Selenium hexafluoride	125	2194
Selenium oxychloride	157	2879
Self-defense spray, non-pressurized	171	3334
Self-heating liquid, corrosive, inorganic, n.o.s.	136	3188
Self-heating liquid, corrosive, organic, n.o.s.	136	3185
Self-heating liquid, inorganic, n.o.s.	135	3186
Self-heating liquid, organic, n.o.s.	135	3183
Self-heating liquid, poisonous, inorganic, n.o.s.	136	3187
Self-heating liquid, poisonous, organic, n.o.s.	136	3184
Self-heating liquid, toxic, inorganic, n.o.s.	136	3187
Self-heating liquid, toxic, organic, n.o.s.	136	3184
Self-heating metal powders, n.o.s.	135	3189
Self-heating solid, corrosive, inorganic, n.o.s.	136	3192

Name of Material	Guide No.	ID No.
Self-heating solid, corrosive, organic, n.o.s.	136	3126
Self-heating solid, inorganic, n.o.s.	135	3190
Self-heating solid, inorganic, poisonous, n.o.s.	136	3191
Self-heating solid, inorganic, toxic, n.o.s.	136	3191
Self-heating solid, organic, n.o.s.	135	3088
Self-heating solid, oxidizing, n.o.s.	135	3127
Self-heating solid, poisonous, inorganic, n.o.s.	136	3191
Self-heating solid, poisonous, organic, n.o.s.	136	3128
Self-heating solid, toxic, inorganic, n.o.s.	136	3191
Self-heating solid, toxic, organic, n.o.s.	136	3128
Self-reactive liquid type B	149	3221
Self-reactive liquid type B, temperature controlled	150	3231
Self-reactive liquid type C	149	3223
Self-reactive liquid type C, temperature controlled	150	3233
Self-reactive liquid type D	149	3225
Self-reactive liquid type D, temperature controlled	150	3235
Self-reactive liquid type E	149	3227
Self-reactive liquid type E, temperature controlled	150	3237
Self-reactive liquid type F	149	3229
Self-reactive liquid type F, temperature controlled	150	3239
Self-reactive solid type B	149	3222
Self-reactive solid type B, temperature controlled	150	3232
Self-reactive solid type C	149	3224
Self-reactive solid type C, temperature controlled	150	3234

Name of Material	Guide No.	ID No.
Self-reactive solid type D	149	3226
Self-reactive solid type D, temperature controlled	150	3236
Self-reactive solid type E	149	3228
Self-reactive solid type E, temperature controlled	150	3238
Self-reactive solid type F	149	3230
Self-reactive solid type F, temperature controlled	150	3240
Shale oil	128	1288
Silane	116	2203
Silicofluorides, n.o.s.	151	2856
Silane, compressed	116	2203
Silicon powder, amorphous	170	1346
Silicon tetrachloride	157	1818
Silicon tetrafluoride	125	1859
Silicon tetrafluoride, compressed	125	1859
Silver arsenite	151	1683
Silver cyanide	151	1684
Silver nitrate	140	1493
Silver picrate, wetted with not less than 30% water	113	1347
Sludge acid	153	1906
Smokeless powder for small arms	133	3178
Soda lime, with more than 4% Sodium hydroxide	154	1907
Sodium	138	1428
Sodium aluminate, solid	154	2812
Sodium aluminate, solution	154	1819
Sodium aluminum hydride	138	2835
Sodium ammonium vanadate	154	2863
Sodium arsanilate	154	2473
Sodium arsenate	151	1685

Name of Material	Guide No.	ID No.	Name of Material	Guide No.	ID No.
Sodium arsenite, aqueous solution	154	1686	Sodium dinitro-ortho-cresolate, wetted	113	1348
Sodium arsenite, solid	151	2027	Sodium dithionite	135	1384
Sodium azide	153	1687	Sodium fluoride	154	1690
Sodium bisulfate, solution	154	2837	Sodium fluoride, solid	154	1690
Sodium bisulphate, solution	154	2837	Sodium fluoride, solution	154	3415
Sodium borohydride	138	1426	Sodium fluoroacetate	151	2629
Sodium borohydride and Sodium hydroxide solution, with not more than 12% Sodium borohydride and not more than 40% Sodium hydroxide	157	3320	Sodium fluorosilicate	154	2674
			Sodium hydride	138	1427
			Sodium hydrogendifluoride	154	2439
Sodium bromate	141	1494	Sodium hydrogen sulfate, solution	154	2837
Sodium cacodylate	152	1688	Sodium hydrogen sulphate, solution	154	2837
Sodium carbonate peroxyhydrate	140	3378	Sodium hydrosulfide, solid, with less than 25% water of crystallization	135	2318
Sodium chlorate	140	1495			
Sodium chlorate, aqueous solution	140	2428	Sodium hydrosulfide, with less than 25% water of crystallization	135	2318
Sodium chlorite	143	1496	Sodium hydrosulfide, with not less than 25% water of crystallization	154	2949
Sodium chlorite, solution, with more than 5% available Chlorine	154	1908	Sodium hydrosulfite	135	1384
Sodium chloroacetate	151	2659	Sodium hydrosulphide, solid, with less than 25% water of crystallization	135	2318
Sodium cuprocyanide, solid	157	2316			
Sodium cuprocyanide, solution	157	2317	Sodium hydrosulphide, with less than 25% water of crystallization	135	2318
Sodium cyanide	157	1689			
Sodium cyanide, solid	157	1689	Sodium hydrosulphide, with not less than 25% water of crystallization	154	2949
Sodium cyanide, solution	157	3414			
Sodium dichloroisocyanurate	140	2465	Sodium hydrosulphite	135	1384
Sodium dichloro-s-triazinetrione	140	2465	Sodium hydroxide, bead	154	1823
Sodium dinitro-o-cresolate, wetted with not less than 10% water	113	3369	Sodium hydroxide, dry	154	1823
			Sodium hydroxide, flake	154	1823
			Sodium hydroxide, granular	154	1823
Sodium dinitro-o-cresolate, wetted with not less than 15% water	113	1348	Sodium hydroxide, solid	154	1823

Name of Material	Guide No.	ID No.
Sodium hydroxide, solution	154	1824
Sodium methylate	138	1431
Sodium methylate, dry	138	1431
Sodium methylate, solution in alcohol	132	1289
Sodium monoxide	157	1825
Sodium nitrate	140	1498
Sodium nitrate and Potassium nitrate mixture	140	1499
Sodium nitrite	140	1500
Sodium nitrite and Potassium nitrate mixture	140	1487
Sodium pentachlorophenate	154	2567
Sodium perborate monohydrate	140	3377
Sodium perchlorate	140	1502
Sodium permanganate	140	1503
Sodium peroxide	144	1504
Sodium peroxoborate, anhydrous	140	3247
Sodium persulfate	140	1505
Sodium persulphate	140	1505
Sodium phosphide	139	1432
Sodium picramate, wetted with not less than 20% water	113	1349
Sodium potassium alloys	138	1422
Sodium potassium alloys, liquid	138	1422
Sodium potassium alloys, solid	138	3404
Sodium silicofluoride	154	2674
Sodium sulfide, anhydrous	135	1385
Sodium sulfide, hydrated, with not less than 30% water	153	1849
Sodium sulfide, with less than 30% water of crystallization	135	1385
Sodium sulphide, anhydrous	135	1385

Name of Material	Guide No.	ID No.
Sodium sulphide, hydrated, with not less than 30% water	153	1849
Sodium sulphide, with less than 30% water of crystallization	135	1385
Sodium superoxide	143	2547
Solids containing corrosive liquid, n.o.s.	154	3244
Solids containing flammable liquid, n.o.s.	133	3175
Solids containing poisonous liquid, n.o.s.	151	3243
Solids containing toxic liquid, n.o.s.	151	3243
Soman	153	2810
Stannic chloride, anhydrous	137	1827
Stannic chloride, pentahydrate	154	2440
Stannic phosphides	139	1433
Stibine	119	2676
Straw, wet, damp or contaminated with oil	133	1327
Strontium arsenite	151	1691
Strontium chlorate	143	1506
Strontium chlorate, solid	143	1506
Strontium chlorate, solution	143	1506
Strontium nitrate	140	1507
Strontium perchlorate	140	1508
Strontium peroxide	143	1509
Strontium phosphide	139	2013
Strychnine	151	1692
Strychnine salts	151	1692
Styrene monomer, stabilized	128P	2055
Substituted nitrophenol pesticide, liquid, flammable, poisonous	131	2780

Name of Material	Guide No.	ID No.
Substituted nitrophenol pesticide, liquid, flammable, toxic	131	2780
Substituted nitrophenol pesticide, liquid, poisonous	153	3014
Substituted nitrophenol pesticide, liquid, poisonous, flammable	131	3013
Substituted nitrophenol pesticide, liquid, toxic	153	3014
Substituted nitrophenol pesticide, liquid, toxic, flammable	131	3013
Substituted nitrophenol pesticide, solid, poisonous	153	2779
Substituted nitrophenol pesticide, solid, toxic	153	2779
Sulfamic acid	154	2967
Sulfur	133	1350
Sulfur, molten	133	2448
Sulfur chlorides	137	1828
Sulfur dioxide	125	1079
Sulfur hexafluoride	126	1080
Sulfuric acid	137	1830
Sulfuric acid, fuming	137	1831
Sulfuric acid, fuming, with less than 30% free Sulfur trioxide	137	1831
Sulfuric acid, fuming, with not less than 30% free Sulfur trioxide	137	1831
Sulfuric acid, spent	137	1832
Sulfuric acid, with more than 51% acid	137	1830
Sulfuric acid, with not more than 51% acid	157	2796
Sulfuric acid and Hydrofluoric acid mixture	157	1786
Sulfurous acid	154	1833
Sulfur tetrafluoride	125	2418

Name of Material	Guide No.	ID No.
Sulfur trioxide, stabilized	137	1829
Sulfur trioxide and Chlorosulfonic acid mixture	137	1754
Sulfuryl chloride	137	1834
Sulfuryl fluoride	123	2191
Sulphamic acid	154	2967
Sulphur	133	1350
Sulphur, molten	133	2448
Sulphur chlorides	137	1828
Sulphur dioxide	125	1079
Sulphur hexafluoride	126	1080
Sulphuric acid	137	1830
Sulphuric acid, fuming	137	1831
Sulphuric acid, fuming, with less than 30% free Sulphur trioxide	137	1831
Sulphuric acid, fuming, with not less than 30% free Sulphur trioxide	137	1831
Sulphuric acid, spent	137	1832
Sulphuric acid, with more than 51% acid	137	1830
Sulphuric acid, with not more than 51% acid	157	2796
Sulphuric acid and Hydrofluoric acid mixture	157	1786
Sulphurous acid	154	1833
Sulphur tetrafluoride	125	2418
Sulphur trioxide, stabilized	137	1829
Sulphur trioxide and Chlorosulphonic acid mixture	137	1754
Sulphuryl chloride	137	1834
Sulphuryl fluoride	123	2191
Tabun	153	2810
Tars, liquid	130	1999

Name of Material	Guide No.	ID No.	Name of Material	Guide No.	ID No.
Tear gas candles	159	1700	Tetrahydrophthalic anhydrides	156	2698
Tear gas devices	159	1693	1,2,3,6-Tetrahydropyridine	129	2410
Tear gas grenades	159	1700	1,2,5,6-Tetrahydropyridine	129	2410
Tear gas substance, liquid, n.o.s.	159	1693	Tetrahydrothiophene	130	2412
Tear gas substance, solid, n.o.s.	159	1693	Tetramethylammonium hydroxide	153	1835
Tear gas substance, solid, n.o.s.	159	3448	Tetramethylammonium hydroxide, solid	153	3423
Tellurium compound, n.o.s.	151	3284	Tetramethylammonium hydroxide, solution	153	1835
Tellurium hexafluoride	125	2195	Tetramethylsilane	130	2749
Terpene hydrocarbons, n.o.s.	128	2319	Tetranitromethane	143	1510
Terpinolene	128	2541	Tetrapropyl orthotitanate	128	2413
Tetrabromoethane	159	2504	Textile waste, wet	133	1857
1,1,2,2-Tetrachloroethane	151	1702	Thallium chlorate	141	2573
Tetrachloroethane	151	1702	Thallium compound, n.o.s.	151	1707
Tetrachloroethylene	160	1897	Thallium nitrate	141	2727
Tetraethyl dithiopyrophosphate	153	1704	4-Thiapentanal	152	2785
Tetraethyl dithiopyrophosphate, mixture, dry or liquid	153	1704	Thia-4-pentanal	152	2785
Tetraethylenepentamine	153	2320	Thickened GD	153	2810
Tetraethyl silicate	129	1292	Thioacetic acid	129	2436
1,1,1,2-Tetrafluoroethane	126	3159	Thiocarbamate pesticide, liquid, flammable, poisonous	131	2772
Tetrafluoroethane and Ethylene oxide mixture, with not more than 5.6% Ethylene oxide	126	3299	Thiocarbamate pesticide, liquid, flammable, toxic	131	2772
Tetrafluoroethylene, stabilized	116P	1081	Thiocarbamate pesticide, liquid, poisonous	151	3006
Tetrafluoromethane	126	1982	Thiocarbamate pesticide, liquid, poisonous, flammable	131	3005
Tetrafluoromethane, compressed	126	1982	Thiocarbamate pesticide, liquid, toxic	151	3006
1,2,3,6-Tetrahydrobenzaldehyde	129	2498	Thiocarbamate pesticide, liquid, toxic, flammable	131	3005
Tetrahydrofuran	127	2056	Thiocarbamate pesticide, solid, poisonous	151	2771
Tetrahydrofurfurylamine	129	2943			

Name of Material	Guide No.	ID No.	Name of Material	Guide No.	ID No.
Thiocarbamate pesticide, solid, toxic	151	2771	Toluene	130	1294
Thioglycol	153	2966	2,4-Toluenediamine	151	1709
Thioglycolic acid	153	1940	Toluene diisocyanate	156	2078
Thiolactic acid	153	2936	Toluidines	153	1708
Thionyl chloride	137	1836	Toluidines, liquid	153	1708
Thiophene	130	2414	Toluidines, solid	153	1708
Thiophosgene	157	2474	Toluidines, solid	153	3451
Thiophosphoryl chloride	157	1837	2,4-Toluylenediamine	151	1709
Thiourea dioxide	135	3341	2,4-Toluylenediamine, solid	151	1709
Thorium metal, pyrophoric	162	2975	2,4-Toluylenediamine, solution	151	3418
Thorium nitrate, solid	162	2976	Toxic by inhalation liquid, corrosive, flammable, n.o.s. (Inhalation Hazard Zone A)	131	3492
Tinctures, medicinal	127	1293			
Tin tetrachloride	137	1827	Toxic by inhalation liquid, corrosive, flammable, n.o.s. (Inhalation Hazard Zone B)	131	3493
Tin tetrachloride, pentahydrate	154	2440			
Titanium disulfide	135	3174	Toxic by inhalation liquid, corrosive, n.o.s. (Inhalation Hazard Zone A)	154	3389
Titanium disulphide	135	3174			
Titanium hydride	170	1871	Toxic by inhalation liquid, corrosive, n.o.s. (Inhalation Hazard Zone B)	154	3390
Titanium powder, dry	135	2546			
Titanium powder, wetted with not less than 25% water	170	1352	Toxic by inhalation liquid, flammable, corrosive, n.o.s. (Inhalation Hazard Zone A)	131	3488
Titanium sponge granules	170	2878			
Titanium sponge powders	170	2878	Toxic by inhalation liquid, flammable, corrosive, n.o.s. (Inhalation Hazard Zone B)	131	3489
Titanium tetrachloride	137	1838			
Titanium trichloride, pyrophoric	135	2441	Toxic by inhalation liquid, flammable, n.o.s. (Inhalation Hazard Zone A)	131	3383
Titanium trichloride mixture	157	2869			
Titanium trichloride mixture, pyrophoric	135	2441	Toxic by inhalation liquid, flammable, n.o.s. (Inhalation Hazard Zone B)	131	3384
TNT, wetted with not less than 10% water	113	3366	Toxic by inhalation liquid, n.o.s. (Inhalation Hazard Zone A)	151	3381
TNT, wetted with not less than 30% water	113	1356			
Toe puffs, nitrocellulose base	133	1353	Toxic by inhalation liquid, n.o.s. (Inhalation Hazard Zone B)	151	3382

Name of Material	Guide No.	ID No.
Toxic by inhalation liquid, oxidizing, n.o.s. (Inhalation Hazard Zone A)	142	3387
Toxic by inhalation liquid, oxidizing, n.o.s. (Inhalation Hazard Zone B)	142	3388
Toxic by inhalation liquid, water-reactive, flammable, n.o.s. (Inhalation Hazard Zone A)	155	3490
Toxic by inhalation liquid, water-reactive, flammable, n.o.s. (Inhalation Hazard Zone B)	155	3491
Toxic by inhalation liquid, water-reactive, n.o.s. (Inhalation Hazard Zone A)	139	3385
Toxic by inhalation liquid, water-reactive, n.o.s. (Inhalation Hazard Zone B)	139	3386
Toxic liquid, corrosive, inorganic, n.o.s.	154	3289
Toxic liquid, corrosive, inorganic, n.o.s. (Inhalation Hazard Zone A)	154	3289
Toxic liquid, corrosive, inorganic, n.o.s. (Inhalation Hazard Zone B)	154	3289
Toxic liquid, corrosive, n.o.s.	154	2927
Toxic liquid, corrosive, n.o.s. (Inhalation Hazard Zone A)	154	2927
Toxic liquid, corrosive, n.o.s. (Inhalation Hazard Zone B)	154	2927
Toxic liquid, corrosive, organic, n.o.s.	154	2927
Toxic liquid, corrosive, organic, n.o.s. (Inhalation Hazard Zone A)	154	2927
Toxic liquid, corrosive, organic, n.o.s. (Inhalation Hazard Zone B)	154	2927
Toxic liquid, flammable, n.o.s.	131	2929
Toxic liquid, flammable, n.o.s. (Inhalation Hazard Zone A)	131	2929
Toxic liquid, flammable, n.o.s. (Inhalation Hazard Zone B)	131	2929
Toxic liquid, flammable, organic, n.o.s.	131	2929
Toxic liquid, flammable, organic, n.o.s. (Inhalation Hazard Zone A)	131	2929
Toxic liquid, flammable, organic, n.o.s. (Inhalation Hazard Zone B)	131	2929
Toxic liquid, inorganic, n.o.s.	151	3287
Toxic liquid, inorganic, n.o.s. (Inhalation Hazard Zone A)	151	3287
Toxic liquid, inorganic, n.o.s. (Inhalation Hazard Zone B)	151	3287
Toxic liquid, n.o.s.	153	2810
Toxic liquid, n.o.s. (Inhalation Hazard Zone A)	153	2810
Toxic liquid, n.o.s. (Inhalation Hazard Zone B)	153	2810
Toxic liquid, organic, n.o.s.	153	2810
Toxic liquid, organic, n.o.s. (Inhalation Hazard Zone A)	153	2810
Toxic liquid, organic, n.o.s. (Inhalation Hazard Zone B)	153	2810
Toxic liquid, oxidizing, n.o.s.	142	3122
Toxic liquid, oxidizing, n.o.s. (Inhalation Hazard Zone A)	142	3122
Toxic liquid, oxidizing, n.o.s. (Inhalation Hazard Zone B)	142	3122
Toxic liquid, water-reactive, n.o.s.	139	3123
Toxic liquid, water-reactive, n.o.s. (Inhalation Hazard Zone A)	139	3123
Toxic liquid, water-reactive, n.o.s. (Inhalation Hazard Zone B)	139	3123
Toxic liquid, which in contact with water emits flammable gases, n.o.s.	139	3123

Name of Material	Guide No.	ID No.
Toxic liquid, which in contact with water emits flammable gases, n.o.s. (Inhalation Hazard Zone A)	139	3123
Toxic liquid, which in contact with water emits flammable gases, n.o.s. (Inhalation Hazard Zone B)	139	3123
Toxic solid, corrosive, inorganic, n.o.s.	154	3290
Toxic solid, corrosive, organic, n.o.s.	154	2928
Toxic solid, flammable, n.o.s.	134	2930
Toxic solid, flammable, organic, n.o.s.	134	2930
Toxic solid, inorganic, n.o.s.	151	3288
Toxic solid, organic, n.o.s.	154	2811
Toxic solid, oxidizing, n.o.s.	141	3086
Toxic solid, self-heating, n.o.s.	136	3124
Toxic solid, water-reactive, n.o.s.	139	3125
Toxic solid, which in contact with water emits flammable gases, n.o.s.	139	3125
Toxins	153	——
Toxins, extracted from living sources, liquid, n.o.s.	153	3172
Toxins, extracted from living sources, n.o.s.	153	3172
Toxins, extracted from living sources, solid, n.o.s.	153	3172
Toxins, extracted from living sources, solid, n.o.s.	153	3462
Triallylamine	132	2610
Triallyl borate	156	2609
Triazine pesticide, liquid, flammable, poisonous	131	2764
Triazine pesticide, liquid, flammable, toxic	131	2764

Name of Material	Guide No.	ID No.
Triazine pesticide, liquid, poisonous	151	2998
Triazine pesticide, liquid, poisonous, flammable	131	2997
Triazine pesticide, liquid, toxic	151	2998
Triazine pesticide, liquid, toxic, flammable	131	2997
Triazine pesticide, solid, poisonous	151	2763
Triazine pesticide, solid, toxic	151	2763
Tri-(1-aziridinyl)phosphine oxide, solution	152	2501
Tributylamine	153	2542
Tributylphosphane	135	3254
Tributylphosphine	135	3254
Trichloroacetic acid	153	1839
Trichloroacetic acid, solution	153	2564
Trichloroacetyl chloride	156	2442
Trichlorobenzenes, liquid	153	2321
Trichlorobutene	152	2322
1,1,1-Trichloroethane	160	2831
Trichloroethylene	160	1710
Trichloroisocyanuric acid, dry	140	2468
Trichlorosilane	139	1295
Tricresyl phosphate	151	2574
Triethylamine	132	1296
Triethylenetetramine	153	2259
Triethyl phosphite	130	2323
Trifluoroacetic acid	154	2699
Trifluoroacetyl chloride	125	3057
Trifluorochloroethylene, stabilized	119P	1082
1,1,1-Trifluoroethane	115	2035
Trifluoroethane, compressed	115	2035
Trifluoromethane	126	1984

Name of Material	Guide No.	ID No.	Name of Material	Guide No.	ID No.
Trifluoromethane, refrigerated liquid	120	3136	Trinitrotoluene, wetted with not less than 10% water	113	3366
Trifluoromethane and Chlorotrifluoromethane azeotropic mixture with approximately 60% Chlorotrifluoromethane	126	2599	Trinitrotoluene, wetted with not less than 30% water	113	1356
			Tripropylamine	132	2260
			Tripropylene	128	2057
2-Trifluoromethylaniline	153	2942	Tris-(1-aziridinyl)phosphine oxide, solution	152	2501
3-Trifluoromethylaniline	153	2948			
Triisobutylene	128	2324	Tungsten hexafluoride	125	2196
Triisopropyl borate	129	2616	Turpentine	128	1299
Trimethoxysilane	132	9269	Turpentine substitute	128	1300
Trimethylacetyl chloride	132	2438	Undecane	128	2330
Trimethylamine, anhydrous	118	1083	Uranium hexafluoride	166	2978
Trimethylamine, aqueous solution	132	1297	Uranium hexafluoride, fissile containing more than 1% Uranium-235	166	2977
1,3,5-Trimethylbenzene	129	2325	Uranium hexafluoride, non fissile or fissile-excepted	166	2978
Trimethyl borate	129	2416			
Trimethylchlorosilane	155	1298	Uranium metal, pyrophoric	162	2979
Trimethylcyclohexylamine	153	2326	Uranyl nitrate, hexahydrate, solution	162	2980
Trimethylhexamethylenediamines	153	2327			
Trimethylhexamethylene diisocyanate	156	2328	Uranyl nitrate, solid	162	2981
			Urea hydrogen peroxide	140	1511
Trimethyl phosphite	130	2329	Urea nitrate, wetted with not less than 10% water	113	3370
Trinitrobenzene, wetted with not less than 10% water	113	3367			
Trinitrobenzene, wetted with not less than 30% water	113	1354	Urea nitrate, wetted with not less than 20% water	113	1357
			Valeraldehyde	129	2058
Trinitrobenzoic acid, wetted with not less than 10% water	113	3368	Valeryl chloride	132	2502
			Vanadium compound, n.o.s.	151	3285
Trinitrobenzoic acid, wetted with not less than 30% water	113	1355	Vanadium oxytrichloride	137	2443
Trinitrochlorobenzene, wetted with not less than 10% water	113	3365	Vanadium pentoxide	151	2862
			Vanadium tetrachloride	137	2444
Trinitrophenol, wetted with not less than 10% water	113	3364	Vanadium trichloride	157	2475
Trinitrophenol, wetted with not less than 30% water	113	1344	Vanadyl sulfate	151	2931

Name of Material	Guide No.	ID No.	Name of Material	Guide No.	ID No.
Vanadyl sulphate	151	2931	Water-reactive solid, oxidizing, n.o.s.	138	3133
Vehicle, flammable gas powered	128	3166	Water-reactive solid, poisonous, n.o.s.	139	3134
Vehicle, flammable liquid powered	128	3166	Water-reactive solid, self-heating, n.o.s.	138	3135
Vehicle, fuel cell, flammable gas powered	128	3166	Water-reactive solid, toxic, n.o.s.	139	3134
Vehicle, fuel cell, flammable liquid powered	128	3166	Wheelchair, electric, with batteries	154	3171
Vinyl acetate, stabilized	129P	1301	White asbestos	171	2590
Vinyl bromide, stabilized	116P	1085	White phosphorus, dry	136	1381
Vinyl butyrate, stabilized	129P	2838	White phosphorus, in solution	136	1381
Vinyl chloride, stabilized	116P	1086	White phosphorus, molten	136	2447
Vinyl chloroacetate	155	2589	White phosphorus, under water	136	1381
Vinyl ethyl ether, stabilized	127P	1302	Wood preservatives, liquid	129	1306
Vinyl fluoride, stabilized	116P	1860	Wool waste, wet	133	1387
Vinylidene chloride, stabilized	130P	1303	Xanthates	135	3342
Vinyl isobutyl ether, stabilized	127P	1304	Xenon	121	2036
Vinyl methyl ether, stabilized	116P	1087	Xenon, compressed	121	2036
Vinylpyridines, stabilized	131P	3073	Xenon, refrigerated liquid (cryogenic liquid)	120	2591
Vinyltoluenes, stabilized	130P	2618	Xylenes	130	1307
Vinyltrichlorosilane	155P	1305	Xylenols	153	2261
Vinyltrichlorosilane, stabilized	155P	1305	Xylenols, liquid	153	3430
VX	153	2810	Xylenols, solid	153	2261
Water-reactive liquid, corrosive, n.o.s.	138	3129	Xylidines	153	1711
Water-reactive liquid, n.o.s.	138	3148	Xylidines, liquid	153	1711
Water-reactive liquid, poisonous, n.o.s.	139	3130	Xylidines, solid	153	1711
Water-reactive liquid, toxic, n.o.s.	139	3130	Xylidines, solid	153	3452
Water-reactive solid, corrosive, n.o.s.	138	3131	Xylyl bromide	152	1701
Water-reactive solid, flammable, n.o.s.	138	3132	Xylyl bromide, liquid	152	1701
Water-reactive solid, n.o.s.	138	2813	Xylyl bromide, solid	152	3417
			Yellow phosphorus, dry	136	1381

Name of Material	Guide No.	ID No.	Name of Material	Guide No.	ID No.
Yellow phosphorus, in solution	136	1381	Zirconium, dry, coiled wire, finished metal sheets or strips	170	2858
Yellow phosphorus, molten	136	2447			
Yellow phosphorus, under water	136	1381	Zirconium, dry, finished sheets, strips or coiled wire	135	2009
Zinc ammonium nitrite	140	1512	Zirconium hydride	138	1437
Zinc arsenate	151	1712	Zirconium metal, liquid suspension	170	1308
Zinc arsenate and Zinc arsenite mixture	151	1712	Zirconium metal, powder, wet	170	1358
Zinc arsenite	151	1712	Zirconium nitrate	140	2728
Zinc arsenite and Zinc arsenate mixture	151	1712	Zirconium picramate, wetted with not less than 20% water	113	1517
Zinc ashes	138	1435	Zirconium powder, dry	135	2008
Zinc bromate	140	2469	Zirconium powder, wetted with not less than 25% water	170	1358
Zinc chlorate	140	1513			
Zinc chloride, anhydrous	154	2331	Zirconium scrap	135	1932
Zinc chloride, solution	154	1840	Zirconium suspended in a flammable liquid	170	1308
Zinc cyanide	151	1713	Zirconium suspended in a liquid (flammable)	170	1308
Zinc dithionite	171	1931			
Zinc dross	138	1435	Zirconium tetrachloride	137	2503
Zinc dust	138	1436			
Zinc fluorosilicate	151	2855			
Zinc hydrosulfite	171	1931			
Zinc hydrosulphite	171	1931			
Zinc nitrate	140	1514			
Zinc permanganate	140	1515			
Zinc peroxide	143	1516			
Zinc phosphide	139	1714			
Zinc powder	138	1436			
Zinc residue	138	1435			
Zinc resinate	133	2714			
Zinc silicofluoride	151	2855			
Zinc skimmings	138	1435			

GUIDES

POTENTIAL HAZARDS

FIRE OR EXPLOSION

- May explode from heat, shock, friction or contamination.
- May react violently or explosively on contact with air, water or foam.
- May be ignited by heat, sparks or flames.
- Vapors may travel to source of ignition and flash back.
- Containers may explode when heated.
- Ruptured cylinders may rocket.

HEALTH

- Inhalation, ingestion or contact with substance may cause severe injury, infection, disease or death.
- High concentration of gas may cause asphyxiation without warning.
- Contact may cause burns to skin and eyes.
- Fire or contact with water may produce irritating, toxic and/or corrosive gases.
- Runoff from fire control may cause pollution.

PUBLIC SAFETY

- **CALL EMERGENCY RESPONSE Telephone Number on Shipping Paper first. If Shipping Paper not available or no answer, refer to appropriate telephone number listed on the inside back cover.**
- As an immediate precautionary measure, isolate spill or leak area for at least 100 meters (330 feet) in all directions.
- Keep unauthorized personnel away.
- Stay upwind.
- Keep out of low areas.

PROTECTIVE CLOTHING

- Wear positive pressure self-contained breathing apparatus (SCBA).
- Structural firefighters' protective clothing provides limited protection in fire situations ONLY; it may not be effective in spill situations.

EVACUATION

Fire
- If tank, rail car or tank truck is involved in a fire, ISOLATE for 800 meters (1/2 mile) in all directions; also, consider initial evacuation for 800 meters (1/2 mile) in all directions.

EMERGENCY RESPONSE

FIRE

CAUTION: Material may react with extinguishing agent.

Small Fire
- Dry chemical, CO_2, water spray or regular foam.

Large Fire
- Water spray, fog or regular foam.
- Move containers from fire area if you can do it without risk.

Fire involving Tanks
- Cool containers with flooding quantities of water until well after fire is out.
- Do not get water inside containers.
- Withdraw immediately in case of rising sound from venting safety devices or discoloration of tank.
- ALWAYS stay away from tanks engulfed in fire.

SPILL OR LEAK

- Do not touch or walk through spilled material.
- ELIMINATE all ignition sources (no smoking, flares, sparks or flames in immediate area).
- All equipment used when handling the product must be grounded.
- Keep combustibles (wood, paper, oil, etc.) away from spilled material.
- Use water spray to reduce vapors or divert vapor cloud drift. Avoid allowing water runoff to contact spilled material.
- Prevent entry into waterways, sewers, basements or confined areas.

Small Spill
- Take up with sand or other non-combustible absorbent material and place into containers for later disposal.

Large Spill
- Dike far ahead of liquid spill for later disposal.

FIRST AID

- Move victim to fresh air.
- Call 911 or emergency medical service.
- Give artificial respiration if victim is not breathing.
- **Do not use mouth-to-mouth method if victim ingested or inhaled the substance; give artificial respiration with the aid of a pocket mask equipped with a one-way valve or other proper respiratory medical device.**
- Administer oxygen if breathing is difficult.
- Remove and isolate contaminated clothing and shoes.
- In case of contact with substance, immediately flush skin or eyes with running water for at least 20 minutes.
- Shower and wash with soap and water.
- Keep victim warm and quiet.
- Effects of exposure (inhalation, ingestion or skin contact) to substance may be delayed.
- Ensure that medical personnel are aware of the material(s) involved and take precautions to protect themselves.

GUIDE 112

POTENTIAL HAZARDS

FIRE OR EXPLOSION
- MAY EXPLODE AND THROW FRAGMENTS 1600 meters (1 MILE) OR MORE IF FIRE REACHES CARGO.
- For information on "Compatibility Group" letters, refer to Glossary section.

HEALTH
- Fire may produce irritating, corrosive and/or toxic gases.

PUBLIC SAFETY

- CALL EMERGENCY RESPONSE Telephone Number on Shipping Paper first. If Shipping Paper not available or no answer, refer to appropriate telephone number listed on the inside back cover.
- Isolate spill or leak area immediately for at least 500 meters (1/3 mile) in all directions.
- Move people out of line of sight of the scene and away from windows.
- Keep unauthorized personnel away.
- Stay upwind.
- Ventilate closed spaces before entering.

PROTECTIVE CLOTHING
- Wear positive pressure self-contained breathing apparatus (SCBA).
- Structural firefighters' protective clothing will only provide limited protection.

EVACUATION

Large Spill
- Consider initial EVACUATION for 800 meters (1/2 mile) in all directions.

Fire
- If rail car or trailer is involved in a fire, ISOLATE for 1600 meters (1 mile) in all directions; also, initiate evacuation including emergency responders for 1600 meters (1 mile) in all directions.

* FOR INFORMATION ON "COMPATIBILITY GROUP" LETTERS, REFER TO THE GLOSSARY SECTION.

EMERGENCY RESPONSE

FIRE

CARGO Fire

- **DO NOT fight fire when fire reaches cargo! Cargo may EXPLODE!**
- Stop all traffic and clear the area for at least 1600 meters (1 mile) in all directions and let burn.
- **Do not move cargo or vehicle if cargo has been exposed to heat.**

TIRE or VEHICLE Fire

- **Use plenty of water - FLOOD it! If water is not available, use CO_2, dry chemical or dirt.**
- If possible, and WITHOUT RISK, use unmanned hose holders or monitor nozzles from maximum distance to prevent fire from spreading to cargo area.
- Pay special attention to tire fires as re-ignition may occur. Stand by with extinguisher ready.

SPILL OR LEAK

- ELIMINATE all ignition sources (no smoking, flares, sparks or flames in immediate area).
- All equipment used when handling the product must be grounded.
- Do not touch or walk through spilled material.
- DO NOT OPERATE RADIO TRANSMITTERS WITHIN 100 meters (330 feet) OF ELECTRIC DETONATORS.
- **DO NOT CLEAN-UP OR DISPOSE OF, EXCEPT UNDER SUPERVISION OF A SPECIALIST.**

FIRST AID

- Move victim to fresh air.
- Call 911 or emergency medical service.
- Give artificial respiration if victim is not breathing.
- Administer oxygen if breathing is difficult.
- Remove and isolate contaminated clothing and shoes.
- In case of contact with substance, immediately flush skin or eyes with running water for at least 20 minutes.
- Ensure that medical personnel are aware of the material(s) involved and take precautions to protect themselves.

* FOR INFORMATION ON "COMPATIBILITY GROUP" LETTERS, REFER TO THE GLOSSARY SECTION.

GUIDE 113

FLAMMABLE SOLIDS - TOXIC
(WET/DESENSITIZED EXPLOSIVE)

ERG201

POTENTIAL HAZARDS

FIRE OR EXPLOSION
- Flammable/combustible material.
- May be ignited by heat, sparks or flames.
- **DRIED OUT material may explode if exposed to heat, flame, friction or shock; Treat as an explosive (GUIDE 112).**
- **Keep material wet with water or treat as an explosive (GUIDE 112).**
- Runoff to sewer may create fire or explosion hazard.

HEALTH
- Some are toxic and may be fatal if inhaled, swallowed or absorbed through skin.
- Contact may cause burns to skin and eyes.
- Fire may produce irritating, corrosive and/or toxic gases.
- Runoff from fire control or dilution water may cause pollution.

PUBLIC SAFETY
- **CALL EMERGENCY RESPONSE Telephone Number on Shipping Paper first. If Shipping Paper not available or no answer, refer to appropriate telephone number listed on the inside back cover.**
- Isolate spill or leak area immediately for at least 100 meters (330 feet) in all directions.
- Keep unauthorized personnel away.
- Stay upwind.
- Ventilate closed spaces before entering.

PROTECTIVE CLOTHING
- Wear positive pressure self-contained breathing apparatus (SCBA).
- Structural firefighters' protective clothing will only provide limited protection.

EVACUATION
Large Spill
- **Consider initial EVACUATION for 500 meters (1/3 mile) in all directions.**
Fire
- If tank, rail car or tank truck is involved in a fire, ISOLATE for 800 meters (1/2 mile) in all directions; also, consider initial evacuation for 800 meters (1/2 mile) in all directions.

EMERGENCY RESPONSE

FIRE

CARGO Fire
- **DO NOT fight fire when fire reaches cargo! Cargo may EXPLODE!**
- Stop all traffic and clear the area for at least 800 meters (1/2 mile) in all directions and let burn.
- **Do not move cargo or vehicle if cargo has been exposed to heat.**

TIRE or VEHICLE Fire
- **Use plenty of water - FLOOD it! If water is not available, use CO_2, dry chemical or dirt.**
- If possible, and WITHOUT RISK, use unmanned hose holders or monitor nozzles from maximum distance to prevent fire from spreading to cargo area.
- Pay special attention to tire fires as re-ignition may occur. Stand by with extinguisher ready.

SPILL OR LEAK

- ELIMINATE all ignition sources (no smoking, flares, sparks or flames in immediate area).
- All equipment used when handling the product must be grounded.
- Do not touch or walk through spilled material.

Small Spill
- Flush area with flooding quantities of water.

Large Spill
- Wet down with water and dike for later disposal.
- KEEP "WETTED" PRODUCT WET BY SLOWLY ADDING FLOODING QUANTITIES OF WATER.

FIRST AID

- Move victim to fresh air.
- Call 911 or emergency medical service.
- Give artificial respiration if victim is not breathing.
- Administer oxygen if breathing is difficult.
- Remove and isolate contaminated clothing and shoes.
- In case of contact with substance, immediately flush skin or eyes with running water for at least 20 minutes.
- Ensure that medical personnel are aware of the material(s) involved and take precautions to protect themselves.

POTENTIAL HAZARDS

FIRE OR EXPLOSION

- MAY EXPLODE AND THROW FRAGMENTS 500 meters (1/3 MILE) OR MORE IF FIRE REACHES CARGO.
- For information on "Compatibility Group" letters, refer to Glossary section.

HEALTH

- Fire may produce irritating, corrosive and/or toxic gases.

PUBLIC SAFETY

- CALL EMERGENCY RESPONSE Telephone Number on Shipping Paper first. If Shipping Paper not available or no answer, refer to appropriate telephone number listed on the inside back cover.
- Isolate spill or leak area immediately for at least 100 meters (330 feet) in all directions.
- Move people out of line of sight of the scene and away from windows.
- Keep unauthorized personnel away.
- Stay upwind.
- Ventilate closed spaces before entering.

PROTECTIVE CLOTHING

- Wear positive pressure self-contained breathing apparatus (SCBA).
- Structural firefighters' protective clothing will only provide limited protection.

EVACUATION

Large Spill

- Consider initial EVACUATION for 250 meters (800 feet) in all directions.

Fire

- If rail car or trailer is involved in a fire, ISOLATE for 500 meters (1/3 mile) in all directions; also initiate evacuation including emergency responders for 500 meters (1/3 mile) in all directions.

* For information on "Compatibility Group" Letters, refer to the Glossary section.

EMERGENCY RESPONSE

FIRE

CARGO Fire
- **DO NOT fight fire when fire reaches cargo! Cargo may EXPLODE!**
- Stop all traffic and clear the area for at least 500 meters (1/3 mile) in all directions and let burn.
- **Do not move cargo or vehicle if cargo has been exposed to heat.**

TIRE or VEHICLE Fire
- **Use plenty of water - FLOOD it! If water is not available, use CO_2, dry chemical or dirt.**
- If possible, and WITHOUT RISK, use unmanned hose holders or monitor nozzles from maximum distance to prevent fire from spreading to cargo area.
- Pay special attention to tire fires as re-ignition may occur. Stand by with extinguisher ready.

SPILL OR LEAK
- ELIMINATE all ignition sources (no smoking, flares, sparks or flames in immediate area).
- All equipment used when handling the product must be grounded.
- Do not touch or walk through spilled material.
- DO NOT OPERATE RADIO TRANSMITTERS WITHIN 100 meters (330 feet) OF ELECTRIC DETONATORS.
- **DO NOT CLEAN-UP OR DISPOSE OF, EXCEPT UNDER SUPERVISION OF A SPECIALIST.**

FIRST AID
- Move victim to fresh air.
- Call 911 or emergency medical service.
- Give artificial respiration if victim is not breathing.
- Administer oxygen if breathing is difficult.
- Remove and isolate contaminated clothing and shoes.
- In case of contact with substance, immediately flush skin or eyes with running water for at least 20 minutes.
- Ensure that medical personnel are aware of the material(s) involved and take precautions to protect themselves.

SUPPLEMENTAL INFORMATION
- Packages bearing the 1.4S label or packages containing material classified as 1.4S are designed or packaged in such a manner that when involved in a fire, may burn vigorously with localized detonations and projection of fragments.
- Effects are usually confined to immediate vicinity of packages.
- If fire threatens cargo area containing packages bearing the 1.4S label or packages containing material classified as 1.4S, consider isolating at least 15 meters (50 feet) in all directions. Fight fire with normal precautions from a reasonable distance.

* FOR INFORMATION ON "COMPATIBILITY GROUP" LETTERS,
REFER TO THE GLOSSARY SECTION.

GUIDE 115

GASES - FLAMMABLE
(INCLUDING REFRIGERATED LIQUIDS)

POTENTIAL HAZARDS

FIRE OR EXPLOSION
- **EXTREMELY FLAMMABLE.**
- Will be easily ignited by heat, sparks or flames.
- Will form explosive mixtures with air.
- Vapors from liquefied gas are initially heavier than air and spread along ground.
- **CAUTION: Hydrogen (UN1049), Deuterium (UN1957), Hydrogen, refrigerated liquid (UN1966) and Methane (UN1971) are lighter than air and will rise. Hydrogen and Deuterium fires are difficult to detect since they burn with an invisible flame. Use an alternate method of detection (thermal camera, broom handle, etc.)**
- Vapors may travel to source of ignition and flash back.
- Cylinders exposed to fire may vent and release flammable gas through pressure relief devices.
- Containers may explode when heated.
- Ruptured cylinders may rocket.

HEALTH
- Vapors may cause dizziness or asphyxiation without warning.
- Some may be irritating if inhaled at high concentrations.
- Contact with gas or liquefied gas may cause burns, severe injury and/or frostbite.
- Fire may produce irritating and/or toxic gases.

PUBLIC SAFETY
- **CALL EMERGENCY RESPONSE Telephone Number on Shipping Paper first. If Shipping Paper not available or no answer, refer to appropriate telephone number listed on the inside back cover.**
- As an immediate precautionary measure, isolate spill or leak area for at least 100 meters (330 feet) in all directions.
- Keep unauthorized personnel away.
- Stay upwind.
- Many gases are heavier than air and will spread along ground and collect in low or confined areas (sewers, basements, tanks).
- Keep out of low areas.

PROTECTIVE CLOTHING
- Wear positive pressure self-contained breathing apparatus (SCBA).
- Structural firefighters' protective clothing will only provide limited protection.
- Always wear thermal protective clothing when handling refrigerated/cryogenic liquids.

EVACUATION
Large Spill
- Consider initial downwind evacuation for at least 800 meters (1/2 mile).
Fire
- If tank, rail car or tank truck is involved in a fire, ISOLATE for 1600 meters (1 mile) in all directions; also, consider initial evacuation for 1600 meters (1 mile) in all directions.

EMERGENCY RESPONSE

FIRE

- **DO NOT EXTINGUISH A LEAKING GAS FIRE UNLESS LEAK CAN BE STOPPED.**
  CAUTION: Hydrogen (UN1049), Deuterium (UN1957) and Hydrogen, refrigerated liquid (UN1966) burn with an invisible flame. Hydrogen and Methane mixture, compressed (UN2034) may burn with an invisible flame.

Small Fire
- Dry chemical or CO_2.

Large Fire
- Water spray or fog.
- Move containers from fire area if you can do it without risk.

Fire involving Tanks
- Fight fire from maximum distance or use unmanned hose holders or monitor nozzles.
- Cool containers with flooding quantities of water until well after fire is out.
- Do not direct water at source of leak or safety devices; icing may occur.
- Withdraw immediately in case of rising sound from venting safety devices or discoloration of tank.
- ALWAYS stay away from tanks engulfed in fire.
- For massive fire, use unmanned hose holders or monitor nozzles; if this is impossible, withdraw from area and let fire burn.

SPILL OR LEAK

- ELIMINATE all ignition sources (no smoking, flares, sparks or flames in immediate area).
- All equipment used when handling the product must be grounded.
- Do not touch or walk through spilled material.
- Stop leak if you can do it without risk.
- If possible, turn leaking containers so that gas escapes rather than liquid.
- Use water spray to reduce vapors or divert vapor cloud drift. Avoid allowing water runoff to contact spilled material.
- Do not direct water at spill or source of leak.
- Prevent spreading of vapors through sewers, ventilation systems and confined areas.
- Isolate area until gas has dispersed.
- **CAUTION: When in contact with refrigerated/cryogenic liquids, many materials become brittle and are likely to break without warning.**

FIRST AID

- Move victim to fresh air.
- Call 911 or emergency medical service.
- Give artificial respiration if victim is not breathing.
- Administer oxygen if breathing is difficult.
- Remove and isolate contaminated clothing and shoes.
- Clothing frozen to the skin should be thawed before being removed.
- In case of contact with liquefied gas, thaw frosted parts with lukewarm water.
- In case of burns, immediately cool affected skin for as long as possible with cold water. Do not remove clothing if adhering to skin.
- Keep victim warm and quiet.
- Ensure that medical personnel are aware of the material(s) involved and take precautions to protect themselves.

POTENTIAL HAZARDS

FIRE OR EXPLOSION

- **EXTREMELY FLAMMABLE.**
- Will be easily ignited by heat, sparks or flames.
- Will form explosive mixtures with air.
- Silane will ignite spontaneously in air.
- Those substances designated with a **(P)** may polymerize explosively when heated or involved in a fire.
- Vapors from liquefied gas are initially heavier than air and spread along ground.
- Vapors may travel to source of ignition and flash back.
- Cylinders exposed to fire may vent and release flammable gas through pressure relief devices.
- Containers may explode when heated.
- Ruptured cylinders may rocket.

HEALTH

- Vapors may cause dizziness or asphyxiation without warning.
- Some may be toxic if inhaled at high concentrations.
- Contact with gas or liquefied gas may cause burns, severe injury and/or frostbite.
- Fire may produce irritating and/or toxic gases.

PUBLIC SAFETY

- **CALL EMERGENCY RESPONSE Telephone Number on Shipping Paper first. If Shipping Paper not available or no answer, refer to appropriate telephone number listed on the inside back cover.**
- As an immediate precautionary measure, isolate spill or leak area for at least 100 meters (330 feet) in all directions.
- Keep unauthorized personnel away.
- Stay upwind.
- Many gases are heavier than air and will spread along ground and collect in low or confined areas (sewers, basements, tanks).
- Keep out of low areas.

PROTECTIVE CLOTHING

- Wear positive pressure self-contained breathing apparatus (SCBA).
- Structural firefighters' protective clothing will only provide limited protection.

EVACUATION

Large Spill
- Consider initial downwind evacuation for at least 800 meters (1/2 mile).

Fire
- If tank, rail car or tank truck is involved in a fire, ISOLATE for 1600 meters (1 mile) in all directions; also, consider initial evacuation for 1600 meters (1 mile) in all directions.

EMERGENCY RESPONSE

FIRE

- **DO NOT EXTINGUISH A LEAKING GAS FIRE UNLESS LEAK CAN BE STOPPED.**

Small Fire
- Dry chemical or CO_2.

Large Fire
- Water spray or fog.
- Move containers from fire area if you can do it without risk.

Fire involving Tanks
- Fight fire from maximum distance or use unmanned hose holders or monitor nozzles.
- Cool containers with flooding quantities of water until well after fire is out.
- Do not direct water at source of leak or safety devices; icing may occur.
- Withdraw immediately in case of rising sound from venting safety devices or discoloration of tank.
- ALWAYS stay away from tanks engulfed in fire.
- For massive fire, use unmanned hose holders or monitor nozzles; if this is impossible, withdraw from area and let fire burn.

SPILL OR LEAK

- ELIMINATE all ignition sources (no smoking, flares, sparks or flames in immediate area).
- All equipment used when handling the product must be grounded.
- Stop leak if you can do it without risk.
- Do not touch or walk through spilled material.
- Do not direct water at spill or source of leak.
- Use water spray to reduce vapors or divert vapor cloud drift. Avoid allowing water runoff to contact spilled material.
- If possible, turn leaking containers so that gas escapes rather than liquid.
- Prevent entry into waterways, sewers, basements or confined areas.
- Isolate area until gas has dispersed.

FIRST AID

- Move victim to fresh air.
- Call 911 or emergency medical service.
- Give artificial respiration if victim is not breathing.
- Administer oxygen if breathing is difficult.
- Remove and isolate contaminated clothing and shoes.
- In case of contact with liquefied gas, thaw frosted parts with lukewarm water.
- In case of burns, immediately cool affected skin for as long as possible with cold water. Do not remove clothing if adhering to skin.
- Keep victim warm and quiet.
- Ensure that medical personnel are aware of the material(s) involved and take precautions to protect themselves.

POTENTIAL HAZARDS

HEALTH

- **TOXIC; Extremely Hazardous.**
- May be fatal if inhaled or absorbed through skin.
- Initial odor may be irritating or foul and may deaden your sense of smell.
- Contact with gas or liquefied gas may cause burns, severe injury and/or frostbite.
- Fire will produce irritating, corrosive and/or toxic gases.
- Runoff from fire control may cause pollution.

FIRE OR EXPLOSION

- These materials are extremely flammable.
- May form explosive mixtures with air.
- May be ignited by heat, sparks or flames.
- Vapors from liquefied gas are initially heavier than air and spread along ground.
- Vapors may travel to source of ignition and flash back.
- Runoff may create fire or explosion hazard.
- Cylinders exposed to fire may vent and release toxic and flammable gas through pressure relief devices.
- Containers may explode when heated.
- Ruptured cylinders may rocket.

PUBLIC SAFETY

- **CALL EMERGENCY RESPONSE Telephone Number on Shipping Paper first. If Shipping Paper not available or no answer, refer to appropriate telephone number listed on the inside back cover.**
- As an immediate precautionary measure, isolate spill or leak area for at least 100 meters (330 feet) in all directions.
- Keep unauthorized personnel away.
- Stay upwind.
- Many gases are heavier than air and will spread along ground and collect in low or confined areas (sewers, basements, tanks).
- Keep out of low areas.
- Ventilate closed spaces before entering.

PROTECTIVE CLOTHING

- Wear positive pressure self-contained breathing apparatus (SCBA).
- Wear chemical protective clothing that is specifically recommended by the manufacturer. It may provide little or no thermal protection.
- Structural firefighters' protective clothing provides limited protection in fire situations ONLY; it is not effective in spill situations where direct contact with the substance is possible.

EVACUATION

Spill
- See Table 1 - Initial Isolation and Protective Action Distances.

Fire
- If tank, rail car or tank truck is involved in a fire, ISOLATE for 1600 meters (1 mile) in all directions; also, consider initial evacuation for 1600 meters (1 mile) in all directions.

EMERGENCY RESPONSE

FIRE

DO NOT EXTINGUISH A LEAKING GAS FIRE UNLESS LEAK CAN BE STOPPED.

Small Fire
- Dry chemical, CO_2, water spray or regular foam.

Large Fire
- Water spray, fog or regular foam.
- Move containers from fire area if you can do it without risk.
- Damaged cylinders should be handled only by specialists.

Fire involving Tanks
- Fight fire from maximum distance or use unmanned hose holders or monitor nozzles.
- Cool containers with flooding quantities of water until well after fire is out.
- Do not direct water at source of leak or safety devices; icing may occur.
- Withdraw immediately in case of rising sound from venting safety devices or discoloration of tank.
- ALWAYS stay away from tanks engulfed in fire.

SPILL OR LEAK

- ELIMINATE all ignition sources (no smoking, flares, sparks or flames in immediate area).
- All equipment used when handling the product must be grounded.
- Fully encapsulating, vapor protective clothing should be worn for spills and leaks with no fire.
- Do not touch or walk through spilled material.
- Stop leak if you can do it without risk.
- Use water spray to reduce vapors or divert vapor cloud drift. Avoid allowing water runoff to contact spilled material.
- Do not direct water at spill or source of leak.
- If possible, turn leaking containers so that gas escapes rather than liquid.
- Prevent entry into waterways, sewers, basements or confined areas.
- Isolate area until gas has dispersed.
- Consider igniting spill or leak to eliminate toxic gas concerns.

FIRST AID

- Move victim to fresh air.
- Call 911 or emergency medical service.
- Give artificial respiration if victim is not breathing.
- **Do not use mouth-to-mouth method if victim ingested or inhaled the substance; give artificial respiration with the aid of a pocket mask equipped with a one-way valve or other proper respiratory medical device.**
- Administer oxygen if breathing is difficult.
- Remove and isolate contaminated clothing and shoes.
- In case of contact with substance, immediately flush skin or eyes with running water for at least 20 minutes.
- In case of contact with liquefied gas, thaw frosted parts with lukewarm water.
- In case of burns, immediately cool affected skin for as long as possible with cold water. Do not remove clothing if adhering to skin.
- Keep victim warm and quiet.
- Keep victim under observation.
- Effects of contact or inhalation may be delayed.
- Ensure that medical personnel are aware of the material(s) involved and take precautions to protect themselves.

POTENTIAL HAZARDS

FIRE OR EXPLOSION
- **EXTREMELY FLAMMABLE.**
- May be ignited by heat, sparks or flames.
- May form explosive mixtures with air.
- Vapors from liquefied gas are initially heavier than air and spread along ground.
- Vapors may travel to source of ignition and flash back.
- Some of these materials may react violently with water.
- Cylinders exposed to fire may vent and release flammable gas through pressure relief devices.
- Containers may explode when heated.
- Ruptured cylinders may rocket.

HEALTH
- May cause toxic effects if inhaled.
- Vapors are extremely irritating.
- Contact with gas or liquefied gas may cause burns, severe injury and/or frostbite.
- Fire will produce irritating, corrosive and/or toxic gases.
- Runoff from fire control may cause pollution.

PUBLIC SAFETY
- **CALL EMERGENCY RESPONSE Telephone Number on Shipping Paper first. If Shipping Paper not available or no answer, refer to appropriate telephone number listed on the inside back cover.**
- As an immediate precautionary measure, isolate spill or leak area for at least 100 meters (330 feet) in all directions.
- Keep unauthorized personnel away.
- Stay upwind.
- Many gases are heavier than air and will spread along ground and collect in low or confined areas (sewers, basements, tanks).
- Keep out of low areas.
- Ventilate closed spaces before entering.

PROTECTIVE CLOTHING
- Wear positive pressure self-contained breathing apparatus (SCBA).
- Wear chemical protective clothing that is specifically recommended by the manufacturer. It may provide little or no thermal protection.
- Structural firefighters' protective clothing provides limited protection in fire situations ONLY; it is not effective in spill situations where direct contact with the substance is possible.

EVACUATION
Large Spill
- Consider initial downwind evacuation for at least 800 meters (1/2 mile).

Fire
- If tank, rail car or tank truck is involved in a fire, ISOLATE for 1600 meters (1 mile) in all directions; also, consider initial evacuation for 1600 meters (1 mile) in all directions.

EMERGENCY RESPONSE

FIRE
- **DO NOT EXTINGUISH A LEAKING GAS FIRE UNLESS LEAK CAN BE STOPPED.**

Small Fire
- Dry chemical or CO_2.

Large Fire
- Water spray, fog or regular foam.
- Move containers from fire area if you can do it without risk.
- Damaged cylinders should be handled only by specialists.

Fire involving Tanks
- Fight fire from maximum distance or use unmanned hose holders or monitor nozzles.
- Cool containers with flooding quantities of water until well after fire is out.
- Do not direct water at source of leak or safety devices; icing may occur.
- Withdraw immediately in case of rising sound from venting safety devices or discoloration of tank.
- ALWAYS stay away from tanks engulfed in fire.

SPILL OR LEAK
- ELIMINATE all ignition sources (no smoking, flares, sparks or flames in immediate area).
- All equipment used when handling the product must be grounded.
- Fully encapsulating, vapor protective clothing should be worn for spills and leaks with no fire.
- Do not touch or walk through spilled material.
- Stop leak if you can do it without risk.
- If possible, turn leaking containers so that gas escapes rather than liquid.
- Use water spray to reduce vapors or divert vapor cloud drift. Avoid allowing water runoff to contact spilled material.
- Do not direct water at spill or source of leak.
- Isolate area until gas has dispersed.

FIRST AID
- Move victim to fresh air.
- Call 911 or emergency medical service.
- Give artificial respiration if victim is not breathing.
- **Do not use mouth-to-mouth method if victim ingested or inhaled the substance; give artificial respiration with the aid of a pocket mask equipped with a one-way valve or other proper respiratory medical device.**
- Administer oxygen if breathing is difficult.
- Remove and isolate contaminated clothing and shoes.
- In case of contact with liquefied gas, thaw frosted parts with lukewarm water.
- In case of burns, immediately cool affected skin for as long as possible with cold water. Do not remove clothing if adhering to skin.
- Keep victim warm and quiet.
- Keep victim under observation.
- Effects of contact or inhalation may be delayed.
- Ensure that medical personnel are aware of the material(s) involved and take precautions to protect themselves.

GUIDE 119

GASES - TOXIC - FLAMMABLE

POTENTIAL HAZARDS

HEALTH

- **TOXIC; may be fatal if inhaled or absorbed through skin.**
- Contact with gas or liquefied gas may cause burns, severe injury and/or frostbite.
- Fire will produce irritating, corrosive and/or toxic gases.
- Runoff from fire control may cause pollution.

FIRE OR EXPLOSION

- Flammable; may be ignited by heat, sparks or flames.
- May form explosive mixtures with air.
- Those substances designated with a **(P)** may polymerize explosively when heated or involved in a fire.
- Vapors from liquefied gas are initially heavier than air and spread along ground.
- Vapors may travel to source of ignition and flash back.
- Some of these materials may react violently with water.
- Cylinders exposed to fire may vent and release toxic and flammable gas through pressure relief devices.
- Containers may explode when heated.
- Ruptured cylinders may rocket.
- Runoff may create fire or explosion hazard.

PUBLIC SAFETY

- **CALL EMERGENCY RESPONSE Telephone Number on Shipping Paper first. If Shipping Paper not available or no answer, refer to appropriate telephone number listed on the inside back cover.**
- As an immediate precautionary measure, isolate spill or leak area for at least 100 meters (330 feet) in all directions.
- Keep unauthorized personnel away.
- Stay upwind.
- Many gases are heavier than air and will spread along ground and collect in low or confined areas (sewers, basements, tanks).
- Keep out of low areas.
- Ventilate closed spaces before entering.

PROTECTIVE CLOTHING

- Wear positive pressure self-contained breathing apparatus (SCBA).
- Wear chemical protective clothing that is specifically recommended by the manufacturer. It may provide little or no thermal protection.
- Structural firefighters' protective clothing provides limited protection in fire situations ONLY; it is not effective in spill situations where direct contact with the substance is possible.

EVACUATION

Spill
- See Table 1 - Initial Isolation and Protective Action Distances for highlighted materials. For non-highlighted materials, increase, in the downwind direction, as necessary, the isolation distance shown under "PUBLIC SAFETY".

Fire
- If tank, rail car or tank truck is involved in a fire, ISOLATE for 1600 meters (1 mile) in all directions; also, consider initial evacuation for 1600 meters (1 mile) in all directions.

POTENTIAL HAZARDS

HEALTH

- Vapors may cause dizziness or asphyxiation without warning.
- Vapors from liquefied gas are initially heavier than air and spread along ground.
- Contact with gas or liquefied gas may cause burns, severe injury and/or frostbite.

FIRE OR EXPLOSION

- **Non-flammable gases.**
- Containers may explode when heated.
- Ruptured cylinders may rocket.

PUBLIC SAFETY

- **CALL EMERGENCY RESPONSE Telephone Number on Shipping Paper first. If Shipping Paper not available or no answer, refer to appropriate telephone number listed on the inside back cover.**
- As an immediate precautionary measure, isolate spill or leak area for at least 100 meters (330 feet) in all directions.
- Keep unauthorized personnel away.
- Stay upwind.
- Many gases are heavier than air and will spread along ground and collect in low or confined areas (sewers, basements, tanks).
- Keep out of low areas.
- Ventilate closed spaces before entering.

PROTECTIVE CLOTHING

- Wear positive pressure self-contained breathing apparatus (SCBA).
- Structural firefighters' protective clothing will only provide limited protection.
- Always wear thermal protective clothing when handling refrigerated/cryogenic liquids or solids.

EVACUATION

Large Spill
- Consider initial downwind evacuation for at least 100 meters (330 feet).

Fire
- If tank, rail car or tank truck is involved in a fire, ISOLATE for 800 meters (1/2 mile) in all directions; also, consider initial evacuation for 800 meters (1/2 mile) in all directions.

EMERGENCY RESPONSE

FIRE
- Use extinguishing agent suitable for type of surrounding fire.
- Move containers from fire area if you can do it without risk.
- Damaged cylinders should be handled only by specialists.

Fire involving Tanks
- Fight fire from maximum distance or use unmanned hose holders or monitor nozzles.
- Cool containers with flooding quantities of water until well after fire is out.
- Do not direct water at source of leak or safety devices; icing may occur.
- Withdraw immediately in case of rising sound from venting safety devices or discoloration of tank.
- ALWAYS stay away from tanks engulfed in fire.

SPILL OR LEAK
- Do not touch or walk through spilled material.
- Stop leak if you can do it without risk.
- Use water spray to reduce vapors or divert vapor cloud drift. Avoid allowing water runoff to contact spilled material.
- Do not direct water at spill or source of leak.
- If possible, turn leaking containers so that gas escapes rather than liquid.
- Prevent entry into waterways, sewers, basements or confined areas.
- Allow substance to evaporate.
- Ventilate the area.

CAUTION: When in contact with refrigerated/cryogenic liquids, many materials become brittle and are likely to break without warning.

FIRST AID
- Move victim to fresh air.
- Call 911 or emergency medical service.
- Give artificial respiration if victim is not breathing.
- Administer oxygen if breathing is difficult.
- Clothing frozen to the skin should be thawed before being removed.
- In case of contact with liquefied gas, thaw frosted parts with lukewarm water.
- Keep victim warm and quiet.
- Ensure that medical personnel are aware of the material(s) involved and take precautions to protect themselves.

POTENTIAL HAZARDS

HEALTH
- Vapors may cause dizziness or asphyxiation without warning.
- Vapors from liquefied gas are initially heavier than air and spread along ground.

FIRE OR EXPLOSION
- **Non-flammable gases.**
- Containers may explode when heated.
- Ruptured cylinders may rocket.

PUBLIC SAFETY
- **CALL EMERGENCY RESPONSE Telephone Number on Shipping Paper first. If Shipping Paper not available or no answer, refer to appropriate telephone number listed on the inside back cover.**
- As an immediate precautionary measure, isolate spill or leak area for at least 100 meters (330 feet) in all directions.
- Keep unauthorized personnel away.
- Stay upwind.
- Many gases are heavier than air and will spread along ground and collect in low or confined areas (sewers, basements, tanks).
- Keep out of low areas.
- Ventilate closed spaces before entering.

PROTECTIVE CLOTHING
- Wear positive pressure self-contained breathing apparatus (SCBA).
- Structural firefighters' protective clothing will only provide limited protection.

EVACUATION
Large Spill
- Consider initial downwind evacuation for at least 100 meters (330 feet).

Fire
- If tank, rail car or tank truck is involved in a fire, ISOLATE for 800 meters (1/2 mile) in all directions; also, consider initial evacuation for 800 meters (1/2 mile) in all directions.

EMERGENCY RESPONSE

FIRE
- Use extinguishing agent suitable for type of surrounding fire.
- Move containers from fire area if you can do it without risk.
- Damaged cylinders should be handled only by specialists.

Fire involving Tanks
- Fight fire from maximum distance or use unmanned hose holders or monitor nozzles.
- Cool containers with flooding quantities of water until well after fire is out.
- Do not direct water at source of leak or safety devices; icing may occur.
- Withdraw immediately in case of rising sound from venting safety devices or discoloration of tank.
- ALWAYS stay away from tanks engulfed in fire.

SPILL OR LEAK
- Do not touch or walk through spilled material.
- Stop leak if you can do it without risk.
- Use water spray to reduce vapors or divert vapor cloud drift. Avoid allowing water runoff to contact spilled material.
- Do not direct water at spill or source of leak.
- If possible, turn leaking containers so that gas escapes rather than liquid.
- Prevent entry into waterways, sewers, basements or confined areas.
- Allow substance to evaporate.
- Ventilate the area.

FIRST AID
- Move victim to fresh air.
- Call 911 or emergency medical service.
- Give artificial respiration if victim is not breathing.
- Administer oxygen if breathing is difficult.
- Keep victim warm and quiet.
- Ensure that medical personnel are aware of the material(s) involved and take precautions to protect themselves.

GUIDE
122

GASES - OXIDIZING
(INCLUDING REFRIGERATED LIQUIDS)

ERG2012

POTENTIAL HAZARDS

FIRE OR EXPLOSION
- Substance does not burn but will support combustion.
- Some may react explosively with fuels.
- May ignite combustibles (wood, paper, oil, clothing, etc.).
- Vapors from liquefied gas are initially heavier than air and spread along ground.
- Runoff may create fire or explosion hazard.
- Containers may explode when heated.
- Ruptured cylinders may rocket.

HEALTH
- Vapors may cause dizziness or asphyxiation without warning.
- Contact with gas or liquefied gas may cause burns, severe injury and/or frostbite.
- Fire may produce irritating and/or toxic gases.

PUBLIC SAFETY
- **CALL EMERGENCY RESPONSE Telephone Number on Shipping Paper first. If Shipping Paper not available or no answer, refer to appropriate telephone number listed on the inside back cover.**
- As an immediate precautionary measure, isolate spill or leak area for at least 100 meters (330 feet) in all directions.
- Keep unauthorized personnel away.
- Stay upwind.
- Many gases are heavier than air and will spread along ground and collect in low or confined areas (sewers, basements, tanks).
- Keep out of low areas.
- Ventilate closed spaces before entering.

PROTECTIVE CLOTHING
- Wear positive pressure self-contained breathing apparatus (SCBA).
- Wear chemical protective clothing that is specifically recommended by the manufacturer. It may provide little or no thermal protection.
- Structural firefighters' protective clothing provides limited protection in fire situations ONLY; it is not effective in spill situations where direct contact with the substance is possible.
- Always wear thermal protective clothing when handling refrigerated/cryogenic liquids.

EVACUATION
Large Spill
- Consider initial downwind evacuation for at least 500 meters (1/3 mile).

Fire
- If tank, rail car or tank truck is involved in a fire, ISOLATE for 800 meters (1/2 mile) in all directions; also, consider initial evacuation for 800 meters (1/2 mile) in all directions.

EMERGENCY RESPONSE

FIRE
- Use extinguishing agent suitable for type of surrounding fire.

Small Fire
- Dry chemical or CO_2.

Large Fire
- Water spray, fog or regular foam.
- Move containers from fire area if you can do it without risk.
- Damaged cylinders should be handled only by specialists.

Fire involving Tanks
- Fight fire from maximum distance or use unmanned hose holders or monitor nozzles.
- Cool containers with flooding quantities of water until well after fire is out.
- Do not direct water at source of leak or safety devices; icing may occur.
- Withdraw immediately in case of rising sound from venting safety devices or discoloration of tank.
- ALWAYS stay away from tanks engulfed in fire.
- For massive fire, use unmanned hose holders or monitor nozzles; if this is impossible, withdraw from area and let fire burn.

SPILL OR LEAK
- Keep combustibles (wood, paper, oil, etc.) away from spilled material.
- Do not touch or walk through spilled material.
- Stop leak if you can do it without risk.
- If possible, turn leaking containers so that gas escapes rather than liquid.
- Do not direct water at spill or source of leak.
- Use water spray to reduce vapors or divert vapor cloud drift. Avoid allowing water runoff to contact spilled material.
- Prevent entry into waterways, sewers, basements or confined areas.
- Allow substance to evaporate.
- Isolate area until gas has dispersed.
- **CAUTION: When in contact with refrigerated/cryogenic liquids, many materials become brittle and are likely to break without warning.**

FIRST AID
- Move victim to fresh air.
- Call 911 or emergency medical service.
- Give artificial respiration if victim is not breathing.
- Administer oxygen if breathing is difficult.
- Remove and isolate contaminated clothing and shoes.
- Clothing frozen to the skin should be thawed before being removed.
- In case of contact with liquefied gas, thaw frosted parts with lukewarm water.
- Keep victim warm and quiet.
- Ensure that medical personnel are aware of the material(s) involved and take precautions to protect themselves.

POTENTIAL HAZARDS

HEALTH

- **TOXIC; may be fatal if inhaled or absorbed through skin.**
- Vapors may be irritating.
- Contact with gas or liquefied gas may cause burns, severe injury and/or frostbite.
- Fire will produce irritating, corrosive and/or toxic gases.
- Runoff from fire control may cause pollution.

FIRE OR EXPLOSION

- Some may burn but none ignite readily.
- Vapors from liquefied gas are initially heavier than air and spread along ground.
- Cylinders exposed to fire may vent and release toxic and/or corrosive gas through pressure relief devices.
- Containers may explode when heated.
- Ruptured cylinders may rocket.

PUBLIC SAFETY

- **CALL EMERGENCY RESPONSE Telephone Number on Shipping Paper first. If Shipping Paper not available or no answer, refer to appropriate telephone number listed on the inside back cover.**
- As an immediate precautionary measure, isolate spill or leak area for at least 100 meters (330 feet) in all directions.
- Keep unauthorized personnel away.
- Stay upwind.
- Many gases are heavier than air and will spread along ground and collect in low or confined areas (sewers, basements, tanks).
- Keep out of low areas.
- Ventilate closed spaces before entering.

PROTECTIVE CLOTHING

- Wear positive pressure self-contained breathing apparatus (SCBA).
- Wear chemical protective clothing that is specifically recommended by the manufacturer. It may provide little or no thermal protection.
- Structural firefighters' protective clothing provides limited protection in fire situations ONLY; it is not effective in spill situations where direct contact with the substance is possible.

EVACUATION

Spill

- See Table 1 - Initial Isolation and Protective Action Distances for highlighted materials. For non-highlighted materials, increase, in the downwind direction, as necessary, the isolation distance shown under "PUBLIC SAFETY".

Fire

- If tank, rail car or tank truck is involved in a fire, ISOLATE for 800 meters (1/2 mile) in all directions; also, consider initial evacuation for 800 meters (1/2 mile) in all directions.

EMERGENCY RESPONSE

FIRE
Small Fire
- Dry chemical or CO_2.

Large Fire
- Water spray, fog or regular foam.
- Do not get water inside containers.
- Move containers from fire area if you can do it without risk.
- Damaged cylinders should be handled only by specialists.

Fire involving Tanks
- Fight fire from maximum distance or use unmanned hose holders or monitor nozzles.
- Cool containers with flooding quantities of water until well after fire is out.
- Do not direct water at source of leak or safety devices; icing may occur.
- Withdraw immediately in case of rising sound from venting safety devices or discoloration of tank.
- ALWAYS stay away from tanks engulfed in fire.

SPILL OR LEAK
- Fully encapsulating, vapor protective clothing should be worn for spills and leaks with no fire.
- Do not touch or walk through spilled material.
- Stop leak if you can do it without risk.
- If possible, turn leaking containers so that gas escapes rather than liquid.
- Prevent entry into waterways, sewers, basements or confined areas.
- Use water spray to reduce vapors or divert vapor cloud drift. Avoid allowing water runoff to contact spilled material.
- Do not direct water at spill or source of leak.
- Isolate area until gas has dispersed.

FIRST AID
- Move victim to fresh air.
- Call 911 or emergency medical service.
- Give artificial respiration if victim is not breathing.
- **Do not use mouth-to-mouth method if victim ingested or inhaled the substance; give artificial respiration with the aid of a pocket mask equipped with a one-way valve or other proper respiratory medical device.**
- Administer oxygen if breathing is difficult.
- Remove and isolate contaminated clothing and shoes.
- In case of contact with liquefied gas, thaw frosted parts with lukewarm water.
- In case of contact with substance, immediately flush skin or eyes with running water for at least 20 minutes.
- Keep victim warm and quiet.
- Keep victim under observation.
- Effects of contact or inhalation may be delayed.
- Ensure that medical personnel are aware of the material(s) involved and take precautions to protect themselves.

POTENTIAL HAZARDS

HEALTH

- **TOXIC; may be fatal if inhaled or absorbed through skin.**
- Fire will produce irritating, corrosive and/or toxic gases.
- Contact with gas or liquefied gas may cause burns, severe injury and/or frostbite.
- Runoff from fire control may cause pollution.

FIRE OR EXPLOSION

- Substance does not burn but will support combustion.
- Vapors from liquefied gas are initially heavier than air and spread along ground.
- These are strong oxidizers and will react vigorously or explosively with many materials including fuels.
- May ignite combustibles (wood, paper, oil, clothing, etc.).
- Some will react violently with air, moist air and/or water.
- Cylinders exposed to fire may vent and release toxic and/or corrosive gas through pressure relief devices.
- Containers may explode when heated.
- Ruptured cylinders may rocket.

PUBLIC SAFETY

- **CALL EMERGENCY RESPONSE Telephone Number on Shipping Paper first. If Shipping Paper not available or no answer, refer to appropriate telephone number listed on the inside back cover.**
- As an immediate precautionary measure, isolate spill or leak area for at least 100 meters (330 feet) in all directions.
- Keep unauthorized personnel away.
- Stay upwind.
- Many gases are heavier than air and will spread along ground and collect in low or confined areas (sewers, basements, tanks).
- Keep out of low areas.
- Ventilate closed spaces before entering.

PROTECTIVE CLOTHING

- Wear positive pressure self-contained breathing apparatus (SCBA).
- Wear chemical protective clothing that is specifically recommended by the manufacturer. It may provide little or no thermal protection.
- Structural firefighters' protective clothing provides limited protection in fire situations ONLY; it is not effective in spill situations where direct contact with the substance is possible.

EVACUATION

Spill
- See Table 1 - Initial Isolation and Protective Action Distances.

Fire
- If tank, rail car or tank truck is involved in a fire, ISOLATE for 800 meters (1/2 mile) in all directions; also, consider initial evacuation for 800 meters (1/2 mile) in all directions.

EMERGENCY RESPONSE

FIRE
Small Fire
CAUTION: These materials do not burn but will support combustion. Some will react violently with water.
- Contain fire and let burn. If fire must be fought, water spray or fog is recommended.
- **Water only; no dry chemical, CO$_2$ or Halon®.**
- Do not get water inside containers.
- Move containers from fire area if you can do it without risk.
- Damaged cylinders should be handled only by specialists.

Fire involving Tanks
- Fight fire from maximum distance or use unmanned hose holders or monitor nozzles.
- Cool containers with flooding quantities of water until well after fire is out.
- Do not direct water at source of leak or safety devices; icing may occur.
- Withdraw immediately in case of rising sound from venting safety devices or discoloration of tank.
- ALWAYS stay away from tanks engulfed in fire.
- For massive fire, use unmanned hose holders or monitor nozzles; if this is impossible, withdraw from area and let fire burn.

SPILL OR LEAK
- Fully encapsulating, vapor protective clothing should be worn for spills and leaks with no fire.
- Do not touch or walk through spilled material.
- Keep combustibles (wood, paper, oil, etc.) away from spilled material.
- Stop leak if you can do it without risk.
- Use water spray to reduce vapors or divert vapor cloud drift. Avoid allowing water runoff to contact spilled material.
- Do not direct water at spill or source of leak.
- If possible, turn leaking containers so that gas escapes rather than liquid.
- Prevent entry into waterways, sewers, basements or confined areas.
- Isolate area until gas has dispersed.
- Ventilate the area.

FIRST AID
- Move victim to fresh air.
- Call 911 or emergency medical service.
- Give artificial respiration if victim is not breathing.
- **Do not use mouth-to-mouth method if victim ingested or inhaled the substance; give artificial respiration with the aid of a pocket mask equipped with a one-way valve or other proper respiratory medical device.**
- Administer oxygen if breathing is difficult.
- Clothing frozen to the skin should be thawed before being removed.
- Remove and isolate contaminated clothing and shoes.
- In case of contact with substance, immediately flush skin or eyes with running water for at least 20 minutes.
- Keep victim warm and quiet.
- Keep victim under observation.
- Effects of contact or inhalation may be delayed.
- Ensure that medical personnel are aware of the material(s) involved and take precautions to protect themselves.

POTENTIAL HAZARDS

HEALTH

- **TOXIC; may be fatal if inhaled, ingested or absorbed through skin.**
- Vapors are extremely irritating and corrosive.
- Contact with gas or liquefied gas may cause burns, severe injury and/or frostbite.
- Fire will produce irritating, corrosive and/or toxic gases.
- Runoff from fire control may cause pollution.

FIRE OR EXPLOSION

- Some may burn but none ignite readily.
- Vapors from liquefied gas are initially heavier than air and spread along ground.
- Some of these materials may react violently with water.
- Cylinders exposed to fire may vent and release toxic and/or corrosive gas through pressure relief devices.
- Containers may explode when heated.
- Ruptured cylinders may rocket.

PUBLIC SAFETY

- **CALL EMERGENCY RESPONSE Telephone Number on Shipping Paper first. If Shipping Paper not available or no answer, refer to appropriate telephone number listed on the inside back cover.**
- As an immediate precautionary measure, isolate spill or leak area for at least 100 meters (330 feet) in all directions.
- Keep unauthorized personnel away.
- Stay upwind.
- Many gases are heavier than air and will spread along ground and collect in low or confined areas (sewers, basements, tanks).
- Keep out of low areas.
- Ventilate closed spaces before entering.

PROTECTIVE CLOTHING

- Wear positive pressure self-contained breathing apparatus (SCBA).
- Wear chemical protective clothing that is specifically recommended by the manufacturer. It may provide little or no thermal protection.
- Structural firefighters' protective clothing provides limited protection in fire situations ONLY; it is not effective in spill situations where direct contact with the substance is possible.

EVACUATION

Spill

- See Table 1 - Initial Isolation and Protective Action Distances for highlighted materials. For non-highlighted materials, increase, in the downwind direction, as necessary, the isolation distance shown under "PUBLIC SAFETY".

Fire

- If tank, rail car or tank truck is involved in a fire, ISOLATE for 1600 meters (1 mile) in all directions; also, consider initial evacuation for 1600 meters (1 mile) in all directions.

EMERGENCY RESPONSE

FIRE

Small Fire
- Dry chemical or CO_2.

Large Fire
- Water spray, fog or regular foam.
- Move containers from fire area if you can do it without risk.
- Do not get water inside containers.
- Damaged cylinders should be handled only by specialists.

Fire involving Tanks
- Fight fire from maximum distance or use unmanned hose holders or monitor nozzles.
- Cool containers with flooding quantities of water until well after fire is out.
- Do not direct water at source of leak or safety devices; icing may occur.
- Withdraw immediately in case of rising sound from venting safety devices or discoloration of tank.
- ALWAYS stay away from tanks engulfed in fire.

SPILL OR LEAK

- Fully encapsulating, vapor protective clothing should be worn for spills and leaks with no fire.
- Do not touch or walk through spilled material.
- Stop leak if you can do it without risk.
- If possible, turn leaking containers so that gas escapes rather than liquid.
- Prevent entry into waterways, sewers, basements or confined areas.
- Do not direct water at spill or source of leak.
- Use water spray to reduce vapors or divert vapor cloud drift. Avoid allowing water runoff to contact spilled material.
- Isolate area until gas has dispersed.

FIRST AID

- Move victim to fresh air.
- Call 911 or emergency medical service.
- Give artificial respiration if victim is not breathing.
- **Do not use mouth-to-mouth method if victim ingested or inhaled the substance; give artificial respiration with the aid of a pocket mask equipped with a one-way valve or other proper respiratory medical device.**
- Administer oxygen if breathing is difficult.
- Remove and isolate contaminated clothing and shoes.
- In case of contact with liquefied gas, thaw frosted parts with lukewarm water.
- In case of contact with substance, immediately flush skin or eyes with running water for at least 20 minutes.
- **In case of contact with Hydrogen fluoride, anhydrous (UN1052),** flush skin and eyes with water for 5 minutes; then, for skin exposures rub on a calcium/gel combination; for eyes flush with a water/calcium solution for 15 minutes.
- Keep victim warm and quiet.
- Keep victim under observation.
- Effects of contact or inhalation may be delayed.
- Ensure that medical personnel are aware of the material(s) involved and take precautions to protect themselves.

POTENTIAL HAZARDS

FIRE OR EXPLOSION
- Some may burn but none ignite readily.
- Containers may explode when heated.
- Ruptured cylinders may rocket.

HEALTH
- Vapors may cause dizziness or asphyxiation without warning.
- Vapors from liquefied gas are initially heavier than air and spread along ground.
- Contact with gas or liquefied gas may cause burns, severe injury and/or frostbite.
- Fire may produce irritating, corrosive and/or toxic gases.

PUBLIC SAFETY

- **CALL EMERGENCY RESPONSE Telephone Number on Shipping Paper first. If Shipping Paper not available or no answer, refer to appropriate telephone number listed on the inside back cover.**
- As an immediate precautionary measure, isolate spill or leak area for at least 100 meters (330 feet) in all directions.
- Keep unauthorized personnel away.
- Stay upwind.
- Many gases are heavier than air and will spread along ground and collect in low or confined areas (sewers, basements, tanks).
- Keep out of low areas.
- Ventilate closed spaces before entering.

PROTECTIVE CLOTHING
- Wear positive pressure self-contained breathing apparatus (SCBA).
- Wear chemical protective clothing that is specifically recommended by the manufacturer. It may provide little or no thermal protection.
- Structural firefighters' protective clothing will only provide limited protection.

EVACUATION
Large Spill
- Consider initial downwind evacuation for at least 500 meters (1/3 mile).

Fire
- If tank, rail car or tank truck is involved in a fire, ISOLATE for 800 meters (1/2 mile) in all directions; also, consider initial evacuation for 800 meters (1/2 mile) in all directions.

EMERGENCY RESPONSE

FIRE
- Use extinguishing agent suitable for type of surrounding fire.

Small Fire
- Dry chemical or CO_2.

Large Fire
- Water spray, fog or regular foam.
- Move containers from fire area if you can do it without risk.
- Damaged cylinders should be handled only by specialists.

Fire involving Tanks
- Fight fire from maximum distance or use unmanned hose holders or monitor nozzles.
- Cool containers with flooding quantities of water until well after fire is out.
- Do not direct water at source of leak or safety devices; icing may occur.
- Withdraw immediately in case of rising sound from venting safety devices or discoloration of tank.
- ALWAYS stay away from tanks engulfed in fire.
- Some of these materials, if spilled, may evaporate leaving a flammable residue.

SPILL OR LEAK
- Do not touch or walk through spilled material.
- Stop leak if you can do it without risk.
- Do not direct water at spill or source of leak.
- Use water spray to reduce vapors or divert vapor cloud drift. Avoid allowing water runoff to contact spilled material.
- If possible, turn leaking containers so that gas escapes rather than liquid.
- Prevent entry into waterways, sewers, basements or confined areas.
- Allow substance to evaporate.
- Ventilate the area.

FIRST AID
- Move victim to fresh air.
- Call 911 or emergency medical service.
- Give artificial respiration if victim is not breathing.
- Administer oxygen if breathing is difficult.
- Remove and isolate contaminated clothing and shoes.
- In case of contact with liquefied gas, thaw frosted parts with lukewarm water.
- Keep victim warm and quiet.
- Ensure that medical personnel are aware of the material(s) involved and take precautions to protect themselves.

POTENTIAL HAZARDS

FIRE OR EXPLOSION

- **HIGHLY FLAMMABLE: Will be easily ignited by heat, sparks or flames.**
- Vapors may form explosive mixtures with air.
- Vapors may travel to source of ignition and flash back.
- Most vapors are heavier than air. They will spread along ground and collect in low or confined areas (sewers, basements, tanks).
- Vapor explosion hazard indoors, outdoors or in sewers.
- Those substances designated with a **(P)** may polymerize explosively when heated or involved in a fire.
- Runoff to sewer may create fire or explosion hazard.
- Containers may explode when heated.
- Many liquids are lighter than water.

HEALTH

- Inhalation or contact with material may irritate or burn skin and eyes.
- Fire may produce irritating, corrosive and/or toxic gases.
- Vapors may cause dizziness or suffocation.
- Runoff from fire control may cause pollution.

PUBLIC SAFETY

- **CALL EMERGENCY RESPONSE Telephone Number on Shipping Paper first. If Shipping Paper not available or no answer, refer to appropriate telephone number listed on the inside back cover.**
- As an immediate precautionary measure, isolate spill or leak area for at least 50 meters (150 feet) in all directions.
- Keep unauthorized personnel away.
- Stay upwind.
- Keep out of low areas.
- Ventilate closed spaces before entering.

PROTECTIVE CLOTHING

- Wear positive pressure self-contained breathing apparatus (SCBA).
- Structural firefighters' protective clothing will only provide limited protection.

EVACUATION

Large Spill

- Consider initial downwind evacuation for at least 300 meters (1000 feet).

Fire

- If tank, rail car or tank truck is involved in a fire, ISOLATE for 800 meters (1/2 mile) in all directions; also, consider initial evacuation for 800 meters (1/2 mile) in all directions.

EMERGENCY RESPONSE

FIRE

CAUTION: All these products have a very low flash point: Use of water spray when fighting fire may be inefficient.

Small Fire

- Dry chemical, CO_2, water spray or alcohol-resistant foam.

Large Fire

- Water spray, fog or alcohol-resistant foam.
- **Do not use straight streams**.
- Move containers from fire area if you can do it without risk.

Fire involving Tanks or Car/Trailer Loads

- Fight fire from maximum distance or use unmanned hose holders or monitor nozzles.
- Cool containers with flooding quantities of water until well after fire is out.
- Withdraw immediately in case of rising sound from venting safety devices or discoloration of tank.
- ALWAYS stay away from tanks engulfed in fire.
- For massive fire, use unmanned hose holders or monitor nozzles; if this is impossible, withdraw from area and let fire burn.

SPILL OR LEAK

- ELIMINATE all ignition sources (no smoking, flares, sparks or flames in immediate area).
- All equipment used when handling the product must be grounded.
- Do not touch or walk through spilled material.
- Stop leak if you can do it without risk.
- Prevent entry into waterways, sewers, basements or confined areas.
- A vapor suppressing foam may be used to reduce vapors.
- Absorb or cover with dry earth, sand or other non-combustible material and transfer to containers.
- Use clean non-sparking tools to collect absorbed material.

Large Spill

- Dike far ahead of liquid spill for later disposal.
- Water spray may reduce vapor; but may not prevent ignition in closed spaces.

FIRST AID

- Move victim to fresh air.
- Call 911 or emergency medical service.
- Give artificial respiration if victim is not breathing.
- Administer oxygen if breathing is difficult.
- Remove and isolate contaminated clothing and shoes.
- In case of contact with substance, immediately flush skin or eyes with running water for at least 20 minutes.
- Wash skin with soap and water.
- In case of burns, immediately cool affected skin for as long as possible with cold water. Do not remove clothing if adhering to skin.
- Keep victim warm and quiet.
- Ensure that medical personnel are aware of the material(s) involved and take precautions to protect themselves.

POTENTIAL HAZARDS

FIRE OR EXPLOSION
- **HIGHLY FLAMMABLE: Will be easily ignited by heat, sparks or flames.**
- Vapors may form explosive mixtures with air.
- Vapors may travel to source of ignition and flash back.
- Most vapors are heavier than air. They will spread along ground and collect in low or confined areas (sewers, basements, tanks).
- Vapor explosion hazard indoors, outdoors or in sewers.
- Those substances designated with a **(P)** may polymerize explosively when heated or involved in a fire.
- Runoff to sewer may create fire or explosion hazard.
- Containers may explode when heated.
- Many liquids are lighter than water.
- Substance may be transported hot.
- For UN3166, if Lithium ion batteries are involved, also consult GUIDE 147.
- **If molten aluminum is involved, refer to GUIDE 169.**

HEALTH
- Inhalation or contact with material may irritate or burn skin and eyes.
- Fire may produce irritating, corrosive and/or toxic gases.
- Vapors may cause dizziness or suffocation.
- Runoff from fire control or dilution water may cause pollution.

PUBLIC SAFETY
- **CALL EMERGENCY RESPONSE Telephone Number on Shipping Paper first. If Shipping Paper not available or no answer, refer to appropriate telephone number listed on the inside back cover.**
- As an immediate precautionary measure, isolate spill or leak area for at least 50 meters (150 feet) in all directions.
- Keep unauthorized personnel away.
- Stay upwind.
- Keep out of low areas.
- Ventilate closed spaces before entering.

PROTECTIVE CLOTHING
- Wear positive pressure self-contained breathing apparatus (SCBA).
- Structural firefighters' protective clothing will only provide limited protection.

EVACUATION
Large Spill
- Consider initial downwind evacuation for at least 300 meters (1000 feet).

Fire
- If tank, rail car or tank truck is involved in a fire, ISOLATE for 800 meters (1/2 mile) in all directions; also, consider initial evacuation for 800 meters (1/2 mile) in all directions.

EMERGENCY RESPONSE

FIRE

CAUTION: All these products have a very low flash point: Use of water spray when fighting fire may be inefficient.

CAUTION: For mixtures containing alcohol or polar solvent, alcohol-resistant foam may be more effective.

Small Fire
- Dry chemical, CO_2, water spray or regular foam.

Large Fire
- Water spray, fog or regular foam.
- **Do not use straight streams**.
- Move containers from fire area if you can do it without risk.

Fire involving Tanks or Car/Trailer Loads
- Fight fire from maximum distance or use unmanned hose holders or monitor nozzles.
- Cool containers with flooding quantities of water until well after fire is out.
- Withdraw immediately in case of rising sound from venting safety devices or discoloration of tank.
- ALWAYS stay away from tanks engulfed in fire.
- For massive fire, use unmanned hose holders or monitor nozzles; if this is impossible, withdraw from area and let fire burn.

SPILL OR LEAK

- ELIMINATE all ignition sources (no smoking, flares, sparks or flames in immediate area).
- All equipment used when handling the product must be grounded.
- Do not touch or walk through spilled material.
- Stop leak if you can do it without risk.
- Prevent entry into waterways, sewers, basements or confined areas.
- A vapor suppressing foam may be used to reduce vapors.
- Absorb or cover with dry earth, sand or other non-combustible material and transfer to containers.
- Use clean non-sparking tools to collect absorbed material.

Large Spill
- Dike far ahead of liquid spill for later disposal.
- Water spray may reduce vapor; but may not prevent ignition in closed spaces.

FIRST AID

- Move victim to fresh air.
- Call 911 or emergency medical service.
- Give artificial respiration if victim is not breathing.
- Administer oxygen if breathing is difficult.
- Remove and isolate contaminated clothing and shoes.
- In case of contact with substance, immediately flush skin or eyes with running water for at least 20 minutes.
- Wash skin with soap and water.
- In case of burns, immediately cool affected skin for as long as possible with cold water. Do not remove clothing if adhering to skin.
- Keep victim warm and quiet.
- Ensure that medical personnel are aware of the material(s) involved and take precautions to protect themselves.

POTENTIAL HAZARDS

FIRE OR EXPLOSION

- **HIGHLY FLAMMABLE: Will be easily ignited by heat, sparks or flames.**
- Vapors may form explosive mixtures with air.
- Vapors may travel to source of ignition and flash back.
- Most vapors are heavier than air. They will spread along ground and collect in low or confined areas (sewers, basements, tanks).
- Vapor explosion hazard indoors, outdoors or in sewers.
- Those substances designated with a **(P)** may polymerize explosively when heated or involved in a fire.
- Runoff to sewer may create fire or explosion hazard.
- Containers may explode when heated.
- Many liquids are lighter than water.

HEALTH

- May cause toxic effects if inhaled or absorbed through skin.
- Inhalation or contact with material may irritate or burn skin and eyes.
- Fire will produce irritating, corrosive and/or toxic gases.
- Vapors may cause dizziness or suffocation.
- Runoff from fire control or dilution water may cause pollution.

PUBLIC SAFETY

- **CALL EMERGENCY RESPONSE Telephone Number on Shipping Paper first. If Shipping Paper not available or no answer, refer to appropriate telephone number listed on the inside back cover.**
- As an immediate precautionary measure, isolate spill or leak area for at least 50 meters (150 feet) in all directions.
- Keep unauthorized personnel away.
- Stay upwind.
- Keep out of low areas.
- Ventilate closed spaces before entering.

PROTECTIVE CLOTHING

- Wear positive pressure self-contained breathing apparatus (SCBA).
- Structural firefighters' protective clothing will only provide limited protection.

EVACUATION

Large Spill
- Consider initial downwind evacuation for at least 300 meters (1000 feet).

Fire
- If tank, rail car or tank truck is involved in a fire, ISOLATE for 800 meters (1/2 mile) in all directions; also, consider initial evacuation for 800 meters (1/2 mile) in all directions.

EMERGENCY RESPONSE

FIRE

CAUTION: All these products have a very low flash point: Use of water spray when fighting fire may be inefficient.

Small Fire
- Dry chemical, CO_2, water spray or alcohol-resistant foam.
- **Do not use dry chemical extinguishers to control fires involving nitromethane or nitroethane.**

Large Fire
- Water spray, fog or alcohol-resistant foam.
- **Do not use straight streams.**
- Move containers from fire area if you can do it without risk.

Fire involving Tanks or Car/Trailer Loads
- Fight fire from maximum distance or use unmanned hose holders or monitor nozzles.
- Cool containers with flooding quantities of water until well after fire is out.
- Withdraw immediately in case of rising sound from venting safety devices or discoloration of tank.
- ALWAYS stay away from tanks engulfed in fire.
- For massive fire, use unmanned hose holders or monitor nozzles; if this is impossible, withdraw from area and let fire burn.

SPILL OR LEAK

- ELIMINATE all ignition sources (no smoking, flares, sparks or flames in immediate area).
- All equipment used when handling the product must be grounded.
- Do not touch or walk through spilled material.
- Stop leak if you can do it without risk.
- Prevent entry into waterways, sewers, basements or confined areas.
- A vapor suppressing foam may be used to reduce vapors.
- Absorb or cover with dry earth, sand or other non-combustible material and transfer to containers.
- Use clean non-sparking tools to collect absorbed material.

Large Spill
- Dike far ahead of liquid spill for later disposal.
- Water spray may reduce vapor; but may not prevent ignition in closed spaces.

FIRST AID

- Move victim to fresh air.
- Call 911 or emergency medical service.
- Give artificial respiration if victim is not breathing.
- Administer oxygen if breathing is difficult.
- Remove and isolate contaminated clothing and shoes.
- In case of contact with substance, immediately flush skin or eyes with running water for at least 20 minutes.
- Wash skin with soap and water.
- In case of burns, immediately cool affected skin for as long as possible with cold water. Do not remove clothing if adhering to skin.
- Keep victim warm and quiet.
- Effects of exposure (inhalation, ingestion or skin contact) to substance may be delayed.
- Ensure that medical personnel are aware of the material(s) involved and take precautions to protect themselves.

GUIDE 130

FLAMMABLE LIQUIDS
(NON-POLAR/WATER-IMMISCIBLE/NOXIOUS)

ERG2012

POTENTIAL HAZARDS

FIRE OR EXPLOSION

- **HIGHLY FLAMMABLE: Will be easily ignited by heat, sparks or flames.**
- Vapors may form explosive mixtures with air.
- Vapors may travel to source of ignition and flash back.
- Most vapors are heavier than air. They will spread along ground and collect in low or confined areas (sewers, basements, tanks).
- Vapor explosion hazard indoors, outdoors or in sewers.
- Those substances designated with a **(P)** may polymerize explosively when heated or involved in a fire.
- Runoff to sewer may create fire or explosion hazard.
- Containers may explode when heated.
- Many liquids are lighter than water.

HEALTH

- May cause toxic effects if inhaled or absorbed through skin.
- Inhalation or contact with material may irritate or burn skin and eyes.
- Fire will produce irritating, corrosive and/or toxic gases.
- Vapors may cause dizziness or suffocation.
- Runoff from fire control or dilution water may cause pollution.

PUBLIC SAFETY

- **CALL EMERGENCY RESPONSE Telephone Number on Shipping Paper first. If Shipping Paper not available or no answer, refer to appropriate telephone number listed on the inside back cover.**
- As an immediate precautionary measure, isolate spill or leak area for at least 50 meters (150 feet) in all directions.
- Keep unauthorized personnel away.
- Stay upwind.
- Keep out of low areas.
- Ventilate closed spaces before entering.

PROTECTIVE CLOTHING

- Wear positive pressure self-contained breathing apparatus (SCBA).
- Structural firefighters' protective clothing will only provide limited protection.

EVACUATION

Large Spill
- Consider initial downwind evacuation for at least 300 meters (1000 feet).

Fire
- If tank, rail car or tank truck is involved in a fire, ISOLATE for 800 meters (1/2 mile) in all directions; also, consider initial evacuation for 800 meters (1/2 mile) in all directions.

EMERGENCY RESPONSE

FIRE
CAUTION: All these products have a very low flash point: Use of water spray when fighting fire may be inefficient.

Small Fire
- Dry chemical, CO_2, water spray or regular foam.

Large Fire
- Water spray, fog or regular foam.
- **Do not use straight streams.**
- Move containers from fire area if you can do it without risk.

Fire involving Tanks or Car/Trailer Loads
- Fight fire from maximum distance or use unmanned hose holders or monitor nozzles.
- Cool containers with flooding quantities of water until well after fire is out.
- Withdraw immediately in case of rising sound from venting safety devices or discoloration of tank.
- ALWAYS stay away from tanks engulfed in fire.
- For massive fire, use unmanned hose holders or monitor nozzles; if this is impossible, withdraw from area and let fire burn.

SPILL OR LEAK
- ELIMINATE all ignition sources (no smoking, flares, sparks or flames in immediate area).
- All equipment used when handling the product must be grounded.
- Do not touch or walk through spilled material.
- Stop leak if you can do it without risk.
- Prevent entry into waterways, sewers, basements or confined areas.
- A vapor suppressing foam may be used to reduce vapors.
- Absorb or cover with dry earth, sand or other non-combustible material and transfer to containers.
- Use clean non-sparking tools to collect absorbed material.

Large Spill
- Dike far ahead of liquid spill for later disposal.
- Water spray may reduce vapor; but may not prevent ignition in closed spaces.

FIRST AID
- Move victim to fresh air.
- Call 911 or emergency medical service.
- Give artificial respiration if victim is not breathing.
- Administer oxygen if breathing is difficult.
- Remove and isolate contaminated clothing and shoes.
- In case of contact with substance, immediately flush skin or eyes with running water for at least 20 minutes.
- Wash skin with soap and water.
- In case of burns, immediately cool affected skin for as long as possible with cold water. Do not remove clothing if adhering to skin.
- Keep victim warm and quiet.
- Effects of exposure (inhalation, ingestion or skin contact) to substance may be delayed.
- Ensure that medical personnel are aware of the material(s) involved and take precautions to protect themselves.

POTENTIAL HAZARDS

HEALTH

- **TOXIC; may be fatal if inhaled, ingested or absorbed through skin.**
- Inhalation or contact with some of these materials will irritate or burn skin and eyes.
- Fire will produce irritating, corrosive and/or toxic gases.
- Vapors may cause dizziness or suffocation.
- Runoff from fire control or dilution water may cause pollution.

FIRE OR EXPLOSION

- **HIGHLY FLAMMABLE: Will be easily ignited by heat, sparks or flames.**
- Vapors may form explosive mixtures with air.
- Vapors may travel to source of ignition and flash back.
- Most vapors are heavier than air. They will spread along ground and collect in low or confined areas (sewers, basements, tanks).
- Vapor explosion and poison hazard indoors, outdoors or in sewers.
- Those substances designated with a **(P)** may polymerize explosively when heated or involved in a fire.
- Runoff to sewer may create fire or explosion hazard.
- Containers may explode when heated.
- Many liquids are lighter than water.

PUBLIC SAFETY

- **CALL EMERGENCY RESPONSE Telephone Number on Shipping Paper first. If Shipping Paper not available or no answer, refer to appropriate telephone number listed on the inside back cover.**
- As an immediate precautionary measure, isolate spill or leak area for at least 50 meters (150 feet) in all directions.
- Keep unauthorized personnel away.
- Stay upwind.
- Keep out of low areas.
- Ventilate closed spaces before entering.

PROTECTIVE CLOTHING

- Wear positive pressure self-contained breathing apparatus (SCBA).
- Wear chemical protective clothing that is specifically recommended by the manufacturer. It may provide little or no thermal protection.
- Structural firefighters' protective clothing provides limited protection in fire situations ONLY; it is not effective in spill situations where direct contact with the substance is possible.

EVACUATION

Spill

- See Table 1 - Initial Isolation and Protective Action Distances for highlighted materials. For non-highlighted materials, increase, in the downwind direction, as necessary, the isolation distance shown under "PUBLIC SAFETY".

Fire

- If tank, rail car or tank truck is involved in a fire, ISOLATE for 800 meters (1/2 mile) in all directions; also, consider initial evacuation for 800 meters (1/2 mile) in all directions.

EMERGENCY RESPONSE

FIRE

CAUTION: All these products have a very low flash point: Use of water spray when fighting fire may be inefficient.

Small Fire

- Dry chemical, CO_2, water spray or alcohol-resistant foam.

Large Fire

- Water spray, fog or alcohol-resistant foam.
- Move containers from fire area if you can do it without risk.
- Dike fire-control water for later disposal; do not scatter the material.
- Use water spray or fog; do not use straight streams.

Fire involving Tanks or Car/Trailer Loads

- Fight fire from maximum distance or use unmanned hose holders or monitor nozzles.
- Cool containers with flooding quantities of water until well after fire is out.
- Withdraw immediately in case of rising sound from venting safety devices or discoloration of tank.
- ALWAYS stay away from tanks engulfed in fire.
- For massive fire, use unmanned hose holders or monitor nozzles; if this is impossible, withdraw from area and let fire burn.

SPILL OR LEAK

- Fully encapsulating, vapor protective clothing should be worn for spills and leaks with no fire.
- ELIMINATE all ignition sources (no smoking, flares, sparks or flames in immediate area).
- All equipment used when handling the product must be grounded.
- Do not touch or walk through spilled material.
- Stop leak if you can do it without risk.
- Prevent entry into waterways, sewers, basements or confined areas.
- A vapor suppressing foam may be used to reduce vapors.
- **Small Spill** •Absorb with earth, sand or other non-combustible material and transfer to containers for later disposal.
- Use clean non-sparking tools to collect absorbed material.
- **Large Spill** • Dike far ahead of liquid spill for later disposal.
- Water spray may reduce vapor; but may not prevent ignition in closed spaces.

FIRST AID

- Move victim to fresh air.   • Call 911 or emergency medical service.
- Give artificial respiration if victim is not breathing.
- **Do not use mouth-to-mouth method if victim ingested or inhaled the substance; give artificial respiration with the aid of a pocket mask equipped with a one-way valve or other proper respiratory medical device.**
- Administer oxygen if breathing is difficult.
- Remove and isolate contaminated clothing and shoes.
- In case of contact with substance, immediately flush skin or eyes with running water for at least 20 minutes.
- Wash skin with soap and water.
- In case of burns, immediately cool affected skin for as long as possible with cold water. Do not remove clothing if adhering to skin.   • Keep victim warm and quiet.
- Effects of exposure (inhalation, ingestion or skin contact) to substance may be delayed.
- Ensure that medical personnel are aware of the material(s) involved and take precautions to protect themselves.

POTENTIAL HAZARDS

FIRE OR EXPLOSION

- Flammable/combustible material.
- May be ignited by heat, sparks or flames.
- Vapors may form explosive mixtures with air.
- Vapors may travel to source of ignition and flash back.
- Most vapors are heavier than air. They will spread along ground and collect in low or confined areas (sewers, basements, tanks).
- Vapor explosion hazard indoors, outdoors or in sewers.
- Those substances designated with a **(P)** may polymerize explosively when heated or involved in a fire.
- Runoff to sewer may create fire or explosion hazard.
- Containers may explode when heated.
- Many liquids are lighter than water.

HEALTH

- May cause toxic effects if inhaled or ingested/swallowed.
- Contact with substance may cause severe burns to skin and eyes.
- Fire will produce irritating, corrosive and/or toxic gases.
- Vapors may cause dizziness or suffocation.
- Runoff from fire control or dilution water may cause pollution.

PUBLIC SAFETY

- **CALL EMERGENCY RESPONSE Telephone Number on Shipping Paper first. If Shipping Paper not available or no answer, refer to appropriate telephone number listed on the inside back cover.**
- As an immediate precautionary measure, isolate spill or leak area for at least 50 meters (150 feet) in all directions.
- Keep unauthorized personnel away.
- Stay upwind.
- Keep out of low areas.
- Ventilate closed spaces before entering.

PROTECTIVE CLOTHING

- Wear positive pressure self-contained breathing apparatus (SCBA).
- Wear chemical protective clothing that is specifically recommended by the manufacturer. It may provide little or no thermal protection.
- Structural firefighters' protective clothing provides limited protection in fire situations ONLY; it is not effective in spill situations where direct contact with the substance is possible.

EVACUATION

Spill

- See Table 1 - Initial Isolation and Protective Action Distances for highlighted materials. For non-highlighted materials, increase, in the downwind direction, as necessary, the isolation distance shown under "PUBLIC SAFETY".

Fire

- If tank, rail car or tank truck is involved in a fire, ISOLATE for 800 meters (1/2 mile) in all directions; also, consider initial evacuation for 800 meters (1/2 mile) in all directions.

EMERGENCY RESPONSE

FIRE
- Some of these materials may react violently with water.

Small Fire
- Dry chemical, CO_2, water spray or alcohol-resistant foam.

Large Fire
- Water spray, fog or alcohol-resistant foam.
- Move containers from fire area if you can do it without risk.
- Dike fire-control water for later disposal; do not scatter the material.
- Do not get water inside containers.

Fire involving Tanks or Car/Trailer Loads
- Fight fire from maximum distance or use unmanned hose holders or monitor nozzles.
- Cool containers with flooding quantities of water until well after fire is out.
- Withdraw immediately in case of rising sound from venting safety devices or discoloration of tank.
- ALWAYS stay away from tanks engulfed in fire.
- For massive fire, use unmanned hose holders or monitor nozzles; if this is impossible, withdraw from area and let fire burn.

SPILL OR LEAK
- Fully encapsulating, vapor protective clothing should be worn for spills and leaks with no fire.
- ELIMINATE all ignition sources (no smoking, flares, sparks or flames in immediate area).
- All equipment used when handling the product must be grounded.
- Do not touch or walk through spilled material.
- Stop leak if you can do it without risk.
- Prevent entry into waterways, sewers, basements or confined areas.
- A vapor suppressing foam may be used to reduce vapors.
- Absorb with earth, sand or other non-combustible material and transfer to containers (except for Hydrazine).
- Use clean non-sparking tools to collect absorbed material.

Large Spill
- Dike far ahead of liquid spill for later disposal.
- Water spray may reduce vapor; but may not prevent ignition in closed spaces.

FIRST AID
- Move victim to fresh air. • Call 911 or emergency medical service.
- Give artificial respiration if victim is not breathing.
- **Do not use mouth-to-mouth method if victim ingested or inhaled the substance; give artificial respiration with the aid of a pocket mask equipped with a one-way valve or other proper respiratory medical device.**
- Administer oxygen if breathing is difficult.
- Remove and isolate contaminated clothing and shoes.
- In case of contact with substance, immediately flush skin or eyes with running water for at least 20 minutes.
- In case of burns, immediately cool affected skin for as long as possible with cold water. Do not remove clothing if adhering to skin.
- Keep victim warm and quiet.
- Effects of exposure (inhalation, ingestion or skin contact) to substance may be delayed.
- Ensure that medical personnel are aware of the material(s) involved and take precautions to protect themselves.

POTENTIAL HAZARDS

FIRE OR EXPLOSION
- Flammable/combustible material.
- May be ignited by friction, heat, sparks or flames.
- Some may burn rapidly with flare burning effect.
- Powders, dusts, shavings, borings, turnings or cuttings may explode or burn with explosive violence.
- Substance may be transported in a molten form at a temperature that may be above its flash point.
- May re-ignite after fire is extinguished.

HEALTH
- Fire may produce irritating and/or toxic gases.
- Contact may cause burns to skin and eyes.
- Contact with molten substance may cause severe burns to skin and eyes.
- Runoff from fire control may cause pollution.

PUBLIC SAFETY
- **CALL EMERGENCY RESPONSE Telephone Number on Shipping Paper first. If Shipping Paper not available or no answer, refer to appropriate telephone number listed on the inside back cover.**
- As an immediate precautionary measure, isolate spill or leak area for at least 25 meters (75 feet) in all directions.
- Keep unauthorized personnel away.
- Stay upwind.
- Keep out of low areas.

PROTECTIVE CLOTHING
- Wear positive pressure self-contained breathing apparatus (SCBA).
- Structural firefighters' protective clothing will only provide limited protection.

EVACUATION
Large Spill
- Consider initial downwind evacuation for at least 100 meters (330 feet).

Fire
- If tank, rail car or tank truck is involved in a fire, ISOLATE for 800 meters (1/2 mile) in all directions; also, consider initial evacuation for 800 meters (1/2 mile) in all directions.

EMERGENCY RESPONSE

FIRE

Small Fire
- Dry chemical, CO_2, sand, earth, water spray or regular foam.

Large Fire
- Water spray, fog or regular foam.
- Move containers from fire area if you can do it without risk.

Fire Involving Metal Pigments or Pastes (e.g. "Aluminum Paste")
- Aluminum Paste fires should be treated as a combustible metal fire. Use DRY sand, graphite powder, dry sodium chloride based extinguishers, G-1® or Met-L-X® powder. Also, see GUIDE 170.

Fire involving Tanks or Car/Trailer Loads
- Cool containers with flooding quantities of water until well after fire is out.
- For massive fire, use unmanned hose holders or monitor nozzles; if this is impossible, withdraw from area and let fire burn.
- Withdraw immediately in case of rising sound from venting safety devices or discoloration of tank.
- ALWAYS stay away from tanks engulfed in fire.

SPILL OR LEAK

- ELIMINATE all ignition sources (no smoking, flares, sparks or flames in immediate area).
- Do not touch or walk through spilled material.

Small Dry Spill
- With clean shovel place material into clean, dry container and cover loosely; move containers from spill area.

Large Spill
- Wet down with water and dike for later disposal.
- Prevent entry into waterways, sewers, basements or confined areas.

FIRST AID

- Move victim to fresh air.
- Call 911 or emergency medical service.
- Give artificial respiration if victim is not breathing.
- Administer oxygen if breathing is difficult.
- Remove and isolate contaminated clothing and shoes.
- In case of contact with substance, immediately flush skin or eyes with running water for at least 20 minutes.
- Removal of solidified molten material from skin requires medical assistance.
- Keep victim warm and quiet.
- Ensure that medical personnel are aware of the material(s) involved and take precautions to protect themselves.

POTENTIAL HAZARDS

FIRE OR EXPLOSION

- Flammable/combustible material.
- May be ignited by heat, sparks or flames.
- When heated, vapors may form explosive mixtures with air: indoors, outdoors and sewers explosion hazards.
- Contact with metals may evolve flammable hydrogen gas.
- Containers may explode when heated.

HEALTH

- **TOXIC;** inhalation, ingestion or skin contact with material may cause severe injury or death.
- Fire will produce irritating, corrosive and/or toxic gases.
- Runoff from fire control or dilution water may be corrosive and/or toxic and cause pollution.

PUBLIC SAFETY

- **CALL EMERGENCY RESPONSE Telephone Number on Shipping Paper first. If Shipping Paper not available or no answer, refer to appropriate telephone number listed on the inside back cover.**
- As an immediate precautionary measure, isolate spill or leak area for at least 25 meters (75 feet) in all directions.
- Stay upwind.
- Keep unauthorized personnel away.
- Keep out of low areas.
- Ventilate enclosed areas.

PROTECTIVE CLOTHING

- Wear positive pressure self-contained breathing apparatus (SCBA).
- Wear chemical protective clothing that is specifically recommended by the manufacturer. It may provide little or no thermal protection.
- Structural firefighters' protective clothing provides limited protection in fire situations ONLY; it is not effective in spill situations where direct contact with the substance is possible.

EVACUATION

Large Spill

- Consider initial downwind evacuation for at least 100 meters (330 feet).

Fire

- If tank, rail car or tank truck is involved in a fire, ISOLATE for 800 meters (1/2 mile) in all directions; also, consider initial evacuation for 800 meters (1/2 mile) in all directions.

EMERGENCY RESPONSE

FIRE
Small Fire
- Dry chemical, CO_2, water spray or alcohol-resistant foam.

Large Fire
- Water spray, fog or alcohol-resistant foam.
- Move containers from fire area if you can do it without risk.
- Use water spray or fog; do not use straight streams.
- Do not get water inside containers.
- Dike fire-control water for later disposal; do not scatter the material.

Fire involving Tanks or Car/Trailer Loads
- Fight fire from maximum distance or use unmanned hose holders or monitor nozzles.
- Cool containers with flooding quantities of water until well after fire is out.
- Withdraw immediately in case of rising sound from venting safety devices or discoloration of tank.
- ALWAYS stay away from tanks engulfed in fire.

SPILL OR LEAK
- Fully encapsulating, vapor protective clothing should be worn for spills and leaks with no fire.
- ELIMINATE all ignition sources (no smoking, flares, sparks or flames in immediate area).
- Stop leak if you can do it without risk.
- Do not touch damaged containers or spilled material unless wearing appropriate protective clothing.
- Prevent entry into waterways, sewers, basements or confined areas.
- Use clean non-sparking tools to collect material and place it into loosely covered plastic containers for later disposal.

FIRST AID
- Move victim to fresh air.
- Call 911 or emergency medical service.
- Give artificial respiration if victim is not breathing.
- **Do not use mouth-to-mouth method if victim ingested or inhaled the substance; give artificial respiration with the aid of a pocket mask equipped with a one-way valve or other proper respiratory medical device.**
- Administer oxygen if breathing is difficult.
- Remove and isolate contaminated clothing and shoes.
- In case of contact with substance, immediately flush skin or eyes with running water for at least 20 minutes.
- For minor skin contact, avoid spreading material on unaffected skin.
- Keep victim warm and quiet.
- Effects of exposure (inhalation, ingestion or skin contact) to substance may be delayed.
- Ensure that medical personnel are aware of the material(s) involved and take precautions to protect themselves.

POTENTIAL HAZARDS

FIRE OR EXPLOSION
- Flammable/combustible material.
- May ignite on contact with moist air or moisture.
- May burn rapidly with flare-burning effect.
- Some react vigorously or explosively on contact with water.
- Some may decompose explosively when heated or involved in a fire.
- May re-ignite after fire is extinguished.
- Runoff may create fire or explosion hazard.
- Containers may explode when heated.

HEALTH
- Fire will produce irritating, corrosive and/or toxic gases.
- Inhalation of decomposition products may cause severe injury or death.
- Contact with substance may cause severe burns to skin and eyes.
- Runoff from fire control may cause pollution.

PUBLIC SAFETY
- **CALL EMERGENCY RESPONSE Telephone Number on Shipping Paper first. If Shipping Paper not available or no answer, refer to appropriate telephone number listed on the inside back cover.**
- As an immediate precautionary measure, isolate spill or leak area in all directions for at least 50 meters (150 feet) for liquids and at least 25 meters (75 feet) for solids.
- Stay upwind.
- Keep unauthorized personnel away.
- Keep out of low areas.

PROTECTIVE CLOTHING
- Wear positive pressure self-contained breathing apparatus (SCBA).
- Wear chemical protective clothing that is specifically recommended by the manufacturer. It may provide little or no thermal protection.
- Structural firefighters' protective clothing will only provide limited protection.

EVACUATION
Spill
- See Table 1 - Initial Isolation and Protective Action Distances for highlighted materials. For non-highlighted materials, increase, in the downwind direction, as necessary, the isolation distance shown under "PUBLIC SAFETY".

Fire
- If tank, rail car or tank truck is involved in a fire, ISOLATE for 800 meters (1/2 mile) in all directions; also, consider initial evacuation for 800 meters (1/2 mile) in all directions.

EMERGENCY RESPONSE

FIRE

- **DO NOT USE WATER, CO_2 OR FOAM ON MATERIAL ITSELF.**
- Some of these materials may react violently with water.

EXCEPTION: For Xanthates, UN3342 and for Dithionite (Hydrosulfite/Hydrosulphite) UN1384, UN1923 and UN1929, USE FLOODING AMOUNTS OF WATER for SMALL AND LARGE fires to stop the reaction. Smothering will not work for these materials, they do not need air to burn.

Small Fire
- Dry chemical, soda ash, lime or DRY sand, **EXCEPT for UN1384, UN1923, UN1929 and UN3342.**

Large Fire
- DRY sand, dry chemical, soda ash or lime **EXCEPT for UN1384, UN1923, UN1929 and UN3342**, or withdraw from area and let fire burn.
- **CAUTION**: UN3342 when flooded with water will continue to evolve flammable Carbon disulfide/Carbon disulphide vapors.
- Move containers from fire area if you can do it without risk.

Fire involving Tanks or Car/Trailer Loads
- Fight fire from maximum distance or use unmanned hose holders or monitor nozzles.
- Do not get water inside containers or in contact with substance.
- Cool containers with flooding quantities of water until well after fire is out.
- Withdraw immediately in case of rising sound from venting safety devices or discoloration of tank.
- ALWAYS stay away from tanks engulfed in fire.

SPILL OR LEAK

- Fully encapsulating, vapor protective clothing should be worn for spills and leaks with no fire.
- ELIMINATE all ignition sources (no smoking, flares, sparks or flames in immediate area).
- Do not touch or walk through spilled material.
- Stop leak if you can do it without risk.

Small Spill

EXCEPTION: For spills of Xanthates, UN3342 and for Dithionite (Hydrosulfite/Hydrosulphite), UN1384, UN1923 and UN1929, dissolve in 5 parts water and collect for proper disposal.
- **CAUTION**: UN3342 when flooded with water will continue to evolve flammable Carbon disulfide/Carbon disulphide vapors.
- Cover with DRY earth, DRY sand or other non-combustible material followed with plastic sheet to minimize spreading or contact with rain.
- Use clean non-sparking tools to collect material and place it into loosely covered plastic containers for later disposal.
- Prevent entry into waterways, sewers, basements or confined areas.

FIRST AID

- Move victim to fresh air.
- Call 911 or emergency medical service.
- Give artificial respiration if victim is not breathing.
- Administer oxygen if breathing is difficult.
- Remove and isolate contaminated clothing and shoes.
- In case of contact with substance, immediately flush skin or eyes with running water for at least 20 minutes.
- Keep victim warm and quiet.
- Ensure that medical personnel are aware of the material(s) involved and take precautions to protect themselves.

POTENTIAL HAZARDS

FIRE OR EXPLOSION

- Extremely flammable; will ignite itself if exposed to air.
- Burns rapidly, releasing dense, white, irritating fumes.
- Substance may be transported in a molten form.
- May re-ignite after fire is extinguished.
- Corrosive substances in contact with metals may produce flammable hydrogen gas.
- Containers may explode when heated.

HEALTH

- Fire will produce irritating, corrosive and/or toxic gases.
- **TOXIC**; ingestion of substance or inhalation of decomposition products will cause severe injury or death.
- Contact with substance may cause severe burns to skin and eyes.
- Some effects may be experienced due to skin absorption.
- Runoff from fire control may be corrosive and/or toxic and cause pollution.

PUBLIC SAFETY

- **CALL EMERGENCY RESPONSE Telephone Number on Shipping Paper first. If Shipping Paper not available or no answer, refer to appropriate telephone number listed on the inside back cover.**
- As an immediate precautionary measure, isolate spill or leak area in all directions for at least 50 meters (150 feet) for liquids and at least 25 meters (75 feet) for solids.
- Stay upwind.
- Keep unauthorized personnel away.
- Keep out of low areas.

PROTECTIVE CLOTHING

- Wear positive pressure self-contained breathing apparatus (SCBA).
- Wear chemical protective clothing that is specifically recommended by the manufacturer. It may provide little or no thermal protection.
- Structural firefighters' protective clothing provides limited protection in fire situations ONLY; it is not effective in spill situations where direct contact with the substance is possible.
- **For Phosphorus (UN1381): Special aluminized protective clothing should be worn when direct contact with the substance is possible.**

EVACUATION

Spill

- Consider initial downwind evacuation for at least 300 meters (1000 feet).

Fire

- If tank, rail car or tank truck is involved in a fire, ISOLATE for 800 meters (1/2 mile) in all directions; also, consider initial evacuation for 800 meters (1/2 mile) in all directions.

EMERGENCY RESPONSE

FIRE

Small Fire
- Water spray, wet sand or wet earth.

Large Fire
- Water spray or fog.

Do not scatter spilled material with high pressure water streams.
- Move containers from fire area if you can do it without risk.

Fire involving Tanks or Car/Trailer Loads
- Fight fire from maximum distance or use unmanned hose holders or monitor nozzles.
- Cool containers with flooding quantities of water until well after fire is out.
- Withdraw immediately in case of rising sound from venting safety devices or discoloration of tank.
- ALWAYS stay away from tanks engulfed in fire.

SPILL OR LEAK

- Fully encapsulating, vapor protective clothing should be worn for spills and leaks with no fire.
- ELIMINATE all ignition sources (no smoking, flares, sparks or flames in immediate area).
- Do not touch or walk through spilled material.
- Do not touch damaged containers or spilled material unless wearing appropriate protective clothing.
- Stop leak if you can do it without risk.

Small Spill
- Cover with water, sand or earth. Shovel into metal container and keep material under water.

Large Spill
- Dike for later disposal and cover with wet sand or earth.
- Prevent entry into waterways, sewers, basements or confined areas.

FIRST AID

- Move victim to fresh air.
- Call 911 or emergency medical service.
- Give artificial respiration if victim is not breathing.
- Administer oxygen if breathing is difficult.
- In case of contact with substance, keep exposed skin areas immersed in water or covered with wet bandages until medical attention is received.
- Removal of solidified molten material from skin requires medical assistance.
- Remove and isolate contaminated clothing and shoes at the site and place in metal container filled with water. Fire hazard if allowed to dry.
- Effects of exposure (inhalation, ingestion or skin contact) to substance may be delayed.
- Keep victim warm and quiet.
- Ensure that medical personnel are aware of the material(s) involved and take precautions to protect themselves.

POTENTIAL HAZARDS

HEALTH

- CORROSIVE and/or TOXIC; inhalation, ingestion or contact (skin, eyes) with vapors, dusts or substance may cause severe injury, burns or death.
- Fire will produce irritating, corrosive and/or toxic gases.
- Reaction with water may generate much heat that will increase the concentration of fumes in the air.
- Contact with molten substance may cause severe burns to skin and eyes.
- Runoff from fire control or dilution water may cause pollution.

FIRE OR EXPLOSION

- **EXCEPT FOR ACETIC ANHYDRIDE (UN1715), THAT IS FLAMMABLE,** some of these materials may burn, but none ignite readily.
- May ignite combustibles (wood, paper, oil, clothing, etc.).
- Substance will react with water (some violently), releasing corrosive and/or toxic gases and runoff.
- Flammable/toxic gases may accumulate in confined areas (basement, tanks, hopper/tank cars, etc.).
- Contact with metals may evolve flammable hydrogen gas.
- Containers may explode when heated or if contaminated with water.
- Substance may be transported in a molten form.

PUBLIC SAFETY

- **CALL EMERGENCY RESPONSE Telephone Number on Shipping Paper first. If Shipping Paper not available or no answer, refer to appropriate telephone number listed on the inside back cover.**
- As an immediate precautionary measure, isolate spill or leak area in all directions for at least 50 meters (150 feet) for liquids and at least 25 meters (75 feet) for solids.
- Keep unauthorized personnel away.
- Stay upwind.
- Keep out of low areas.
- Ventilate enclosed areas.

PROTECTIVE CLOTHING

- Wear positive pressure self-contained breathing apparatus (SCBA).
- Wear chemical protective clothing that is specifically recommended by the manufacturer. It may provide little or no thermal protection.
- Structural firefighters' protective clothing provides limited protection in fire situations ONLY; it is not effective in spill situations where direct contact with the substance is possible.

EVACUATION

Spill

- See Table 1 - Initial Isolation and Protective Action Distances for highlighted materials. For non-highlighted materials, increase, in the downwind direction, as necessary, the isolation distance shown under "PUBLIC SAFETY".

Fire

- If tank, rail car or tank truck is involved in a fire, ISOLATE for 800 meters (1/2 mile) in all directions; also, consider initial evacuation for 800 meters (1/2 mile) in all directions.

EMERGENCY RESPONSE

FIRE
- When material is not involved in fire, do not use water on material itself.

Small Fire
- Dry chemical or CO_2.
- Move containers from fire area if you can do it without risk.

Large Fire
- Flood fire area with large quantities of water, while knocking down vapors with water fog. If insufficient water supply: knock down vapors only.

Fire involving Tanks or Car/Trailer Loads
- Cool containers with flooding quantities of water until well after fire is out.
- Do not get water inside containers.
- Withdraw immediately in case of rising sound from venting safety devices or discoloration of tank.
- ALWAYS stay away from tanks engulfed in fire.

SPILL OR LEAK
- Fully encapsulating, vapor protective clothing should be worn for spills and leaks with no fire.
- Do not touch damaged containers or spilled material unless wearing appropriate protective clothing.
- Stop leak if you can do it without risk.
- Use water spray to reduce vapors; do not put water directly on leak, spill area or inside container.
- Keep combustibles (wood, paper, oil, etc.) away from spilled material.

Small Spill
- Cover with DRY earth, DRY sand or other non-combustible material followed with plastic sheet to minimize spreading or contact with rain.
- Use clean non-sparking tools to collect material and place it into loosely covered plastic containers for later disposal.
- Prevent entry into waterways, sewers, basements or confined areas.

FIRST AID
- Move victim to fresh air.
- Call 911 or emergency medical service.
- Give artificial respiration if victim is not breathing.
- **Do not use mouth-to-mouth method if victim ingested or inhaled the substance; give artificial respiration with the aid of a pocket mask equipped with a one-way valve or other proper respiratory medical device.**
- Administer oxygen if breathing is difficult.
- Remove and isolate contaminated clothing and shoes.
- In case of contact with substance, immediately flush skin or eyes with running water for at least 20 minutes.
- For minor skin contact, avoid spreading material on unaffected skin.
- Removal of solidified molten material from skin requires medical assistance.
- Keep victim warm and quiet.
- Effects of exposure (inhalation, ingestion or skin contact) to substance may be delayed.
- Ensure that medical personnel are aware of the material(s) involved and take precautions to protect themselves.

POTENTIAL HAZARDS

FIRE OR EXPLOSION

- Produce flammable gases on contact with water.
- May ignite on contact with water or moist air.
- Some react vigorously or explosively on contact with water.
- May be ignited by heat, sparks or flames.
- May re-ignite after fire is extinguished.
- Some are transported in highly flammable liquids.
- Runoff may create fire or explosion hazard.

HEALTH

- Inhalation or contact with vapors, substance or decomposition products may cause severe injury or death.
- May produce corrosive solutions on contact with water.
- Fire will produce irritating, corrosive and/or toxic gases.
- Runoff from fire control may cause pollution.

PUBLIC SAFETY

- **CALL EMERGENCY RESPONSE Telephone Number on Shipping Paper first. If Shipping Paper not available or no answer, refer to appropriate telephone number listed on the inside back cover.**
- As an immediate precautionary measure, isolate spill or leak area in all directions for at least 50 meters (150 feet) for liquids and at least 25 meters (75 feet) for solids.
- Keep unauthorized personnel away.
- Stay upwind.
- Keep out of low areas.
- Ventilate the area before entry.

PROTECTIVE CLOTHING

- Wear positive pressure self-contained breathing apparatus (SCBA).
- Wear chemical protective clothing that is specifically recommended by the manufacturer. It may provide little or no thermal protection.
- Structural firefighters' protective clothing provides limited protection in fire situations ONLY; it is not effective in spill situations where direct contact with the substance is possible.

EVACUATION

Spill

- See Table 1 - Initial Isolation and Protective Action Distances for highlighted materials. For non-highlighted materials, increase, in the downwind direction, as necessary, the isolation distance shown under "PUBLIC SAFETY".

Fire

- If tank, rail car or tank truck is involved in a fire, ISOLATE for 800 meters (1/2 mile) in all directions; also, consider initial evacuation for 800 meters (1/2 mile) in all directions.

EMERGENCY RESPONSE

FIRE
- **DO NOT USE WATER OR FOAM.**

Small Fire
- Dry chemical, soda ash, lime or sand.

Large Fire
- DRY sand, dry chemical, soda ash or lime or withdraw from area and let fire burn.
- Move containers from fire area if you can do it without risk.

Fire Involving Metals or Powders (Aluminum, Lithium, Magnesium, etc.)
- Use dry chemical, DRY sand, sodium chloride powder, graphite powder or Met-L-X® powder; in addition, for Lithium you may use Lith-X® powder or copper powder.
  Also, see GUIDE 170.

Fire involving Tanks or Car/Trailer Loads
- Fight fire from maximum distance or use unmanned hose holders or monitor nozzles.
- Do not get water inside containers.
- Cool containers with flooding quantities of water until well after fire is out.
- Withdraw immediately in case of rising sound from venting safety devices or discoloration of tank.
- ALWAYS stay away from tanks engulfed in fire.

SPILL OR LEAK
- ELIMINATE all ignition sources (no smoking, flares, sparks or flames in immediate area).
- Do not touch or walk through spilled material.
- Stop leak if you can do it without risk.
- Use water spray to reduce vapors or divert vapor cloud drift. Avoid allowing water runoff to contact spilled material.

DO NOT GET WATER on spilled substance or inside containers.

Small Spill
- Cover with DRY earth, DRY sand or other non-combustible material followed with plastic sheet to minimize spreading or contact with rain.
- Dike for later disposal; do not apply water unless directed to do so.

Powder Spill
- Cover powder spill with plastic sheet or tarp to minimize spreading and keep powder dry.
- **DO NOT CLEAN-UP OR DISPOSE OF, EXCEPT UNDER SUPERVISION OF A SPECIALIST.**

FIRST AID
- Move victim to fresh air.
- Call 911 or emergency medical service.
- Give artificial respiration if victim is not breathing.
- Administer oxygen if breathing is difficult.
- Remove and isolate contaminated clothing and shoes.
- In case of contact with substance, wipe from skin immediately; flush skin or eyes with running water for at least 20 minutes.
- Keep victim warm and quiet.
- Ensure that medical personnel are aware of the material(s) involved and take precautions to protect themselves.

POTENTIAL HAZARDS

FIRE OR EXPLOSION

- Produce flammable and toxic gases on contact with water.
- May ignite on contact with water or moist air.
- Some react vigorously or explosively on contact with water.
- May be ignited by heat, sparks or flames.
- May re-ignite after fire is extinguished.
- Some are transported in highly flammable liquids.
- Containers may explode when heated.
- Runoff may create fire or explosion hazard.

HEALTH

- Highly toxic: contact with water produces toxic gas, may be fatal if inhaled.
- Inhalation or contact with vapors, substance or decomposition products may cause severe injury or death.
- May produce corrosive solutions on contact with water.
- Fire will produce irritating, corrosive and/or toxic gases.
- Runoff from fire control may cause pollution.

PUBLIC SAFETY

- **CALL EMERGENCY RESPONSE Telephone Number on Shipping Paper first. If Shipping Paper not available or no answer, refer to appropriate telephone number listed on the inside back cover.**
- As an immediate precautionary measure, isolate spill or leak area in all directions for at least 50 meters (150 feet) for liquids and at least 25 meters (75 feet) for solids.
- Keep unauthorized personnel away.
- Stay upwind.
- Keep out of low areas.
- Ventilate the area before entry.

PROTECTIVE CLOTHING

- Wear positive pressure self-contained breathing apparatus (SCBA).
- Wear chemical protective clothing that is specifically recommended by the manufacturer. It may provide little or no thermal protection.
- Structural firefighters' protective clothing provides limited protection in fire situations ONLY; it is not effective in spill situations where direct contact with the substance is possible.

EVACUATION

Spill
- See Table 1 - Initial Isolation and Protective Action Distances for highlighted materials. For non-highlighted materials, increase, in the downwind direction, as necessary, the isolation distance shown under "PUBLIC SAFETY".

Fire
- If tank, rail car or tank truck is involved in a fire, ISOLATE for 800 meters (1/2 mile) in all directions; also, consider initial evacuation for 800 meters (1/2 mile) in all directions.

EMERGENCY RESPONSE

FIRE
- **DO NOT USE WATER OR FOAM. (FOAM MAY BE USED FOR CHLOROSILANES, SEE BELOW)**

Small Fire
- Dry chemical, soda ash, lime or sand.

Large Fire
- DRY sand, dry chemical, soda ash or lime or withdraw from area and let fire burn.
- **FOR CHLOROSILANES, DO NOT USE WATER**; use AFFF alcohol-resistant medium expansion foam; **DO NOT USE** dry chemicals, soda ash or lime on chlorosilane fires (large or small) as they may release large quantities of hydrogen gas that may explode.
- Move containers from fire area if you can do it without risk.

Fire involving Tanks or Car/Trailer Loads
- Fight fire from maximum distance or use unmanned hose holders or monitor nozzles.
- Cool containers with flooding quantities of water until well after fire is out.
- Do not get water inside containers.
- Withdraw immediately in case of rising sound from venting safety devices or discoloration of tank.
- ALWAYS stay away from tanks engulfed in fire.

SPILL OR LEAK
- Fully encapsulating, vapor protective clothing should be worn for spills and leaks with no fire.
- ELIMINATE all ignition sources (no smoking, flares, sparks or flames in immediate area).
- Do not touch or walk through spilled material.
- Stop leak if you can do it without risk.
- **DO NOT GET WATER on spilled substance or inside containers.**
- Use water spray to reduce vapors or divert vapor cloud drift. Avoid allowing water runoff to contact spilled material.
- **FOR CHLOROSILANES,** use AFFF alcohol-resistant medium expansion foam to reduce vapors.

Small Spill
- Cover with DRY earth, DRY sand or other non-combustible material followed with plastic sheet to minimize spreading or contact with rain.
- Dike for later disposal; do not apply water unless directed to do so.

Powder Spill
- Cover powder spill with plastic sheet or tarp to minimize spreading and keep powder dry.
- **DO NOT CLEAN-UP OR DISPOSE OF, EXCEPT UNDER SUPERVISION OF A SPECIALIST.**

FIRST AID
- Move victim to fresh air.
- Call 911 or emergency medical service.
- Give artificial respiration if victim is not breathing.
- **Do not use mouth-to-mouth method if victim ingested or inhaled the substance; give artificial respiration with the aid of a pocket mask equipped with a one-way valve or other proper respiratory medical device.**
- Administer oxygen if breathing is difficult.
- Remove and isolate contaminated clothing and shoes.
- In case of contact with substance, wipe from skin immediately; flush skin or eyes with running water for at least 20 minutes.
- Keep victim warm and quiet.
- Ensure that medical personnel are aware of the material(s) involved and take precautions to protect themselves.

POTENTIAL HAZARDS

FIRE OR EXPLOSION

- These substances will accelerate burning when involved in a fire.
- Some may decompose explosively when heated or involved in a fire.
- May explode from heat or contamination.
- Some will react explosively with hydrocarbons (fuels).
- May ignite combustibles (wood, paper, oil, clothing, etc.).
- Containers may explode when heated.
- Runoff may create fire or explosion hazard.

HEALTH

- Inhalation, ingestion or contact (skin, eyes) with vapors or substance may cause severe injury, burns or death.
- Fire may produce irritating, corrosive and/or toxic gases.
- Runoff from fire control or dilution water may cause pollution.

PUBLIC SAFETY

- **CALL EMERGENCY RESPONSE Telephone Number on Shipping Paper first. If Shipping Paper not available or no answer, refer to appropriate telephone number listed on the inside back cover.**
- As an immediate precautionary measure, isolate spill or leak area in all directions for at least 50 meters (150 feet) for liquids and at least 25 meters (75 feet) for solids.
- Keep unauthorized personnel away.
- Stay upwind.
- Keep out of low areas.
- Ventilate closed spaces before entering.

PROTECTIVE CLOTHING

- Wear positive pressure self-contained breathing apparatus (SCBA).
- Wear chemical protective clothing that is specifically recommended by the manufacturer. It may provide little or no thermal protection.
- Structural firefighters' protective clothing will only provide limited protection.

EVACUATION

Large Spill

- Consider initial downwind evacuation for at least 100 meters (330 feet).

Fire

- If tank, rail car or tank truck is involved in a fire, ISOLATE for 800 meters (1/2 mile) in all directions; also, consider initial evacuation for 800 meters (1/2 mile) in all directions.

EMERGENCY RESPONSE

FIRE

Small Fire
- Use water. Do not use dry chemicals or foams. CO_2 or Halon® may provide limited control.

Large Fire
- Flood fire area with water from a distance.
- Do not move cargo or vehicle if cargo has been exposed to heat.
- Move containers from fire area if you can do it without risk.

Fire involving Tanks or Car/Trailer Loads
- Fight fire from maximum distance or use unmanned hose holders or monitor nozzles.
- Cool containers with flooding quantities of water until well after fire is out.
- ALWAYS stay away from tanks engulfed in fire.
- For massive fire, use unmanned hose holders or monitor nozzles; if this is impossible, withdraw from area and let fire burn.

SPILL OR LEAK

- Keep combustibles (wood, paper, oil, etc.) away from spilled material.
- Do not touch damaged containers or spilled material unless wearing appropriate protective clothing.
- Stop leak if you can do it without risk.
- Do not get water inside containers.

Small Dry Spill
- With clean shovel place material into clean, dry container and cover loosely; move containers from spill area.

Small Liquid Spill
- Use a non-combustible material like vermiculite or sand to soak up the product and place into a container for later disposal.

Large Spill
- Dike far ahead of liquid spill for later disposal.
- **Following product recovery, flush area with water.**

FIRST AID

- Move victim to fresh air.
- Call 911 or emergency medical service.
- Give artificial respiration if victim is not breathing.
- Administer oxygen if breathing is difficult.
- Remove and isolate contaminated clothing and shoes.
- Contaminated clothing may be a fire risk when dry.
- In case of contact with substance, immediately flush skin or eyes with running water for at least 20 minutes.
- Keep victim warm and quiet.
- Ensure that medical personnel are aware of the material(s) involved and take precautions to protect themselves.

POTENTIAL HAZARDS

FIRE OR EXPLOSION
- These substances will accelerate burning when involved in a fire.
- May explode from heat or contamination.
- Some may burn rapidly.
- Some will react explosively with hydrocarbons (fuels).
- May ignite combustibles (wood, paper, oil, clothing, etc.).
- Containers may explode when heated.
- Runoff may create fire or explosion hazard.

HEALTH
- Toxic by ingestion.
- Inhalation of dust is toxic.
- Fire may produce irritating, corrosive and/or toxic gases.
- Contact with substance may cause severe burns to skin and eyes.
- Runoff from fire control or dilution water may cause pollution.

PUBLIC SAFETY
- **CALL EMERGENCY RESPONSE Telephone Number on Shipping Paper first. If Shipping Paper not available or no answer, refer to appropriate telephone number listed on the inside back cover.**
- As an immediate precautionary measure, isolate spill or leak area in all directions for at least 50 meters (150 feet) for liquids and at least 25 meters (75 feet) for solids.
- Keep unauthorized personnel away.
- Stay upwind.
- Keep out of low areas.
- Ventilate closed spaces before entering.

PROTECTIVE CLOTHING
- Wear positive pressure self-contained breathing apparatus (SCBA).
- Wear chemical protective clothing that is specifically recommended by the manufacturer. It may provide little or no thermal protection.
- Structural firefighters' protective clothing will only provide limited protection.

EVACUATION
Large Spill
- Consider initial downwind evacuation for at least 100 meters (330 feet).

Fire
- If tank, rail car or tank truck is involved in a fire, ISOLATE for 800 meters (1/2 mile) in all directions; also, consider initial evacuation for 800 meters (1/2 mile) in all directions.

EMERGENCY RESPONSE

FIRE
Small Fire
- Use water. Do not use dry chemicals or foams. CO_2 or Halon® may provide limited control.

Large Fire
- Flood fire area with water from a distance.
- Do not move cargo or vehicle if cargo has been exposed to heat.
- Move containers from fire area if you can do it without risk.

Fire involving Tanks or Car/Trailer Loads
- Fight fire from maximum distance or use unmanned hose holders or monitor nozzles.
- Cool containers with flooding quantities of water until well after fire is out.
- ALWAYS stay away from tanks engulfed in fire.
- For massive fire, use unmanned hose holders or monitor nozzles; if this is impossible, withdraw from area and let fire burn.

SPILL OR LEAK
- Keep combustibles (wood, paper, oil, etc.) away from spilled material.
- Do not touch damaged containers or spilled material unless wearing appropriate protective clothing.
- Stop leak if you can do it without risk.

Small Dry Spill
- With clean shovel place material into clean, dry container and cover loosely; move containers from spill area.

Large Spill
- Dike far ahead of spill for later disposal.

FIRST AID
- Move victim to fresh air.
- Call 911 or emergency medical service.
- Give artificial respiration if victim is not breathing.
- Administer oxygen if breathing is difficult.
- Remove and isolate contaminated clothing and shoes.
- Contaminated clothing may be a fire risk when dry.
- In case of contact with substance, immediately flush skin or eyes with running water for at least 20 minutes.
- Keep victim warm and quiet.
- Ensure that medical personnel are aware of the material(s) involved and take precautions to protect themselves.

POTENTIAL HAZARDS

FIRE OR EXPLOSION

- These substances will accelerate burning when involved in a fire.
- May explode from heat or contamination.
- Some will react explosively with hydrocarbons (fuels).
- May ignite combustibles (wood, paper, oil, clothing, etc.).
- Containers may explode when heated.
- Runoff may create fire or explosion hazard.

HEALTH

- **TOXIC;** inhalation, ingestion or contact (skin, eyes) with vapors or substance may cause severe injury, burns or death.
- Fire may produce irritating, corrosive and/or toxic gases.
- Toxic/flammable fumes may accumulate in confined areas (basement, tanks, tank cars, etc.).
- Runoff from fire control or dilution water may cause pollution.

PUBLIC SAFETY

- **CALL EMERGENCY RESPONSE Telephone Number on Shipping Paper first. If Shipping Paper not available or no answer, refer to appropriate telephone number listed on the inside back cover.**
- As an immediate precautionary measure, isolate spill or leak area for at least 50 meters (150 feet) in all directions.
- Keep unauthorized personnel away.
- Stay upwind.
- Keep out of low areas.
- Ventilate closed spaces before entering.

PROTECTIVE CLOTHING

- Wear positive pressure self-contained breathing apparatus (SCBA).
- Wear chemical protective clothing that is specifically recommended by the manufacturer. It may provide little or no thermal protection.
- Structural firefighters' protective clothing provides limited protection in fire situations ONLY; it is not effective in spill situations where direct contact with the substance is possible.

EVACUATION

Spill

- See Table 1 - Initial Isolation and Protective Action Distances for highlighted materials. For non-highlighted materials, increase, in the downwind direction, as necessary, the isolation distance shown under "PUBLIC SAFETY".

Fire

- If tank, rail car or tank truck is involved in a fire, ISOLATE for 800 meters (1/2 mile) in all directions; also, consider initial evacuation for 800 meters (1/2 mile) in all directions.

EMERGENCY RESPONSE

FIRE

Small Fire
- Use water. Do not use dry chemicals or foams. CO_2 or Halon® may provide limited control.

Large Fire
- Flood fire area with water from a distance.
- Do not move cargo or vehicle if cargo has been exposed to heat.
- Move containers from fire area if you can do it without risk.

Fire involving Tanks or Car/Trailer Loads
- Fight fire from maximum distance or use unmanned hose holders or monitor nozzles.
- Cool containers with flooding quantities of water until well after fire is out.
- ALWAYS stay away from tanks engulfed in fire.
- For massive fire, use unmanned hose holders or monitor nozzles; if this is impossible, withdraw from area and let fire burn.

SPILL OR LEAK

- Keep combustibles (wood, paper, oil, etc.) away from spilled material.
- Fully encapsulating, vapor protective clothing should be worn for spills and leaks with no fire.
- Do not touch damaged containers or spilled material unless wearing appropriate protective clothing.
- Stop leak if you can do it without risk.
- Use water spray to reduce vapors or divert vapor cloud drift.
- Do not get water inside containers.

Small Liquid Spill
- Use a non-combustible material like vermiculite or sand to soak up the product and place into a container for later disposal.

Large Spill
- Dike far ahead of liquid spill for later disposal.

FIRST AID

- Move victim to fresh air.
- Call 911 or emergency medical service.
- Give artificial respiration if victim is not breathing.
- **Do not use mouth-to-mouth method if victim ingested or inhaled the substance; give artificial respiration with the aid of a pocket mask equipped with a one-way valve or other proper respiratory medical device.**
- Administer oxygen if breathing is difficult.
- Remove and isolate contaminated clothing and shoes.
- Contaminated clothing may be a fire risk when dry.
- In case of contact with substance, immediately flush skin or eyes with running water for at least 20 minutes.
- Keep victim warm and quiet.
- Ensure that medical personnel are aware of the material(s) involved and take precautions to protect themselves.

POTENTIAL HAZARDS

FIRE OR EXPLOSION

- May explode from friction, heat or contamination.
- These substances will accelerate burning when involved in a fire.
- May ignite combustibles (wood, paper, oil, clothing, etc.).
- Some will react explosively with hydrocarbons (fuels).
- Containers may explode when heated.
- Runoff may create fire or explosion hazard.

HEALTH

- **TOXIC;** inhalation, ingestion or contact (skin, eyes) with vapors, dusts or substance may cause severe injury, burns or death.
- Fire may produce irritating and/or toxic gases.
- Toxic fumes or dust may accumulate in confined areas (basement, tanks, hopper/tank cars, etc.).
- Runoff from fire control or dilution water may cause pollution.

PUBLIC SAFETY

- **CALL EMERGENCY RESPONSE Telephone Number on Shipping Paper first. If Shipping Paper not available or no answer, refer to appropriate telephone number listed on the inside back cover.**
- As an immediate precautionary measure, isolate spill or leak area in all directions for at least 50 meters (150 feet) for liquids and at least 25 meters (75 feet) for solids.
- Keep unauthorized personnel away.
- Stay upwind.
- Keep out of low areas.
- Ventilate closed spaces before entering.

PROTECTIVE CLOTHING

- Wear positive pressure self-contained breathing apparatus (SCBA).
- Wear chemical protective clothing that is specifically recommended by the manufacturer. It may provide little or no thermal protection.
- Structural firefighters' protective clothing provides limited protection in fire situations ONLY; it is not effective in spill situations where direct contact with the substance is possible.

EVACUATION

Spill

- See Table 1 - Initial Isolation and Protective Action Distances for highlighted materials. For non-highlighted materials, increase, in the downwind direction, as necessary, the isolation distance shown under "PUBLIC SAFETY".

Fire

- If tank, rail car or tank truck is involved in a fire, ISOLATE for 800 meters (1/2 mile) in all directions; also, consider initial evacuation for 800 meters (1/2 mile) in all directions.

EMERGENCY RESPONSE

FIRE

Small Fire
- Use water. Do not use dry chemicals or foams. CO_2 or Halon® may provide limited control.

Large Fire
- Flood fire area with water from a distance.
- Do not move cargo or vehicle if cargo has been exposed to heat.
- Move containers from fire area if you can do it without risk.
- Do not get water inside containers: a violent reaction may occur.

Fire involving Tanks or Car/Trailer Loads
- Cool containers with flooding quantities of water until well after fire is out.
- Dike fire-control water for later disposal.
- ALWAYS stay away from tanks engulfed in fire.
- For massive fire, use unmanned hose holders or monitor nozzles; if this is impossible, withdraw from area and let fire burn.

SPILL OR LEAK
- Keep combustibles (wood, paper, oil, etc.) away from spilled material.
- Do not touch damaged containers or spilled material unless wearing appropriate protective clothing.
- Use water spray to reduce vapors or divert vapor cloud drift.
- Prevent entry into waterways, sewers, basements or confined areas.

Small Spill
- Flush area with flooding quantities of water.

Large Spill
- **DO NOT CLEAN-UP OR DISPOSE OF, EXCEPT UNDER SUPERVISION OF A SPECIALIST.**

FIRST AID
- Move victim to fresh air.
- Call 911 or emergency medical service.
- Give artificial respiration if victim is not breathing.
- Administer oxygen if breathing is difficult.
- Remove and isolate contaminated clothing and shoes.
- Contaminated clothing may be a fire risk when dry.
- In case of contact with substance, immediately flush skin or eyes with running water for at least 20 minutes.
- Keep victim warm and quiet.
- Ensure that medical personnel are aware of the material(s) involved and take precautions to protect themselves.

POTENTIAL HAZARDS

FIRE OR EXPLOSION

- May ignite combustibles (wood, paper, oil, clothing, etc.).
- React vigorously and/or explosively with water.
- Produce toxic and/or corrosive substances on contact with water.
- Flammable/toxic gases may accumulate in tanks and hopper cars.
- Some may produce flammable hydrogen gas upon contact with metals.
- Containers may explode when heated.
- Runoff may create fire or explosion hazard.

HEALTH

- **TOXIC;** inhalation or contact with vapor, substance, or decomposition products may cause severe injury or death.
- Fire will produce irritating, corrosive and/or toxic gases.
- Runoff from fire control or dilution water may cause pollution.

PUBLIC SAFETY

- **CALL EMERGENCY RESPONSE Telephone Number on Shipping Paper first. If Shipping Paper not available or no answer, refer to appropriate telephone number listed on the inside back cover.**
- As an immediate precautionary measure, isolate spill or leak area in all directions for at least 50 meters (150 feet) for liquids and at least 25 meters (75 feet) for solids.
- Keep unauthorized personnel away.
- Stay upwind.
- Keep out of low areas.
- Ventilate closed spaces before entering.

PROTECTIVE CLOTHING

- Wear positive pressure self-contained breathing apparatus (SCBA).
- Wear chemical protective clothing that is specifically recommended by the manufacturer. It may provide little or no thermal protection.
- Structural firefighters' protective clothing provides limited protection in fire situations ONLY; it is not effective in spill situations where direct contact with the substance is possible.

EVACUATION

Spill

- See Table 1 - Initial Isolation and Protective Action Distances for highlighted materials. For non-highlighted materials, increase, in the downwind direction, as necessary, the isolation distance shown under "PUBLIC SAFETY".

Fire

- If tank, rail car or tank truck is involved in a fire, ISOLATE for 800 meters (1/2 mile) in all directions; also, consider initial evacuation for 800 meters (1/2 mile) in all directions.

EMERGENCY RESPONSE

FIRE

- **DO NOT USE WATER OR FOAM.**

Small Fire
- Dry chemical, soda ash or lime.

Large Fire
- DRY sand, dry chemical, soda ash or lime or withdraw from area and let fire burn.
- Do not move cargo or vehicle if cargo has been exposed to heat.
- Move containers from fire area if you can do it without risk.

Fire involving Tanks or Car/Trailer Loads
- Fight fire from maximum distance or use unmanned hose holders or monitor nozzles.
- Cool containers with flooding quantities of water until well after fire is out.
- Withdraw immediately in case of rising sound from venting safety devices or discoloration of tank.
- ALWAYS stay away from tanks engulfed in fire.

SPILL OR LEAK

- ELIMINATE all ignition sources (no smoking, flares, sparks or flames in immediate area).
- Do not touch damaged containers or spilled material unless wearing appropriate protective clothing.
- Stop leak if you can do it without risk.
- Use water spray to reduce vapors or divert vapor cloud drift. Avoid allowing water runoff to contact spilled material.
- **DO NOT GET WATER on spilled substance or inside containers.**

Small Spill
- Cover with DRY earth, DRY sand or other non-combustible material followed with plastic sheet to minimize spreading or contact with rain.

Large Spill
- **DO NOT CLEAN-UP OR DISPOSE OF, EXCEPT UNDER SUPERVISION OF A SPECIALIST.**

FIRST AID

- Move victim to fresh air.
- Call 911 or emergency medical service.
- Give artificial respiration if victim is not breathing.
- **Do not use mouth-to-mouth method if victim ingested or inhaled the substance; give artificial respiration with the aid of a pocket mask equipped with a one-way valve or other proper respiratory medical device.**
- Administer oxygen if breathing is difficult.
- Remove and isolate contaminated clothing and shoes.
- Contaminated clothing may be a fire risk when dry.
- In case of contact with substance, immediately flush skin or eyes with running water for at least 20 minutes.
- Keep victim warm and quiet.
- Keep victim under observation.
- Effects of contact or inhalation may be delayed.
- Ensure that medical personnel are aware of the material(s) involved and take precautions to protect themselves.

POTENTIAL HAZARDS

FIRE OR EXPLOSION

- May explode from heat or contamination.
- May ignite combustibles (wood, paper, oil, clothing, etc.).
- May be ignited by heat, sparks or flames.
- May burn rapidly with flare-burning effect.
- Containers may explode when heated.
- Runoff may create fire or explosion hazard.

HEALTH

- Fire may produce irritating, corrosive and/or toxic gases.
- Ingestion or contact (skin, eyes) with substance may cause severe injury or burns.
- Runoff from fire control or dilution water may cause pollution.

PUBLIC SAFETY

- **CALL EMERGENCY RESPONSE Telephone Number on Shipping Paper first. If Shipping Paper not available or no answer, refer to appropriate telephone number listed on the inside back cover.**
- As an immediate precautionary measure, isolate spill or leak area in all directions for at least 50 meters (150 feet) for liquids and at least 25 meters (75 feet) for solids.
- Keep unauthorized personnel away.
- Stay upwind.
- Keep out of low areas.

PROTECTIVE CLOTHING

- Wear positive pressure self-contained breathing apparatus (SCBA).
- Wear chemical protective clothing that is specifically recommended by the manufacturer. It may provide little or no thermal protection.
- Structural firefighters' protective clothing will only provide limited protection.

EVACUATION

Large Spill
- Consider initial evacuation for at least 250 meters (800 feet) in all directions.

Fire
- If tank, rail car or tank truck is involved in a fire, ISOLATE for 800 meters (1/2 mile) in all directions; also, consider initial evacuation for 800 meters (1/2 mile) in all directions.

EMERGENCY RESPONSE

FIRE

Small Fire
- Water spray or fog is preferred; if water not available use dry chemical, CO_2 or regular foam.

Large Fire
- Flood fire area with water from a distance.
- Use water spray or fog; do not use straight streams.
- Do not move cargo or vehicle if cargo has been exposed to heat.
- Move containers from fire area if you can do it without risk.

Fire involving Tanks or Car/Trailer Loads
- Fight fire from maximum distance or use unmanned hose holders or monitor nozzles.
- Cool containers with flooding quantities of water until well after fire is out.
- ALWAYS stay away from tanks engulfed in fire.
- For massive fire, use unmanned hose holders or monitor nozzles; if this is impossible, withdraw from area and let fire burn.

SPILL OR LEAK
- ELIMINATE all ignition sources (no smoking, flares, sparks or flames in immediate area).
- Keep combustibles (wood, paper, oil, etc.) away from spilled material.
- Do not touch damaged containers or spilled material unless wearing appropriate protective clothing.
- Keep substance wet using water spray.
- Stop leak if you can do it without risk.

Small Spill
- Take up with inert, damp, non-combustible material using clean non-sparking tools and place into loosely covered plastic containers for later disposal.

Large Spill
- Wet down with water and dike for later disposal.
- Prevent entry into waterways, sewers, basements or confined areas.
- **DO NOT CLEAN-UP OR DISPOSE OF, EXCEPT UNDER SUPERVISION OF A SPECIALIST.**

FIRST AID
- Move victim to fresh air.
- Call 911 or emergency medical service.
- Give artificial respiration if victim is not breathing.
- Administer oxygen if breathing is difficult.
- Remove and isolate contaminated clothing and shoes.
- Contaminated clothing may be a fire risk when dry.
- Remove material from skin immediately.
- In case of contact with substance, immediately flush skin or eyes with running water for at least 20 minutes.
- Keep victim warm and quiet.
- Ensure that medical personnel are aware of the material(s) involved and take precautions to protect themselves.

POTENTIAL HAZARDS

FIRE OR EXPLOSION
- May explode from heat, shock, friction or contamination.
- May ignite combustibles (wood, paper, oil, clothing, etc.).
- May be ignited by heat, sparks or flames.
- May burn rapidly with flare-burning effect.
- Containers may explode when heated.
- Runoff may create fire or explosion hazard.

HEALTH
- Fire may produce irritating, corrosive and/or toxic gases.
- Ingestion or contact (skin, eyes) with substance may cause severe injury or burns.
- Runoff from fire control or dilution water may cause pollution.

PUBLIC SAFETY
- **CALL EMERGENCY RESPONSE Telephone Number on Shipping Paper first. If Shipping Paper not available or no answer, refer to appropriate telephone number listed on the inside back cover.**
- As an immediate precautionary measure, isolate spill or leak area in all directions for at least 50 meters (150 feet) for liquids and at least 25 meters (75 feet) for solids.
- Keep unauthorized personnel away.
- Stay upwind.
- Keep out of low areas.

PROTECTIVE CLOTHING
- Wear positive pressure self-contained breathing apparatus (SCBA).
- Wear chemical protective clothing that is specifically recommended by the manufacturer. It may provide little or no thermal protection.
- Structural firefighters' protective clothing will only provide limited protection.

EVACUATION
Large Spill
- Consider initial evacuation for at least 250 meters (800 feet) in all directions.

Fire
- If tank, rail car or tank truck is involved in a fire, ISOLATE for 800 meters (1/2 mile) in all directions; also, consider initial evacuation for 800 meters (1/2 mile) in all directions.

EMERGENCY RESPONSE

FIRE
Small Fire
- Water spray or fog is preferred; if water not available use dry chemical, CO_2 or regular foam.

Large Fire
- Flood fire area with water from a distance.
- Use water spray or fog; do not use straight streams.
- Do not move cargo or vehicle if cargo has been exposed to heat.
- Move containers from fire area if you can do it without risk.

Fire involving Tanks or Car/Trailer Loads
- Fight fire from maximum distance or use unmanned hose holders or monitor nozzles.
- Cool containers with flooding quantities of water until well after fire is out.
- ALWAYS stay away from tanks engulfed in fire.
- For massive fire, use unmanned hose holders or monitor nozzles; if this is impossible, withdraw from area and let fire burn.

SPILL OR LEAK
- ELIMINATE all ignition sources (no smoking, flares, sparks or flames in immediate area).
- Keep combustibles (wood, paper, oil, etc.) away from spilled material.
- Do not touch damaged containers or spilled material unless wearing appropriate protective clothing.
- Keep substance wet using water spray.
- Stop leak if you can do it without risk.

Small Spill
- Take up with inert, damp, non-combustible material using clean non-sparking tools and place into loosely covered plastic containers for later disposal.

Large Spill
- Wet down with water and dike for later disposal.
- Prevent entry into waterways, sewers, basements or confined areas.
- **DO NOT CLEAN-UP OR DISPOSE OF, EXCEPT UNDER SUPERVISION OF A SPECIALIST.**

FIRST AID
- Move victim to fresh air.
- Call 911 or emergency medical service.
- Give artificial respiration if victim is not breathing.
- Administer oxygen if breathing is difficult.
- Remove and isolate contaminated clothing and shoes.
- Contaminated clothing may be a fire risk when dry.
- Remove material from skin immediately.
- In case of contact with substance, immediately flush skin or eyes with running water for at least 20 minutes.
- Keep victim warm and quiet.
- Ensure that medical personnel are aware of the material(s) involved and take precautions to protect themselves.

POTENTIAL HAZARDS

FIRE OR EXPLOSION

- Lithium ion batteries contain flammable liquid electrolyte that may vent, ignite and produce sparks when subjected to high temperatures (> 150 ^{0}C (302 ^{0}F)), when damaged or abused (e.g., mechanical damage or electrical overcharging).
- May burn rapidly with flare-burning effect.
- May ignite other batteries in close proximity.

HEALTH

- Contact with battery electrolyte may be irritating to skin, eyes and mucous membranes.
- Fire will produce irritating, corrosive and/or toxic gases.
- Burning batteries may produce toxic hydrogen fluoride gas (see GUIDE 125).
- Fumes may cause dizziness or suffocation.

PUBLIC SAFETY

- **CALL Emergency Response Telephone Number on Shipping Paper first. If Shipping Paper not available or no answer, refer to appropriate telephone number listed on the inside back cover.**
- As an immediate precautionary measure, isolate spill or leak area for at least 25 meters (75 feet) in all directions.
- Keep unauthorized personnel away.
- Stay upwind.
- Keep out of low areas.
- Ventilate closed spaces before entering.

PROTECTIVE CLOTHING

- Wear positive pressure self-contained breathing apparatus (SCBA).
- Structural firefighters' protective clothing will only provide limited protection.

EVACUATION

Large Spill
- Consider initial downwind evacuation for at least 100 meters (330 feet).

Fire
- If rail car or trailer is involved in a fire, ISOLATE for 500 meters (1/3 mile) in all directions; also initiate evacuation including emergency responders for 500 meters (1/3 mile) in all directions.

EMERGENCY RESPONSE

FIRE

Small Fire
- Dry chemical, CO_2, water spray or regular foam.

Large Fire
- Water spray, fog or regular foam.
- Move containers from fire area if you can do it without risk.

SPILL OR LEAK
- ELIMINATE all ignition sources (no smoking, flares, sparks or flames in immediate area).
- Do not touch or walk through spilled material.
- Absorb with earth, sand or other non-combustible material.
- Leaking batteries and contaminated absorbent material should be placed in metal containers.

FIRST AID
- Move victim to fresh air.
- Call 911 or emergency medical service.
- Give artificial respiration if victim is not breathing.
- Administer oxygen if breathing is difficult.
- Remove and isolate contaminated clothing and shoes.
- In case of contact with substance, immediately flush skin or eyes with running water for at least 20 minutes.
- Ensure that medical personnel are aware of the material(s) involved and take precautions to protect themselves.

POTENTIAL HAZARDS

FIRE OR EXPLOSION

- May explode from heat, contamination or loss of temperature control.
- These materials are particularly sensitive to temperature rises. Above a given "Control Temperature" they decompose violently and catch fire.
- May ignite combustibles (wood, paper, oil, clothing, etc.).
- May ignite spontaneously if exposed to air.
- May be ignited by heat, sparks or flames.
- May burn rapidly with flare-burning effect.
- Containers may explode when heated.
- Runoff may create fire or explosion hazard.

HEALTH

- Fire may produce irritating, corrosive and/or toxic gases.
- Ingestion or contact (skin, eyes) with substance may cause severe injury or burns.
- Runoff from fire control or dilution water may cause pollution.

PUBLIC SAFETY

- **CALL EMERGENCY RESPONSE Telephone Number on Shipping Paper first. If Shipping Paper not available or no answer, refer to appropriate telephone number listed on the inside back cover.**
- As an immediate precautionary measure, isolate spill or leak area in all directions for at least 50 meters (150 feet) for liquids and at least 25 meters (75 feet) for solids.
- Keep unauthorized personnel away.
- Stay upwind.
- Keep out of low areas.
- **DO NOT allow the substance to warm up. Obtain liquid nitrogen (wear thermal protective clothing, see GUIDE 120), dry ice or ice for cooling. If this is not possible or none can be obtained, evacuate the area immediately.**

PROTECTIVE CLOTHING

- Wear positive pressure self-contained breathing apparatus (SCBA).
- Wear chemical protective clothing that is specifically recommended by the manufacturer. It may provide little or no thermal protection.
- Structural firefighters' protective clothing will only provide limited protection.

EVACUATION

Large Spill
- Consider initial evacuation for at least 250 meters (800 feet) in all directions.

Fire
- If tank, rail car or tank truck is involved in a fire, ISOLATE for 800 meters (1/2 mile) in all directions; also, consider initial evacuation for 800 meters (1/2 mile) in all directions.

EMERGENCY RESPONSE

FIRE
- The temperature of the substance must be maintained at or below the "Control Temperature" at all times.

Small Fire
- Water spray or fog is preferred; if water not available use dry chemical, CO_2 or regular foam.

Large Fire
- Flood fire area with water from a distance.
- Use water spray or fog; do not use straight streams.
- Do not move cargo or vehicle if cargo has been exposed to heat.
- Move containers from fire area if you can do it without risk.

Fire involving Tanks or Car/Trailer Loads
- Fight fire from maximum distance or use unmanned hose holders or monitor nozzles.
- Cool containers with flooding quantities of water until well after fire is out.
- **BEWARE OF POSSIBLE CONTAINER EXPLOSION.**
- ALWAYS stay away from tanks engulfed in fire.
- For massive fire, use unmanned hose holders or monitor nozzles; if this is impossible, withdraw from area and let fire burn.

SPILL OR LEAK
- ELIMINATE all ignition sources (no smoking, flares, sparks or flames in immediate area).
- Keep combustibles (wood, paper, oil, etc.) away from spilled material.
- Do not touch or walk through spilled material.
- Stop leak if you can do it without risk.

Small Spill
- Take up with inert, damp, non-combustible material using clean non-sparking tools and place into loosely covered plastic containers for later disposal.

Large Spill
- Dike far ahead of liquid spill for later disposal.
- Prevent entry into waterways, sewers, basements or confined areas.
- **DO NOT CLEAN-UP OR DISPOSE OF, EXCEPT UNDER SUPERVISION OF A SPECIALIST.**

FIRST AID
- Move victim to fresh air.
- Call 911 or emergency medical service.
- Give artificial respiration if victim is not breathing.
- Administer oxygen if breathing is difficult.
- Remove and isolate contaminated clothing and shoes.
- Contaminated clothing may be a fire risk when dry.
- Remove material from skin immediately.
- In case of contact with substance, immediately flush skin or eyes with running water for at least 20 minutes.
- Keep victim warm and quiet.
- Ensure that medical personnel are aware of the material(s) involved and take precautions to protect themselves.

POTENTIAL HAZARDS

FIRE OR EXPLOSION

- **Self-decomposition or self-ignition may be triggered by heat, chemical reaction, friction or impact.**
- May be ignited by heat, sparks or flames.
- Some may decompose explosively when heated or involved in a fire.
- May burn violently. Decomposition may be self-accelerating and produce large amounts of gases.
- Vapors or dust may form explosive mixtures with air.

HEALTH

- Inhalation or contact with vapors, substance or decomposition products may cause severe injury or death.
- May produce irritating, toxic and/or corrosive gases.
- Runoff from fire control may cause pollution.

PUBLIC SAFETY

- **CALL EMERGENCY RESPONSE Telephone Number on Shipping Paper first. If Shipping Paper not available or no answer, refer to appropriate telephone number listed on the inside back cover.**
- As an immediate precautionary measure, isolate spill or leak area in all directions for at least 50 meters (150 feet) for liquids and at least 25 meters (75 feet) for solids.
- Keep unauthorized personnel away.
- Stay upwind.
- Keep out of low areas.

PROTECTIVE CLOTHING

- Wear positive pressure self-contained breathing apparatus (SCBA).
- Wear chemical protective clothing that is specifically recommended by the manufacturer. It may provide little or no thermal protection.
- Structural firefighters' protective clothing will only provide limited protection.

EVACUATION

Large Spill

- Consider initial downwind evacuation for at least 250 meters (800 feet) in all directions.

Fire

- If tank, rail car or tank truck is involved in a fire, ISOLATE for 800 meters (1/2 mile) in all directions; also, consider initial evacuation for 800 meters (1/2 mile) in all directions.

EMERGENCY RESPONSE

FIRE

Small Fire
- Dry chemical, CO_2, water spray or regular foam.

Large Fire
- Flood fire area with water from a distance.
- Move containers from fire area if you can do it without risk.

Fire involving Tanks or Car/Trailer Loads
- **BEWARE OF POSSIBLE CONTAINER EXPLOSION.**
- Fight fire from maximum distance or use unmanned hose holders or monitor nozzles.
- Cool containers with flooding quantities of water until well after fire is out.
- Withdraw immediately in case of rising sound from venting safety devices or discoloration of tank.
- ALWAYS stay away from tanks engulfed in fire.

SPILL OR LEAK

- ELIMINATE all ignition sources (no smoking, flares, sparks or flames in immediate area).
- Do not touch or walk through spilled material.
- Stop leak if you can do it without risk.

Small Spill
- Take up with inert, damp, non-combustible material using clean non-sparking tools and place into loosely covered plastic containers for later disposal.
- Prevent entry into waterways, sewers, basements or confined areas.

FIRST AID

- Move victim to fresh air.
- Call 911 or emergency medical service.
- Give artificial respiration if victim is not breathing.
- Administer oxygen if breathing is difficult.
- Remove and isolate contaminated clothing and shoes.
- In case of contact with substance, immediately flush skin or eyes with running water for at least 20 minutes.
- Keep victim warm and quiet.
- Ensure that medical personnel are aware of the material(s) involved and take precautions to protect themselves.

POTENTIAL HAZARDS

FIRE OR EXPLOSION

- **Self-decomposition or self-ignition may be triggered by heat, chemical reaction, friction or impact.**
- Self-accelerating decomposition may occur if the specific control temperature is not maintained.
- These materials are particularly sensitive to temperature rises. Above a given "Control Temperature" they decompose violently and catch fire.
- May be ignited by heat, sparks or flames.
- Some may decompose explosively when heated or involved in a fire.
- May burn violently. Decomposition may be self-accelerating and produce large amounts of gases.
- Vapors or dust may form explosive mixtures with air.

HEALTH

- Inhalation or contact with vapors, substance or decomposition products may cause severe injury or death.
- May produce irritating, toxic and/or corrosive gases.
- Runoff from fire control may cause pollution.

PUBLIC SAFETY

- **CALL EMERGENCY RESPONSE Telephone Number on Shipping Paper first. If Shipping Paper not available or no answer, refer to appropriate telephone number listed on the inside back cover.**
- As an immediate precautionary measure, isolate spill or leak area in all directions for at least 50 meters (150 feet) for liquids and at least 25 meters (75 feet) for solids.
- Keep unauthorized personnel away.
- Stay upwind.
- Keep out of low areas.
- **DO NOT allow the substance to warm up. Obtain liquid nitrogen (wear thermal protective clothing, see GUIDE 120), dry ice or ice for cooling. If this is not possible or none can be obtained, evacuate the area immediately.**

PROTECTIVE CLOTHING

- Wear positive pressure self-contained breathing apparatus (SCBA).
- Wear chemical protective clothing that is specifically recommended by the manufacturer. It may provide little or no thermal protection.
- Structural firefighters' protective clothing will only provide limited protection.

EVACUATION

Large Spill
- Consider initial evacuation for at least 250 meters (800 feet) in all directions.

Fire
- If tank, rail car or tank truck is involved in a fire, ISOLATE for 800 meters (1/2 mile) in all directions; also, consider initial evacuation for 800 meters (1/2 mile) in all directions.

EMERGENCY RESPONSE

FIRE

- The temperature of the substance must be maintained at or below the "Control Temperature" at all times.

Small Fire

- Dry chemical, CO_2, water spray or regular foam.

Large Fire

- Flood fire area with water from a distance.
- Move containers from fire area if you can do it without risk.

Fire involving Tanks or Car/Trailer Loads

- **BEWARE OF POSSIBLE CONTAINER EXPLOSION.**
- Fight fire from maximum distance or use unmanned hose holders or monitor nozzles.
- Cool containers with flooding quantities of water until well after fire is out.
- Withdraw immediately in case of rising sound from venting safety devices or discoloration of tank.
- ALWAYS stay away from tanks engulfed in fire.

SPILL OR LEAK

- ELIMINATE all ignition sources (no smoking, flares, sparks or flames in immediate area).
- Do not touch or walk through spilled material.
- Stop leak if you can do it without risk.

Small Spill

- Take up with inert, damp, non-combustible material using clean non-sparking tools and place into loosely covered plastic containers for later disposal.
- Prevent entry into waterways, sewers, basements or confined areas.
- **DO NOT CLEAN-UP OR DISPOSE OF, EXCEPT UNDER SUPERVISION OF A SPECIALIST.**

FIRST AID

- Move victim to fresh air.
- Call 911 or emergency medical service.
- Give artificial respiration if victim is not breathing.
- Administer oxygen if breathing is difficult.
- Remove and isolate contaminated clothing and shoes.
- In case of contact with substance, immediately flush skin or eyes with running water for at least 20 minutes.
- Keep victim warm and quiet.
- Ensure that medical personnel are aware of the material(s) involved and take precautions to protect themselves.

POTENTIAL HAZARDS

HEALTH

- **Highly toxic**, may be fatal if inhaled, swallowed or absorbed through skin.
- Avoid any skin contact.
- Effects of contact or inhalation may be delayed.
- Fire may produce irritating, corrosive and/or toxic gases.
- Runoff from fire control or dilution water may be corrosive and/or toxic and cause pollution.

FIRE OR EXPLOSION

- Non-combustible, substance itself does not burn but may decompose upon heating to produce corrosive and/or toxic fumes.
- Containers may explode when heated.
- Runoff may pollute waterways.

PUBLIC SAFETY

- **CALL EMERGENCY RESPONSE Telephone Number on Shipping Paper first. If Shipping Paper not available or no answer, refer to appropriate telephone number listed on the inside back cover.**
- As an immediate precautionary measure, isolate spill or leak area in all directions for at least 50 meters (150 feet) for liquids and at least 25 meters (75 feet) for solids.
- Keep unauthorized personnel away.
- Stay upwind.
- Keep out of low areas.

PROTECTIVE CLOTHING

- Wear positive pressure self-contained breathing apparatus (SCBA).
- Wear chemical protective clothing that is specifically recommended by the manufacturer. It may provide little or no thermal protection.
- Structural firefighters' protective clothing provides limited protection in fire situations ONLY; it is not effective in spill situations where direct contact with the substance is possible.

EVACUATION

Spill

- See Table 1 - Initial Isolation and Protective Action Distances for highlighted materials. For non-highlighted materials, increase, in the downwind direction, as necessary, the isolation distance shown under "PUBLIC SAFETY".

Fire

- If tank, rail car or tank truck is involved in a fire, ISOLATE for 800 meters (1/2 mile) in all directions; also, consider initial evacuation for 800 meters (1/2 mile) in all directions.

EMERGENCY RESPONSE

FIRE

Small Fire
- Dry chemical, CO_2 or water spray.

Large Fire
- Water spray, fog or regular foam.
- Move containers from fire area if you can do it without risk.
- Dike fire-control water for later disposal; do not scatter the material.
- Use water spray or fog; do not use straight streams.

Fire involving Tanks or Car/Trailer Loads
- Fight fire from maximum distance or use unmanned hose holders or monitor nozzles.
- Do not get water inside containers.
- Cool containers with flooding quantities of water until well after fire is out.
- Withdraw immediately in case of rising sound from venting safety devices or discoloration of tank.
- ALWAYS stay away from tanks engulfed in fire.
- For massive fire, use unmanned hose holders or monitor nozzles; if this is impossible, withdraw from area and let fire burn.

SPILL OR LEAK

- Do not touch damaged containers or spilled material unless wearing appropriate protective clothing.
- Stop leak if you can do it without risk.
- Prevent entry into waterways, sewers, basements or confined areas.
- Cover with plastic sheet to prevent spreading.
- Absorb or cover with dry earth, sand or other non-combustible material and transfer to containers.
- DO NOT GET WATER INSIDE CONTAINERS.

FIRST AID

- Move victim to fresh air.
- Call 911 or emergency medical service.
- Give artificial respiration if victim is not breathing.
- **Do not use mouth-to-mouth method if victim ingested or inhaled the substance; give artificial respiration with the aid of a pocket mask equipped with a one-way valve or other proper respiratory medical device.**
- Administer oxygen if breathing is difficult.
- Remove and isolate contaminated clothing and shoes.
- In case of contact with substance, immediately flush skin or eyes with running water for at least 20 minutes.
- For minor skin contact, avoid spreading material on unaffected skin.
- Keep victim warm and quiet.
- Effects of exposure (inhalation, ingestion or skin contact) to substance may be delayed.
- Ensure that medical personnel are aware of the material(s) involved and take precautions to protect themselves.

POTENTIAL HAZARDS

HEALTH

- **Highly toxic,** may be fatal if inhaled, swallowed or absorbed through skin.
- Contact with molten substance may cause severe burns to skin and eyes.
- Avoid any skin contact.
- Effects of contact or inhalation may be delayed.
- Fire may produce irritating, corrosive and/or toxic gases.
- Runoff from fire control or dilution water may be corrosive and/or toxic and cause pollution.

FIRE OR EXPLOSION

- Combustible material: may burn but does not ignite readily.
- Containers may explode when heated.
- Runoff may pollute waterways.
- Substance may be transported in a molten form.

PUBLIC SAFETY

- **CALL EMERGENCY RESPONSE Telephone Number on Shipping Paper first. If Shipping Paper not available or no answer, refer to appropriate telephone number listed on the inside back cover.**
- As an immediate precautionary measure, isolate spill or leak area in all directions for at least 50 meters (150 feet) for liquids and at least 25 meters (75 feet) for solids.
- Keep unauthorized personnel away.
- Stay upwind.
- Keep out of low areas.

PROTECTIVE CLOTHING

- Wear positive pressure self-contained breathing apparatus (SCBA).
- Wear chemical protective clothing that is specifically recommended by the manufacturer. It may provide little or no thermal protection.
- Structural firefighters' protective clothing provides limited protection in fire situations ONLY; it is not effective in spill situations where direct contact with the substance is possible.

EVACUATION

Spill

- See Table 1 - Initial Isolation and Protective Action Distances for highlighted materials. For non-highlighted materials, increase, in the downwind direction, as necessary, the isolation distance shown under "PUBLIC SAFETY".

Fire

- If tank, rail car or tank truck is involved in a fire, ISOLATE for 800 meters (1/2 mile) in all directions; also, consider initial evacuation for 800 meters (1/2 mile) in all directions.

GUIDE
152

SUBSTANCES - TOXIC (COMBUSTIBLE)

EMERGENCY RESPONSE

FIRE

Small Fire
- Dry chemical, CO_2 or water spray.

Large Fire
- Water spray, fog or regular foam.
- Move containers from fire area if you can do it without risk.
- Dike fire-control water for later disposal; do not scatter the material.
- Use water spray or fog; do not use straight streams.

Fire involving Tanks or Car/Trailer Loads
- Fight fire from maximum distance or use unmanned hose holders or monitor nozzles.
- Do not get water inside containers.
- Cool containers with flooding quantities of water until well after fire is out.
- Withdraw immediately in case of rising sound from venting safety devices or discoloration of tank.
- ALWAYS stay away from tanks engulfed in fire.
- For massive fire, use unmanned hose holders or monitor nozzles; if this is impossible, withdraw from area and let fire burn.

SPILL OR LEAK
- ELIMINATE all ignition sources (no smoking, flares, sparks or flames in immediate area).
- Do not touch damaged containers or spilled material unless wearing appropriate protective clothing.
- Stop leak if you can do it without risk.
- Prevent entry into waterways, sewers, basements or confined areas.
- Cover with plastic sheet to prevent spreading.
- Absorb or cover with dry earth, sand or other non-combustible material and transfer to containers.
- DO NOT GET WATER INSIDE CONTAINERS.

FIRST AID
- Move victim to fresh air.
- Call 911 or emergency medical service.
- Give artificial respiration if victim is not breathing.
- **Do not use mouth-to-mouth method if victim ingested or inhaled the substance; give artificial respiration with the aid of a pocket mask equipped with a one-way valve or other proper respiratory medical device.**
- Administer oxygen if breathing is difficult.
- Remove and isolate contaminated clothing and shoes.
- In case of contact with substance, immediately flush skin or eyes with running water for at least 20 minutes.
- For minor skin contact, avoid spreading material on unaffected skin.
- Keep victim warm and quiet.
- Effects of exposure (inhalation, ingestion or skin contact) to substance may be delayed.
- Ensure that medical personnel are aware of the material(s) involved and take precautions to protect themselves.

POTENTIAL HAZARDS

HEALTH

- **TOXIC**; inhalation, ingestion or skin contact with material may cause severe injury or death.
- Contact with molten substance may cause severe burns to skin and eyes.
- Avoid any skin contact.
- Effects of contact or inhalation may be delayed.
- Fire may produce irritating, corrosive and/or toxic gases.
- Runoff from fire control or dilution water may be corrosive and/or toxic and cause pollution.

FIRE OR EXPLOSION

- Combustible material: may burn but does not ignite readily.
- When heated, vapors may form explosive mixtures with air: indoors, outdoors and sewers explosion hazards.
- Those substances designated with a **(P)** may polymerize explosively when heated or involved in a fire.
- Contact with metals may evolve flammable hydrogen gas.
- Containers may explode when heated.
- Runoff may pollute waterways.
- Substance may be transported in a molten form.

PUBLIC SAFETY

- **CALL EMERGENCY RESPONSE Telephone Number on Shipping Paper first. If Shipping Paper not available or no answer, refer to appropriate telephone number listed on the inside back cover.**
- As an immediate precautionary measure, isolate spill or leak area in all directions for at least 50 meters (150 feet) for liquids and at least 25 meters (75 feet) for solids.
- Keep unauthorized personnel away.
- Stay upwind.
- Keep out of low areas.
- Ventilate enclosed areas.

PROTECTIVE CLOTHING

- Wear positive pressure self-contained breathing apparatus (SCBA).
- Wear chemical protective clothing that is specifically recommended by the manufacturer. It may provide little or no thermal protection.
- Structural firefighters' protective clothing provides limited protection in fire situations ONLY; it is not effective in spill situations where direct contact with the substance is possible.

EVACUATION

Spill

- See Table 1 - Initial Isolation and Protective Action Distances for highlighted materials. For non-highlighted materials, increase, in the downwind direction, as necessary, the isolation distance shown under "PUBLIC SAFETY".

Fire

- If tank, rail car or tank truck is involved in a fire, ISOLATE for 800 meters (1/2 mile) in all directions; also, consider initial evacuation for 800 meters (1/2 mile) in all directions.

EMERGENCY RESPONSE

FIRE

Small Fire

- Dry chemical, CO_2 or water spray.

Large Fire

- Dry chemical, CO_2, alcohol-resistant foam or water spray.
- Move containers from fire area if you can do it without risk.
- Dike fire-control water for later disposal; do not scatter the material.

Fire involving Tanks or Car/Trailer Loads

- Fight fire from maximum distance or use unmanned hose holders or monitor nozzles.
- Do not get water inside containers.
- Cool containers with flooding quantities of water until well after fire is out.
- Withdraw immediately in case of rising sound from venting safety devices or discoloration of tank.
- ALWAYS stay away from tanks engulfed in fire.

SPILL OR LEAK

- ELIMINATE all ignition sources (no smoking, flares, sparks or flames in immediate area).
- Do not touch damaged containers or spilled material unless wearing appropriate protective clothing.
- Stop leak if you can do it without risk.
- Prevent entry into waterways, sewers, basements or confined areas.
- Absorb or cover with dry earth, sand or other non-combustible material and transfer to containers.
- DO NOT GET WATER INSIDE CONTAINERS.

FIRST AID

- Move victim to fresh air.
- Call 911 or emergency medical service.
- Give artificial respiration if victim is not breathing.
- **Do not use mouth-to-mouth method if victim ingested or inhaled the substance; give artificial respiration with the aid of a pocket mask equipped with a one-way valve or other proper respiratory medical device.**
- Administer oxygen if breathing is difficult.
- Remove and isolate contaminated clothing and shoes.
- In case of contact with substance, immediately flush skin or eyes with running water for at least 20 minutes.
- For minor skin contact, avoid spreading material on unaffected skin.
- Keep victim warm and quiet.
- Effects of exposure (inhalation, ingestion or skin contact) to substance may be delayed.
- Ensure that medical personnel are aware of the material(s) involved and take precautions to protect themselves.

POTENTIAL HAZARDS

HEALTH

- **TOXIC**; inhalation, ingestion or skin contact with material may cause severe injury or death.
- Contact with molten substance may cause severe burns to skin and eyes.
- Avoid any skin contact.
- Effects of contact or inhalation may be delayed.
- Fire may produce irritating, corrosive and/or toxic gases.
- Runoff from fire control or dilution water may be corrosive and/or toxic and cause pollution.

FIRE OR EXPLOSION

- Non-combustible, substance itself does not burn but may decompose upon heating to produce corrosive and/or toxic fumes.
- Some are oxidizers and may ignite combustibles (wood, paper, oil, clothing, etc.).
- Contact with metals may evolve flammable hydrogen gas.
- Containers may explode when heated.
- For UN3171, if Lithium ion batteries are involved, also consult GUIDE 147.

PUBLIC SAFETY

- **CALL EMERGENCY RESPONSE Telephone Number on Shipping Paper first. If Shipping Paper not available or no answer, refer to appropriate telephone number listed on the inside back cover.**
- As an immediate precautionary measure, isolate spill or leak area in all directions for at least 50 meters (150 feet) for liquids and at least 25 meters (75 feet) for solids.
- Keep unauthorized personnel away.
- Stay upwind.
- Keep out of low areas.
- Ventilate enclosed areas.

PROTECTIVE CLOTHING

- Wear positive pressure self-contained breathing apparatus (SCBA).
- Wear chemical protective clothing that is specifically recommended by the manufacturer. It may provide little or no thermal protection.
- Structural firefighters' protective clothing provides limited protection in fire situations ONLY; it is not effective in spill situations where direct contact with the substance is possible.

EVACUATION

Spill

- See Table 1 - Initial Isolation and Protective Action Distances for highlighted materials. For non-highlighted materials, increase, in the downwind direction, as necessary, the isolation distance shown under "PUBLIC SAFETY".

Fire

- If tank, rail car or tank truck is involved in a fire, ISOLATE for 800 meters (1/2 mile) in all directions; also, consider initial evacuation for 800 meters (1/2 mile) in all directions.

ERG2012

SUBSTANCES - TOXIC AND/OR CORROSIVE (NON-COMBUSTIBLE)

GUIDE 154

EMERGENCY RESPONSE

FIRE

Small Fire
- Dry chemical, CO_2 or water spray.

Large Fire
- Dry chemical, CO_2, alcohol-resistant foam or water spray.
- Move containers from fire area if you can do it without risk.
- Dike fire-control water for later disposal; do not scatter the material.

Fire involving Tanks or Car/Trailer Loads
- Fight fire from maximum distance or use unmanned hose holders or monitor nozzles.
- Do not get water inside containers.
- Cool containers with flooding quantities of water until well after fire is out.
- Withdraw immediately in case of rising sound from venting safety devices or discoloration of tank.
- ALWAYS stay away from tanks engulfed in fire.

SPILL OR LEAK
- ELIMINATE all ignition sources (no smoking, flares, sparks or flames in immediate area).
- Do not touch damaged containers or spilled material unless wearing appropriate protective clothing.
- Stop leak if you can do it without risk.
- Prevent entry into waterways, sewers, basements or confined areas.
- Absorb or cover with dry earth, sand or other non-combustible material and transfer to containers.
- DO NOT GET WATER INSIDE CONTAINERS.

FIRST AID
- Move victim to fresh air.
- Call 911 or emergency medical service.
- Give artificial respiration if victim is not breathing.
- **Do not use mouth-to-mouth method if victim ingested or inhaled the substance; give artificial respiration with the aid of a pocket mask equipped with a one-way valve or other proper respiratory medical device.**
- Administer oxygen if breathing is difficult.
- Remove and isolate contaminated clothing and shoes.
- In case of contact with substance, immediately flush skin or eyes with running water for at least 20 minutes.
- For minor skin contact, avoid spreading material on unaffected skin.
- Keep victim warm and quiet.
- Effects of exposure (inhalation, ingestion or skin contact) to substance may be delayed.
- Ensure that medical personnel are aware of the material(s) involved and take precautions to protect themselves.

POTENTIAL HAZARDS

FIRE OR EXPLOSION
- **HIGHLY FLAMMABLE: Will be easily ignited by heat, sparks or flames.**
- Vapors form explosive mixtures with air: indoors, outdoors and sewers explosion hazards.
- Most vapors are heavier than air. They will spread along ground and collect in low or confined areas (sewers, basements, tanks).
- Vapors may travel to source of ignition and flash back.
- Those substances designated with a **(P)** may polymerize explosively when heated or involved in a fire.
- Substance will react with water (some violently) releasing flammable, toxic or corrosive gases and runoff.
- Contact with metals may evolve flammable hydrogen gas.
- Containers may explode when heated or if contaminated with water.

HEALTH
- **TOXIC**; inhalation, ingestion or contact (skin, eyes) with vapors, dusts or substance may cause severe injury, burns or death.
- **Bromoacetates and chloroacetates are extremely irritating/lachrymators.**
- Reaction with water or moist air will release toxic, corrosive or flammable gases.
- Reaction with water may generate much heat that will increase the concentration of fumes in the air.
- Fire will produce irritating, corrosive and/or toxic gases.
- Runoff from fire control or dilution water may be corrosive and/or toxic and cause pollution.

PUBLIC SAFETY
- **CALL EMERGENCY RESPONSE Telephone Number on Shipping Paper first. If Shipping Paper not available or no answer, refer to appropriate telephone number listed on the inside back cover.**
- As an immediate precautionary measure, isolate spill or leak area in all directions for at least 50 meters (150 feet) for liquids and at least 25 meters (75 feet) for solids.
- Keep unauthorized personnel away.
- Stay upwind.
- Keep out of low areas.
- Ventilate enclosed areas.

PROTECTIVE CLOTHING
- Wear positive pressure self-contained breathing apparatus (SCBA).
- Wear chemical protective clothing that is specifically recommended by the manufacturer. It may provide little or no thermal protection.
- Structural firefighters' protective clothing provides limited protection in fire situations ONLY; it is not effective in spill situations where direct contact with the substance is possible.

EVACUATION
Spill
- See Table 1 - Initial Isolation and Protective Action Distances for highlighted materials. For non-highlighted materials, increase, in the downwind direction, as necessary, the isolation distance shown under "PUBLIC SAFETY".

Fire
- If tank, rail car or tank truck is involved in a fire, ISOLATE for 800 meters (1/2 mile) in all directions; also, consider initial evacuation for 800 meters (1/2 mile) in all directions.

EMERGENCY RESPONSE

FIRE
- Note: Most foams will react with the material and release corrosive/toxic gases.
- **CAUTION: For Acetyl chloride (UN1717), use CO$_2$ or dry chemical only.**

Small Fire
- CO$_2$, dry chemical, dry sand, alcohol-resistant foam.

Large Fire
- Water spray, fog or alcohol-resistant foam.
- **FOR CHLOROSILANES, DO NOT USE WATER**; use AFFF alcohol-resistant medium expansion foam.
- Move containers from fire area if you can do it without risk.
- Use water spray or fog; do not use straight streams.

Fire involving Tanks or Car/Trailer Loads
- Fight fire from maximum distance or use unmanned hose holders or monitor nozzles.
- Do not get water inside containers.
- Cool containers with flooding quantities of water until well after fire is out.
- Withdraw immediately in case of rising sound from venting safety devices or discoloration of tank.
- ALWAYS stay away from tanks engulfed in fire.

SPILL OR LEAK
- ELIMINATE all ignition sources (no smoking, flares, sparks or flames in immediate area).
- All equipment used when handling the product must be grounded.
- Do not touch damaged containers or spilled material unless wearing appropriate protective clothing.
- Stop leak if you can do it without risk.
- A vapor suppressing foam may be used to reduce vapors.
- **FOR CHLOROSILANES**, use AFFF alcohol-resistant medium expansion foam to reduce vapors.
- **DO NOT GET WATER on spilled substance or inside containers.**
- Use water spray to reduce vapors or divert vapor cloud drift. Avoid allowing water runoff to contact spilled material.
- Prevent entry into waterways, sewers, basements or confined areas.

Small Spill
- Cover with DRY earth, DRY sand or other non-combustible material followed with plastic sheet to minimize spreading or contact with rain.
- Use clean non-sparking tools to collect material and place it into loosely covered plastic containers for later disposal.

FIRST AID
- Move victim to fresh air.   • Call 911 or emergency medical service.
- Give artificial respiration if victim is not breathing.
- **Do not use mouth-to-mouth method if victim ingested or inhaled the substance; give artificial respiration with the aid of a pocket mask equipped with a one-way valve or other proper respiratory medical device.**
- Administer oxygen if breathing is difficult.
- Remove and isolate contaminated clothing and shoes.
- In case of contact with substance, immediately flush skin or eyes with running water for at least 20 minutes.
- For minor skin contact, avoid spreading material on unaffected skin.
- Keep victim warm and quiet.
- Effects of exposure (inhalation, ingestion or skin contact) to substance may be delayed.
- Ensure that medical personnel are aware of the material(s) involved and take precautions to protect themselves.

POTENTIAL HAZARDS

FIRE OR EXPLOSION
- Combustible material: may burn but does not ignite readily.
- Substance will react with water (some violently) releasing flammable, toxic or corrosive gases and runoff.
- When heated, vapors may form explosive mixtures with air: indoors, outdoors and sewers explosion hazards.
- Most vapors are heavier than air. They will spread along ground and collect in low or confined areas (sewers, basements, tanks).
- Vapors may travel to source of ignition and flash back.
- Contact with metals may evolve flammable hydrogen gas.
- Containers may explode when heated or if contaminated with water.

HEALTH
- **TOXIC;** inhalation, ingestion or contact (skin, eyes) with vapors, dusts or substance may cause severe injury, burns or death.
- Contact with molten substance may cause severe burns to skin and eyes.
- Reaction with water or moist air will release toxic, corrosive or flammable gases.
- Reaction with water may generate much heat that will increase the concentration of fumes in the air.
- Fire will produce irritating, corrosive and/or toxic gases.
- Runoff from fire control or dilution water may be corrosive and/or toxic and cause pollution.

PUBLIC SAFETY
- **CALL EMERGENCY RESPONSE Telephone Number on Shipping Paper first. If Shipping Paper not available or no answer, refer to appropriate telephone number listed on the inside back cover.**
- As an immediate precautionary measure, isolate spill or leak area in all directions for at least 50 meters (150 feet) for liquids and at least 25 meters (75 feet) for solids.
- Keep unauthorized personnel away.
- Stay upwind.
- Keep out of low areas.
- Ventilate enclosed areas.

PROTECTIVE CLOTHING
- Wear positive pressure self-contained breathing apparatus (SCBA).
- Wear chemical protective clothing that is specifically recommended by the manufacturer. It may provide little or no thermal protection.
- Structural firefighters' protective clothing provides limited protection in fire situations ONLY; it is not effective in spill situations where direct contact with the substance is possible.

EVACUATION
Spill
- See Table 1 - Initial Isolation and Protective Action Distances for highlighted materials. For non-highlighted materials, increase, in the downwind direction, as necessary, the isolation distance shown under "PUBLIC SAFETY".

Fire
- If tank, rail car or tank truck is involved in a fire, ISOLATE for 800 meters (1/2 mile) in all directions; also, consider initial evacuation for 800 meters (1/2 mile) in all directions.

EMERGENCY RESPONSE

FIRE
- Note: Most foams will react with the material and release corrosive/toxic gases.

Small Fire
- CO_2, dry chemical, dry sand, alcohol-resistant foam.

Large Fire
- Water spray, fog or alcohol-resistant foam.
- **FOR CHLOROSILANES, DO NOT USE WATER**; use AFFF alcohol-resistant medium expansion foam.
- Move containers from fire area if you can do it without risk.
- Use water spray or fog; do not use straight streams.

Fire involving Tanks or Car/Trailer Loads
- Fight fire from maximum distance or use unmanned hose holders or monitor nozzles.
- Do not get water inside containers.
- Cool containers with flooding quantities of water until well after fire is out.
- Withdraw immediately in case of rising sound from venting safety devices or discoloration of tank.
- ALWAYS stay away from tanks engulfed in fire.

SPILL OR LEAK
- ELIMINATE all ignition sources (no smoking, flares, sparks or flames in immediate area).
- All equipment used when handling the product must be grounded.
- Do not touch damaged containers or spilled material unless wearing appropriate protective clothing.
- Stop leak if you can do it without risk.
- A vapor suppressing foam may be used to reduce vapors.
- **FOR CHLOROSILANES**, use AFFF alcohol-resistant medium expansion foam to reduce vapors.
- **DO NOT GET WATER on spilled substance or inside containers.**
- Use water spray to reduce vapors or divert vapor cloud drift. Avoid allowing water runoff to contact spilled material.
- Prevent entry into waterways, sewers, basements or confined areas.

Small Spill
- Cover with DRY earth, DRY sand or other non-combustible material followed with plastic sheet to minimize spreading or contact with rain.
- Use clean non-sparking tools to collect material and place it into loosely covered plastic containers for later disposal.

FIRST AID
- Move victim to fresh air.   • Call 911 or emergency medical service.
- Give artificial respiration if victim is not breathing.
- **Do not use mouth-to-mouth method if victim ingested or inhaled the substance; give artificial respiration with the aid of a pocket mask equipped with a one-way valve or other proper respiratory medical device.**
- Administer oxygen if breathing is difficult.
- Remove and isolate contaminated clothing and shoes.
- In case of contact with substance, immediately flush skin or eyes with running water for at least 20 minutes.
- For minor skin contact, avoid spreading material on unaffected skin.
- Keep victim warm and quiet.
- Effects of exposure (inhalation, ingestion or skin contact) to substance may be delayed.
- Ensure that medical personnel are aware of the material(s) involved and take precautions to protect themselves.

POTENTIAL HAZARDS

HEALTH

- **TOXIC**; inhalation, ingestion or contact (skin, eyes) with vapors, dusts or substance may cause severe injury, burns or death.
- Reaction with water or moist air may release toxic, corrosive or flammable gases.
- Reaction with water may generate much heat that will increase the concentration of fumes in the air.
- Fire will produce irritating, corrosive and/or toxic gases.
- Runoff from fire control or dilution water may be corrosive and/or toxic and cause pollution.

FIRE OR EXPLOSION

- Non-combustible, substance itself does not burn but may decompose upon heating to produce corrosive and/or toxic fumes.
- For UN1796, UN1826, UN2031 at high concentrations and for UN2032, these may act as oxidizers, also consult GUIDE 140.
- Vapors may accumulate in confined areas (basement, tanks, hopper/tank cars etc.).
- Substance may react with water (some violently), releasing corrosive and/or toxic gases and runoff.
- Contact with metals may evolve flammable hydrogen gas.
- Containers may explode when heated or if contaminated with water.

PUBLIC SAFETY

- **CALL EMERGENCY RESPONSE Telephone Number on Shipping Paper first. If Shipping Paper not available or no answer, refer to appropriate telephone number listed on the inside back cover.**
- As an immediate precautionary measure, isolate spill or leak area in all directions for at least 50 meters (150 feet) for liquids and at least 25 meters (75 feet) for solids.
- Keep unauthorized personnel away.
- Stay upwind.
- Keep out of low areas.
- Ventilate enclosed areas.

PROTECTIVE CLOTHING

- Wear positive pressure self-contained breathing apparatus (SCBA).
- Wear chemical protective clothing that is specifically recommended by the manufacturer. It may provide little or no thermal protection.
- Structural firefighters' protective clothing provides limited protection in fire situations ONLY; it is not effective in spill situations where direct contact with the substance is possible.

EVACUATION

Spill

- See Table 1 - Initial Isolation and Protective Action Distances for highlighted materials. For non-highlighted materials, increase, in the downwind direction, as necessary, the isolation distance shown under "PUBLIC SAFETY".

Fire

- If tank, rail car or tank truck is involved in a fire, ISOLATE for 800 meters (1/2 mile) in all directions; also, consider initial evacuation for 800 meters (1/2 mile) in all directions.

EMERGENCY RESPONSE

FIRE
- Note: Some foams will react with the material and release corrosive/toxic gases.

Small Fire
- CO_2 (except for Cyanides), dry chemical, dry sand, alcohol-resistant foam.

Large Fire
- Water spray, fog or alcohol-resistant foam.
- Move containers from fire area if you can do it without risk.
- Use water spray or fog; do not use straight streams.
- Dike fire-control water for later disposal; do not scatter the material.

Fire involving Tanks or Car/Trailer Loads
- Fight fire from maximum distance or use unmanned hose holders or monitor nozzles.
- Do not get water inside containers.
- Cool containers with flooding quantities of water until well after fire is out.
- Withdraw immediately in case of rising sound from venting safety devices or discoloration of tank.
- ALWAYS stay away from tanks engulfed in fire.

SPILL OR LEAK
- ELIMINATE all ignition sources (no smoking, flares, sparks or flames in immediate area).
- All equipment used when handling the product must be grounded.
- Do not touch damaged containers or spilled material unless wearing appropriate protective clothing.
- Stop leak if you can do it without risk.
- A vapor suppressing foam may be used to reduce vapors.
- DO NOT GET WATER INSIDE CONTAINERS.
- Use water spray to reduce vapors or divert vapor cloud drift. Avoid allowing water runoff to contact spilled material.
- Prevent entry into waterways, sewers, basements or confined areas.

Small Spill
- Cover with DRY earth, DRY sand or other non-combustible material followed with plastic sheet to minimize spreading or contact with rain.
- Use clean non-sparking tools to collect material and place it into loosely covered plastic containers for later disposal.

FIRST AID
- Move victim to fresh air. • Call 911 or emergency medical service.
- Give artificial respiration if victim is not breathing.
- **Do not use mouth-to-mouth method if victim ingested or inhaled the substance; give artificial respiration with the aid of a pocket mask equipped with a one-way valve or other proper respiratory medical device.**
- Administer oxygen if breathing is difficult.
- Remove and isolate contaminated clothing and shoes.
- In case of contact with substance, immediately flush skin or eyes with running water for at least 20 minutes.
- **In case of contact with Hydrofluoric acid (UN1790),** flush skin and eyes with water for 5 minutes; then, for skin exposures rub on a calcium/gel combination; for eyes flush with a water/calcium solution if available, otherwise continue with water for 15 minutes.
- For minor skin contact, avoid spreading material on unaffected skin.
- Keep victim warm and quiet.
- Effects of exposure (inhalation, ingestion or skin contact) to substance may be delayed.
- Ensure that medical personnel are aware of the material(s) involved and take precautions to protect themselves.

POTENTIAL HAZARDS

HEALTH

- Inhalation or contact with substance may cause infection, disease or death.
- Runoff from fire control may cause pollution.
- **Note: Damaged packages containing solid CO_2 as a refrigerant may produce water or frost from condensation of air. Do not touch this liquid as it could be contaminated by the contents of the parcel.**

FIRE OR EXPLOSION

- Some of these materials may burn, but none ignite readily.
- Some may be transported in flammable liquids.

PUBLIC SAFETY

- **CALL EMERGENCY RESPONSE Telephone Number on Shipping Paper first. If Shipping Paper not available or no answer, refer to appropriate telephone number listed on the inside back cover.**
- As an immediate precautionary measure, isolate spill or leak area for at least 25 meters (75 feet) in all directions.
- Keep unauthorized personnel away.
- Stay upwind.
- Obtain identity of substance involved.

PROTECTIVE CLOTHING

- Wear positive pressure self-contained breathing apparatus (SCBA).
- Structural firefighters' protective clothing will only provide limited protection.

EMERGENCY RESPONSE

FIRE
Small Fire
- Dry chemical, soda ash, lime or sand.

Large Fire
- Use extinguishing agent suitable for type of surrounding fire.
- Do not scatter spilled material with high pressure water streams.
- Move containers from fire area if you can do it without risk.

SPILL OR LEAK
- Do not touch or walk through spilled material.
- Do not touch damaged containers or spilled material unless wearing appropriate protective clothing.
- Absorb with earth, sand or other non-combustible material.
- Cover damaged package or spilled material with damp towel or rag and keep wet with liquid bleach or other disinfectant.
- **DO NOT CLEAN-UP OR DISPOSE OF, EXCEPT UNDER SUPERVISION OF A SPECIALIST.**

FIRST AID
- Move victim to a safe isolated area.

CAUTION: Victim may be a source of contamination.
- Call 911 or emergency medical service.
- Remove and isolate contaminated clothing and shoes.
- In case of contact with substance, immediately flush skin or eyes with running water for at least 20 minutes.
- Effects of exposure (inhalation, ingestion or skin contact) to substance may be delayed.
- **For further assistance, contact your local Poison Control Center.**
- Ensure that medical personnel are aware of the material(s) involved and take precautions to protect themselves.

POTENTIAL HAZARDS

HEALTH

- Inhalation of vapors or dust is extremely irritating.
- May cause burning of eyes and flow of tears.
- May cause coughing, difficult breathing and nausea.
- Brief exposure effects last only a few minutes.
- Exposure in an enclosed area may be very harmful.
- Fire will produce irritating, corrosive and/or toxic gases.
- Runoff from fire control or dilution water may cause pollution.

FIRE OR EXPLOSION

- Some of these materials may burn, but none ignite readily.
- Containers may explode when heated.

PUBLIC SAFETY

- **CALL EMERGENCY RESPONSE Telephone Number on Shipping Paper first. If Shipping Paper not available or no answer, refer to appropriate telephone number listed on the inside back cover.**
- As an immediate precautionary measure, isolate spill or leak area in all directions for at least 50 meters (150 feet) for liquids and at least 25 meters (75 feet) for solids.
- Keep unauthorized personnel away.
- Stay upwind.
- Keep out of low areas.
- Ventilate closed spaces before entering.

PROTECTIVE CLOTHING

- Wear positive pressure self-contained breathing apparatus (SCBA).
- Wear chemical protective clothing that is specifically recommended by the manufacturer. It may provide little or no thermal protection.
- Structural firefighters' protective clothing provides limited protection in fire situations ONLY; it is not effective in spill situations where direct contact with the substance is possible.

EVACUATION

Spill

- See Table 1 - Initial Isolation and Protective Action Distances for highlighted materials. For non-highlighted materials, increase, in the downwind direction, as necessary, the isolation distance shown under "PUBLIC SAFETY".

Fire

- If tank, rail car or tank truck is involved in a fire, ISOLATE for 800 meters (1/2 mile) in all directions; also, consider initial evacuation for 800 meters (1/2 mile) in all directions.

EMERGENCY RESPONSE

FIRE

Small Fire

- Dry chemical, CO_2, water spray or regular foam.

Large Fire

- Water spray, fog or regular foam.
- Move containers from fire area if you can do it without risk.
- Dike fire-control water for later disposal; do not scatter the material.

Fire involving Tanks or Car/Trailer Loads

- Fight fire from maximum distance or use unmanned hose holders or monitor nozzles.
- Do not get water inside containers.
- Cool containers with flooding quantities of water until well after fire is out.
- Withdraw immediately in case of rising sound from venting safety devices or discoloration of tank.
- ALWAYS stay away from tanks engulfed in fire.
- For massive fire, use unmanned hose holders or monitor nozzles; if this is impossible, withdraw from area and let fire burn.

SPILL OR LEAK

- Do not touch or walk through spilled material.
- Stop leak if you can do it without risk.
- Fully encapsulating, vapor protective clothing should be worn for spills and leaks with no fire.

Small Spill

- Take up with sand or other non-combustible absorbent material and place into containers for later disposal.

Large Spill

- Dike far ahead of liquid spill for later disposal.
- Prevent entry into waterways, sewers, basements or confined areas.

FIRST AID

- Move victim to fresh air.
- Call 911 or emergency medical service.
- Give artificial respiration if victim is not breathing.
- **Do not use mouth-to-mouth method if victim ingested or inhaled the substance; give artificial respiration with the aid of a pocket mask equipped with a one-way valve or other proper respiratory medical device.**
- Administer oxygen if breathing is difficult.
- Remove and isolate contaminated clothing and shoes.
- In case of contact with substance, immediately flush skin or eyes with running water for at least 20 minutes.
- For minor skin contact, avoid spreading material on unaffected skin.
- Keep victim warm and quiet.
- Effects should disappear after individual has been exposed to fresh air for approximately 10 minutes.
- Ensure that medical personnel are aware of the material(s) involved and take precautions to protect themselves.

POTENTIAL HAZARDS

HEALTH
- Toxic by ingestion.
- Vapors may cause dizziness or suffocation.
- Exposure in an enclosed area may be very harmful.
- Contact may irritate or burn skin and eyes.
- Fire may produce irritating and/or toxic gases.
- Runoff from fire control or dilution water may cause pollution.

FIRE OR EXPLOSION
- Some of these materials may burn, but none ignite readily.
- Most vapors are heavier than air.
- Air/vapor mixtures may explode when ignited.
- Container may explode in heat of fire.

PUBLIC SAFETY
- **CALL EMERGENCY RESPONSE Telephone Number on Shipping Paper first. If Shipping Paper not available or no answer, refer to appropriate telephone number listed on the inside back cover.**
- As an immediate precautionary measure, isolate spill or leak area for at least 50 meters (150 feet) in all directions.
- Keep unauthorized personnel away.
- Stay upwind.
- Many gases are heavier than air and will spread along ground and collect in low or confined areas (sewers, basements, tanks).
- Keep out of low areas.
- Ventilate closed spaces before entering.

PROTECTIVE CLOTHING
- Wear positive pressure self-contained breathing apparatus (SCBA).
- Wear chemical protective clothing that is specifically recommended by the manufacturer.
- Structural firefighters' protective clothing will only provide limited protection.

EVACUATION
Large Spill
- Consider initial downwind evacuation for at least 100 meters (330 feet).

Fire
- If tank, rail car or tank truck is involved in a fire, ISOLATE for 800 meters (1/2 mile) in all directions; also, consider initial evacuation for 800 meters (1/2 mile) in all directions.

EMERGENCY RESPONSE

FIRE

Small Fire
- Dry chemical, CO_2 or water spray.

Large Fire
- Dry chemical, CO_2, alcohol-resistant foam or water spray.
- Move containers from fire area if you can do it without risk.
- Dike fire-control water for later disposal; do not scatter the material.

Fire involving Tanks or Car/Trailer Loads
- Fight fire from maximum distance or use unmanned hose holders or monitor nozzles.
- Cool containers with flooding quantities of water until well after fire is out.
- Withdraw immediately in case of rising sound from venting safety devices or discoloration of tank.
- ALWAYS stay away from tanks engulfed in fire.

SPILL OR LEAK

- ELIMINATE all ignition sources (no smoking, flares, sparks or flames in immediate area).
- Stop leak if you can do it without risk.

Small Liquid Spill
- Take up with sand, earth or other non-combustible absorbent material.

Large Spill
- Dike far ahead of liquid spill for later disposal.
- Prevent entry into waterways, sewers, basements or confined areas.

FIRST AID

- Move victim to fresh air.
- Call 911 or emergency medical service.
- Give artificial respiration if victim is not breathing.
- Administer oxygen if breathing is difficult.
- Remove and isolate contaminated clothing and shoes.
- In case of contact with substance, immediately flush skin or eyes with running water for at least 20 minutes.
- For minor skin contact, avoid spreading material on unaffected skin.
- Wash skin with soap and water.
- Keep victim warm and quiet.
- Ensure that medical personnel are aware of the material(s) involved and take precautions to protect themselves.

POTENTIAL HAZARDS

HEALTH

- Radiation presents minimal risk to transport workers, emergency response personnel and the public during transportation accidents. Packaging durability increases as potential hazard of radioactive content increases.
- Very low levels of contained radioactive materials and low radiation levels outside packages result in low risks to people. Damaged packages may release measurable amounts of radioactive material, but the resulting risks are expected to be low.
- Some radioactive materials cannot be detected by commonly available instruments.
- Packages do not have RADIOACTIVE I, II, or III labels. Some may have EMPTY labels or may have the word "Radioactive" in the package marking.

FIRE OR EXPLOSION

- Some of these materials may burn, but most do not ignite readily.
- Many have cardboard outer packaging; content (physically large or small) can be of many different physical forms.
- Radioactivity does not change flammability or other properties of materials.

PUBLIC SAFETY

- **CALL EMERGENCY RESPONSE Telephone Number on Shipping Paper first. If Shipping Paper not available or no answer, refer to appropriate telephone number listed on the inside back cover.**
- **Priorities for rescue, life-saving, first aid, fire control and other hazards are higher than the priority for measuring radiation levels.**
- Radiation Authority must be notified of accident conditions. Radiation Authority is usually responsible for decisions about radiological consequences and closure of emergencies.
- As an immediate precautionary measure, isolate spill or leak area for at least 25 meters (75 feet) in all directions.
- Stay upwind.
- Keep unauthorized personnel away.
- Detain or isolate uninjured persons or equipment suspected to be contaminated; delay decontamination and cleanup until instructions are received from Radiation Authority.

PROTECTIVE CLOTHING

- Positive pressure self-contained breathing apparatus (SCBA) and structural firefighters' protective clothing will provide adequate protection.

EVACUATION

Large Spill
- Consider initial downwind evacuation for at least 100 meters (330 feet).

Fire
- When a large quantity of this material is involved in a major fire, consider an initial evacuation distance of 300 meters (1000 feet) in all directions.

EMERGENCY RESPONSE

FIRE
- Presence of radioactive material will not influence the fire control processes and should not influence selection of techniques.
- Move containers from fire area if you can do it without risk.
- Do not move damaged packages; move undamaged packages out of fire zone.

Small Fire
- Dry chemical, CO_2, water spray or regular foam.

Large Fire
- Water spray, fog (flooding amounts).

SPILL OR LEAK
- Do not touch damaged packages or spilled material.
- Cover liquid spill with sand, earth or other non-combustible absorbent material.
- Cover powder spill with plastic sheet or tarp to minimize spreading.

FIRST AID
- Call 911 or emergency medical service.
- Medical problems take priority over radiological concerns.
- Use first aid treatment according to the nature of the injury.
- Do not delay care and transport of a seriously injured person.
- Give artificial respiration if victim is not breathing.
- Administer oxygen if breathing is difficult.
- In case of contact with substance, immediately flush skin or eyes with running water for at least 20 minutes.
- Injured persons contaminated by contact with released material are not a serious hazard to health care personnel, equipment or facilities.
- Ensure that medical personnel are aware of the material(s) involved, take precautions to protect themselves and prevent spread of contamination.

POTENTIAL HAZARDS

HEALTH

- Radiation presents minimal risk to transport workers, emergency response personnel and the public during transportation accidents. Packaging durability increases as potential hazard of radioactive content increases.
- Undamaged packages are safe. Contents of damaged packages may cause higher external radiation exposure, or both external and internal radiation exposure if contents are released.
- Low radiation hazard when material is inside container. If material is released from package or bulk container, hazard will vary from low to moderate. Level of hazard will depend on the type and amount of radioactivity, the kind of material it is in, and/or the surfaces it is on.
- Some material may be released from packages during accidents of moderate severity but risks to people are not great.
- Released radioactive materials or contaminated objects usually will be visible if packaging fails.
- Some exclusive use shipments of bulk and packaged materials will not have "RADIOACTIVE" labels. Placards, markings and shipping papers provide identification.
- Some packages may have a "RADIOACTIVE" label and a second hazard label. The second hazard is usually greater than the radiation hazard; so follow this GUIDE as well as the response GUIDE for the second hazard class label.
- Some radioactive materials cannot be detected by commonly available instruments.
- Runoff from control of cargo fire may cause low-level pollution.

FIRE OR EXPLOSION

- Some of these materials may burn, but most do not ignite readily.
- Uranium and Thorium metal cuttings may ignite spontaneously if exposed to air (see GUIDE 136).
- Nitrates are oxidizers and may ignite other combustibles (see GUIDE 141).

PUBLIC SAFETY

- **CALL EMERGENCY RESPONSE Telephone Number on Shipping Paper first. If Shipping Paper not available or no answer, refer to appropriate telephone number listed on the inside back cover.**
- **Priorities for rescue, life-saving, first aid, fire control and other hazards are higher than the priority for measuring radiation levels.**
- Radiation Authority must be notified of accident conditions. Radiation Authority is usually responsible for decisions about radiological consequences and closure of emergencies.
- As an immediate precautionary measure, isolate spill or leak area for at least 25 meters (75 feet) in all directions.
- Stay upwind.
- Keep unauthorized personnel away.
- Detain or isolate uninjured persons or equipment suspected to be contaminated; delay decontamination and cleanup until instructions are received from Radiation Authority.

PROTECTIVE CLOTHING

- Positive pressure self-contained breathing apparatus (SCBA) and structural firefighters' protective clothing will provide adequate protection.

EVACUATION

Large Spill
- Consider initial downwind evacuation for at least 100 meters (330 feet).

Fire
- When a large quantity of this material is involved in a major fire, consider an initial evacuation distance of 300 meters (1000 feet) in all directions.

EMERGENCY RESPONSE

FIRE
- Presence of radioactive material will not influence the fire control processes and should not influence selection of techniques.
- Move containers from fire area if you can do it without risk.
- Do not move damaged packages; move undamaged packages out of fire zone.

Small Fire
- Dry chemical, CO_2, water spray or regular foam.

Large Fire
- Water spray, fog (flooding amounts).
- Dike fire-control water for later disposal.

SPILL OR LEAK
- Do not touch damaged packages or spilled material.
- Cover liquid spill with sand, earth or other non-combustible absorbent material.
- Dike to collect large liquid spills.
- Cover powder spill with plastic sheet or tarp to minimize spreading.

FIRST AID
- Call 911 or emergency medical service.
- Medical problems take priority over radiological concerns.
- Use first aid treatment according to the nature of the injury.
- Do not delay care and transport of a seriously injured person.
- Give artificial respiration if victim is not breathing.
- Administer oxygen if breathing is difficult.
- In case of contact with substance, wipe from skin immediately; flush skin or eyes with running water for at least 20 minutes.
- Injured persons contaminated by contact with released material are not a serious hazard to health care personnel, equipment or facilities.
- Ensure that medical personnel are aware of the material(s) involved, take precautions to protect themselves and prevent spread of contamination.

POTENTIAL HAZARDS

HEALTH

- Radiation presents minimal risk to transport workers, emergency response personnel and the public during transportation accidents. Packaging durability increases as potential hazard of radioactive content increases.
- Undamaged packages are safe. Contents of damaged packages may cause higher external radiation exposure, or both external and internal radiation exposure if contents are released.
- Type A packages (cartons, boxes, drums, articles, etc.) identified as "Type A" by marking on packages or by shipping papers contain non-life endangering amounts. Partial releases might be expected if "Type A" packages are damaged in moderately severe accidents.
- Type B packages, and the rarely occurring Type C packages, (large and small, usually metal) contain the most hazardous amounts. They can be identified by package markings or by shipping papers. Life threatening conditions may exist only if contents are released or package shielding fails. Because of design, evaluation and testing of packages, these conditions would be expected only for accidents of utmost severity.
- The rarely occurring "Special Arrangement" shipments may be of Type A, Type B or Type C packages. Package type will be marked on packages, and shipment details will be on shipping papers.
- Radioactive White-I labels indicate radiation levels outside single, isolated, undamaged packages are very low (less than 0.005 mSv/h (0.5 mrem/h)).
- Radioactive Yellow-II and Yellow-III labeled packages have higher radiation levels. The transport index (TI) on the label identifies the maximum radiation level in mrem/h one meter from a single, isolated, undamaged package.
- Some radioactive materials cannot be detected by commonly available instruments.
- Water from cargo fire control may cause pollution.

FIRE OR EXPLOSION

- Some of these materials may burn, but most do not ignite readily.
- Radioactivity does not change flammability or other properties of materials.
- Type B packages are designed and evaluated to withstand total engulfment in flames at temperatures of 800°C (1475°F) for a period of 30 minutes.

PUBLIC SAFETY

- **CALL EMERGENCY RESPONSE Telephone Number on Shipping Paper first. If Shipping Paper not available or no answer, refer to appropriate telephone number listed on the inside back cover.**
- **Priorities for rescue, life-saving, first aid, fire control and other hazards are higher than the priority for measuring radiation levels.**
- Radiation Authority must be notified of accident conditions. Radiation Authority is usually responsible for decisions about radiological consequences and closure of emergencies.
- As an immediate precautionary measure, isolate spill or leak area for at least 25 meters (75 feet) in all directions. • Stay upwind. • Keep unauthorized personnel away.
- Detain or isolate uninjured persons or equipment suspected to be contaminated; delay decontamination and cleanup until instructions are received from Radiation Authority.

PROTECTIVE CLOTHING

- Positive pressure self-contained breathing apparatus (SCBA) and structural firefighters' protective clothing will provide adequate protection against internal radiation exposure, but not external radiation exposure.

EVACUATION

Large Spill
- Consider initial downwind evacuation for at least 100 meters (330 feet).

Fire
- When a large quantity of this material is involved in a major fire, consider an initial evacuation distance of 300 meters (1000 feet) in all directions.

EMERGENCY RESPONSE

FIRE
- Presence of radioactive material will not influence the fire control processes and should not influence selection of techniques.
- Move containers from fire area if you can do it without risk.
- Do not move damaged packages; move undamaged packages out of fire zone.

Small Fire
- Dry chemical, CO_2, water spray or regular foam.

Large Fire
- Water spray, fog (flooding amounts).
- Dike fire-control water for later disposal.

SPILL OR LEAK
- Do not touch damaged packages or spilled material.
- Damp surfaces on undamaged or slightly damaged packages are seldom an indication of packaging failure. Most packaging for liquid content have inner containers and/or inner absorbent materials.
- Cover liquid spill with sand, earth or other non-combustible absorbent material.

FIRST AID
- Call 911 or emergency medical service.
- Medical problems take priority over radiological concerns.
- Use first aid treatment according to the nature of the injury.
- Do not delay care and transport of a seriously injured person.
- Give artificial respiration if victim is not breathing.
- Administer oxygen if breathing is difficult.
- In case of contact with substance, immediately flush skin or eyes with running water for at least 20 minutes.
- Injured persons contaminated by contact with released material are not a serious hazard to health care personnel, equipment or facilities.
- Ensure that medical personnel are aware of the material(s) involved, take precautions to protect themselves and prevent spread of contamination.

POTENTIAL HAZARDS

HEALTH

- Radiation presents minimal risk to transport workers, emergency response personnel and the public during transportation accidents. Packaging durability increases as potential hazard of radioactive content increases.
- Undamaged packages are safe; contents of damaged packages may cause external radiation exposure, and much higher external exposure if contents (source capsules) are released.
- Contamination and internal radiation hazards are not expected, but not impossible.
- Type A packages (cartons, boxes, drums, articles, etc.) identified as "Type A" by marking on packages or by shipping papers contain non-life endangering amounts. Radioactive sources may be released if "Type A" packages are damaged in moderately severe accidents.
- Type B packages, and the rarely occurring Type C packages, (large and small, usually metal) contain the most hazardous amounts. They can be identified by package markings or by shipping papers. Life threatening conditions may exist only if contents are released or package shielding fails. Because of design, evaluation and testing of packages, these conditions would be expected only for accidents of utmost severity.
- Radioactive White-I labels indicate radiation levels outside single, isolated, undamaged packages are very low (less than 0.005 mSv/h (0.5 mrem/h)).
- Radioactive Yellow-II and Yellow-III labeled packages have higher radiation levels. The transport index (TI) on the label identifies the maximum radiation level in mrem/h one meter from a single, isolated, undamaged package.
- Radiation from the package contents, usually in durable metal capsules, can be detected by most radiation instruments.
- Water from cargo fire control is not expected to cause pollution.

FIRE OR EXPLOSION

- Packagings can burn completely without risk of content loss from sealed source capsule.
- Radioactivity does not change flammability or other properties of materials.
- Radioactive source capsules and Type B packages are designed and evaluated to withstand total engulfment in flames at temperatures of 800°C (1475°F) for a period of 30 minutes.

PUBLIC SAFETY

- **CALL EMERGENCY RESPONSE Telephone Number on Shipping Paper first. If Shipping Paper not available or no answer, refer to appropriate telephone number listed on the inside back cover.**
- **Priorities for rescue, life-saving, first aid, fire control and other hazards are higher than the priority for measuring radiation levels.**
- Radiation Authority must be notified of accident conditions. Radiation Authority is usually responsible for decisions about radiological consequences and closure of emergencies.
- As an immediate precautionary measure, isolate spill or leak area for at least 25 meters (75 feet) in all directions.
- Stay upwind.   • Keep unauthorized personnel away.
- Delay final cleanup until instructions or advice is received from Radiation Authority.

PROTECTIVE CLOTHING

- Positive pressure self-contained breathing apparatus (SCBA) and structural firefighters' protective clothing will provide adequate protection against internal radiation exposure, but not external radiation exposure.

EVACUATION

Large Spill
- Consider initial downwind evacuation for at least 100 meters (330 feet).

Fire
- When a large quantity of this material is involved in a major fire, consider an initial evacuation distance of 300 meters (1000 feet) in all directions.

EMERGENCY RESPONSE

FIRE
- Presence of radioactive material will not influence the fire control processes and should not influence selection of techniques.
- Move containers from fire area if you can do it without risk.
- Do not move damaged packages; move undamaged packages out of fire zone.

Small Fire
- Dry chemical, CO_2, water spray or regular foam.

Large Fire
- Water spray, fog (flooding amounts).

SPILL OR LEAK
- Do not touch damaged packages or spilled material.
- Damp surfaces on undamaged or slightly damaged packages are seldom an indication of packaging failure. Contents are seldom liquid. Content is usually a metal capsule, easily seen if released from package.
- If source capsule is identified as being out of package, **DO NOT TOUCH**. Stay away and await advice from Radiation Authority.

FIRST AID
- Call 911 or emergency medical service.
- Medical problems take priority over radiological concerns.
- Use first aid treatment according to the nature of the injury.
- Do not delay care and transport of a seriously injured person.
- Persons exposed to special form sources are not likely to be contaminated with radioactive material.
- Give artificial respiration if victim is not breathing.
- Administer oxygen if breathing is difficult.
- Injured persons contaminated by contact with released material are not a serious hazard to health care personnel, equipment or facilities.
- Ensure that medical personnel are aware of the material(s) involved, take precautions to protect themselves and prevent spread of contamination.

GUIDE
165

RADIOACTIVE MATERIALS
(FISSILE/LOW TO HIGH LEVEL RADIATION)

ERG2012

POTENTIAL HAZARDS

HEALTH

- Radiation presents minimal risk to transport workers, emergency response personnel and the public during transportation accidents. Packaging durability increases as potential radiation and criticality hazards of the content increase.
- Undamaged packages are safe. Contents of damaged packages may cause higher external radiation exposure, or both external and internal radiation exposure if contents are released.
- Type AF or IF packages, identified by package markings, do not contain life-threatening amounts of material. External radiation levels are low and packages are designed, evaluated and tested to control releases and to prevent a fission chain reaction under severe transport conditions.
- Type B(U)F, B(M)F and CF packages (identified by markings on packages or shipping papers) contain potentially life endangering amounts. Because of design, evaluation and testing of packages, fission chain reactions are prevented and releases are not expected to be life endangering for all accidents except those of utmost severity.
- The rarely occurring "Special Arrangement" shipments may be of Type AF, BF or CF packages. Package type will be marked on packages, and shipment details will be on shipping papers.
- The transport index (TI) shown on labels or a shipping paper might not indicate the radiation level at one meter from a single, isolated, undamaged package; instead, it might relate to controls needed during transport because of the fissile properties of the materials. Alternatively, the fissile nature of the contents may be indicated by a criticality safety index (CSI) on a special FISSILE label or on the shipping paper.
- Some radioactive materials cannot be detected by commonly available instruments.
- Water from cargo fire control is not expected to cause pollution.

FIRE OR EXPLOSION

- These materials are seldom flammable. Packages are designed to withstand fires without damage to contents.
- Radioactivity does not change flammability or other properties of materials.
- Type AF, IF, B(U)F, B(M)F and CF packages are designed and evaluated to withstand total engulfment in flames at temperatures of 800°C (1475°F) for a period of 30 minutes.

PUBLIC SAFETY

- **CALL EMERGENCY RESPONSE Telephone Number on Shipping Paper first. If Shipping Paper not available or no answer, refer to appropriate telephone number listed on the inside back cover**
- **Priorities for rescue, life-saving, first aid, fire control and other hazards are higher than the priority for measuring radiation levels.**
- Radiation Authority must be notified of accident conditions. Radiation Authority is usually responsible for decisions about radiological consequences and closure of emergencies.
- As an immediate precautionary measure, isolate spill or leak area for at least 25 meters (75 feet) in all directions. • Stay upwind. • Keep unauthorized personnel away.
- Detain or isolate uninjured persons or equipment suspected to be contaminated; delay decontamination and cleanup until instructions are received from Radiation Authority.

PROTECTIVE CLOTHING

- Positive pressure self-contained breathing apparatus (SCBA) and structural firefighters' protective clothing will provide adequate protection against internal radiation exposure, but not external radiation exposure.

EVACUATION

Large Spill
- Consider initial downwind evacuation for at least 100 meters (330 feet).

Fire
- When a large quantity of this material is involved in a major fire, consider an initial evacuation distance of 300 meters (1000 feet) in all directions.

Page 268

EMERGENCY RESPONSE

FIRE

- Presence of radioactive material will not influence the fire control processes and should not influence selection of techniques.
- Move containers from fire area if you can do it without risk.
- Do not move damaged packages; move undamaged packages out of fire zone.

Small Fire
- Dry chemical, CO_2, water spray or regular foam.

Large Fire
- Water spray, fog (flooding amounts).

SPILL OR LEAK

- Do not touch damaged packages or spilled material.
- Damp surfaces on undamaged or slightly damaged packages are seldom an indication of packaging failure. Most packaging for liquid content have inner containers and/or inner absorbent materials.

Liquid Spill
- Package contents are seldom liquid. If any radioactive contamination resulting from a liquid release is present, it probably will be low-level.

FIRST AID

- Call 911 or emergency medical service.
- Medical problems take priority over radiological concerns.
- Use first aid treatment according to the nature of the injury.
- Do not delay care and transport of a seriously injured person.
- Give artificial respiration if victim is not breathing.
- Administer oxygen if breathing is difficult.
- In case of contact with substance, immediately flush skin or eyes with running water for at least 20 minutes.
- Injured persons contaminated by contact with released material are not a serious hazard to health care personnel, equipment or facilities.
- Ensure that medical personnel are aware of the material(s) involved, take precautions to protect themselves and prevent spread of contamination.

POTENTIAL HAZARDS

HEALTH

- Radiation presents minimal risk to transport workers, emergency response personnel and the public during transportation accidents. Packaging durability increases as potential radiation and criticality hazards of the content increase.
- Chemical hazard greatly exceeds radiation hazard.
- Substance reacts with water and water vapor in air to form toxic and corrosive hydrogen fluoride gas and an extremely irritating and corrosive, white-colored, water-soluble residue.
- If inhaled, may be fatal.
- Direct contact causes burns to skin, eyes, and respiratory tract.
- Low-level radioactive material; very low radiation hazard to people.
- Runoff from control of cargo fire may cause low-level pollution.

FIRE OR EXPLOSION

- Substance does not burn.
- The material may react violently with fuels.
- Containers in protective overpacks (horizontal cylindrical shape with short legs for tie-downs), are identified with "AF", "B(U)F" or "H(U)" on shipping papers or by markings on the overpacks. They are designed and evaluated to withstand severe conditions including total engulfment in flames at temperatures of 800°C (1475°F) for a period of 30 minutes.
- Bare filled cylinders, identified with UN2978 as part of the marking (may also be marked H(U) or H(M)), may rupture in heat of engulfing fire; bare empty (except for residue) cylinders will not rupture in fires.
- Radioactivity does not change flammability or other properties of materials.

PUBLIC SAFETY

- **CALL EMERGENCY RESPONSE Telephone Number on Shipping Paper first. If Shipping Paper not available or no answer, refer to appropriate telephone number listed on the inside back cover.**
- **Priorities for rescue, life-saving, first aid, fire control and other hazards are higher than the priority for measuring radiation levels.**
- Radiation Authority must be notified of accident conditions. Radiation Authority is usually responsible for decisions about radiological consequences and closure of emergencies.
- As an immediate precautionary measure, isolate spill or leak area for at least 25 meters (75 feet) in all directions.
- Stay upwind.
- Keep unauthorized personnel away.
- Detain or isolate uninjured persons or equipment suspected to be contaminated; delay decontamination and cleanup until instructions are received from Radiation Authority.

PROTECTIVE CLOTHING

- Wear positive pressure self-contained breathing apparatus (SCBA).
- Wear chemical protective clothing that is specifically recommended by the manufacturer. It may provide little or no thermal protection.
- Structural firefighters' protective clothing provides limited protection in fire situations ONLY; it is not effective in spill situations where direct contact with the substance is possible.

EVACUATION

Spill
- See Table 1 - Initial Isolation and Protective Action Distances.

Fire
- When a large quantity of this material is involved in a major fire, consider an initial evacuation distance of 300 meters (1000 feet) in all directions.

EMERGENCY RESPONSE

FIRE

- DO NOT USE WATER OR FOAM ON MATERIAL ITSELF.
- Move containers from fire area if you can do it without risk.

Small Fire

- Dry chemical or CO_2.

Large Fire

- Water spray, fog or regular foam.
- Cool containers with flooding quantities of water until well after fire is out.
- If this is impossible, withdraw from area and let fire burn.
- ALWAYS stay away from tanks engulfed in fire.

SPILL OR LEAK

- Do not touch damaged packages or spilled material.
- Without fire or smoke, leak will be evident by visible and irritating vapors and residue forming at the point of release.
- Use fine water spray to reduce vapors; do not put water directly on point of material release from container.
- Residue buildup may self-seal small leaks.
- Dike far ahead of spill to collect runoff water.

FIRST AID

- Call 911 or emergency medical service.
- Medical problems take priority over radiological concerns.
- Use first aid treatment according to the nature of the injury.
- Do not delay care and transport of a seriously injured person.
- Give artificial respiration if victim is not breathing.
- Administer oxygen if breathing is difficult.
- In case of contact with substance, immediately flush skin or eyes with running water for at least 20 minutes.
- Effects of exposure (inhalation, ingestion or skin contact) to substance may be delayed.
- Injured persons contaminated by contact with released material are not a serious hazard to health care personnel, equipment or facilities.
- Ensure that medical personnel are aware of the material(s) involved, take precautions to protect themselves and prevent spread of contamination.

GUIDE 167

FLUORINE (REFRIGERATED LIQUID)

ERG2012

POTENTIAL HAZARDS

HEALTH
- **TOXIC; may be fatal if inhaled.**
- Vapors are extremely irritating.
- Contact with gas or liquefied gas will cause burns, severe injury and/or frostbite.
- Vapors from liquefied gas are initially heavier than air and spread along ground.
- Runoff from fire control may cause pollution.

FIRE OR EXPLOSION
- Substance does not burn but will support combustion.
- This is a strong oxidizer and will react vigorously or explosively with many materials including fuels.
- May ignite combustibles (wood, paper, oil, clothing, etc.).
- Vapor explosion and poison hazard indoors, outdoors or in sewers.
- Containers may explode when heated.
- Ruptured cylinders may rocket.

PUBLIC SAFETY
- **CALL EMERGENCY RESPONSE Telephone Number on Shipping Paper first. If Shipping Paper not available or no answer, refer to appropriate telephone number listed on the inside back cover.**
- As an immediate precautionary measure, isolate spill or leak area for at least 100 meters (330 feet) in all directions.
- Keep unauthorized personnel away.
- Stay upwind.
- Many gases are heavier than air and will spread along ground and collect in low or confined areas (sewers, basements, tanks).
- Keep out of low areas.
- Ventilate closed spaces before entering.

PROTECTIVE CLOTHING
- Wear positive pressure self-contained breathing apparatus (SCBA).
- Wear chemical protective clothing that is specifically recommended by the manufacturer. It may provide little or no thermal protection.
- Structural firefighters' protective clothing provides limited protection in fire situations ONLY; it is not effective in spill situations where direct contact with the substance is possible.
- Always wear thermal protective clothing when handling refrigerated/cryogenic liquids.

EVACUATION
Spill
- See Table 1 - Initial Isolation and Protective Action Distances.
Fire
- If tank, rail car or tank truck is involved in a fire, ISOLATE for 1600 meters (1 mile) in all directions; also, consider initial evacuation for 1600 meters (1 mile) in all directions.

EMERGENCY RESPONSE

FIRE

Small Fire
- Dry chemical, soda ash, lime or sand.

Large Fire
- Water spray, fog (flooding amounts).
- Do not get water inside containers.
- Move containers from fire area if you can do it without risk.

Fire involving Tanks
- Fight fire from maximum distance or use unmanned hose holders or monitor nozzles.
- Cool containers with flooding quantities of water until well after fire is out.
- Do not direct water at source of leak or safety devices; icing may occur.
- Withdraw immediately in case of rising sound from venting safety devices or discoloration of tank.
- ALWAYS stay away from tanks engulfed in fire.
- For massive fire, use unmanned hose holders or monitor nozzles; if this is impossible, withdraw from area and let fire burn.

SPILL OR LEAK

- Do not touch or walk through spilled material.
- If you have not donned special protective clothing approved for this material, do not expose yourself to any risk of this material touching you.
- **Do not direct water at spill or source of leak.**
- A fine water spray remotely directed to the edge of the spill pool can be used to direct and maintain a hot flare fire that will burn the spilled material in a controlled manner.
- Keep combustibles (wood, paper, oil, etc.) away from spilled material.
- Stop leak if you can do it without risk.
- Use water spray to reduce vapors or divert vapor cloud drift. Avoid allowing water runoff to contact spilled material.
- If possible, turn leaking containers so that gas escapes rather than liquid.
- Prevent entry into waterways, sewers, basements or confined areas.
- Isolate area until gas has dispersed.
- Ventilate the area.

FIRST AID

- Move victim to fresh air.
- Call 911 or emergency medical service.
- Give artificial respiration if victim is not breathing.
- Administer oxygen if breathing is difficult.
- Clothing frozen to the skin should be thawed before being removed.
- Remove and isolate contaminated clothing and shoes.
- In case of contact with substance, immediately flush skin or eyes with running water for at least 20 minutes.
- Keep victim warm and quiet.
- Keep victim under observation.
- Effects of contact or inhalation may be delayed.
- Ensure that medical personnel are aware of the material(s) involved and take precautions to protect themselves.

POTENTIAL HAZARDS

HEALTH

- **TOXIC; Extremely Hazardous.**
- Inhalation extremely dangerous; may be fatal.
- Contact with gas or liquefied gas may cause burns, severe injury and/or frostbite.
- Odorless, will not be detected by sense of smell.

FIRE OR EXPLOSION

- **EXTREMELY FLAMMABLE.**
- May be ignited by heat, sparks or flames.
- Flame may be invisible.
- Containers may explode when heated.
- Vapor explosion and poison hazard indoors, outdoors or in sewers.
- Vapors from liquefied gas are initially heavier than air and spread along ground.
- Vapors may travel to source of ignition and flash back.
- Runoff may create fire or explosion hazard.

PUBLIC SAFETY

- **CALL EMERGENCY RESPONSE Telephone Number on Shipping Paper first. If Shipping Paper not available or no answer, refer to appropriate telephone number listed on the inside back cover.**
- As an immediate precautionary measure, isolate spill or leak area for at least 100 meters (330 feet) in all directions.
- Keep unauthorized personnel away.
- Stay upwind.
- Many gases are heavier than air and will spread along ground and collect in low or confined areas (sewers, basements, tanks).
- Keep out of low areas.
- Ventilate closed spaces before entering.

PROTECTIVE CLOTHING

- Wear positive pressure self-contained breathing apparatus (SCBA).
- Wear chemical protective clothing that is specifically recommended by the manufacturer. It may provide little or no thermal protection.
- Structural firefighters' protective clothing provides limited protection in fire situations ONLY; it is not effective in spill situations where direct contact with the substance is possible.
- Always wear thermal protective clothing when handling refrigerated/cryogenic liquids.

EVACUATION

Spill
- See Table 1 - Initial Isolation and Protective Action Distances.

Fire
- If tank, rail car or tank truck is involved in a fire, ISOLATE for 800 meters (1/2 mile) in all directions; also, consider initial evacuation for 800 meters (1/2 mile) in all directions.

EMERGENCY RESPONSE

FIRE

- **DO NOT EXTINGUISH A LEAKING GAS FIRE UNLESS LEAK CAN BE STOPPED.**

Small Fire

- Dry chemical, CO_2 or water spray.

Large Fire

- Water spray, fog or regular foam.
- Move containers from fire area if you can do it without risk.

Fire involving Tanks

- Fight fire from maximum distance or use unmanned hose holders or monitor nozzles.
- Cool containers with flooding quantities of water until well after fire is out.
- Do not direct water at source of leak or safety devices; icing may occur.
- Withdraw immediately in case of rising sound from venting safety devices or discoloration of tank.
- ALWAYS stay away from tanks engulfed in fire.

SPILL OR LEAK

- ELIMINATE all ignition sources (no smoking, flares, sparks or flames in immediate area).
- All equipment used when handling the product must be grounded.
- Fully encapsulating, vapor protective clothing should be worn for spills and leaks with no fire.
- Do not touch or walk through spilled material.
- Stop leak if you can do it without risk.
- Use water spray to reduce vapors or divert vapor cloud drift. Avoid allowing water runoff to contact spilled material.
- Do not direct water at spill or source of leak.
- If possible, turn leaking containers so that gas escapes rather than liquid.
- Prevent entry into waterways, sewers, basements or confined areas.
- Isolate area until gas has dispersed.

FIRST AID

- Move victim to fresh air.
- Call 911 or emergency medical service.
- Give artificial respiration if victim is not breathing.
- Administer oxygen if breathing is difficult.
- Remove and isolate contaminated clothing and shoes.
- In case of contact with substance, immediately flush skin or eyes with running water for at least 20 minutes.
- In case of contact with liquefied gas, thaw frosted parts with lukewarm water.
- Keep victim warm and quiet.
- Keep victim under observation.
- Effects of contact or inhalation may be delayed.
- Ensure that medical personnel are aware of the material(s) involved and take precautions to protect themselves.

POTENTIAL HAZARDS

FIRE OR EXPLOSION

- Substance is transported in molten form at a temperature above 705°C (1300°F).
- Violent reaction with water; contact may cause an explosion or may produce a flammable gas.
- Will ignite combustible materials (wood, paper, oil, debris, etc.).
- Contact with nitrates or other oxidizers may cause an explosion.
- Contact with containers or other materials, including cold, wet or dirty tools, may cause an explosion.
- Contact with concrete will cause spalling and small pops.

HEALTH

- Contact causes severe burns to skin and eyes.
- Fire may produce irritating and/or toxic gases.

PUBLIC SAFETY

- **CALL EMERGENCY RESPONSE Telephone Number on Shipping Paper first. If Shipping Paper not available or no answer, refer to appropriate telephone number listed on the inside back cover.**
- As an immediate precautionary measure, isolate spill or leak area for at least 50 meters (150 feet) in all directions.
- Keep unauthorized personnel away.
- Ventilate closed spaces before entering.

PROTECTIVE CLOTHING

- Wear positive pressure self-contained breathing apparatus (SCBA).
- Wear flame retardant structural firefighters' protective clothing, including faceshield, helmet and gloves, this will provide limited thermal protection.

EMERGENCY RESPONSE

FIRE

- **Do Not Use Water, except in life threatening situations and then only in a fine spray.**
- **Do not use halogenated extinguishing agents or foam.**
- Move combustibles out of path of advancing pool if you can do so without risk.
- Extinguish fires started by molten material by using appropriate method for the burning material; keep water, halogenated extinguishing agents and foam away from the molten material.

SPILL OR LEAK

- Do not touch or walk through spilled material.
- Do not attempt to stop leak, due to danger of explosion.
- Keep combustibles (wood, paper, oil, etc.) away from spilled material.
- Substance is very fluid, spreads quickly, and may splash. Do not try to stop it with shovels or other objects.
- Dike far ahead of spill; use dry sand to contain the flow of material.
- Where possible allow molten material to solidify naturally.
- Avoid contact even after material solidifies. Molten, heated and cold aluminum look alike; do not touch unless you know it is cold.
- Clean up under the supervision of an expert after material has solidified.

FIRST AID

- Move victim to fresh air.
- Call 911 or emergency medical service.
- Give artificial respiration if victim is not breathing.
- Administer oxygen if breathing is difficult.
- For severe burns, immediate medical attention is required.
- Removal of solidified molten material from skin requires medical assistance.
- Remove and isolate contaminated clothing and shoes.
- In case of contact with substance, immediately flush skin or eyes with running water for at least 20 minutes.
- Keep victim warm and quiet.

POTENTIAL HAZARDS

FIRE OR EXPLOSION
- May react violently or explosively on contact with water.
- Some are transported in flammable liquids.
- May be ignited by friction, heat, sparks or flames.
- Some of these materials will burn with intense heat.
- Dusts or fumes may form explosive mixtures in air.
- Containers may explode when heated.
- May re-ignite after fire is extinguished.

HEALTH
- Oxides from metallic fires are a severe health hazard.
- Inhalation or contact with substance or decomposition products may cause severe injury or death.
- Fire may produce irritating, corrosive and/or toxic gases.
- Runoff from fire control or dilution water may cause pollution.

PUBLIC SAFETY
- **CALL EMERGENCY RESPONSE Telephone Number on Shipping Paper first. If Shipping Paper not available or no answer, refer to appropriate telephone number listed on the inside back cover.**
- As an immediate precautionary measure, isolate spill or leak area in all directions for at least 50 meters (150 feet) for liquids and at least 25 meters (75 feet) for solids.
- Stay upwind.
- Keep unauthorized personnel away.

PROTECTIVE CLOTHING
- Wear positive pressure self-contained breathing apparatus (SCBA).
- Structural firefighters' protective clothing will only provide limited protection.

EVACUATION
Large Spill
- Consider initial downwind evacuation for at least 50 meters (160 feet).

Fire
- If tank, rail car or tank truck is involved in a fire, ISOLATE for 800 meters (1/2 mile) in all directions; also, consider initial evacuation for 800 meters (1/2 mile) in all directions.

EMERGENCY RESPONSE

FIRE

- **DO NOT USE WATER, FOAM OR CO$_2$.**
- Dousing metallic fires with water will generate hydrogen gas, an extremely dangerous explosion hazard, particularly if fire is in a confined environment (i.e., building, cargo hold, etc.).
- Use DRY sand, graphite powder, dry sodium chloride based extinguishers, G-1® or Met-L-X® powder.
- Confining and smothering metal fires is preferable rather than applying water.
- Move containers from fire area if you can do it without risk.

Fire involving Tanks or Car/Trailer Loads

- If impossible to extinguish, protect surroundings and allow fire to burn itself out.

SPILL OR LEAK

- ELIMINATE all ignition sources (no smoking, flares, sparks or flames in immediate area).
- Do not touch or walk through spilled material.
- Stop leak if you can do it without risk.
- Prevent entry into waterways, sewers, basements or confined areas.

FIRST AID

- Move victim to fresh air.
- Call 911 or emergency medical service.
- Give artificial respiration if victim is not breathing.
- Administer oxygen if breathing is difficult.
- Remove and isolate contaminated clothing and shoes.
- In case of contact with substance, immediately flush skin or eyes with running water for at least 20 minutes.
- Keep victim warm and quiet.
- Ensure that medical personnel are aware of the material(s) involved and take precautions to protect themselves.

POTENTIAL HAZARDS

FIRE OR EXPLOSION

- Some may burn but none ignite readily.
- Containers may explode when heated.
- Some may be transported hot.

HEALTH

- Inhalation of material may be harmful.
- Contact may cause burns to skin and eyes.
- Inhalation of Asbestos dust may have a damaging effect on the lungs.
- Fire may produce irritating, corrosive and/or toxic gases.
- Some liquids produce vapors that may cause dizziness or suffocation.
- Runoff from fire control may cause pollution.

PUBLIC SAFETY

- **CALL EMERGENCY RESPONSE Telephone Number on Shipping Paper first. If Shipping Paper not available or no answer, refer to appropriate telephone number listed on the inside back cover.**
- As an immediate precautionary measure, isolate spill or leak area in all directions for at least 50 meters (150 feet) for liquids and at least 25 meters (75 feet) for solids.
- Keep unauthorized personnel away.
- Stay upwind.

PROTECTIVE CLOTHING

- Wear positive pressure self-contained breathing apparatus (SCBA).
- Structural firefighters' protective clothing will only provide limited protection.

EVACUATION

Spill

- See Table 1 - Initial Isolation and Protective Action Distances for highlighted materials. For non-highlighted materials, increase, in the downwind direction, as necessary, the isolation distance shown under "PUBLIC SAFETY".

Fire

- If tank, rail car or tank truck is involved in a fire, ISOLATE for 800 meters (1/2 mile) in all directions; also, consider initial evacuation for 800 meters (1/2 mile) in all directions.

EMERGENCY RESPONSE

FIRE

Small Fire
- Dry chemical, CO_2, water spray or regular foam.

Large Fire
- Water spray, fog or regular foam.
- Do not scatter spilled material with high pressure water streams.
- Move containers from fire area if you can do it without risk.
- Dike fire-control water for later disposal.

Fire involving Tanks
- Cool containers with flooding quantities of water until well after fire is out.
- Withdraw immediately in case of rising sound from venting safety devices or discoloration of tank.
- ALWAYS stay away from tanks engulfed in fire.

SPILL OR LEAK

- Do not touch or walk through spilled material.
- Stop leak if you can do it without risk.
- Prevent dust cloud.
- Avoid inhalation of asbestos dust.

Small Dry Spill
- With clean shovel place material into clean, dry container and cover loosely; move containers from spill area.

Small Spill
- Take up with sand or other non-combustible absorbent material and place into containers for later disposal.

Large Spill
- Dike far ahead of liquid spill for later disposal.
- Cover powder spill with plastic sheet or tarp to minimize spreading.
- Prevent entry into waterways, sewers, basements or confined areas.

FIRST AID

- Move victim to fresh air.
- Call 911 or emergency medical service.
- Give artificial respiration if victim is not breathing.
- Administer oxygen if breathing is difficult.
- Remove and isolate contaminated clothing and shoes.
- In case of contact with substance, immediately flush skin or eyes with running water for at least 20 minutes.
- Ensure that medical personnel are aware of the material(s) involved and take precautions to protect themselves.

POTENTIAL HAZARDS

HEALTH

- Inhalation of vapors or contact with substance will result in contamination and potential harmful effects.
- Fire will produce irritating, corrosive and/or toxic gases.

FIRE OR EXPLOSION

- Non-combustible, substance itself does not burn but may react upon heating to produce corrosive and/or toxic fumes.
- Runoff may pollute waterways.

PUBLIC SAFETY

- **CALL EMERGENCY RESPONSE Telephone Number on Shipping Paper first. If Shipping Paper not available or no answer, refer to appropriate telephone number listed on the inside back cover.**
- As an immediate precautionary measure, isolate spill or leak area for at least 50 meters (150 feet) in all directions.
- Stay upwind.
- Keep unauthorized personnel away.

PROTECTIVE CLOTHING

- Wear positive pressure self-contained breathing apparatus (SCBA).
- Structural firefighters' protective clothing will only provide limited protection.

EVACUATION

Large Spill

- Consider initial downwind evacuation for at least 100 meters (330 feet).

Fire

- When any large container is involved in a fire, consider initial evacuation for 500 meters (1/3 mile) in all directions.

EMERGENCY RESPONSE

FIRE
- Use extinguishing agent suitable for type of surrounding fire.
- **Do not direct water at the heated metal.**

SPILL OR LEAK
- Do not touch or walk through spilled material.
- Do not touch damaged containers or spilled material unless wearing appropriate protective clothing.
- Stop leak if you can do it without risk.
- Prevent entry into waterways, sewers, basements or confined areas.
- Do not use steel or aluminum tools or equipment.
- Cover with earth, sand or other non-combustible material followed with plastic sheet to minimize spreading or contact with rain.
- For mercury, use a mercury spill kit.
- Mercury spill areas may be subsequently treated with calcium sulphide/calcium sulfide or with sodium thiosulphate/sodium thiosulfate wash to neutralize any residual mercury.

FIRST AID
- Move victim to fresh air.
- Call 911 or emergency medical service.
- Give artificial respiration if victim is not breathing.
- Administer oxygen if breathing is difficult.
- Remove and isolate contaminated clothing and shoes.
- In case of contact with substance, immediately flush skin or eyes with running water for at least 20 minutes.
- Keep victim warm and quiet.
- Ensure that medical personnel are aware of the material(s) involved and take precautions to protect themselves.

NOTES

INTRODUCTION TO GREEN TABLES - INITIAL ISOLATION
AND PROTECTIVE ACTION DISTANCES

Table 1 - Initial Isolation and Protective Action Distances suggests distances useful to protect people from vapors resulting from spills involving dangerous goods that are considered toxic by inhalation (TIH). This list includes certain chemical warfare agents and materials that produce toxic gases upon contact with water. Table 1 provides first responders with initial guidance until technically qualified emergency response personnel are available.

The **Initial Isolation Zone** defines an area SURROUNDING the incident in which persons may be exposed to dangerous (upwind) and life threatening (downwind) concentrations of material. The **Protective Action Zone** defines an area DOWNWIND from the incident in which persons may become incapacitated and unable to take protective action and/or incur serious or irreversible health effects. Table 1 provides specific guidance for small and large spills occurring day or night.

Adjusting distances for a specific incident involves many interdependent variables and should be made only by personnel technically qualified to make such adjustments. For this reason, no precise guidance can be provided in this document to aid in adjusting the table distances; however, general guidance follows.

Factors That May Change the Protective Action Distances

The orange-bordered guide for a material clearly indicates under the section EVACUATION – Fire, the evacuation distance required to protect against fragmentation hazard of a large container. If the material becomes involved in a **FIRE**, the toxic hazard may be less than the fire or explosion hazard. In these cases, the **Fire** hazard distance should be used.

Initial isolation and protective action distances in this guidebook are derived from historical data on transportation incidents and the use of statistical models. For worst-case scenarios involving the instantaneous release of the entire contents of a package (e.g., as a result of terrorism, sabotage or catastrophic accident) the distances may increase substantially. For such events, doubling of the initial isolation and protective action distances is appropriate in absence of other information.

If more than one tank car containing TIH materials involved in the incident is leaking, LARGE SPILL distances may need to be increased.

For a material with a protective action distance of 11.0+ km (7.0+ miles), the actual distance can be larger in certain atmospheric conditions. If the dangerous goods vapor plume is channeled in a valley or between many tall buildings, distances may be larger than shown in Table 1 due to less mixing of the plume with the atmosphere. Daytime spills in regions with known strong inversions or snow cover, or occurring near sunset, may require an increase of the protective action distance because airborne contaminants mix and disperse more slowly and may travel much farther downwind. In such cases, the nighttime protective action distance may be more appropriate. In addition, protective action distances may be larger for liquid spills when either the material or outdoor temperature exceeds 30°C (86°F).

Materials which react with water to produce large amounts of toxic gases are included in Table 1 - Initial Isolation and Protective Action Distances. Note that some water-reactive materials (WRM) which are also TIH (e.g., Bromine trifluoride (1746), Thionyl chloride (1836), etc.) produce additional TIH materials when spilled in water. For these materials, two entries are provided in Table 1 - Initial Isolation and Protective Action Distances (i.e., for spills on land and for spills in water). **If it is not clear whether the spill is on land or in water, or in cases where the spill occurs both on land and in water, choose the larger Protective Action Distance.**

Following Table 1, **Table 2** – Water-Reactive Materials Which Produce Toxic Gases lists materials that produce large amounts of Toxic Inhalation Hazard gases (TIH) when spilled in water as well as the toxic gases that are produced when spilled in water.

When a water-reactive TIH producing material is spilled into a river or stream, the source of the toxic gas may move with the current and stretch from the spill point downstream for a substantial distance.

Finally, **Table 3** lists Initial Isolation and Protective Action Distances for Toxic Inhalation Hazard materials that may be more commonly encountered.

The selected materials are:

- Ammonia, anhydrous (UN1005)
- Chlorine (UN1017)
- Ethylene oxide (UN1040)
- Hydrogen chloride (UN1050) and Hydrogen chloride, refrigerated liquid (UN2186)
- Hydrogen fluoride (UN1052)
- Sulfur dioxide/Sulphur dioxide (UN1079)

The materials are presented in alphabetical order and provide Initial Isolation and Protective Action Distances for large spills (more than 208 liters or 55 US gallons) involving different container types (therefore different volume capacities) for day time and night time situations and for different wind speeds.

PROTECTIVE ACTION DECISION FACTORS TO CONSIDER

The choice of protective actions for a given situation depends on a number of factors. For some cases, evacuation may be the best option; in others, sheltering in-place may be the best course. Sometimes, these two actions may be used in combination. In any emergency, officials need to quickly give the public instructions. The public will need continuing information and instructions while being evacuated or sheltered in-place.

Proper evaluation of the factors listed below will determine the effectiveness of evacuation or in-place protection (shelter in-place). The importance of these factors can vary with emergency conditions. In specific emergencies, other factors may need to be identified and considered as well. This list indicates what kind of information may be needed to make the initial decision.

The Dangerous Goods

- Degree of health hazard
- Chemical and physical properties
- Amount involved
- Containment/control of release
- Rate of vapor movement

The Population Threatened

- Location
- Number of people
- Time available to evacuate or shelter in-place
- Ability to control evacuation or shelter in-place
- Building types and availability
- Special institutions or populations, e.g., nursing homes, hospitals, prisons

Weather Conditions

- Effect on vapor and cloud movement
- Potential for change
- Effect on evacuation or shelter in-place

PROTECTIVE ACTIONS

Protective Actions are those steps taken to preserve the health and safety of emergency responders and the public during an incident involving releases of dangerous goods. Table 1 - Initial Isolation and Protective Action Distances (green-bordered pages) predicts the size of downwind areas which could be affected by a cloud of toxic gas. People in this area should be evacuated and/or sheltered in-place inside buildings.

Isolate Hazard Area and Deny Entry means to keep everybody away from the area if they are not directly involved in emergency response operations. Unprotected emergency responders should not be allowed to enter the isolation zone. This "isolation" task is done first to establish control over the area of operations. This is the first step for any protective actions that may follow. See Table 1 - Initial Isolation and Protective Action Distances (green-bordered pages) for more detailed information on specific materials.

Evacuate means to move all people from a threatened area to a safer place. To perform an evacuation, there must be enough time for people to be warned, to get ready, and to leave an area. If there is enough time, evacuation is the best protective action. Begin evacuating people nearby and those outdoors in direct view of the scene. When additional help arrives, expand the area to be evacuated downwind and crosswind to at least the extent recommended in this guidebook. Even after people move to the distances recommended, they may not be completely safe from harm. They should not be permitted to congregate at such distances. Send evacuees to a definite place, by a specific route, far enough away so they will not have to be moved again if the wind shifts.

Shelter In-Place means people should seek shelter inside a building and remain inside until the danger passes. **Sheltering in-place is used when evacuating the public would cause greater risk than staying where they are, or when an evacuation cannot be performed.** Direct the people inside to **close all doors and windows** and to **shut off all ventilating, heating and cooling systems.** In-place protection (shelter in-place) may not be the best option if (a) the vapors are flammable; (b) if it will take a long time for the gas to clear the area; or (c) if buildings cannot be closed tightly. Vehicles can offer some protection for a short period if the windows are closed and the ventilating systems are shut off. Vehicles are not as effective as buildings for in-place protection.

It is vital to maintain communications with competent persons inside the building so that they are advised about changing conditions. **Persons protected-in-place should be warned to stay far from windows** because of the danger from glass and projected metal fragments in a fire and/or explosion.

Every dangerous goods incident is different. Each will have special problems and concerns. Action to protect the public must be selected carefully. These pages can help with **initial** decisions on how to protect the public. Officials must continue to gather information and monitor the situation until the threat is removed.

BACKGROUND ON TABLE 1 - INITIAL ISOLATION
AND PROTECTIVE ACTION DISTANCES

Initial Isolation and Protective Action Distances in this guidebook were determined for small and large spills occurring during day or night. The overall analysis was statistical in nature and utilized state-of-the-art emission rate and dispersion models; statistical release data from the U.S. DOT HMIS (Hazardous Materials Information System) database; meteorological observations from over 120 locations in United States, Canada and Mexico; and the most current toxicological exposure guidelines.

For each chemical, thousands of hypothetical releases were modeled to account for the statistical variation in both release amount and atmospheric conditions. Based on this statistical sample, the 90th percentile Protective Action Distance for each chemical and category was selected to appear in the Table. A brief description of the analysis is provided below. A detailed report outlining the methodology and data used in the generation of the Initial Isolation and Protective Action Distances may be obtained from the U.S. Department of Transportation, Pipeline and Hazardous Materials Safety Administration.

Release amounts and emission rates into the atmosphere were statistically modeled based on (1) data from the U.S. DOT HMIS database; (2) container types and sizes authorized for transport as specified in 49 CFR §172.101 and Part 173; (3) physical properties of the individual materials, and (4) atmospheric data from a historical database. The emission model calculated the release of vapor due to evaporation of pools on the ground, direct release of vapors from the container, or a combination of both, as would occur for liquefied gases which can flash to form both a vapor/aerosol mixture and an evaporating pool. In addition, the emission model also calculated the emission of toxic vapor by-products generated from spilling water-reactive materials in water. Spills that involve releases of approximately 208 liters for liquids (55 US gallons) and 300 kg for solids (660 pounds) or less are considered Small Spills, while spills that involve greater quantities are considered Large Spills. An exception to this is certain chemical warfare agents where Small Spills include releases up to 2 kg (4.4 lbs), and Large Spills include releases up to 25 kg (55 lbs). These agents are BZ, CX, GA, GB, GD, GF, HD, HL, HN1, HN2, HN3, L and VX.

Downwind dispersion of the vapor was estimated for each case modeled. Atmospheric parameters affecting the dispersion, and the emission rate, were selected in a statistical fashion from a database containing hourly meteorological data from 120 cities in the United States, Canada and Mexico. The dispersion calculation accounted for the time dependent emission rate from the source as well as the density of the vapor plume (i.e., heavy gas effects). Since atmospheric mixing is less effective at dispersing vapor plumes during nighttime, day and night were separated in the analysis. In Table 1, "Day" refers to time periods after sunrise and before sunset, while "Night" includes all hours between sunset and sunrise.

Toxicological short-term exposure guidelines for the materials were applied to determine the downwind distance to which persons may become incapacitated and unable to take protective action or may incur serious health effects after a once-in-a-lifetime, or rare, exposure. When available, toxicological exposure guidelines were chosen from AEGL-2 or ERPG-2 emergency response guidelines, with AEGL-2 values being the first choice. For materials that do not have AEGL-2 or ERPG-2 values, emergency response guidelines estimated from lethal concentration limits derived from animal studies were used, as recommended by an independent panel of toxicological experts from industry and academia.

HOW TO USE TABLE 1 - INITIAL ISOLATION AND PROTECTIVE ACTION DISTANCES

(1) The responder should already have:

  • Identified the material by its ID Number and Name; (if an ID Number cannot be found, use the Name of Material index in the blue-bordered pages to locate that number.)

  • Found the three-digit guide for that material in order to consult the emergency actions recommended jointly with this table;

  • **Noted the wind direction.**

(2) Look in Table 1 (the green-bordered pages) for the ID Number and Name of the Material involved in the incident. Some ID Numbers have more than one shipping name listed— look for the specific name of the material. (If the shipping name is not known and Table 1 lists more than one name for the same ID Number, use the entry with the largest protective action distances.)

(3) Determine if the incident involves a SMALL or LARGE spill and if DAY or NIGHT. Generally, a SMALL SPILL is one which involves a single, small package (e.g., a drum containing up to approximately 208 liters (55 US gallons)), a small cylinder, or a small leak from a large package. A LARGE SPILL is one which involves a spill from a large package, or multiple spills from many small packages. DAY is any time after sunrise and before sunset. NIGHT is any time between sunset and sunrise.

(4) Look up the INITIAL ISOLATION DISTANCE. Direct all persons to move, in a crosswind direction, away from the spill to the distance specified—in meters and feet.

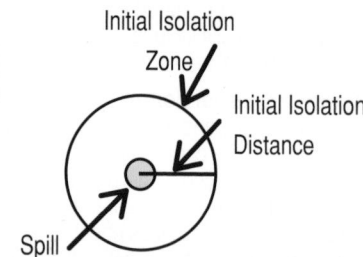

(5) Look up the initial PROTECTIVE ACTION DISTANCE shown in Table 1. For a given material, spill size, and whether day or night, Table 1 gives the downwind distance—in kilometers and miles— for which protective actions should be considered. For practical purposes, the Protective Action Zone (i.e., the area in which people are at risk of harmful exposure) is a square, whose length and width are the same as the downwind distance shown in Table 1.

(6) Initiate Protective Actions to the extent possible, beginning with those closest to the spill site and working away from the site in the downwind direction. When a water-reactive TIH producing material is spilled into a river or stream, the source of the toxic gas may move with the current or stretch from the spill point downstream for a substantial distance.

The shape of the area in which protective actions should be taken (the Protective Action Zone) is shown in this figure. The spill is located at the center of the small circle. The larger circle represents the INITIAL ISOLATION zone around the spill.

NOTE 1: See "Introduction To Green Tables – Initial Isolation And Protective Action Distances" under "Factors That May Change the Protective Action Distances" (page 285)

NOTE 2: See Table 2 – Water-Reactive Materials which Produce Toxic Gases for the list of gases produced when these materials are spilled in water.

Call the emergency response telephone number listed on the shipping paper or the appropriate response agency as soon as possible for additional information on the material, safety precautions and mitigation procedures.

TABLE 1 - INITIAL ISOLATION AND PROTECTIVE ACTION DISTANCES

ID No.	Guide	NAME OF MATERIAL	SMALL SPILLS (From a small package or small leak from a large package) First ISOLATE in all Directions Meters (Feet)	Then PROTECT persons Downwind during- DAY Kilometers (Miles)	NIGHT Kilometers (Miles)	LARGE SPILLS (From a large package or from many small packages) First ISOLATE in all Directions Meters (Feet)	Then PROTECT persons Downwind during- DAY Kilometers (Miles)	NIGHT Kilometers (Miles)
1005 *	125	Ammonia, anhydrous	30 m (100 ft)	0.1 km (0.1 mi)	0.2 km (0.1 mi)	150 m (500 ft)	0.8 km (0.5 mi)	2.0 km (1.3 mi)
1005 *	125	Anhydrous ammonia						
1008	125	Boron trifluoride	30 m (100 ft)	0.1 km (0.1 mi)	0.5 km (0.4 mi)	300 m (1000 ft)	1.7 km (1.1 mi)	4.8 km (3.0 mi)
1008	125	Boron trifluoride, compressed						
1016	119	Carbon monoxide	30 m (100 ft)	0.1 km (0.1 mi)	0.2 km (0.1 mi)	200 m (600 ft)	1.2 km (0.8 mi)	4.8 km (3.0 mi)
1016	119	Carbon monoxide, compressed						
1017 *	124	Chlorine	60 m (200 ft)	0.4 km (0.2 mi)	1.5 km (1.0 mi)	500 m (1500 ft)	3.0 km (1.9 mi)	7.9 km (4.9 mi)
1023	119	Coal gas	60 m (200 ft)	0.2 km (0.1 mi)	0.2 km (0.1 mi)	100 m (300 ft)	0.4 km (0.2 mi)	0.5 km (0.3 mi)
1023	119	Coal gas, compressed						
1026	119	Cyanogen	30 m (100 ft)	0.1 km (0.1 mi)	0.5 km (0.3 mi)	60 m (200 ft)	0.4 km (0.2 mi)	1.7 km (1.0 mi)
1026	119	Cyanogen gas						
1040 *	119P	Ethylene oxide	30 m (100 ft)	0.1 km (0.1 mi)	0.2 km (0.1 mi)	150 m (500 ft)	0.9 km (0.5 mi)	2.0 km (1.3 mi)
1040 *	119P	Ethylene oxide with Nitrogen						
1045	124	Fluorine	30 m (100 ft)	0.1 km (0.1 mi)	0.2 km (0.1 mi)	100 m (300 ft)	0.5 km (0.3 mi)	2.3 km (1.4 mi)
1045	124	Fluorine, compressed						
1048	125	Hydrogen bromide, anhydrous	30 m (100 ft)	0.1 km (0.1 mi)	0.3 km (0.2 mi)	200 m (600 ft)	1.2 km (0.8 mi)	3.9 km (2.4 mi)
1050 *	125	Hydrogen chloride, anhydrous	30 m (100 ft)	0.1 km (0.1 mi)	0.3 km (0.2 mi)	60 m (200 ft)	0.3 km (0.2 mi)	1.3 km (0.8 mi)
1051	117	AC (when used as a weapon)	60 m (200 ft)	0.3 km (0.2 mi)	1.0 km (0.6 mi)	1000 m (3000 ft)	3.7 km (2.3 mi)	8.4 km (5.3 mi)

ID No.	Guide No.	Name of Material	SMALL SPILLS First ISOLATE in all Directions	SMALL SPILLS Then PROTECT persons Downwind during- DAY	SMALL SPILLS Then PROTECT persons Downwind during- NIGHT	LARGE SPILLS First ISOLATE in all Directions	LARGE SPILLS Then PROTECT persons Downwind during- DAY	LARGE SPILLS Then PROTECT persons Downwind during- NIGHT
1051	117	Hydrocyanic acid, aqueous solutions, with more than 20% Hydrogen cyanide	60 m (200 ft)	0.2 km (0.1 mi)	0.6 km (0.4 mi)	400 m (1250 ft)	1.4 km (0.9 mi)	3.8 km (2.4 mi)
1051	117	Hydrogen cyanide, anhydrous, stabilized						
1051	117	Hydrogen cyanide, stabilized						
1052 *	125	Hydrogen fluoride, anhydrous	30 m (100 ft)	0.1 km (0.1 mi)	0.5 km (0.3 mi)	300 m (1000 ft)	1.5 km (0.9 mi)	3.2 km (2.0 mi)
1053	117	Hydrogen sulfide	30 m (100 ft)	0.1 km (0.1 mi)	0.4 km (0.3 mi)	300 m (1000 ft)	1.7 km (1.0 mi)	5.6 km (3.5 mi)
1053	117	Hydrogen sulphide						
1062	123	Methyl bromide	30 m (100 ft)	0.1 km (0.1 mi)	0.2 km (0.2 mi)	100 m (300 ft)	0.6 km (0.4 mi)	1.9 km (1.2 mi)
1064	117	Methyl mercaptan	30 m (100 ft)	0.1 km (0.1 mi)	0.3 km (0.2 mi)	150 m (500 ft)	1.0 km (0.7 mi)	3.2 km (2.0 mi)
1067	124	Dinitrogen tetroxide	30 m (100 ft)	0.1 km (0.1 mi)	0.4 km (0.2 mi)	300 m (1000 ft)	1.1 km (0.7 mi)	2.7 km (1.7 mi)
1067	124	Nitrogen dioxide						
1069	125	Nitrosyl chloride	30 m (100 ft)	0.2 km (0.2 mi)	1.1 km (0.7 mi)	600 m (2000 ft)	3.6 km (2.3 mi)	9.5 km (5.9 mi)
1071	119	Oil gas	60 m (200 ft)	0.2 km (0.1 mi)	0.2 km (0.1 mi)	100 m (300 ft)	0.4 km (0.2 mi)	0.5 km (0.3 mi)
1071	119	Oil gas, compressed						
1076	125	CG (when used as a weapon)	150 m (500 ft)	0.8 km (0.5 mi)	3.2 km (2.0 mi)	1000 m (3000 ft)	7.5 km (4.7 mi)	11.0+ km (7.0+ mi)
1076	125	Diphosgene	30 m (100 ft)	0.2 km (0.1 mi)	0.2 km (0.1 mi)	30 m (100 ft)	0.3 km (0.2 mi)	0.5 km (0.3 mi)
1076	125	DP (when used as a weapon)	30 m (100 ft)	0.2 km (0.1 mi)	0.7 km (0.4 mi)	200 m (600 ft)	1.0 km (0.7 mi)	2.4 km (1.5 mi)
1076	125	Phosgene	100 m (300 ft)	0.6 km (0.4 mi)	2.7 km (1.7 mi)	500 m (1500 ft)	3.1 km (1.9 mi)	10.8 km (6.7 mi)
1079 *	125	Sulfur dioxide	100 m (300 ft)	0.7 km (0.4 mi)	2.8 km (1.7 mi)	1000 m (3000 ft)	5.6 km (3.5 mi)	11.0+ km (7.0+ mi)
1079 *	125	Sulphur dioxide						
1082	119P	Trifluorochloroethylene, stabilized	30 m (100 ft)	0.1 km (0.1 mi)	0.2 km (0.1 mi)	60 m (200 ft)	0.4 km (0.3 mi)	0.9 km (0.6 mi)
1092	131P	Acrolein, stabilized	150 m (500 ft)	1.4 km (0.9 mi)	4.0 km (2.5 mi)	800 m (2500 ft)	9.3 km (5.8 mi)	11.0+ km (7.0+ mi)
1098	131	Allyl alcohol	30 m (100 ft)	0.1 km (0.1 mi)	0.1 km (0.1 mi)	60 m (200 ft)	0.3 km (0.2 mi)	0.5 km (0.3 mi)

"+" means distance can be larger in certain atmospheric conditions   * PLEASE ALSO CONSULT TABLE 3 FOR THIS MATERIAL

TABLE 1 - INITIAL ISOLATION AND PROTECTIVE ACTION DISTANCES

ID No.	Guide	NAME OF MATERIAL	SMALL SPILLS (From a small package or small leak from a large package) First ISOLATE in all Directions Meters (Feet)	Then PROTECT persons Downwind during- DAY Kilometers (Miles)	NIGHT Kilometers (Miles)	LARGE SPILLS (From a large package or from many small packages) First ISOLATE in all Directions Meters (Feet)	Then PROTECT persons Downwind during- DAY Kilometers (Miles)	NIGHT Kilometers (Miles)
1135	131	Ethylene chlorohydrin	30 m (100 ft)	0.1 km (0.1 mi)	0.1 km (0.1 mi)	60 m (200 ft)	0.3 km (0.2 mi)	0.4 km (0.3 mi)
1143	131P	Crotonaldehyde	30 m (100 ft)	0.1 km (0.1 mi)	0.2 km (0.1 mi)	60 m (200 ft)	0.5 km (0.3 mi)	1.0 km (0.6 mi)
1143	131P	Crotonaldehyde, stabilized						
1162	155	Dimethyldichlorosilane (when spilled in water)	30 m (100 ft)	0.1 km (0.1 mi)	0.2 km (0.2 mi)	60 m (200 ft)	0.6 km (0.4 mi)	1.9 km (1.2 mi)
1163	131	1,1-Dimethylhydrazine	30 m (100 ft)	0.2 km (0.1 mi)	0.5 km (0.4 mi)	100 m (300 ft)	1.1 km (0.7 mi)	2.2 km (1.4 mi)
1163	131	Dimethylhydrazine, unsymmetrical						
1182	155	Ethyl chloroformate	30 m (100 ft)	0.1 km (0.1 mi)	0.2 km (0.1 mi)	60 m (200 ft)	0.4 km (0.2 mi)	0.6 km (0.4 mi)
1183	139	Ethyldichlorosilane (when spilled in water)	30 m (100 ft)	0.1 km (0.1 mi)	0.3 km (0.2 mi)	60 m (200 ft)	0.7 km (0.5 mi)	2.2 km (1.4 mi)
1185	131P	Ethyleneimine, stabilized	30 m (100 ft)	0.2 km (0.1 mi)	0.5 km (0.3 mi)	100 m (300 ft)	1.0 km (0.6 mi)	2.0 km (1.3 mi)
1196	155	Ethyltrichlorosilane (when spilled in water)	30 m (100 ft)	0.2 km (0.1 mi)	0.7 km (0.5 mi)	200 m (600 ft)	2.1 km (1.3 mi)	6.3 km (3.9 mi)
1238	155	Methyl chloroformate	30 m (100 ft)	0.2 km (0.2 mi)	0.6 km (0.4 mi)	150 m (500 ft)	1.1 km (0.7 mi)	2.3 km (1.4 mi)
1239	131	Methyl chloromethyl ether	30 m (100 ft)	0.3 km (0.2 mi)	1.1 km (0.7 mi)	200 m (600 ft)	2.2 km (1.4 mi)	4.6 km (2.9 mi)
1242	139	Methyldichlorosilane (when spilled in water)	30 m (100 ft)	0.1 km (0.1 mi)	0.3 km (0.2 mi)	60 m (200 ft)	0.8 km (0.5 mi)	2.5 km (1.6 mi)
1244	131	Methylhydrazine	30 m (100 ft)	0.3 km (0.2 mi)	0.6 km (0.4 mi)	100 m (300 ft)	1.4 km (0.9 mi)	2.3 km (1.4 mi)
1250	155	Methyltrichlorosilane (when spilled in water)	30 m (100 ft)	0.1 km (0.1 mi)	0.3 km (0.2 mi)	100 m (300 ft)	0.9 km (0.6 mi)	2.6 km (1.7 mi)

ID No.	Guide No.	Name of Material	SMALL SPILLS First ISOLATE	SMALL SPILLS Then PROTECT Day	SMALL SPILLS Then PROTECT Night	LARGE SPILLS First ISOLATE	LARGE SPILLS Then PROTECT Day	LARGE SPILLS Then PROTECT Night
1251	131P	Methyl vinyl ketone, stabilized	100 m (300 ft)	0.3 km (0.2 mi)	0.8 km (0.5 mi)	800 m (2500 ft)	1.5 km (1.0 mi)	3.0 km (1.9 mi)
1259	131	Nickel carbonyl	100 m (300 ft)	1.4 km (0.9 mi)	5.4 km (3.4 mi)	1000 m (3000 ft)	11.0+ km (7.0+ mi)	11.0+ km (7.0+ mi)
1295	139	Trichlorosilane **(when spilled in water)**	30 m (100 ft)	0.1 km (0.1 mi)	0.3 km (0.2 mi)	60 m (200 ft)	0.7 km (0.4 mi)	2.2 km (1.4 mi)
1298	155	Trimethylchlorosilane **(when spilled in water)**	30 m (100 ft)	0.1 km (0.1 mi)	0.2 km (0.1 mi)	60 m (200 ft)	0.6 km (0.4 mi)	1.6 km (1.0 mi)
1305	155P	Vinyltrichlorosilane **(when spilled in water)**	30 m (100 ft)	0.1 km (0.1 mi)	0.2 km (0.1 mi)	60 m (200 ft)	0.6 km (0.4 mi)	2.0 km (1.3 mi)
1305	155P	Vinyltrichlorosilane, stabilized **(when spilled in water)**						
1340	139	Phosphorus pentasulfide, free from yellow and white Phosphorus **(when spilled in water)**	30 m (100 ft)	0.1 km (0.1 mi)	0.2 km (0.1 mi)	60 m (200 ft)	0.4 km (0.2 mi)	1.4 km (0.9 mi)
1340	139	Phosphorus pentasulphide, free from yellow and white Phosphorus **(when spilled in water)**						
1360	139	Calcium phosphide **(when spilled in water)**	30 m (100 ft)	0.2 km (0.1 mi)	0.7 km (0.4 mi)	300 m (1000 ft)	1.1 km (0.7 mi)	3.8 km (2.4 mi)
1380	135	Pentaborane	60 m (200 ft)	0.6 km (0.4 mi)	2.0 km (1.2 mi)	200 m (600 ft)	2.7 km (1.7 mi)	8.2 km (5.1 mi)
1384	135	Sodium dithionite **(when spilled in water)**	30 m (100 ft)	0.2 km (0.1 mi)	0.6 km (0.4 mi)	60 m (200 ft)	0.8 km (0.5 mi)	2.7 km (1.7 mi)
1384	135	Sodium hydrosulfite **(when spilled in water)**						
1384	135	Sodium hydrosulphite **(when spilled in water)**						
1397	139	Aluminum phosphide **(when spilled in water)**	60 m (200 ft)	0.2 km (0.2 mi)	0.9 km (0.6 mi)	500 m (1500 ft)	2.1 km (1.3 mi)	7.5 km (4.7 mi)

"+" means distance can be larger in certain atmospheric conditions

TABLE 1 - INITIAL ISOLATION AND PROTECTIVE ACTION DISTANCES

ID No.	Guide	NAME OF MATERIAL	SMALL SPILLS (From a small package or small leak from a large package)				LARGE SPILLS (From a large package or from many small packages)			
			First ISOLATE in all Directions	Then PROTECT persons Downwind during-			First ISOLATE in all Directions	Then PROTECT persons Downwind during-		
			Meters (Feet)	DAY Kilometers (Miles)	NIGHT Kilometers (Miles)		Meters (Feet)	DAY Kilometers (Miles)	NIGHT Kilometers (Miles)	
1419	139	Magnesium aluminum phosphide (when spilled in water)	60 m (200 ft)	0.2 km (0.1 mi)	0.9 km (0.5 mi)		500 m (1500 ft)	1.9 km (1.2 mi)	6.5 km (4.1 mi)	
1432	139	Sodium phosphide (when spilled in water)	30 m (100 ft)	0.2 km (0.1 mi)	0.6 km (0.4 mi)		400 m (1250 ft)	1.4 km (0.9 mi)	4.2 km (2.6 mi)	
1510	143	Tetranitromethane	30 m (100 ft)	0.2 km (0.2 mi)	0.4 km (0.2 mi)		60 m (200 ft)	0.5 km (0.4 mi)	1.0 km (0.6 mi)	
1541	155	Acetone cyanohydrin, stabilized (when spilled in water)	30 m (100 ft)	0.1 km (0.1 mi)	0.1 km (0.1 mi)		100 m (300 ft)	0.3 km (0.2 mi)	1.0 km (0.7 mi)	
1556	152	MD (when used as a weapon)	300 m (1000 ft)	1.6 km (1.0 mi)	4.3 km (2.7 mi)		1000 m (3000 ft)	11.0+ km (7.0+ mi)	11.0+ km (7.0+ mi)	
1556	152	Methyldichloroarsine	100 m (300 ft)	1.4 km (0.9 mi)	2.2 km (1.4 mi)		300 m (1000 ft)	3.8 km (2.4 mi)	6.9 km (4.3 mi)	
1556	152	PD (when used as a weapon)	60 m (200 ft)	0.4 km (0.3 mi)	0.4 km (0.3 mi)		300 m (1000 ft)	1.6 km (1.0 mi)	1.6 km (1.0 mi)	
1560 1560	157 157	Arsenic chloride Arsenic trichloride	30 m (100 ft)	0.2 km (0.1 mi)	0.3 km (0.2 mi)		100 m (300 ft)	1.0 km (0.6 mi)	1.6 km (1.0 mi)	
1569	131	Bromoacetone	30 m (100 ft)	0.4 km (0.3 mi)	1.2 km (0.8 mi)		150 m (500 ft)	1.9 km (1.2 mi)	3.6 km (2.3 mi)	
1580	154	Chloropicrin	30 m (100 ft)	0.4 km (0.3 mi)	1.0 km (0.6 mi)		150 m (500 ft)	1.6 km (1.0 mi)	3.1 km (1.9 mi)	
1581	123	Chloropicrin and Methyl bromide mixture	30 m (100 ft)	0.1 km (0.1 mi)	0.6 km (0.4 mi)		300 m (1000 ft)	2.1 km (1.3 mi)	5.9 km (3.7 mi)	
1581	123	Methyl bromide and Chloropicrin mixture								

ID No.	Guide No.	Name of Material	SMALL SPILLS First ISOLATE in all Directions	SMALL SPILLS Then PROTECT DAY	SMALL SPILLS Then PROTECT NIGHT	LARGE SPILLS First ISOLATE in all Directions	LARGE SPILLS Then PROTECT DAY	LARGE SPILLS Then PROTECT NIGHT
1582	119	Chloropicrin and Methyl chloride mixture	30 m (100 ft)	0.1 km (0.1 mi)	0.4 km (0.3 mi)	60 m (200 ft)	0.4 km (0.2 mi)	1.7 km (1.1 mi)
1582	119	Methyl chloride and Chloropicrin mixture						
1583	154	Chloropicrin mixture, n.o.s.	30 m (100 ft)	0.4 km (0.3 mi)	1.0 km (0.6 mi)	150 m (500 ft)	1.6 km (1.0 mi)	3.1 km (1.9 mi)
1589	125	CK (when used as a weapon)	150 m (500 ft)	1.0 km (0.6 mi)	3.8 km (2.4 mi)	800 m (2500 ft)	5.7 km (3.6 mi)	11.0+ km (7.0+ mi)
1589	125	Cyanogen chloride, stabilized	100 m (300 ft)	0.5 km (0.3 mi)	2.2 km (1.4 mi)	400 m (1250 ft)	2.6 km (1.7 mi)	8.6 km (5.4 mi)
1595	156	Dimethyl sulfate	30 m (100 ft)	0.2 km (0.1 mi)	0.2 km (0.1 mi)	60 m (200 ft)	0.5 km (0.3 mi)	0.8 km (0.5 mi)
1595	156	Dimethyl sulphate						
1605	154	Ethylene dibromide	30 m (100 ft)	0.1 km (0.1 mi)	0.1 km (0.1 mi)	30 m (100 ft)	0.2 km (0.1 mi)	0.2 km (0.1 mi)
1612	123	Hexaethyl tetraphosphate and compressed gas mixture	100 m (300 ft)	0.8 km (0.5 mi)	2.7 km (1.7 mi)	400 m (1250 ft)	3.5 km (2.2 mi)	8.1 km (5.1 mi)
1613	154	Hydrocyanic acid, aqueous solution, with not more than 20% Hydrogen cyanide	60 m (200 ft)	0.2 km (0.1 mi)	0.2 km (0.1 mi)	150 m (500 ft)	0.5 km (0.3 mi)	1.3 km (0.8 mi)
1613	154	Hydrogen cyanide, aqueous solution, with not more than 20% Hydrogen cyanide						
1614	152	Hydrogen cyanide, stabilized (absorbed)	60 m (200 ft)	0.2 km (0.1 mi)	0.7 km (0.4 mi)	150 m (500 ft)	0.5 km (0.4 mi)	1.7 km (1.1 mi)
1647	151	Ethylene dibromide and Methyl bromide mixture, liquid	30 m (100 ft)	0.1 km (0.1 mi)	0.2 km (0.2 mi)	100 m (300 ft)	0.6 km (0.4 mi)	1.9 km (1.2 mi)
1647	151	Methyl bromide and Ethylene dibromide mixture, liquid						
1660	124	Nitric oxide	30 m (100 ft)	0.1 km (0.1 mi)	0.6 km (0.4 mi)	100 m (300 ft)	0.6 km (0.4 mi)	2.3 km (1.5 mi)
1660	124	Nitric oxide, compressed						
1670	157	Perchloromethyl mercaptan	30 m (100 ft)	0.2 km (0.2 mi)	0.4 km (0.2 mi)	100 m (300 ft)	0.7 km (0.5 mi)	1.3 km (0.8 mi)

"+" means distance can be larger in certain atmospheric conditions

TABLE 1 - INITIAL ISOLATION AND PROTECTIVE ACTION DISTANCES

ID No.	Guide	NAME OF MATERIAL	SMALL SPILLS (From a small package or small leak from a large package)				LARGE SPILLS (From a large package or from many small packages)				
			First ISOLATE in all Directions	Then PROTECT persons Downwind during-			First ISOLATE in all Directions	Then PROTECT persons Downwind during-			
				DAY	NIGHT			DAY		NIGHT	
			Meters (Feet)	Kilometers (Miles)	Kilometers (Miles)		Meters (Feet)	Kilometers (Miles)		Kilometers (Miles)	
1680	157	Potassium cyanide (when spilled in water)	30 m (100 ft)	0.1 km (0.1 mi)	0.2 km (0.1 mi)		100 m (300 ft)	0.3 km (0.2 mi)		1.2 km (0.8 mi)	
1680	157	Potassium cyanide, solid (when spilled in water)									
1689	157	Sodium cyanide (when spilled in water)	30 m (100 ft)	0.1 km (0.1 mi)	0.2 km (0.1 mi)		100 m (300 ft)	0.4 km (0.2 mi)		1.4 km (0.9 mi)	
1689	157	Sodium cyanide, solid (when spilled in water)									
1694	159	CA (when used as a weapon)	30 m (100 ft)	0.1 km (0.1 mi)	0.4 km (0.3 mi)		100 m (300 ft)	0.5 km (0.4 mi)		2.6 km (1.6 mi)	
1695	131	Chloroacetone, stabilized	30 m (100 ft)	0.1 km (0.1 mi)	0.2 km (0.1 mi)		60 m (200 ft)	0.4 km (0.3 mi)		0.8 km (0.5 mi)	
1697	153	CN (when used as a weapon)	30 m (100 ft)	0.1 km (0.1 mi)	0.2 km (0.1 mi)		60 m (200 ft)	0.3 km (0.2 mi)		1.2 km (0.8 mi)	
1698	154	Adamsite (when used as a weapon)	30 m (100 ft)	0.1 km (0.1 mi)	0.3 km (0.2 mi)		60 m (200 ft)	0.3 km (0.2 mi)		1.4 km (0.9 mi)	
1698	154	DM (when used as a weapon)									
1699	151	DA (when used as a weapon)	30 m (100 ft)	0.2 km (0.1 mi)	0.8 km (0.5 mi)		300 m (1000 ft)	1.9 km (1.2 mi)		7.5 km (4.7 mi)	
1716	156	Acetyl bromide (when spilled in water)	30 m (100 ft)	0.1 km (0.1 mi)	0.2 km (0.1 mi)		60 m (200 ft)	0.5 km (0.3 mi)		1.3 km (0.8 mi)	
1717	155	Acetyl chloride (when spilled in water)	30 m (100 ft)	0.1 km (0.1 mi)	0.3 km (0.2 mi)		100 m (300 ft)	1.0 km (0.6 mi)		2.8 km (1.7 mi)	
1722	155	Allyl chlorocarbonate	100 m (300 ft)	0.4 km (0.2 mi)	0.9 km (0.6 mi)		400 m (1250 ft)	1.5 km (1.0 mi)		3.0 km (1.9 mi)	
1722	155	Allyl chloroformate									

ID No.	Guide No.	NAME OF MATERIAL	SMALL SPILLS First ISOLATE in all Directions	SMALL SPILLS Then PROTECT Downwind DAY	SMALL SPILLS Then PROTECT Downwind NIGHT	LARGE SPILLS First ISOLATE in all Directions	LARGE SPILLS Then PROTECT Downwind DAY	LARGE SPILLS Then PROTECT Downwind NIGHT
1724	155	Allyltrichlorosilane, stabilized (when spilled in water)	30 m (100 ft)	0.1 km (0.1 mi)	0.2 km (0.2 mi)	60 m (200 ft)	0.6 km (0.4 mi)	1.9 km (1.2 mi)
1725	137	Aluminum bromide, anhydrous (when spilled in water)	30 m (100 ft)	0.1 km (0.1 mi)	0.1 km (0.1 mi)	30 m (100 ft)	0.2 km (0.1 mi)	0.6 km (0.4 mi)
1726	137	Aluminum chloride, anhydrous (when spilled in water)	30 m (100 ft)	0.1 km (0.1 mi)	0.3 km (0.2 mi)	60 m (200 ft)	0.6 km (0.4 mi)	2.2 km (1.4 mi)
1728	155	Amyltrichlorosilane (when spilled in water)	30 m (100 ft)	0.1 km (0.1 mi)	0.2 km (0.2 mi)	60 m (200 ft)	0.6 km (0.4 mi)	1.9 km (1.2 mi)
1732	157	Antimony pentafluoride (when spilled in water)	30 m (100 ft)	0.1 km (0.1 mi)	0.5 km (0.3 mi)	150 m (500 ft)	1.2 km (0.7 mi)	4.2 km (2.6 mi)
1741	125	Boron trichloride (when spilled on land)	30 m (100 ft)	0.1 km (0.1 mi)	0.3 km (0.2 mi)	100 m (300 ft)	0.6 km (0.4 mi)	1.4 km (0.9 mi)
1741	125	Boron trichloride (when spilled in water)	30 m (100 ft)	0.1 km (0.1 mi)	0.5 km (0.3 mi)	100 m (300 ft)	1.3 km (0.8 mi)	3.8 km (2.4 mi)
1744 1744 1744	154 154 154	Bromine Bromine, solution Bromine, solution (Inhalation Hazard Zone A)	60 m (200 ft)	0.6 km (0.4 mi)	1.9 km (1.2 mi)	300 m (1000 ft)	2.8 km (1.8 mi)	6.5 km (4.0 mi)
1744	154	Bromine, solution (Inhalation Hazard Zone B)	60 m (200 ft)	0.5 km (0.3 mi)	1.3 km (0.8 mi)	150 m (500 ft)	1.8 km (1.1 mi)	4.2 km (2.6 mi)
1745	144	Bromine pentafluoride (when spilled on land)	30 m (100 ft)	0.4 km (0.2 mi)	1.4 km (0.9 mi)	200 m (600 ft)	2.3 km (1.4 mi)	5.1 km (3.2 mi)
1745	144	Bromine pentafluoride (when spilled in water)	30 m (100 ft)	0.1 km (0.1 mi)	0.6 km (0.4 mi)	150 m (500 ft)	1.2 km (0.8 mi)	4.4 km (2.7 mi)
1746	144	Bromine trifluoride (when spilled on land)	30 m (100 ft)	0.1 km (0.1 mi)	0.2 km (0.1 mi)	30 m (100 ft)	0.3 km (0.2 mi)	0.5 km (0.4 mi)
1746	144	Bromine trifluoride (when spilled in water)	30 m (100 ft)	0.1 km (0.1 mi)	0.5 km (0.3 mi)	100 m (300 ft)	1.1 km (0.7 mi)	4.1 km (2.5 mi)

"+" means distance can be larger in certain atmospheric conditions

TABLE 1 - INITIAL ISOLATION AND PROTECTIVE ACTION DISTANCES

ID No.	Guide	NAME OF MATERIAL	SMALL SPILLS (From a small package or small leak from a large package) First ISOLATE in all Directions Meters (Feet)	SMALL SPILLS Then PROTECT persons Downwind during- DAY Kilometers (Miles)	SMALL SPILLS Then PROTECT persons Downwind during- NIGHT Kilometers (Miles)	LARGE SPILLS (From a large package or from many small packages) First ISOLATE in all Directions Meters (Feet)	LARGE SPILLS Then PROTECT persons Downwind during- DAY Kilometers (Miles)	LARGE SPILLS Then PROTECT persons Downwind during- NIGHT Kilometers (Miles)
1747	155	Butyltrichlorosilane (when spilled in water)	30 m (100 ft)	0.1 km (0.1 mi)	0.2 km (0.2 mi)	60 m (200 ft)	0.6 km (0.4 mi)	1.8 km (1.1 mi)
1749	124	Chlorine trifluoride	60 m (200 ft)	0.3 km (0.2 mi)	1.2 km (0.8 mi)	300 m (1000 ft)	1.5 km (0.9 mi)	4.6 km (2.9 mi)
1752	156	Chloroacetyl chloride (when spilled on land)	30 m (100 ft)	0.3 km (0.2 mi)	0.6 km (0.4 mi)	100 m (300 ft)	1.2 km (0.8 mi)	2.3 km (1.4 mi)
1752	156	Chloroacetyl chloride (when spilled in water)	30 m (100 ft)	0.1 km (0.1 mi)	0.1 km (0.1 mi)	30 m (100 ft)	0.3 km (0.2 mi)	0.9 km (0.6 mi)
1753	156	Chlorophenyltrichlorosilane (when spilled in water)	30 m (100 ft)	0.1 km (0.1 mi)	0.1 km (0.1 mi)	30 m (100 ft)	0.3 km (0.2 mi)	1.0 km (0.7 mi)
1754	137	Chlorosulfonic acid (when spilled on land)	30 m (100 ft)	0.1 km (0.1 mi)	0.1 km (0.1 mi)	30 m (100 ft)	0.3 km (0.2 mi)	0.4 km (0.2 mi)
1754	137	Chlorosulfonic acid (when spilled in water)	30 m (100 ft)	0.1 km (0.1 mi)	0.3 km (0.2 mi)	60 m (200 ft)	0.7 km (0.5 mi)	2.5 km (1.5 mi)
1754	137	Chlorosulfonic acid and Sulfur trioxide mixture (when spilled on land)	100 m (300 ft)	0.4 km (0.2 mi)	0.9 km (0.5 mi)	400 m (1250 ft)	2.9 km (1.8 mi)	5.7 km (3.5 mi)
1754	137	Chlorosulfonic acid and Sulfur trioxide mixture (when spilled in water)	30 m (100 ft)	0.1 km (0.1 mi)	0.3 km (0.2 mi)	60 m (200 ft)	0.7 km (0.5 mi)	2.5 km (1.5 mi)
1754	137	Chlorosulphonic acid (when spilled on land)	30 m (100 ft)	0.1 km (0.1 mi)	0.1 km (0.1 mi)	30 m (100 ft)	0.3 km (0.2 mi)	0.4 km (0.2 mi)

ID No.	Guide No.	NAME OF MATERIAL	SMALL SPILLS First ISOLATE in all Directions	SMALL SPILLS Then PROTECT persons Downwind during DAY	SMALL SPILLS Then PROTECT persons Downwind during NIGHT	LARGE SPILLS First ISOLATE in all Directions	LARGE SPILLS Then PROTECT persons Downwind during DAY	LARGE SPILLS Then PROTECT persons Downwind during NIGHT
1754	137	Chlorosulphonic acid (when spilled in water)	30 m (100 ft)	0.1 km (0.1 mi)	0.3 km (0.2 mi)	60 m (200 ft)	0.7 km (0.5 mi)	2.5 km (1.5 mi)
1754	137	Chlorosulphonic acid and Sulphur trioxide mixture (when spilled on land)	100 m (300 ft)	0.4 km (0.2 mi)	0.9 km (0.5 mi)	400 m (1250 ft)	2.9 km (1.8 mi)	5.7 km (3.5 mi)
1754	137	Chlorosulphonic acid and Sulphur trioxide mixture (when spilled in water)	30 m (100 ft)	0.1 km (0.1 mi)	0.3 km (0.2 mi)	60 m (200 ft)	0.7 km (0.5 mi)	2.5 km (1.5 mi)
1754	137	Sulfur trioxide and Chlorosulfonic acid mixture (when spilled on land)	100 m (300 ft)	0.4 km (0.2 mi)	0.9 km (0.5 mi)	400 m (1250 ft)	2.9 km (1.8 mi)	5.7 km (3.5 mi)
1754	137	Sulfur trioxide and Chlorosulfonic acid mixture (when spilled in water)	30 m (100 ft)	0.1 km (0.1 mi)	0.3 km (0.2 mi)	60 m (200 ft)	0.7 km (0.5 mi)	2.5 km (1.5 mi)
1754	137	Sulphur trioxide and Chlorosulphonic acid mixture (when spilled on land)	100 m (300 ft)	0.4 km (0.2 mi)	0.9 km (0.5 mi)	400 m (1250 ft)	2.9 km (1.8 mi)	5.7 km (3.5 mi)
1754	137	Sulphur trioxide and Chlorosulphonic acid mixture (when spilled in water)	30 m (100 ft)	0.1 km (0.1 mi)	0.3 km (0.2 mi)	60 m (200 ft)	0.7 km (0.5 mi)	2.5 km (1.5 mi)
1758	137	Chromium oxychloride (when spilled in water)	30 m (100 ft)	0.1 km (0.1 mi)	0.1 km (0.1 mi)	30 m (100 ft)	0.2 km (0.2 mi)	0.8 km (0.5 mi)
1762	156	Cyclohexenyltrichlorosilane (when spilled in water)	30 m (100 ft)	0.1 km (0.1 mi)	0.2 km (0.1 mi)	30 m (100 ft)	0.4 km (0.3 mi)	1.4 km (0.9 mi)
1763	156	Cyclohexyltrichlorosilane (when spilled in water)	30 m (100 ft)	0.1 km (0.1 mi)	0.2 km (0.1 mi)	30 m (100 ft)	0.4 km (0.3 mi)	1.4 km (0.9 mi)

"+" means distance can be larger in certain atmospheric conditions

TABLE 1 - INITIAL ISOLATION AND PROTECTIVE ACTION DISTANCES

ID No.	Guide	NAME OF MATERIAL	SMALL SPILLS (From a small package or small leak from a large package)				LARGE SPILLS (From a large package or from many small packages)				
			First ISOLATE in all Directions	Then PROTECT persons Downwind during-			First ISOLATE in all Directions	Then PROTECT persons Downwind during-			
					DAY	NIGHT			DAY		NIGHT
			Meters (Feet)	Kilometers (Miles)		Kilometers (Miles)	Meters (Feet)	Kilometers (Miles)		Kilometers (Miles)	
1765	156	Dichloroacetyl chloride (when spilled in water)	30 m (100 ft)	0.1 km (0.1 mi)	0.1 km (0.1 mi)		30 m (100 ft)	0.3 km (0.2 mi)		1.0 km (0.6 mi)	
1766	156	Dichlorophenyltrichlorosilane (when spilled in water)	30 m (100 ft)	0.1 km (0.1 mi)	0.2 km (0.2 mi)		60 m (200 ft)	0.6 km (0.4 mi)		2.1 km (1.3 mi)	
1767	155	Diethyldichlorosilane (when spilled in water)	30 m (100 ft)	0.1 km (0.1 mi)	0.1 km (0.1 mi)		30 m (100 ft)	0.4 km (0.3 mi)		1.1 km (0.7 mi)	
1769	156	Diphenyldichlorosilane (when spilled in water)	30 m (100 ft)	0.1 km (0.1 mi)	0.2 km (0.1 mi)		30 m (100 ft)	0.4 km (0.3 mi)		1.3 km (0.8 mi)	
1771	156	Dodecyltrichlorosilane (when spilled in water)	30 m (100 ft)	0.1 km (0.1 mi)	0.2 km (0.1 mi)		60 m (200 ft)	0.5 km (0.3 mi)		1.4 km (0.9 mi)	
1777	137	Fluorosulfonic acid (when spilled in water)	30 m (100 ft)	0.1 km (0.1 mi)	0.1 km (0.1 mi)		30 m (100 ft)	0.2 km (0.2 mi)		0.8 km (0.5 mi)	
1777	137	Fluorosulphonic acid (when spilled in water)									
1781	156	Hexadecyltrichlorosilane (when spilled in water)	30 m (100 ft)	0.1 km (0.1 mi)	0.1 km (0.1 mi)		30 m (100 ft)	0.2 km (0.2 mi)		0.7 km (0.4 mi)	
1784	156	Hexyltrichlorosilane (when spilled in water)	30 m (100 ft)	0.1 km (0.1 mi)	0.2 km (0.1 mi)		60 m (200 ft)	0.5 km (0.3 mi)		1.5 km (0.9 mi)	
1799	156	Nonyltrichlorosilane (when spilled in water)	30 m (100 ft)	0.1 km (0.1 mi)	0.2 km (0.1 mi)		60 m (200 ft)	0.5 km (0.3 mi)		1.6 km (1.0 mi)	
1800	156	Octadecyltrichlorosilane (when spilled in water)	30 m (100 ft)	0.1 km (0.1 mi)	0.2 km (0.1 mi)		60 m (200 ft)	0.5 km (0.3 mi)		1.5 km (1.0 mi)	

ID No.	Guide No.	Name of Material	SMALL SPILLS — First ISOLATE	SMALL SPILLS — Then PROTECT (day)	SMALL SPILLS — Then PROTECT (night)	LARGE SPILLS — First ISOLATE	LARGE SPILLS — Then PROTECT (day)	LARGE SPILLS — Then PROTECT (night)
1801	156	Octyltrichlorosilane (when spilled in water)	30 m (100 ft)	0.1 km (0.1 mi)	0.2 km (0.1 mi)	60 m (200 ft)	0.5 km (0.3 mi)	1.6 km (1.0 mi)
1804	156	Phenyltrichlorosilane (when spilled in water)	30 m (100 ft)	0.1 km (0.1 mi)	0.2 km (0.1 mi)	60 m (200 ft)	0.5 km (0.3 mi)	1.5 km (1.0 mi)
1806	137	Phosphorus pentachloride (when spilled in water)	30 m (100 ft)	0.1 km (0.1 mi)	0.2 km (0.2 mi)	30 m (100 ft)	0.4 km (0.3 mi)	1.5 km (0.9 mi)
1808	137	Phosphorus tribromide (when spilled in water)	30 m (100 ft)	0.1 km (0.1 mi)	0.4 km (0.2 mi)	60 m (200 ft)	0.6 km (0.4 mi)	2.0 km (1.2 mi)
1809	137	Phosphorus trichloride (when spilled on land)	30 m (100 ft)	0.2 km (0.1 mi)	0.5 km (0.3 mi)	100 m (300 ft)	1.0 km (0.6 mi)	2.2 km (1.4 mi)
1809	137	Phosphorus trichloride (when spilled in water)	30 m (100 ft)	0.1 km (0.1 mi)	0.3 km (0.2 mi)	60 m (200 ft)	0.8 km (0.5 mi)	2.5 km (1.6 mi)
1810	137	Phosphorus oxychloride (when spilled on land)	30 m (100 ft)	0.3 km (0.2 mi)	0.7 km (0.4 mi)	100 m (300 ft)	1.2 km (0.7 mi)	2.2 km (1.4 mi)
1810	137	Phosphorus oxychloride (when spilled in water)	30 m (100 ft)	0.1 km (0.1 mi)	0.3 km (0.2 mi)	60 m (200 ft)	0.7 km (0.4 mi)	2.3 km (1.4 mi)
1815	132	Propionyl chloride (when spilled in water)	30 m (100 ft)	0.1 km (0.1 mi)	0.1 km (0.1 mi)	30 m (100 ft)	0.3 km (0.2 mi)	0.8 km (0.5 mi)
1816	155	Propyltrichlorosilane (when spilled in water)	30 m (100 ft)	0.1 km (0.1 mi)	0.3 km (0.2 mi)	60 m (200 ft)	0.6 km (0.4 mi)	2.0 km (1.3 mi)
1818	157	Silicon tetrachloride (when spilled in water)	30 m (100 ft)	0.1 km (0.1 mi)	0.3 km (0.2 mi)	100 m (300 ft)	0.9 km (0.6 mi)	2.8 km (1.7 mi)
1828	137	Sulfur chlorides (when spilled on land)	30 m (100 ft)	0.1 km (0.1 mi)	0.1 km (0.1 mi)	60 m (200 ft)	0.3 km (0.2 mi)	0.5 km (0.3 mi)
1828	137	Sulfur chlorides (when spilled in water)	30 m (100 ft)	0.2 km (0.1 mi)	0.2 km (0.1 mi)	30 m (100 ft)	0.4 km (0.2 mi)	1.2 km (0.8 mi)
1828	137	Sulphur chlorides (when spilled on land)	30 m (100 ft)	0.1 km (0.1 mi)	0.1 km (0.1 mi)	60 m (200 ft)	0.3 km (0.2 mi)	0.5 km (0.3 mi)

"+" means distance can be larger in certain atmospheric conditions

TABLE 1 - INITIAL ISOLATION AND PROTECTIVE ACTION DISTANCES

ID No.	Guide	NAME OF MATERIAL	SMALL SPILLS (From a small package or small leak from a large package)			LARGE SPILLS (From a large package or from many small packages)		
			First ISOLATE in all Directions Meters (Feet)	Then PROTECT persons Downwind during— DAY Kilometers (Miles)	NIGHT Kilometers (Miles)	First ISOLATE in all Directions Meters (Feet)	Then PROTECT persons Downwind during— DAY Kilometers (Miles)	NIGHT Kilometers (Miles)
1828	137	Sulphur chlorides (when spilled in water)	30 m (100 ft)	0.1 km (0.1 mi)	0.2 km (0.1 mi)	30 m (100 ft)	0.4 km (0.2 mi)	1.2 km (0.8 mi)
1829 1829	137 137	Sulfur trioxide, stabilized Sulphur trioxide, stabilized	100 m (300 ft)	0.4 km (0.2 mi)	0.9 km (0.5 mi)	400 m (1250 ft)	2.9 km (1.8 mi)	5.7 km (3.5 mi)
1831 1831	137 137	Sulfuric acid, fuming Sulfuric acid, fuming, with not less than 30% free Sulfur trioxide	100 m (300 ft)	0.4 km (0.2 mi)	0.9 km (0.5 mi)	400 m (1250 ft)	2.9 km (1.8 mi)	5.7 km (3.5 mi)
1831 1831	137 137	Sulphuric acid, fuming Sulphuric acid, fuming, with not less than 30% free Sulphur trioxide						
1834	137	Sulfuryl chloride (when spilled on land)	30 m (100 ft)	0.2 km (0.1 mi)	0.5 km (0.4 mi)	100 m (300 ft)	0.9 km (0.6 mi)	2.0 km (1.3 mi)
1834	137	Sulfuryl chloride (when spilled in water)	30 m (100 ft)	0.1 km (0.1 mi)	0.2 km (0.1 mi)	60 m (200 ft)	0.5 km (0.3 mi)	1.8 km (1.1 mi)
1834	137	Sulphuryl chloride (when spilled on land)	30 m (100 ft)	0.2 km (0.1 mi)	0.5 km (0.4 mi)	100 m (300 ft)	0.9 km (0.6 mi)	2.0 km (1.3 mi)
1834	137	Sulphuryl chloride (when spilled in water)	30 m (100 ft)	0.1 km (0.1 mi)	0.2 km (0.1 mi)	60 m (200 ft)	0.5 km (0.3 mi)	1.8 km (1.1 mi)
1836	137	Thionyl chloride (when spilled on land)	30 m (100 ft)	0.2 km (0.2 mi)	0.7 km (0.5 mi)	100 m (300 ft)	0.9 km (0.6 mi)	1.9 km (1.2 mi)

ID No.	Guide No.	NAME OF MATERIAL	SMALL SPILLS First ISOLATE in all Directions	SMALL SPILLS Then PROTECT persons Downwind DAY	SMALL SPILLS Then PROTECT persons Downwind NIGHT	LARGE SPILLS First ISOLATE in all Directions	LARGE SPILLS Then PROTECT persons Downwind DAY	LARGE SPILLS Then PROTECT persons Downwind NIGHT
1836	137	Thionyl chloride (when spilled in water)	100 m (300 ft)	1.1 km (0.7 mi)	3.0 km (1.9 mi)	800 m (2500 ft)	9.9 km (6.2 mi)	11.0+ km (7.0+ mi)
1838	137	Titanium tetrachloride (when spilled on land)	30 m (100 ft)	0.1 km (0.1 mi)	0.2 km (0.1 mi)	30 m (100 ft)	0.4 km (0.3 mi)	0.7 km (0.4 mi)
1838	137	Titanium tetrachloride (when spilled in water)	30 m (100 ft)	0.1 km (0.1 mi)	0.2 km (0.1 mi)	60 m (200 ft)	0.5 km (0.3 mi)	1.8 km (1.1 mi)
1859	125	Silicon tetrafluoride / Silicon tetrafluoride, compressed	30 m (100 ft)	0.2 km (0.1 mi)	0.8 km (0.5 mi)	100 m (300 ft)	0.6 km (0.4 mi)	2.5 km (1.6 mi)
1892	151	ED (when used as a weapon)	150 m (500 ft)	2.0 km (1.2 mi)	2.9 km (1.8 mi)	1000 m (3000 ft)	10.4 km (6.5 mi)	11.0+ km (7.0+ mi)
1892	151	Ethyldichloroarsine	150 m (500 ft)	1.5 km (1.0 mi)	2.4 km (1.5 mi)	500 m (1500 ft)	5.2 km (3.3 mi)	10.2 km (6.1 mi)
1898	156	Acetyl iodide (when spilled in water)	30 m (100 ft)	0.1 km (0.1 mi)	0.2 km (0.2 mi)	60 m (200 ft)	0.5 km (0.3 mi)	1.1 km (0.7 mi)
1911	119	Diborane / Diborane, compressed	60 m (200 ft)	0.3 km (0.2 mi)	1.0 km (0.7 mi)	200 m (600 ft)	1.3 km (0.8 mi)	3.9 km (2.5 mi)
1923	135	Calcium dithionite (when spilled in water)	30 m (100 ft)	0.2 km (0.1 mi)	0.7 km (0.4 mi)	60 m (200 ft)	0.8 km (0.5 mi)	2.8 km (1.7 mi)
1923	135	Calcium hydrosulfite (when spilled in water)						
1923	135	Calcium hydrosulfite (when spilled in water) / Calcium hydrosulphite (when spilled in water)						
1929	135	Potassium dithionite (when spilled in water)	30 m (100 ft)	0.2 km (0.1 mi)	0.6 km (0.4 mi)	60 m (200 ft)	0.7 km (0.4 mi)	2.5 km (1.5 mi)
1929	135	Potassium hydrosulfite (when spilled in water)						
1929	135	Potassium hydrosulphite (when spilled in water)						

"+" means distance can be larger in certain atmospheric conditions

TABLE 1 - INITIAL ISOLATION AND PROTECTIVE ACTION DISTANCES

ID No.	Guide	NAME OF MATERIAL	SMALL SPILLS (From a small package or small leak from a large package)				LARGE SPILLS (From a large package or from many small packages)			
			First ISOLATE in all Directions	Then PROTECT persons Downwind during-			First ISOLATE in all Directions	Then PROTECT persons Downwind during-		
					DAY	NIGHT			DAY	NIGHT
			Meters (Feet)		Kilometers (Miles)	Kilometers (Miles)	Meters (Feet)		Kilometers (Miles)	Kilometers (Miles)
1931	171	Zinc dithionite **(when spilled in water)**	30 m (100 ft)		0.2 km (0.1 mi)	0.6 km (0.4 mi)	60 m (200 ft)		0.7 km (0.5 mi)	2.5 km (1.6 mi)
1931	171	Zinc hydrosulfite **(when spilled in water)**								
1931	171	Zinc hydrosulphite **(when spilled in water)**								
1953	119	Compressed gas, flammable, poisonous, n.o.s. (Inhalation Hazard Zone A)	100 m (300 ft)		0.5 km (0.3 mi)	2.2 km (1.4 mi)	600 m (2000 ft)		2.6 km (1.7 mi)	8.6 km (5.4 mi)
1953	119	Compressed gas, flammable, poisonous, n.o.s. (Inhalation Hazard Zone B)	30 m (100 ft)		0.1 km (0.1 mi)	0.3 km (0.2 mi)	300 m (1000 ft)		1.3 km (0.8 mi)	3.5 km (2.2 mi)
1953	119	Compressed gas, flammable, poisonous, n.o.s. (Inhalation Hazard Zone C)	30 m (100 ft)		0.1 km (0.1 mi)	0.3 km (0.2 mi)	200 m (600 ft)		1.0 km (0.7 mi)	3.2 km (2.0 mi)
1953	119	Compressed gas, flammable, poisonous, n.o.s. (Inhalation Hazard Zone D)	30 m (100 ft)		0.1 km (0.1 mi)	0.2 km (0.1 mi)	200 m (600 ft)		0.8 km (0.5 mi)	2.0 km (1.3 mi)
1953	119	Compressed gas, flammable, toxic, n.o.s. (Inhalation Hazard Zone A)	100 m (300 ft)		0.5 km (0.3 mi)	2.2 km (1.4 mi)	600 m (2000 ft)		2.6 km (1.7 mi)	8.6 km (5.4 mi)
1953	119	Compressed gas, flammable, toxic, n.o.s. (Inhalation Hazard Zone B)	30 m (100 ft)		0.1 km (0.1 mi)	0.3 km (0.2 mi)	300 m (1000 ft)		1.3 km (0.8 mi)	3.5 km (2.2 mi)

ID No.	Guide No.	NAME OF MATERIAL	SMALL SPILLS First ISOLATE in all Directions	SMALL SPILLS Then PROTECT persons Downwind during DAY	SMALL SPILLS Then PROTECT persons Downwind during NIGHT	LARGE SPILLS First ISOLATE in all Directions	LARGE SPILLS Then PROTECT persons Downwind during DAY	LARGE SPILLS Then PROTECT persons Downwind during NIGHT
1953	119	Compressed gas, flammable, toxic, n.o.s. (Inhalation Hazard Zone C)	30 m (100 ft)	0.1 km (0.1 mi)	0.3 km (0.2 mi)	200 m (600 ft)	1.0 km (0.7 mi)	3.2 km (2.0 mi)
1953	119	Compressed gas, flammable, toxic, n.o.s. (Inhalation Hazard Zone D)	30 m (100 ft)	0.1 km (0.1 mi)	0.2 km (0.1 mi)	200 m (600 ft)	0.8 km (0.5 mi)	2.0 km (1.3 mi)
1953	119	Compressed gas, poisonous, flammable, n.o.s.	100 m (300 ft)	0.5 km (0.3 mi)	2.2 km (1.4 mi)	600 m (2000 ft)	2.6 km (1.7 mi)	8.6 km (5.4 mi)
1953	119	Compressed gas, poisonous, flammable, n.o.s. (Inhalation Hazard Zone A)						
1953	119	Compressed gas, poisonous, flammable, n.o.s. (Inhalation Hazard Zone B)	30 m (100 ft)	0.1 km (0.1 mi)	0.3 km (0.2 mi)	300 m (1000 ft)	1.3 km (0.8 mi)	3.5 km (2.2 mi)
1953	119	Compressed gas, poisonous, flammable, n.o.s. (Inhalation Hazard Zone C)	30 m (100 ft)	0.1 km (0.1 mi)	0.3 km (0.2 mi)	200 m (600 ft)	1.0 km (0.7 mi)	3.2 km (2.0 mi)
1953	119	Compressed gas, poisonous, flammable, n.o.s. (Inhalation Hazard Zone D)	30 m (100 ft)	0.1 km (0.1 mi)	0.2 km (0.1 mi)	200 m (600 ft)	0.8 km (0.5 mi)	2.0 km (1.3 mi)
1953	119	Compressed gas, toxic, flammable, n.o.s.	100 m (300 ft)	0.5 km (0.3 mi)	2.2 km (1.4 mi)	600 m (2000 ft)	2.6 km (1.7 mi)	8.6 km (5.4 mi)
1953	119	Compressed gas, toxic, flammable, n.o.s. (Inhalation Hazard Zone A)						
1953	119	Compressed gas, toxic, flammable, n.o.s. (Inhalation Hazard Zone B)	30 m (100 ft)	0.1 km (0.1 mi)	0.3 km (0.2 mi)	300 m (1000 ft)	1.3 km (0.8 mi)	3.5 km (2.2 mi)
1953	119	Compressed gas, toxic, flammable, n.o.s. (Inhalation Hazard Zone C)	30 m (100 ft)	0.1 km (0.1 mi)	0.3 km (0.2 mi)	200 m (600 ft)	1.0 km (0.7 mi)	3.2 km (2.0 mi)

"+" means distance can be larger in certain atmospheric conditions

TABLE 1 - INITIAL ISOLATION AND PROTECTIVE ACTION DISTANCES

ID No.	Guide	NAME OF MATERIAL	SMALL SPILLS (From a small package or small leak from a large package) First ISOLATE in all Directions Meters (Feet)	Then PROTECT persons Downwind during DAY Kilometers (Miles)	Then PROTECT persons Downwind during NIGHT Kilometers (Miles)	LARGE SPILLS (From a large package or from many small packages) First ISOLATE in all Directions Meters (Feet)	Then PROTECT persons Downwind during DAY Kilometers (Miles)	Then PROTECT persons Downwind during NIGHT Kilometers (Miles)
1953	119	Compressed gas, toxic, flammable, n.o.s. (Inhalation Hazard Zone D)	30 m (100 ft)	0.1 km (0.1 mi)	0.2 km (0.1 mi)	200 m (600 ft)	0.8 km (0.5 mi)	2.0 km (1.3 mi)
1955 1955	123 123	Compressed gas, poisonous, n.o.s. Compressed gas, poisonous, n.o.s. (Inhalation Hazard Zone A)	100 m (300 ft)	0.5 km (0.3 mi)	2.2 km (1.4 mi)	600 m (2000 ft)	3.5 km (2.2 mi)	9.4 km (5.9 mi)
1955	123	Compressed gas, poisonous, n.o.s. (Inhalation Hazard Zone B)	30 m (100 ft)	0.2 km (0.1 mi)	0.8 km (0.5 mi)	300 m (1000 ft)	1.5 km (0.9 mi)	4.6 km (2.9 mi)
1955	123	Compressed gas, poisonous, n.o.s. (Inhalation Hazard Zone C)	30 m (100 ft)	0.1 km (0.1 mi)	0.3 km (0.2 mi)	150 m (500 ft)	0.9 km (0.6 mi)	2.8 km (1.7 mi)
1955	123	Compressed gas, poisonous, n.o.s. (Inhalation Hazard Zone D)	30 m (100 ft)	0.1 km (0.1 mi)	0.2 km (0.1 mi)	150 m (500 ft)	0.8 km (0.5 mi)	2.0 km (1.3 mi)
1955 1955	123 123	Compressed gas, toxic, n.o.s. Compressed gas, toxic, n.o.s. (Inhalation Hazard Zone A)	100 m (300 ft)	0.5 km (0.3 mi)	2.2 km (1.4 mi)	600 m (2000 ft)	3.5 km (2.2 mi)	9.4 km (5.9 mi)
1955	123	Compressed gas, toxic, n.o.s. (Inhalation Hazard Zone B)	30 m (100 ft)	0.2 km (0.1 mi)	0.8 km (0.5 mi)	300 m (1000 ft)	1.5 km (0.9 mi)	4.6 km (2.9 mi)
1955	123	Compressed gas, toxic, n.o.s. (Inhalation Hazard Zone C)	30 m (100 ft)	0.1 km (0.1 mi)	0.3 km (0.2 mi)	150 m (500 ft)	0.9 km (0.6 mi)	2.8 km (1.7 mi)

ID No.	Guide No.	Name of Material	First ISOLATE in all Directions	Then PROTECT persons Downwind during DAY	during NIGHT	First ISOLATE in all Directions	Then PROTECT persons Downwind during DAY	during NIGHT
1955	123	Compressed gas, toxic, n.o.s. (Inhalation Hazard Zone D)	30 m (100 ft)	0.1 km (0.1 mi)	0.2 km (0.1 mi)	150 m (500 ft)	0.8 km (0.5 mi)	2.0 km (1.3 mi)
1955	123	Organic phosphate compound mixed with compressed gas	100 m (300 ft)	0.9 km (0.6 mi)	2.6 km (1.6 mi)	500 m (1500 ft)	3.9 km (2.4 mi)	9.4 km (5.9 mi)
1955	123	Organic phosphate mixed with compressed gas						
1955	123	Organic phosphorus compound mixed with compressed gas						
1967	123	Insecticide gas, poisonous, n.o.s.	100 m (300 ft)	0.9 km (0.6 mi)	2.6 km (1.6 mi)	500 m (1500 ft)	3.9 km (2.4 mi)	9.4 km (5.9 mi)
1967	123	Insecticide gas, toxic, n.o.s.						
1967	123	Parathion and compressed gas mixture						
1975	124	Dinitrogen tetroxide and Nitric oxide mixture	30 m (100 ft)	0.1 km (0.1 mi)	0.6 km (0.4 mi)	100 m (300 ft)	0.6 km (0.4 mi)	2.3 km (1.5 mi)
1975	124	Nitric oxide and Dinitrogen tetroxide mixture						
1975	124	Nitric oxide and Nitrogen dioxide mixture						
1975	124	Nitric oxide and Nitrogen tetroxide mixture						
1975	124	Nitrogen dioxide and Nitric oxide mixture						
1975	124	Nitrogen tetroxide and Nitric oxide mixture						
1994	131	Iron pentacarbonyl	100 m (300 ft)	0.9 km (0.6 mi)	2.1 km (1.3 mi)	400 m (1250 ft)	4.8 km (3.0 mi)	8.3 km (5.2 mi)
2004	135	Magnesium diamide **(when spilled in water)**	30 m (100 ft)	0.1 km (0.1 mi)	0.5 km (0.3 mi)	100 m (300 ft)	0.7 km (0.5 mi)	2.4 km (1.5 mi)
2011	139	Magnesium phosphide **(when spilled in water)**	60 m (200 ft)	0.2 km (0.1 mi)	0.8 km (0.5 mi)	500 m (1500 ft)	1.8 km (1.1 mi)	6.0 km (3.8 mi)

"+" means distance can be larger in certain atmospheric conditions

TABLE 1 - INITIAL ISOLATION AND PROTECTIVE ACTION DISTANCES

ID No.	Guide	NAME OF MATERIAL	SMALL SPILLS (From a small package or small leak from a large package)						LARGE SPILLS (From a large package or from many small packages)					
			First ISOLATE in all Directions		Then PROTECT persons Downwind during-				First ISOLATE in all Directions		Then PROTECT persons Downwind during-			
					DAY		NIGHT				DAY		NIGHT	
			Meters	(Feet)	Kilometers	(Miles)	Kilometers	(Miles)	Meters	(Feet)	Kilometers	(Miles)	Kilometers	(Miles)
2012	139	Potassium phosphide (when spilled in water)	30 m	(100 ft)	0.1 km	(0.1 mi)	0.6 km	(0.4 mi)	300 m	(1000 ft)	1.2 km	(0.8 mi)	4.0 km	(2.5 mi)
2013	139	Strontium phosphide (when spilled in water)	30 m	(100 ft)	0.1 km	(0.1 mi)	0.6 km	(0.4 mi)	300 m	(1000 ft)	1.2 km	(0.7 mi)	3.8 km	(2.4 mi)
2032 2032	157 157	Nitric acid, fuming Nitric acid, red fuming	30 m	(100 ft)	0.1 km	(0.1 mi)	0.3 km	(0.2 mi)	150 m	(500 ft)	0.5 km	(0.3 mi)	1.1 km	(0.7 mi)
2186 *	125	Hydrogen chloride, refrigerated liquid	30 m	(100 ft)	0.1 km	(0.1 mi)	0.3 km	(0.2 mi)	300 m	(1000 ft)	2.0 km	(1.3 mi)	7.6 km	(4.7 mi)
2188	119	Arsine	150 m	(500 ft)	1.0 km	(0.6 mi)	4.0 km	(2.5 mi)	1000 m	(3000 ft)	5.8 km	(3.6 mi)	11.0+ km	(7.0+ mi)
2188	119	SA (when used as a weapon)	300 m	(1000 ft)	1.9 km	(1.2 mi)	5.7 km	(3.6 mi)	1000 m	(3000 ft)	8.9 km	(5.6 mi)	11.0+ km	(7.0+ mi)
2189	119	Dichlorosilane	30 m	(100 ft)	0.1 km	(0.1 mi)	0.4 km	(0.2 mi)	200 m	(600 ft)	1.2 km	(0.8 mi)	2.9 km	(1.8 mi)
2190 2190	124 124	Oxygen difluoride Oxygen difluoride, compressed	200 m	(600 ft)	0.4 km	(0.3 mi)	2.1 km	(1.3 mi)	1000 m	(3000 ft)	2.2 km	(1.4 mi)	8.6 km	(5.4 mi)
2191 2191	123 123	Sulfuryl fluoride Sulphuryl fluoride	30 m	(100 ft)	0.1 km	(0.1 mi)	0.5 km	(0.3 mi)	300 m	(1000 ft)	1.9 km	(1.2 mi)	5.1 km	(3.2 mi)
2192	119	Germane	150 m	(500 ft)	0.8 km	(0.5 mi)	3.2 km	(2.0 mi)	800 m	(2500 ft)	4.4 km	(2.7 mi)	10.6 km	(6.6 mi)
2194	125	Selenium hexafluoride	200 m	(600 ft)	1.1 km	(0.7 mi)	3.7 km	(2.3 mi)	800 m	(2500 ft)	5.0 km	(3.1 mi)	11.0+ km	(7.0+ mi)
2195	125	Tellurium hexafluoride	200 m	(600 ft)	1.2 km	(0.7 mi)	4.4 km	(2.8 mi)	1000 m	(3000 ft)	6.7 km	(4.2 mi)	11.0+ km	(7.0+ mi)
2196	125	Tungsten hexafluoride	30 m	(100 ft)	0.2 km	(0.1 mi)	0.8 km	(0.5 mi)	150 m	(500 ft)	0.9 km	(0.6 mi)	3.1 km	(2.0 mi)
2197	125	Hydrogen iodide, anhydrous	30 m	(100 ft)	0.1 km	(0.1 mi)	0.3 km	(0.2 mi)	150 m	(500 ft)	0.9 km	(0.6 mi)	2.8 km	(1.7 mi)

ID No.	Guide No.	Name of Material	SMALL SPILLS First ISOLATE in all Directions	SMALL SPILLS Then PROTECT persons Downwind during DAY	SMALL SPILLS Then PROTECT persons Downwind during NIGHT	LARGE SPILLS First ISOLATE in all Directions	LARGE SPILLS Then PROTECT persons Downwind during DAY	LARGE SPILLS Then PROTECT persons Downwind during NIGHT
2198	125	Phosphorus pentafluoride	30 m (100 ft)	0.2 km (0.1 mi)	0.8 km (0.5 mi)	150 m (500 ft)	0.9 km (0.5 mi)	3.3 km (2.0 mi)
2198	125	Phosphorus pentafluoride, compressed						
2199	119	Phosphine	60 m (200 ft)	0.2 km (0.2 mi)	1.0 km (0.7 mi)	400 m (1250 ft)	1.3 km (0.8 mi)	4.1 km (2.5 mi)
2202	117	Hydrogen selenide, anhydrous	200 m (600 ft)	1.1 km (0.7 mi)	4.9 km (3.1 mi)	1000 m (3000 ft)	8.5 km (5.3 mi)	11.0+ km (7.0+ mi)
2204	119	Carbonyl sulfide	30 m (100 ft)	0.1 km (0.1 mi)	0.3 km (0.2 mi)	300 m (1000 ft)	1.3 km (0.8 mi)	3.5 km (2.2 mi)
2204	119	Carbonyl sulphide						
2232	153	Chloroacetaldehyde	30 m (100 ft)	0.2 km (0.1 mi)	0.4 km (0.2 mi)	60 m (200 ft)	0.7 km (0.5 mi)	1.3 km (0.8 mi)
2232	153	2-Chloroethanal						
2308	157	Nitrosylsulfuric acic (when spilled in water)	30 m (100 ft)	0.1 km (0.1 mi)	0.4 km (0.3 mi)	300 m (1000 ft)	0.9 km (0.6 mi)	2.5 km (1.6 mi)
2308	157	Nitrosylsulfuric acic, liquid (when spilled in water)						
2308	157	Nitrosylsulfuric acic, solid (when spilled in water)						
2308	157	Nitrosylsulphuric acic (when spilled in water)						
2308	157	Nitrosylsulphuric acic, liquid (when spilled in water)						
2308	157	Nitrosylsulphuric acic, solid (when spilled in water)						
2334	131	Allylamine	30 m (100 ft)	0.2 km (0.1 mi)	0.6 km (0.4 mi)	150 m (500 ft)	1.5 km (0.9 mi)	2.8 km (1.7 mi)
2337	131	Phenyl mercaptan	30 m (100 ft)	0.1 km (0.1 mi)	0.1 km (0.1 mi)	30 m (100 ft)	0.3 km (0.2 mi)	0.5 km (0.3 mi)
2353	132	Butyryl chloride (when spilled in water)	30 m (100 ft)	0.1 km (0.1 mi)	0.1 km (0.1 mi)	30 m (100 ft)	0.4 km (0.2 mi)	1.0 km (0.6 mi)
2382	131	1,2-Dimethylhydrazine	30 m (100 ft)	0.2 km (0.1 mi)	0.4 km (0.2 mi)	60 m (200 ft)	0.8 km (0.5 mi)	1.5 km (1.0 mi)
2382	131	Dimethylhydrazine, symmetrical						

"+" means distance can be larger in certain atmospheric conditions   * PLEASE ALSO CONSULT TABLE 3 FOR THIS MATERIAL

TABLE 1 - INITIAL ISOLATION AND PROTECTIVE ACTION DISTANCES

ID No.	Guide	NAME OF MATERIAL	SMALL SPILLS (From a small package or small leak from a large package)						LARGE SPILLS (From a large package or from many small packages)					
			First ISOLATE in all Directions		Then PROTECT persons Downwind during-				First ISOLATE in all Directions		Then PROTECT persons Downwind during-			
					DAY		NIGHT				DAY		NIGHT	
			Meters	(Feet)	Kilometers (Miles)		Kilometers (Miles)		Meters (Feet)		Kilometers (Miles)		Kilometers (Miles)	
2395	132	Isobutyryl chloride (when spilled in water)	30 m	(100 ft)	0.1 km	(0.1 mi)	0.1 km	(0.1 mi)	30 m	(100 ft)	0.2 km	(0.2 mi)	0.6 km	(0.4 mi)
2407	155	Isopropyl chloroformate	30 m	(100 ft)	0.1 km	(0.1 mi)	0.2 km	(0.2 mi)	60 m	(200 ft)	0.5 km	(0.3 mi)	1.0 km	(0.6 mi)
2417	125	Carbonyl fluoride	100 m	(300 ft)	0.6 km	(0.4 mi)	2.3 km	(1.4 mi)	600 m	(2000 ft)	3.7 km	(2.3 mi)	8.0 km	(5.0 mi)
2417	125	Carbonyl fluoride, compressed												
2418	125	Sulfur tetrafluoride	100 m	(300 ft)	0.5 km	(0.4 mi)	2.6 km	(1.6 mi)	600 m	(2000 ft)	3.5 km	(2.2 mi)	9.4 km	(5.9 mi)
2418	125	Sulphur tetrafluoride												
2420	125	Hexafluoroacetone	60 m	(200 ft)	0.3 km	(0.2 mi)	1.4 km	(0.9 mi)	1000 m	(3000 ft)	7.6 km	(4.7 mi)	11.0+ km	(7.0+ mi)
2421	124	Nitrogen trioxide	60 m	(200 ft)	0.4 km	(0.3 mi)	1.8 km	(1.1 mi)	300 m	(1000 ft)	1.9 km	(1.2 mi)	6.7 km	(4.2 mi)
2434	156	Dibenzyldichlorosilane (when spilled in water)	30 m	(100 ft)	0.1 km	(0.1 mi)	0.1 km	(0.1 mi)	30 m	(100 ft)	0.2 km	(0.1 mi)	0.6 km	(0.4 mi)
2435	156	Ethylphenyldichlorosilane (when spilled in water)	30 m	(100 ft)	0.1 km	(0.1 mi)	0.1 km	(0.1 mi)	30 m	(100 ft)	0.4 km	(0.2 mi)	1.1 km	(0.7 mi)
2437	156	Methylphenyldichlorosilane (when spilled in water)	30 m	(100 ft)	0.2 km	(0.1 mi)	0.2 km	(0.1 mi)	30 m	(100 ft)	0.4 km	(0.3 mi)	1.4 km	(0.9 mi)
2438	132	Trimethylacetyl chloride	30 m	(100 ft)	0.3 km	(0.2 mi)	0.6 km	(0.4 mi)	100 m	(300 ft)	1.2 km	(0.8 mi)	2.1 km	(1.3 mi)
2442	156	Trichloroacetyl chloride	30 m	(100 ft)	0.2 km	(0.1 mi)	0.3 km	(0.2 mi)	60 m	(200 ft)	0.6 km	(0.4 mi)	1.2 km	(0.8 mi)
2474	157	Thiophosgene	60 m	(200 ft)	0.7 km	(0.4 mi)	2.0 km	(1.2 mi)	300 m	(1000 ft)	2.7 km	(1.7 mi)	5.5 km	(3.4 mi)
2477	131	Methyl isothiocyanate	30 m	(100 ft)	0.1 km	(0.1 mi)	0.1 km	(0.1 mi)	30 m	(100 ft)	0.2 km	(0.2 mi)	0.4 km	(0.2 mi)
2480	155	Methyl isocyanate	150 m	(500 ft)	1.7 km	(1.1 mi)	5.8 km	(3.6 mi)	1000 m	(3000 ft)	11.0+ km	(7.0+ mi)	11.0+ km	(7.0+ mi)

ID No.	Guide No.	Name of Material	SMALL SPILLS First ISOLATE in all Directions	Then PROTECT persons Downwind during DAY	Then PROTECT persons Downwind during NIGHT	LARGE SPILLS First ISOLATE in all Directions	Then PROTECT persons Downwind during DAY	Then PROTECT persons Downwind during NIGHT
2481	155	Ethyl isocyanate	150 m (500 ft)	1.8 km (1.2 mi)	5.9 km (3.7 mi)	1000 m (3000 ft)	11.0+ km (7.0+ mi)	11.0+ km (7.0+ mi)
2482	155	n-Propyl isocyanate	100 m (300 ft)	1.1 km (0.7 mi)	2.8 km (1.7 mi)	600 m (2000 ft)	7.8 km (4.9 mi)	11.0+ km (7.0+ mi)
2483	155	Isopropyl isocyanate	100 m (300 ft)	1.2 km (0.8 mi)	3.1 km (1.9 mi)	800 m (2500 ft)	10.1 km (6.3 mi)	11.0+ km (7.0+ mi)
2484	155	tert-Butyl isocyanate	100 m (300 ft)	1.1 km (0.7 mi)	2.7 km (1.7 mi)	600 m (2000 ft)	7.2 km (4.5 mi)	11.0+ km (7.0+ mi)
2485	155	n-Butyl isocyanate	60 m (200 ft)	0.8 km (0.5 mi)	1.7 km (1.1 mi)	300 m (1000 ft)	4.0 km (2.5 mi)	6.7 km (4.2 mi)
2486	155	Isobutyl isocyanate	60 m (200 ft)	0.8 km (0.5 mi)	1.7 km (1.1 mi)	300 m (1000 ft)	4.0 km (2.5 mi)	6.5 km (4.1 mi)
2487	155	Phenyl isocyanate	30 m (100 ft)	0.2 km (0.2 mi)	0.3 km (0.2 mi)	60 m (200 ft)	0.8 km (0.5 mi)	1.2 km (0.8 mi)
2488	155	Cyclohexyl isocyanate	30 m (100 ft)	0.2 km (0.1 mi)	0.2 km (0.1 mi)	60 m (200 ft)	0.5 km (0.3 mi)	0.7 km (0.5 mi)
2495	144	Iodine pentafluoride (when spilled in water)	30 m (100 ft)	0.1 km (0.1 mi)	0.6 km (0.4 mi)	150 m (500 ft)	1.2 km (0.8 mi)	4.6 km (2.9 mi)
2521	131P	Diketene, stabilized	30 m (100 ft)	0.1 km (0.1 mi)	0.1 km (0.1 mi)	30 m (100 ft)	0.3 km (0.2 mi)	0.5 km (0.3 mi)
2534	119	Methylchlorosilane	30 m (100 ft)	0.1 km (0.1 mi)	0.3 km (0.2 mi)	100 m (300 ft)	0.7 km (0.4 mi)	1.8 km (1.1 mi)
2548	124	Chlorine pentafluoride	30 m (100 ft)	0.2 km (0.2 mi)	1.2 km (0.7 mi)	300 m (1000 ft)	1.8 km (1.1 mi)	7.3 km (4.6 mi)
2600	119	Carbon monoxide and Hydrogen mixture, compressed	30 m (100 ft)	0.1 km (0.1 mi)	0.2 km (0.1 mi)	200 m (600 ft)	1.2 km (0.8 mi)	4.8 km (3.0 mi)
2600	119	Hydrogen and Carbon monoxide mixture, compressed						
2605	155	Methoxymethyl isocyanate	30 m (100 ft)	0.4 km (0.2 mi)	0.5 km (0.4 mi)	100 m (300 ft)	1.2 km (0.8 mi)	1.8 km (1.2 mi)
2606	155	Methyl orthosilicate	30 m (100 ft)	0.1 km (0.1 mi)	0.1 km (0.1 mi)	30 m (100 ft)	0.2 km (0.1 mi)	0.3 km (0.2 mi)
2644	151	Methyl iodide	30 m (100 ft)	0.1 km (0.1 mi)	0.2 km (0.1 mi)	100 m (300 ft)	0.3 km (0.2 mi)	0.7 km (0.5 mi)
2646	151	Hexachlorocyclopentadiene	30 m (100 ft)	0.1 km (0.1 mi)	0.1 km (0.1 mi)	30 m (100 ft)	0.3 km (0.2 mi)	0.4 km (0.3 mi)
2668	131	Chloroacetonitrile	30 m (100 ft)	0.1 km (0.1 mi)	0.1 km (0.1 mi)	30 m (100 ft)	0.1 km (0.1 mi)	0.2 km (0.1 mi)
2676	119	Stibine	60 m (200 ft)	0.4 km (0.2 mi)	1.7 km (1.1 mi)	300 m (1000 ft)	1.9 km (1.2 mi)	6.5 km (4.0 mi)

"+" means distance can be larger in certain atmospheric conditions

TABLE 1 - INITIAL ISOLATION AND PROTECTIVE ACTION DISTANCES

ID No.	Guide	NAME OF MATERIAL	SMALL SPILLS (From a small package or small leak from a large package) First ISOLATE in all Directions Meters (Feet)	Then PROTECT persons Downwind during- DAY Kilometers (Miles)	Then PROTECT persons Downwind during- NIGHT Kilometers (Miles)	LARGE SPILLS (From a large package or from many small packages) First ISOLATE in all Directions Meters (Feet)	Then PROTECT persons Downwind during- DAY Kilometers (Miles)	Then PROTECT persons Downwind during- NIGHT Kilometers (Miles)
2691	137	Phosphorus pentabromide (when spilled in water)	30 m (100 ft)	0.1 km (0.1 mi)	0.2 km (0.1 mi)	30 m (100 ft)	0.3 km (0.2 mi)	1.0 km (0.6 mi)
2692	157	Boron tribromide (when spilled on land)	30 m (100 ft)	0.1 km (0.1 mi)	0.3 km (0.2 mi)	30 m (100 ft)	0.3 km (0.2 mi)	0.7 km (0.4 mi)
2692	157	Boron tribromide (when spilled in water)	30 m (100 ft)	0.1 km (0.1 mi)	0.4 km (0.3 mi)	60 m (200 ft)	0.8 km (0.5 mi)	2.5 km (1.6 mi)
2740	155	n-Propyl chloroformate	30 m (100 ft)	0.1 km (0.1 mi)	0.3 km (0.2 mi)	60 m (200 ft)	0.6 km (0.4 mi)	1.1 km (0.7 mi)
2742	155	sec-Butyl chloroformate	30 m (100 ft)	0.1 km (0.1 mi)	0.2 km (0.1 mi)	30 m (100 ft)	0.4 km (0.3 mi)	0.6 km (0.4 mi)
2742	155	Isobutyl chloroformate	30 m (100 ft)	0.1 km (0.1 mi)	0.2 km (0.1 mi)	30 m (100 ft)	0.3 km (0.2 mi)	0.5 km (0.3 mi)
2743	155	n-Butyl chloroformate	30 m (100 ft)	0.1 km (0.1 mi)	0.2 km (0.1 mi)	30 m (100 ft)	0.4 km (0.2 mi)	0.5 km (0.4 mi)
2806	138	Lithium nitride (when spilled in water)	30 m (100 ft)	0.1 km (0.1 mi)	0.5 km (0.3 mi)	60 m (200 ft)	0.6 km (0.4 mi)	2.1 km (1.3 mi)
2810	153	Buzz (when used as a weapon) BZ (when used as a weapon)	60 m (200 ft)	0.4 km (0.2 mi)	1.7 km (1.1 mi)	400 m (1250 ft)	2.2 km (1.4 mi)	8.1 km (5.0 mi)
2810	153	CS (when used as a weapon)	30 m (100 ft)	0.1 km (0.1 mi)	0.6 km (0.4 mi)	100 m (300 ft)	0.4 km (0.3 mi)	1.9 km (1.2 mi)
2810	153	DC (when used as a weapon)	30 m (100 ft)	0.1 km (0.1 mi)	0.6 km (0.4 mi)	60 m (200 ft)	0.4 km (0.3 mi)	1.8 km (1.1 mi)
2810	153	GA (when used as a weapon)	30 m (100 ft)	0.2 km (0.1 mi)	0.2 km (0.1 mi)	100 m (300 ft)	0.5 km (0.4 mi)	0.6 km (0.4 mi)
2810	153	GB (when used as a weapon)	60 m (200 ft)	0.4 km (0.3 mi)	1.1 km (0.7 mi)	400 m (1250 ft)	2.1 km (1.3 mi)	4.9 km (3.0 mi)
2810	153	GD (when used as a weapon)	60 m (200 ft)	0.4 km (0.3 mi)	0.7 km (0.5 mi)	300 m (1000 ft)	1.8 km (1.1 mi)	2.7 km (1.7 mi)

ID No.	Guide No.	NAME OF MATERIAL	SMALL SPILLS First ISOLATE in all Directions	SMALL SPILLS Then PROTECT persons Downwind during DAY	SMALL SPILLS Then PROTECT persons Downwind during NIGHT	LARGE SPILLS First ISOLATE in all Directions	LARGE SPILLS Then PROTECT persons Downwind during DAY	LARGE SPILLS Then PROTECT persons Downwind during NIGHT
2810	153	GF (when used as a weapon)	30 m (100 ft)	0.2 km (0.2 mi)	0.3 km (0.2 mi)	150 m (500 ft)	0.8 km (0.5 mi)	1.0 km (0.6 mi)
2810 2810	153 153	H (when used as a weapon) HD (when used as a weapon)	30 m (100 ft)	0.1 km (0.1 mi)	0.1 km (0.1 mi)	60 m (200 ft)	0.3 km (0.2 mi)	0.4 km (0.3 mi)
2810	153	HL (when used as a weapon)	30 m (100 ft)	0.1 km (0.1 mi)	0.3 km (0.2 mi)	100 m (300 ft)	0.5 km (0.3 mi)	1.0 km (0.6 mi)
2810	153	HN-1 (when used as a weapon)	60 m (200 ft)	0.3 km (0.2 mi)	0.5 km (0.3 mi)	200 m (600 ft)	1.1 km (0.7 mi)	1.8 km (1.1 mi)
2810	153	HN-2 (when used as a weapon)	60 m (200 ft)	0.3 km (0.2 mi)	0.6 km (0.4 mi)	300 m (1000 ft)	1.3 km (0.8 mi)	2.1 km (1.3 mi)
2810	153	HN-3 (when used as a weapon)	30 m (100 ft)	0.1 km (0.1 mi)	0.1 km (0.1 mi)	60 m (200 ft)	0.3 km (0.2 mi)	0.3 km (0.2 mi)
2810 2810	153 153	L (Lewisite) (when used as a weapon) Lewisite (when used as a weapon)	30 m (100 ft)	0.1 km (0.1 mi)	0.3 km (0.2 mi)	100 m (300 ft)	0.5 km (0.3 mi)	1.0 km (0.6 mi)
2810	153	Mustard (when used as a weapon)	30 m (100 ft)	0.1 km (0.1 mi)	0.1 km (0.1 mi)	60 m (200 ft)	0.3 km (0.2 mi)	0.4 km (0.3 mi)
2810	153	Mustard Lewisite (when used as a weapon)	30 m (100 ft)	0.1 km (0.1 mi)	0.3 km (0.2 mi)	100 m (300 ft)	0.5 km (0.3 mi)	1.0 km (0.6 mi)
2810 2810	153 153	Poisonous liquid, n.o.s. Poisonous liquid, n.o.s. (Inhalation Hazard Zone A)	60 m (200 ft)	0.4 km (0.3 mi)	1.3 km (0.8 mi)	200 m (600 ft)	2.3 km (1.4 mi)	5.1 km (3.2 mi)
2810	153	Poisonous liquid, n.o.s. (Inhalation Hazard Zone B)	30 m (100 ft)	0.2 km (0.1 mi)	0.2 km (0.1 mi)	60 m (200 ft)	0.5 km (0.3 mi)	0.7 km (0.5 mi)
2810 2810	153 153	Poisonous liquid, organic, n.o.s. Poisonous liquid, organic, n.o.s. (Inhalation Hazard Zone A)	30 m (100 ft)	0.3 km (0.2 mi)	1.1 km (0.7 mi)	300 m (1000 ft)	1.8 km (1.1 mi)	4.5 km (2.8 mi)
2810	153	Poisonous liquid, organic, n.o.s. (Inhalation Hazard Zone B)	30 m (100 ft)	0.2 km (0.1 mi)	0.2 km (0.1 mi)	60 m (200 ft)	0.5 km (0.3 mi)	0.7 km (0.5 mi)

"+" means distance can be larger in certain atmospheric conditions

TABLE 1 - INITIAL ISOLATION AND PROTECTIVE ACTION DISTANCES

ID No.	Guide	NAME OF MATERIAL	SMALL SPILLS (From a small package or small leak from a large package) First ISOLATE in all Directions Meters (Feet)		Then PROTECT persons Downwind during- DAY Kilometers (Miles)	Then PROTECT persons Downwind during- NIGHT Kilometers (Miles)	LARGE SPILLS (From a large package or from many small packages) First ISOLATE in all Directions Meters (Feet)		Then PROTECT persons Downwind during- DAY Kilometers (Miles)	Then PROTECT persons Downwind during- NIGHT Kilometers (Miles)
2810	153	Sarin (when used as a weapon)	60 m	(200 ft)	0.4 km (0.3 mi)	1.1 km (0.7 mi)	400 m	(1250 ft)	2.1 km (1.3 mi)	4.9 km (3.0 mi)
2810	153	Soman (when used as a weapon)	60 m	(200 ft)	0.4 km (0.3 mi)	0.7 km (0.5 mi)	300 m	(1000 ft)	1.8 km (1.1 mi)	2.7 km (1.7 mi)
2810	153	Tabun (when used as a weapon)	30 m	(100 ft)	0.2 km (0.1 mi)	0.2 km (0.1 mi)	100 m	(300 ft)	0.5 km (0.4 mi)	0.6 km (0.4 mi)
2810	153	Thickened GD (when used as a weapon)	60 m	(200 ft)	0.4 km (0.3 mi)	0.7 km (0.5 mi)	300 m	(1000 ft)	1.8 km (1.1 mi)	2.7 km (1.7 mi)
2810 2810	153 153	Toxic liquid, n.o.s. Toxic liquid, n.o.s. (Inhalation Hazard Zone A)	60 m	(200 ft)	0.4 km (0.3 mi)	1.3 km (0.8 mi)	200 m	(600 ft)	2.3 km (1.4 mi)	5.1 km (3.2 mi)
2810	153	Toxic liquid, n.o.s. (Inhalation Hazard Zone B)	30 m	(100 ft)	0.2 km (0.1 mi)	0.2 km (0.1 mi)	60 m	(200 ft)	0.5 km (0.3 mi)	0.7 km (0.5 mi)
2810 2810	153 153	Toxic liquid, organic, n.o.s. Toxic liquid, organic, n.o.s. (Inhalation Hazard Zone A)	30 m	(100 ft)	0.3 km (0.2mi)	1.1 km (0.7 mi)	300 m	(1000 ft)	1.8 km (1.1 mi)	4.5 km (2.8 mi)
2810	153	Toxic liquid, organic, n.o.s. (Inhalation Hazard Zone B)	30 m	(100 ft)	0.2 km (0.1 mi)	0.2 km (0.1 mi)	60 m	(200 ft)	0.5 km (0.3 mi)	0.7 km (0.5 mi)
2810	153	VX (when used as a weapon)	30 m	(100 ft)	0.1 km (0.1 mi)	0.1 km (0.1 mi)	60 m	(200 ft)	0.4 km (0.2 mi)	0.3 km (0.2 mi)
2811	154	CX (when used as a weapon)	60 m	(200 ft)	0.2 km (0.2 mi)	1.1 km (0.7 mi)	200 m	(600 ft)	1.2 km (0.7 mi)	5.1 km (3.2 mi)
2826	155	Ethyl chlorothioformate	30 m	(100 ft)	0.1 km (0.1 mi)	0.2 km (0.1 mi)	30 m	(100 ft)	0.4 km (0.3 mi)	0.7 km (0.4 mi)

ID No.	Guide No.	Name of Material	SMALL SPILLS First ISOLATE in all Directions	SMALL SPILLS Then PROTECT persons Downwind during DAY	SMALL SPILLS Then PROTECT persons Downwind during NIGHT	LARGE SPILLS First ISOLATE in all Directions	LARGE SPILLS Then PROTECT persons Downwind during DAY	LARGE SPILLS Then PROTECT persons Downwind during NIGHT
2845	135	Ethyl phosphonous dichloride, anhydrous	30 m (100 ft)	0.3 km (0.2 mi)	0.8 km (0.5 mi)	150 m (500 ft)	1.5 km (0.9 mi)	2.8 km (1.7 mi)
2845	135	Methyl phosphonous dichloride	30 m (100 ft)	0.4 km (0.3 mi)	1.2 km (0.8 mi)	200 m (600 ft)	2.3 km (1.4 mi)	4.3 km (2.7 mi)
2901	124	Bromine chloride	60 m (200 ft)	0.3 km (0.2 mi)	1.1 km (0.7 mi)	400 m (1250 ft)	2.5 km (1.5 mi)	6.7 km (4.2 mi)
2927	154	Ethyl phosphonothioic dichloride, anhydrous	30 m (100 ft)	0.1 km (0.1 mi)	0.1 km (0.1 mi)	30 m (100 ft)	0.2 km (0.1 mi)	0.2 km (0.1 mi)
2927	154	Ethyl phosphorodichloridate	30 m (100 ft)	0.1 km (0.1 mi)	0.1 km (0.1 mi)	30 m (100 ft)	0.2 km (0.1 mi)	0.2 km (0.1 mi)
2927	154	Poisonous liquid, corrosive, n.o.s. (Inhalation Hazard Zone A)	60 m (200 ft)	0.4 km (0.2 mi)	0.9 km (0.6 mi)	200 m (600 ft)	1.5 km (1.0 mi)	3.0 km (1.9 mi)
2927	154	Poisonous liquid, corrosive, n.o.s. (Inhalation Hazard Zone B)	30 m (100 ft)	0.2 km (0.1 mi)	0.2 km (0.1 mi)	30 m (100 ft)	0.4 km (0.3 mi)	0.7 km (0.4 mi)
2927	154	Poisonous liquid, corrosive, organic, n.o.s. (Inhalation Hazard Zone A)	60 m (200 ft)	0.3 km (0.2 mi)	0.8 km (0.5 mi)	300 m (1000 ft)	1.5 km (1.0 mi)	3.0 km (1.9 mi)
2927	154	Poisonous liquid, corrosive, organic, n.o.s. (Inhalation Hazard Zone B)	30 m (100 ft)	0.2 km (0.1 mi)	0.2 km (0.1 mi)	30 m (100 ft)	0.4 km (0.3 mi)	0.6 km (0.4 mi)
2927 / 2927	154 / 154	Toxic liquid, corrosive, n.o.s. / Toxic liquid, corrosive, n.o.s. (Inhalation Hazard Zone A)	60 m (200 ft)	0.4 km (0.2 mi)	0.9 km (0.6 mi)	200 m (600 ft)	1.5 km (1.0 mi)	3.0 km (1.9 mi)
2927	154	Toxic liquid, corrosive, n.o.s. (Inhalation Hazard Zone B)	30 m (100 ft)	0.2 km (0.1 mi)	0.2 km (0.1 mi)	30 m (100 ft)	0.4 km (0.3 mi)	0.7 km (0.4 mi)

"+" means distance can be larger in certain atmospheric conditions

TABLE 1 - INITIAL ISOLATION AND PROTECTIVE ACTION DISTANCES

ID No.	Guide	NAME OF MATERIAL	SMALL SPILLS (From a small package or small leak from a large package) First ISOLATE in all Directions Meters (Feet)	SMALL SPILLS Then PROTECT persons Downwind during- DAY Kilometers (Miles)	SMALL SPILLS Then PROTECT persons Downwind during- NIGHT Kilometers (Miles)	LARGE SPILLS (From a large package or from many small packages) First ISOLATE in all Directions Meters (Feet)	LARGE SPILLS Then PROTECT persons Downwind during- DAY Kilometers (Miles)	LARGE SPILLS Then PROTECT persons Downwind during- NIGHT Kilometers (Miles)
2927	154	Toxic liquid, corrosive, organic, n.o.s.	60 m (200 ft)	0.3 km (0.2 mi)	0.8 km (0.5 mi)	300 m (1000 ft)	1.5 km (1.0 mi)	3.0 km (1.9 mi)
2927	154	Toxic liquid, corrosive, organic, n.o.s. (Inhalation Hazard Zone A)						
2927	154	Toxic liquid, corrosive, organic, n.o.s. (Inhalation Hazard Zone B)	30 m (100 ft)	0.2 km (0.1 mi)	0.2 km (0.1 mi)	30 m (100 ft)	0.4 km (0.3 mi)	0.6 km (0.4 mi)
2929	131	Poisonous liquid, flammable, n.o.s.	60 m (200 ft)	0.8 km (0.5 mi)	1.7 km (1.1 mi)	300 m (1000 ft)	4.0 km (2.5 mi)	6.5 km (4.1 mi)
2929	131	Poisonous liquid, flammable, n.o.s. (Inhalation Hazard Zone A)						
2929	131	Poisonous liquid, flammable, n.o.s. (Inhalation Hazard Zone B)	30 m (100 ft)	0.1 km (0.1 mi)	0.2 km (0.1 mi)	60 m (200 ft)	0.5 km (0.3 mi)	0.7 km (0.5 mi)
2929	131	Poisonous liquid, flammable, organic, n.o.s.	30 m (100 ft)	0.4 km (0.3 mi)	1.2 km (0.8 mi)	200 m (600 ft)	2.2 km (1.4 mi)	4.6 km (2.9 mi)
2929	131	Poisonous liquid, flammable, organic, n.o.s. (Inhalation Hazard Zone A)						
2929	131	Poisonous liquid, flammable, organic, n.o.s. (Inhalation Hazard Zone B)	30 m (100 ft)	0.2 km (0.1 mi)	0.2 km (0.1 mi)	60 m (200 ft)	0.5 km (0.3 mi)	0.7 km (0.5 mi)

ID No.	Guide No.	Name of Material	SMALL SPILLS First ISOLATE in all Directions		Then PROTECT persons Downwind during DAY		Then PROTECT persons Downwind during NIGHT		LARGE SPILLS First ISOLATE in all Directions		Then PROTECT persons Downwind during DAY		Then PROTECT persons Downwind during NIGHT	
2929 2929	131 131	Toxic liquid, flammable, n.o.s. Toxic liquid, flammable, n.o.s. (Inhalation Hazard Zone A)	60 m	(200 ft)	0.8 km	(0.5 mi)	1.7 km	(1.1 mi)	300 m	(1000 ft)	4.0 km	(2.5 mi)	6.5 km	(4.1 mi)
2929	131	Toxic liquid, flammable, n.o.s. (Inhalation Hazard Zone B)	30 m	(100 ft)	0.1 km	(0.1 mi)	0.2 km	(0.1 mi)	60 m	(200 ft)	0.5 km	(0.3 mi)	0.7 km	(0.5 mi)
2929 2929	131 131	Toxic liquid, flammable, organic, n.o.s. Toxic liquid, flammable, organic, n.o.s. (Inhalation Hazard Zone A)	30 m	(100 ft)	0.4 km	(0.3 mi)	1.2 km	(0.8 mi)	200 m	(600 ft)	2.2 km	(1.4 mi)	4.6 km	(2.9 mi)
2929	131	Toxic liquid, flammable, organic, n.o.s. (Inhalation Hazard Zone B)	30 m	(100 ft)	0.1 km	(0.1 mi)	0.2 km	(0.1 mi)	60 m	(200 ft)	0.5 km	(0.3 mi)	0.7 km	(0.5 mi)
2977 2977	166 166	Radioactive material, Uranium hexafluoride, fissile (when spilled in water) Uranium hexafluoride, fissile containing more than 1% Uranium-235 (when spilled in water)	30 m	(100 ft)	0.1 km	(0.1 mi)	0.4 km	(0.3 mi)	60 m	(200 ft)	0.5 km	(0.3 mi)	2.4 km	(1.5 mi)
2978 2978 2978	166 166 166	Radioactive material, Uranium hexafluoride (when spilled in water) Uranium hexafluoride (when spilled in water) Uranium hexafluoride, non-fissile or fissile-excepted (when spilled in water)	30 m	(100 ft)	0.1 km	(0.1 mi)	0.4 km	(0.3 mi)	60 m	(200 ft)	0.5 km	(0.3 mi)	2.3 km	(1.5 mi)

"+" means distance can be larger in certain atmospheric conditions

TABLE 1 - INITIAL ISOLATION AND PROTECTIVE ACTION DISTANCES

ID No.	Guide	NAME OF MATERIAL	SMALL SPILLS (From a small package or small leak from a large package)				LARGE SPILLS (From a large package or from many small packages)				
			First ISOLATE in all Directions	Then PROTECT persons Downwind during-			First ISOLATE in all Directions	Then PROTECT persons Downwind during-			
				DAY	NIGHT			DAY		NIGHT	
			Meters (Feet)	Kilometers (Miles)	Kilometers (Miles)		Meters (Feet)	Kilometers (Miles)		Kilometers (Miles)	
2985	155	Chlorosilanes, flammable, corrosive, n.o.s. (when spilled in water)	30 m (100 ft)	0.1 km (0.1 mi)	0.2 km (0.1 mi)		60 m (200 ft)	0.5 km (0.3 mi)		1.6 km (1.0 mi)	
2985	155	Chlorosilanes, n.o.s. (when spilled in water)									
2986	155	Chlorosilanes, corrosive, flammable, n.o.s. (when spilled in water)	30 m (100 ft)	0.1 km (0.1 mi)	0.2 km (0.1 mi)		60 m (200 ft)	0.5 km (0.3 mi)		1.6 km (1.0 mi)	
2986	155	Chlorosilanes, n.o.s. (when spilled in water)									
2987	156	Chlorosilanes, corrosive, n.o.s. (when spilled in water)	30 m (100 ft)	0.1 km (0.1 mi)	0.2 km (0.1 mi)		60 m (200 ft)	0.5 km (0.3 mi)		1.6 km (1.0 mi)	
2987	156	Chlorosilanes, n.o.s. (when spilled in water)									
2988	139	Chlorosilanes, n.o.s. (when spilled in water)	30 m (100 ft)	0.1 km (0.1 mi)	0.2 km (0.1 mi)		60 m (200 ft)	0.5 km (0.3 mi)		1.6 km (1.0 mi)	
2988	139	Chlorosilanes, water-reactive, flammable, corrosive, n.o.s. (when spilled in water)									
3023	131	2-Methyl-2-heptanethiol	30 m (100 ft)	0.2 km (0.1 mi)	0.2 km (0.2 mi)		60 m (200 ft)	0.5 km (0.3 mi)		0.9 km (0.5 mi)	
3023	131	tert-Octyl mercaptan									
3048	157	Aluminum phosphide pesticide (when spilled in water)	60 m (200 ft)	0.2 km (0.2 mi)	0.9 km (0.6 mi)		500 m (1500 ft)	2.1 km (1.3 mi)		7.4 km (4.6 mi)	

ID No.	Guide No.	Name of Material	SMALL SPILLS First ISOLATE in all Directions	SMALL SPILLS Then PROTECT Downwind DAY	SMALL SPILLS Then PROTECT Downwind NIGHT	LARGE SPILLS First ISOLATE in all Directions	LARGE SPILLS Then PROTECT Downwind DAY	LARGE SPILLS Then PROTECT Downwind NIGHT
3049	138	Metal alkyl halides, water-reactive, n.o.s. **(when spilled in water)**	30 m (100 ft)	0.1 km (0.1 mi)	0.2 km (0.1 mi)	60 m (200 ft)	0.4 km (0.3 mi)	1.3 km (0.8 mi)
3049	138	Metal aryl halides, water-reactive, n.o.s. **(when spilled in water)**						
3052	135	Aluminum alkyl halides **(when spilled in water)**	30 m (100 ft)	0.1 km (0.1 mi)	0.2 km (0.1 mi)	60 m (200 ft)	0.4 km (0.3 mi)	1.3 km (0.8 mi)
3052	135	Aluminum alkyl halides, liquid **(when spilled in water)**						
3052	135	Aluminum alkyl halides, solid **(when spilled in water)**						
3057	125	Trifluoroacetyl chloride	30 m (100 ft)	0.2 km (0.1 mi)	1.0 km (0.6 mi)	800 m (2500 ft)	4.2 km (2.7 mi)	11.0+ km (7.0+ mi)
3079	131P	Methacrylonitrile, stabilized	30 m (100 ft)	0.1 km (0.1 mi)	0.2 km (0.1 mi)	60 m (200 ft)	0.4 km (0.3 mi)	0.8 km (0.5 mi)
3083	124	Perchloryl fluoride	30 m (100 ft)	0.1 km (0.1 mi)	0.6 km (0.4 mi)	400 m (1250 ft)	2.5 km (1.6 mi)	7.7 km (4.8 mi)
3122	142	Poisonous liquid, oxidizing, n.o.s.	30 m (100 ft)	0.4 km (0.2 mi)	1.4 km (0.9 mi)	200 m (600 ft)	2.3 km (1.4 mi)	5.1 km (3.2 mi)
3122	142	Poisonous liquid, oxidizing, n.o.s. (Inhalation Hazard Zone A)						
3122	142	Poisonous liquid, oxidizing, n.o.s. (Inhalation Hazard Zone B)	30 m (100 ft)	0.1 km (0.1 mi)	0.3 km (0.2 mi)	60 m (200 ft)	0.5 km (0.4 mi)	1.0 km (0.6 mi)
3122	142	Toxic liquid, oxidizing, n.o.s.	30 m (100 ft)	0.4 km (0.2 mi)	1.4 km (0.9 mi)	200 m (600 ft)	2.3 km (1.4 mi)	5.1 km (3.2 mi)
3122	142	Toxic liquid, oxidizing, n.o.s. (Inhalation Hazard Zone A)						
3122	142	Toxic liquid, oxidizing, n.o.s. (Inhalation Hazard Zone B)	30 m (100 ft)	0.1 km (0.1 mi)	0.3 km (0.2 mi)	60 m (200 ft)	0.5 km (0.4 mi)	1.0 km (0.6 mi)

"+" means distance can be larger in certain atmospheric conditions

TABLE 1 - INITIAL ISOLATION AND PROTECTIVE ACTION DISTANCES

ID No.	Guide	NAME OF MATERIAL	SMALL SPILLS (From a small package or small leak from a large package)				LARGE SPILLS (From a large package or from many small packages)				
			First ISOLATE in all Directions		Then PROTECT persons Downwind during-		First ISOLATE in all Directions		Then PROTECT persons Downwind during-		
					DAY	NIGHT			DAY	NIGHT	
			Meters	(Feet)	Kilometers (Miles)	Kilometers (Miles)	Meters	(Feet)	Kilometers (Miles)	Kilometers (Miles)	
3123	139	Poisonous liquid, water-reactive, n.o.s.	60 m	(200 ft)	0.4 km (0.3 mi)	1.3 km (0.8 mi)	200 m	(600 ft)	2.3 km (1.4 mi)	5.1 km (3.2 mi)	
3123	139	Poisonous liquid, water-reactive, n.o.s. (Inhalation Hazard Zone A)	30 m	(100 ft)	0.2 km (0.1 mi)	0.2 km (0.1 mi)	60 m	(200 ft)	0.5 km (0.3 mi)	0.7 km (0.5 mi)	
3123	139	Poisonous liquid, water-reactive, n.o.s. (Inhalation Hazard Zone B)	60 m	(200 ft)	0.4 km (0.3 mi)	1.3 km (0.8 mi)	200 m	(600 ft)	2.3 km (1.4 mi)	5.1 km (3.2 mi)	
3123	139	Poisonous liquid, which in contact with water emits flammable gases, n.o.s.	60 m	(200 ft)	0.4 km (0.3 mi)	1.3 km (0.8 mi)	200 m	(600 ft)	2.3 km (1.4 mi)	5.1 km (3.2 mi)	
3123	139	Poisonous liquid, which in contact with water emits flammable gases, n.o.s. (Inhalation Hazard Zone A)	30 m	(100 ft)	0.2 km (0.1 mi)	0.2 km (0.1 mi)	60 m	(200 ft)	0.5 km (0.3 mi)	0.7 km (0.5 mi)	
3123	139	Poisonous liquid, which in contact with water emits flammable gases, n.o.s. (Inhalation Hazard Zone B)	60 m	(200 ft)	0.4 km (0.3 mi)	1.3 km (0.8 mi)	200 m	(600 ft)	2.3 km (1.4 mi)	5.1 km (3.2 mi)	
3123	139	Toxic liquid, water-reactive, n.o.s.									
3123	139	Toxic liquid, water-reactive, n.o.s. (Inhalation Hazard Zone A)									

ID No.	Guide No.	NAME OF MATERIAL	SMALL SPILLS First ISOLATE in all Directions	SMALL SPILLS Then PROTECT persons Downwind during DAY	SMALL SPILLS Then PROTECT persons Downwind during NIGHT	LARGE SPILLS First ISOLATE in all Directions	LARGE SPILLS Then PROTECT persons Downwind during DAY	LARGE SPILLS Then PROTECT persons Downwind during NIGHT
3123	139	Toxic liquid, water-reactive, n.o.s. (Inhalation Hazard Zone B)	30 m (100 ft)	0.2 km (0.1 mi)	0.2 km (0.1 mi)	60 m (200 ft)	0.5 km (0.3 mi)	0.7 km (0.5 mi)
3123	139	Toxic liquid, which in contact with water emits flammable gases, n.o.s.						
3123	139	Toxic liquid, which in contact with water emits flammable gases, n.o.s. (Inhalation Hazard Zone A)	60 m (200 ft)	0.4 km (0.3 mi)	1.3 km (0.8 mi)	200 m (600 ft)	2.3 km (1.4 mi)	5.1 km (3.2 mi)
3123	139	Toxic liquid, which in contact with water emits flammable gases, n.o.s. (Inhalation Hazard Zone B)	30 m (100 ft)	0.2 km (0.1 mi)	0.2 km (0.1 mi)	60 m (200 ft)	0.5 km (0.3 mi)	0.7 km (0.5 mi)
3160	119	Liquefied gas, poisonous, flammable, n.o.s.						
3160	119	Liquefied gas, poisonous, flammable, n.o.s. (Inhalation Hazard Zone A)	100 m (300 ft)	0.5 km (0.3 mi)	2.2 km (1.4 mi)	600 m (2000 ft)	2.6 km (1.7 mi)	8.6 km (5.4 mi)
3160	119	Liquefied gas, poisonous, flammable, n.o.s. (Inhalation Hazard Zone B)	30 m (100 ft)	0.1 km (0.1 mi)	0.3 km (0.2 mi)	300 m (1000 ft)	1.3 km (0.8 mi)	3.5 km (2.2 mi)
3160	119	Liquefied gas, poisonous, flammable, n.o.s. (Inhalation Hazard Zone C)	30 m (100 ft)	0.1 km (0.1 mi)	0.3 km (0.2 mi)	200 m (600 ft)	1.0 km (0.7 mi)	3.2 km (2.0 mi)
3160	119	Liquefied gas, poisonous, flammable, n.o.s. (Inhalation Hazard Zone D)	30 m (100 ft)	0.1 km (0.1 mi)	0.2 km (0.1 mi)	200 m (600 ft)	0.8 km (0.5 mi)	2.0 km (1.3 mi)

"+" means distance can be larger in certain atmospheric conditions

TABLE 1 - INITIAL ISOLATION AND PROTECTIVE ACTION DISTANCES

ID No.	Guide	NAME OF MATERIAL	SMALL SPILLS (From a small package or small leak from a large package)			LARGE SPILLS (From a large package or from many small packages)		
			First ISOLATE in all Directions Meters (Feet)	Then PROTECT persons Downwind during- DAY Kilometers (Miles)	NIGHT Kilometers (Miles)	First ISOLATE in all Directions Meters (Feet)	Then PROTECT persons Downwind during- DAY Kilometers (Miles)	NIGHT Kilometers (Miles)
3160	119	Liquefied gas, toxic, flammable, n.o.s.	100 m (300 ft)	0.5 km (0.3 mi)	2.2 km (1.4 mi)	600 m (2000 ft)	2.6 km (1.7 mi)	8.6 km (5.4 mi)
3160	119	Liquefied gas, toxic, flammable, n.o.s. (Inhalation Hazard Zone A)						
3160	119	Liquefied gas, toxic, flammable, n.o.s. (Inhalation Hazard Zone B)	30 m (100 ft)	0.1 km (0.1 mi)	0.3 km (0.2 mi)	300 m (1000 ft)	1.3 km (0.8 mi)	3.5 km (2.2 mi)
3160	119	Liquefied gas, toxic, flammable, n.o.s. (Inhalation Hazard Zone C)	30 m (100 ft)	0.1 km (0.1 mi)	0.3 km (0.2 mi)	200 m (600 ft)	1.0 km (0.7 mi)	3.2 km (2.0 mi)
3160	119	Liquefied gas, toxic, flammable, n.o.s. (Inhalation Hazard Zone D)	30 m (100 ft)	0.1 km (0.1 mi)	0.2 km (0.1 mi)	200 m (600 ft)	0.8 km (0.5 mi)	2.0 km (1.3 mi)
3162 3162	123 123	Liquefied gas, poisonous, n.o.s. Liquefied gas, poisonous, n.o.s. (Inhalation Hazard Zone A)	100 m (300 ft)	0.5 km (0.3 mi)	2.2 km (1.4 mi)	600 m (2000 ft)	3.5 km (2.2 mi)	9.4 km (5.9 mi)
3162	123	Liquefied gas, poisonous, n.o.s. (Inhalation Hazard Zone B)	30 m (100 ft)	0.2 km (0.1 mi)	0.8 km (0.5 mi)	300 m (1000 ft)	1.5 km (0.9 mi)	4.6 km (2.9 mi)
3162	123	Liquefied gas, poisonous, n.o.s. (Inhalation Hazard Zone C)	30 m (100 ft)	0.1 km (0.1 mi)	0.3 km (0.2 mi)	150 m (500 ft)	0.9 km (0.6 mi)	2.8 km (1.7 mi)
3162	123	Liquefied gas, poisonous, n.o.s. (Inhalation Hazard Zone D)	30 m (100 ft)	0.1 km (0.1 mi)	0.2 km (0.1 mi)	150 m (500 ft)	0.8 km (0.5 mi)	2.0 km (1.3 mi)

ID No.	Guide No.	NAME OF MATERIAL	SMALL SPILLS First ISOLATE in all Directions	SMALL SPILLS Then PROTECT persons Downwind DAY	SMALL SPILLS Then PROTECT persons Downwind NIGHT	LARGE SPILLS First ISOLATE in all Directions	LARGE SPILLS Then PROTECT persons Downwind DAY	LARGE SPILLS Then PROTECT persons Downwind NIGHT
3162	123	Liquefied gas, toxic, n.o.s.						
3162	123	Liquefied gas, toxic, n.o.s. (Inhalation Hazard Zone A)	100 m (300 ft)	0.5 km (0.3 mi)	2.2 km (1.4 mi)	600 m (2000 ft)	3.5 km (2.2 mi)	9.4 km (5.9 mi)
3162	123	Liquefied gas, toxic, n.o.s. (Inhalation Hazard Zone B)	30 m (100 ft)	0.2 km (0.1 mi)	0.8 km (0.5 mi)	300 m (1000 ft)	1.5 km (0.9 mi)	4.6 km (2.9 mi)
3162	123	Liquefied gas, toxic, n.o.s. (Inhalation Hazard Zone C)	30 m (100 ft)	0.1 km (0.1 mi)	0.3 km (0.2 mi)	150 m (500 ft)	0.9 km (0.6 mi)	2.8 km (1.7 mi)
3162	123	Liquefied gas, toxic, n.o.s. (Inhalation Hazard Zone D)	30 m (100 ft)	0.1 km (0.1 mi)	0.2 km (0.1 mi)	150 m (500 ft)	0.8 km (0.5 mi)	2.0 km (1.3 mi)
3246	156	Methanesulfonyl chloride	30 m (100 ft)	0.1 km (0.1 mi)	0.1 km (0.1 mi)	30 m (100 ft)	0.2 km (0.1 mi)	0.3 km (0.2 mi)
3246	156	Methanesulphonyl chloride						
3275	131	Nitriles, poisonous, flammable, n.o.s.	30 m (100 ft)	0.1 km (0.1 mi)	0.2 km (0.1 mi)	60 m (200 ft)	0.4 km (0.3 mi)	0.8 km (0.5 mi)
3275	131	Nitriles, toxic, flammable, n.o.s.						
3276	151	Nitriles, liquid, poisonous, n.o.s.	30 m (100 ft)	0.1 km (0.1 mi)	0.2 km (0.1 mi)	60 m (200 ft)	0.4 km (0.3 mi)	0.8 km (0.5 mi)
3276	151	Nitriles, liquid, toxic, n.o.s.						
3276	151	Nitriles, poisonous, liquid, n.o.s.						
3276	151	Nitriles, poisonous, n.o.s.						
3276	151	Nitriles, toxic, liquid, n.o.s.						
3276	151	Nitriles, toxic, n.o.s.						

"+" means distance can be larger in certain atmospheric conditions

TABLE 1 - INITIAL ISOLATION AND PROTECTIVE ACTION DISTANCES

ID No.	Guide	NAME OF MATERIAL	SMALL SPILLS (From a small package or small leak from a large package)			LARGE SPILLS (From a large package or from many small packages)		
			First ISOLATE in all Directions	Then PROTECT persons Downwind during-		First ISOLATE in all Directions	Then PROTECT persons Downwind during-	
			Meters (Feet)	DAY Kilometers (Miles)	NIGHT Kilometers (Miles)	Meters (Feet)	DAY Kilometers (Miles)	NIGHT Kilometers (Miles)
3278	**151**	Organophosphorus compound, liquid, poisonous, n.o.s.	30 m (100 ft)	0.4 km (0.3 mi)	1.2 km (0.8 mi)	200 m (600 ft)	2.3 km (1.4 mi)	4.3 km (2.7 mi)
3278	**151**	Organophosphorus compound, liquid, toxic, n.o.s.						
3278	**151**	Organophosphorus compound, poisonous, liquid, n.o.s.						
3278	**151**	Organophosphorus compound, poisonous, n.o.s.						
3278	**151**	Organophosphorus compound, toxic, liquid, n.o.s.						
3278	**151**	Organophosphorus compound, toxic, n.o.s.						
3279	**131**	Organophosphorus compound, poisonous, flammable, n.o.s.	30 m (100 ft)	0.4 km (0.3 mi)	1.2 km (0.8 mi)	200 m (600 ft)	2.3 km (1.4 mi)	4.3 km (2.7 mi)
3279	**131**	Organophosphorus compound, toxic, flammable, n.o.s.						
3280	**151**	Organoarsenic compound, liquid, n.o.s.	30 m (100 ft)	0.2 km (0.1 mi)	0.8 km (0.5 mi)	150 m (500 ft)	1.8 km (1.1 mi)	4.5 km (2.8 mi)
3280	**151**	Organoarsenic compound, n.o.s.						
3281	**151**	Metal carbonyls, liquid, n.o.s.	100 m (300 ft)	1.4 km (0.9 mi)	5.4 km (3.4 mi)	1000 m (3000 ft)	11.0+ km (7.0+ mi)	11.0+ km (7.0+ mi)
3281	**151**	Metal carbonyls, n.o.s.						

ID No.	Guide No.	Name of Material	SMALL SPILLS First ISOLATE in all Directions	SMALL SPILLS Then PROTECT persons Downwind during DAY	SMALL SPILLS Then PROTECT persons Downwind during NIGHT	LARGE SPILLS First ISOLATE in all Directions	LARGE SPILLS Then PROTECT persons Downwind during DAY	LARGE SPILLS Then PROTECT persons Downwind during NIGHT
3287	151	Poisonous liquid, inorganic, n.o.s. / Poisonous liquid, inorganic, n.o.s. (Inhalation Hazard Zone A)	60 m (200 ft)	0.6 km (0.4 mi)	2.0 km (1.2 mi)	300 m (1000 ft)	2.8 km (1.8 mi)	6.5 km (4.0 mi)
3287	151	Poisonous liquid, inorganic, n.o.s. (Inhalation Hazard Zone B)	30 m (100 ft)	0.2 km (0.1 mi)	0.3 km (0.2 mi)	100 m (300 ft)	1.0 km (0.6 mi)	1.6 km (1.0 mi)
3287 3287	151 151	Toxic liquid, inorganic, n.o.s. / Toxic liquid, inorganic, n.o.s. (Inhalation Hazard Zone A)	60 m (200 ft)	0.6 km (0.4 mi)	2.0 km (1.2 mi)	300 m (1000 ft)	2.8 km (1.8 mi)	6.5 km (4.0 mi)
3287	151	Toxic liquid, inorganic, n.o.s. (Inhalation Hazard Zone B)	30 m (100 ft)	0.2 km (0.1 mi)	0.3 km (0.2 mi)	100 m (300 ft)	1.0 km (0.6 mi)	1.6 km (1.0 mi)
3289	154	Poisonous liquid, corrosive, inorganic, n.o.s. / Poisonous liquid, corrosive, inorganic, n.o.s. (Inhalation Hazard Zone A)	30 m (100 ft)	0.4 km (0.2 mi)	1.4 km (0.9 mi)	200 m (600 ft)	2.3 km (1.4 mi)	5.1 km (3.2 mi)
3289	154	Poisonous liquid, corrosive, inorganic, n.o.s. (Inhalation Hazard Zone B)	30 m (100 ft)	0.1 km (0.1 mi)	0.3 km (0.2 mi)	100 m (300 ft)	0.5 km (0.3 mi)	1.1 km (0.7 mi)
3289 3289	154 154	Toxic liquid, corrosive, inorganic, n.o.s. / Toxic liquid, corrosive, inorganic, n.o.s. (Inhalation Hazard Zone A)	30 m (100 ft)	0.4 km (0.2 mi)	1.4 km (0.9 mi)	200 m (600 ft)	2.3 km (1.4 mi)	5.1 km (3.2 mi)
3289	154	Toxic liquid, corrosive, inorganic, n.o.s. (Inhalation Hazard Zone B)	30 m (100 ft)	0.1 km (0.1 mi)	0.3 km (0.2 mi)	100 m (300 ft)	0.5 km (0.3 mi)	1.1 km (0.7 mi)

"+" means distance can be larger in certain atmospheric conditions

TABLE 1 - INITIAL ISOLATION AND PROTECTIVE ACTION DISTANCES

ID No.	Guide	NAME OF MATERIAL	SMALL SPILLS (From a small package or small leak from a large package) First ISOLATE in all Directions		Then PROTECT persons Downwind during- DAY		NIGHT		LARGE SPILLS (From a large package or from many small packages) First ISOLATE in all Directions		Then PROTECT persons Downwind during- DAY		NIGHT	
			Meters	(Feet)	Kilometers	(Miles)	Kilometers	(Miles)	Meters	(Feet)	Kilometers	(Miles)	Kilometers	(Miles)
3294	131	Hydrogen cyanide, solution in alcohol, with not more than 45% Hydrogen cyanide	60 m	(200 ft)	0.2 km	(0.1 mi)	0.4 km	(0.2 mi)	200 m	(600 ft)	0.7 km	(0.4 mi)	2.0 km	(1.2 mi)
3300	119P	Carbon dioxide and Ethylene oxide mixture, with more than 87% Ethylene oxide	30 m	(100 ft)	0.1 km	(0.1 mi)	0.2 km	(0.1 mi)	150 m	(500 ft)	0.9 km	(0.5 mi)	2.0 km	(1.3 mi)
3300	119P	Ethylene oxide and Carbon dioxide mixture, with more than 87% Ethylene oxide												
3303	124	Compressed gas, poisonous, oxidizing, n.o.s.	60 m	(200 ft)	0.4 km	(0.3 mi)	2.1 km	(1.3 mi)	600 m	(2000 ft)	2.6 km	(1.7 mi)	8.6 km	(5.4 mi)
3303	124	Compressed gas, poisonous, oxidizing, n.o.s. (Inhalation Hazard Zone A)												
3303	124	Compressed gas, poisonous, oxidizing, n.o.s. (Inhalation Hazard Zone B)	60 m	(200 ft)	0.3 km	(0.2 mi)	1.1 km	(0.7 mi)	400 m	(1250 ft)	2.5 km	(1.5 mi)	6.7 km	(4.2 mi)
3303	124	Compressed gas, poisonous, oxidizing, n.o.s. (Inhalation Hazard Zone C)	30 m	(100 ft)	0.1 km	(0.1 mi)	0.3 km	(0.2 mi)	200 m	(600 ft)	0.9 km	(0.6 mi)	2.8 km	(1.7 mi)
3303	124	Compressed gas, poisonous, oxidizing, n.o.s. (Inhalation Hazard Zone D)	30 m	(100 ft)	0.1 km	(0.1 mi)	0.2 km	(0.1 mi)	200 m	(600 ft)	0.7 km	(0.4 mi)	2.0 km	(1.3 mi)

ID No.	Guide No.	Name of Material	SMALL SPILLS — First ISOLATE (meters/feet)	SMALL SPILLS — Then PROTECT Day (km/mi)	SMALL SPILLS — Then PROTECT Night (km/mi)	LARGE SPILLS — First ISOLATE (meters/feet)	LARGE SPILLS — Then PROTECT Day (km/mi)	LARGE SPILLS — Then PROTECT Night (km/mi)
3303	124	Compressed gas, toxic, oxidizing, n.o.s.						
3303	124	Compressed gas, toxic, oxidizing, n.o.s. (Inhalation Hazard Zone A)	60 m (200 ft)	0.4 km (0.3 mi)	2.1 km (1.3 mi)	600 m (2000 ft)	2.6 km (1.7 mi)	8.6 km (5.4 mi)
3303	124	Compressed gas, toxic, oxidizing, n.o.s. (Inhalation Hazard Zone B)	60 m (200 ft)	0.3 km (0.2 mi)	1.1 km (0.7 mi)	400 m (1250 ft)	2.5 km (1.5 mi)	6.7 km (4.2 mi)
3303	124	Compressed gas, toxic, oxidizing, n.o.s. (Inhalation Hazard Zone C)	30 m (100 ft)	0.1 km (0.1 mi)	0.3 km (0.2 mi)	200 m (600 ft)	0.9 km (0.6 mi)	2.8 km (1.7 mi)
3303	124	Compressed gas, toxic, oxidizing, n.o.s. (Inhalation Hazard Zone D)	30 m (100 ft)	0.1 km (0.1 mi)	0.2 km (0.1 mi)	200 m (600 ft)	0.7 km (0.4 mi)	2.0 km (1.3 mi)
3304	123	Compressed gas, poisonous, corrosive, n.o.s.						
3304	123	Compressed gas, poisonous, corrosive, n.o.s. (Inhalation Hazard Zone A)	100 m (300 ft)	0.5 km (0.4 mi)	2.6 km (1.6 mi)	600 m (2000 ft)	3.5 km (2.2 mi)	9.4 km (5.9 mi)
3304	123	Compressed gas, poisonous, corrosive, n.o.s. (Inhalation Hazard Zone B)	60 m (200 ft)	0.3 km (0.2 mi)	1.2 km (0.8 mi)	300 m (1000 ft)	1.5 km (0.9 mi)	4.6 km (2.9 mi)
3304	123	Compressed gas, poisonous, corrosive, n.o.s. (Inhalation Hazard Zone C)	30 m (100 ft)	0.1 km (0.1 mi)	0.3 km (0.2 mi)	150 m (500 ft)	0.9 km (0.6 mi)	2.8 km (1.7 mi)
3304	123	Compressed gas, poisonous, corrosive, n.o.s. (Inhalation Hazard Zone D)	30 m (100 ft)	0.1 km (0.1 mi)	0.2 km (0.1 mi)	150 m (500 ft)	0.8 km (0.5 mi)	2.0 km (1.3 mi)

"+" means distance can be larger in certain atmospheric conditions

TABLE 1 - INITIAL ISOLATION AND PROTECTIVE ACTION DISTANCES

ID No.	Guide	NAME OF MATERIAL	SMALL SPILLS (From a small package or small leak from a large package) First ISOLATE in all Directions Meters (Feet)	SMALL SPILLS Then PROTECT persons Downwind during- DAY Kilometers (Miles)	SMALL SPILLS Then PROTECT persons Downwind during- NIGHT Kilometers (Miles)	LARGE SPILLS (From a large package or from many small packages) First ISOLATE in all Directions Meters (Feet)	LARGE SPILLS Then PROTECT persons Downwind during- DAY Kilometers (Miles)	LARGE SPILLS Then PROTECT persons Downwind during- NIGHT Kilometers (Miles)
3304	123	Compressed gas, toxic, corrosive, n.o.s.	100 m (300 ft)	0.5 km (0.4 mi)	2.6 km (1.6 mi)	600 m (2000 ft)	3.5 km (2.2 mi)	9.4 km (5.9 mi)
3304	123	Compressed gas, toxic, corrosive, n.o.s. (Inhalation Hazard Zone A)						
3304	123	Compressed gas, toxic, corrosive, n.o.s. (Inhalation Hazard Zone B)	60 m (200 ft)	0.3 km (0.2 mi)	1.2 km (0.8 mi)	300 m (1000 ft)	1.5 km (0.9 mi)	4.6 km (2.9 mi)
3304	123	Compressed gas, toxic, corrosive, n.o.s. (Inhalation Hazard Zone C)	30 m (100 ft)	0.1 km (0.1 mi)	0.3 km (0.2 mi)	150 m (500 ft)	0.9 km (0.6 mi)	2.8 km (1.7 mi)
3304	123	Compressed gas, toxic, corrosive, n.o.s. (Inhalation Hazard Zone D)	30 m (100 ft)	0.1 km (0.1 mi)	0.2 km (0.1 mi)	150 m (500 ft)	0.8 km (0.5 mi)	2.0 km (1.3 mi)
3305	119	Compressed gas, poisonous, flammable, corrosive, n.o.s.	100 m (300 ft)	0.5 km (0.4 mi)	2.6 km (1.6 mi)	600 m (2000 ft)	3.5 km (2.2 mi)	9.4 km (5.9 mi)
3305	119	Compressed gas, poisonous, flammable, corrosive, n.o.s. (Inhalation Hazard Zone A)						
3305	119	Compressed gas, poisonous, flammable, corrosive, n.o.s. (Inhalation Hazard Zone B)	60 m (200 ft)	0.3 km (0.2 mi)	1.2 km (0.8 mi)	300 m (1000 ft)	1.5 km (0.9 mi)	4.6 km (2.9 mi)

ID No.	Guide No.	Name of Material	SMALL SPILLS First ISOLATE in all Directions		Then PROTECT persons Downwind during DAY	Then PROTECT persons Downwind during NIGHT	LARGE SPILLS First ISOLATE in all Directions		Then PROTECT persons Downwind during DAY	Then PROTECT persons Downwind during NIGHT
3305	119	Compressed gas, poisonous, flammable, corrosive, n.o.s. (Inhalation Hazard Zone C)	30 m	(100 ft)	0.1 km (0.1 mi)	0.3 km (0.2 mi)	200 m	(600 ft)	0.9 km (0.6 mi)	2.8 km (1.7 mi)
3305	119	Compressed gas, poisonous, flammable, corrosive, n.o.s. (Inhalation Hazard Zone D)	30 m	(100 ft)	0.1 km (0.1 mi)	0.2 km (0.1 mi)	200 m	(600 ft)	0.8 km (0.5 mi)	2.0 km (1.3 mi)
3305	119	Compressed gas, toxic, flammable, corrosive, n.o.s.	100 m	(300 ft)	0.5 km (0.4 mi)	2.6 km (1.6 mi)	600 m	(2000 ft)	3.5 km (2.2 mi)	9.4 km (5.9 mi)
3305	119	Compressed gas, toxic, flammable, corrosive, n.o.s. (Inhalation Hazard Zone A)								
3305	119	Compressed gas, toxic, flammable, corrosive, n.o.s. (Inhalation Hazard Zone B)	60 m	(200 ft)	0.3 km (0.2 mi)	1.2 km (0.8 mi)	300 m	(1000 ft)	1.5 km (0.9 mi)	4.6 km (2.9 mi)
3305	119	Compressed gas, toxic, flammable, corrosive, n.o.s. (Inhalation Hazard Zone C)	30 m	(100 ft)	0.1 km (0.1 mi)	0.3 km (0.2 mi)	200 m	(600 ft)	0.9 km (0.6 mi)	2.8 km (1.7 mi)
3305	119	Compressed gas, toxic, flammable, corrosive, n.o.s. (Inhalation Hazard Zone D)	30 m	(100 ft)	0.1 km (0.1 mi)	0.2 km (0.1 mi)	200 m	(600 ft)	0.8 km (0.5 mi)	2.0 km (1.3 mi)
3306	124	Compressed gas, poisonous, oxidizing, corrosive, n.o.s.	100 m	(300 ft)	0.5 km (0.4 mi)	2.6 km (1.6 mi)	600 m	(2000 ft)	3.5 km (2.2 mi)	9.4 km (5.9 mi)
3306	124	Compressed gas, poisonous, oxidizing, corrosive, n.o.s. (Inhalation Hazard Zone A)								
3306	124	Compressed gas, poisonous, oxidizing, corrosive, n.o.s. (Inhalation Hazard Zone B)	60 m	(200 ft)	0.3 km (0.2 mi)	1.1 km (0.7 mi)	400 m	(1250 ft)	2.5 km (1.5 mi)	6.7 km (4.2 mi)
3306	124	Compressed gas, poisonous, oxidizing, corrosive, n.o.s. (Inhalation Hazard Zone C)	30 m	(100 ft)	0.1 km (0.1 mi)	0.3 km (0.2 mi)	200 m	(600 ft)	0.9 km (0.6 mi)	2.8 km (1.7 mi)

"+" means distance can be larger in certain atmospheric conditions

TABLE 1 - INITIAL ISOLATION AND PROTECTIVE ACTION DISTANCES

ID No.	Guide	NAME OF MATERIAL	SMALL SPILLS (From a small package or small leak from a large package) First ISOLATE in all Directions Meters (Feet)	Then PROTECT persons Downwind during- DAY Kilometers (Miles)	NIGHT Kilometers (Miles)	LARGE SPILLS (From a large package or from many small packages) First ISOLATE in all Directions Meters (Feet)	Then PROTECT persons Downwind during- DAY Kilometers (Miles)	NIGHT Kilometers (Miles)
3306	124	Compressed gas, poisonous, oxidizing, corrosive, n.o.s. (Inhalation Hazard Zone D)	30 m (100 ft)	0.1 km (0.1 mi)	0.2 km (0.1 mi)	200 m (600 ft)	0.8 km (0.5 mi)	2.0 km (1.3 mi)
3306	124	Compressed gas, toxic, oxidizing, corrosive, n.o.s.	100 m (300 ft)	0.5 km (0.4 mi)	2.6 km (1.6 mi)	600 m (2000 ft)	3.5 km (2.2 mi)	9.4 km (5.9 mi)
3306	124	Compressed gas, toxic, oxidizing, corrosive, n.o.s. (Inhalation Hazard Zone A)						
3306	124	Compressed gas, toxic, oxidizing, corrosive, n.o.s. (Inhalation Hazard Zone B)	60 m (200 ft)	0.3 km (0.2 mi)	1.1 km (0.7 mi)	400 m (1250 ft)	2.5 km (1.5 mi)	6.7 km (4.2 mi)
3306	124	Compressed gas, toxic, oxidizing, corrosive, n.o.s. (Inhalation Hazard Zone C)	30 m (100 ft)	0.1 km (0.1 mi)	0.3 km (0.2 mi)	200 m (600 ft)	0.9 km (0.6 mi)	2.8 km (1.7 mi)
3306	124	Compressed gas, toxic, oxidizing, corrosive, n.o.s. (Inhalation Hazard Zone D)	30 m (100 ft)	0.1 km (0.1 mi)	0.2 km (0.1 mi)	200 m (600 ft)	0.8 km (0.5 mi)	2.0 km (1.3 mi)
3307	124	Liquefied gas, poisonous, oxidizing, n.o.s.	60 m (200 ft)	0.4 km (0.3 mi)	2.1 km (1.3 mi)	600 m (2000 ft)	2.6 km (1.7 mi)	8.6 km (5.4 mi)
3307	124	Liquefied gas, poisonous, oxidizing, n.o.s. (Inhalation Hazard Zone A)						

ID No.	Guide No.	Name of Material	SMALL SPILLS First ISOLATE	SMALL SPILLS Then PROTECT (Day)	SMALL SPILLS Then PROTECT (Night)	LARGE SPILLS First ISOLATE	LARGE SPILLS Then PROTECT (Day)	LARGE SPILLS Then PROTECT (Night)
3307	124	Liquefied gas, poisonous, oxidizing, n.o.s. (Inhalation Hazard Zone B)	60 m (200 ft)	0.3 km (0.2 mi)	1.1 km (0.7 mi)	400 m (1250 ft)	2.5 km (1.5 mi)	6.7 km (4.2 mi)
3307	124	Liquefied gas, poisonous, oxidizing, n.o.s. (Inhalation Hazard Zone C)	30 m (100 ft)	0.1 km (0.1 mi)	0.3 km (0.2 mi)	200 m (600 ft)	0.9 km (0.6 mi)	2.8 km (1.7 mi)
3307	124	Liquefied gas, poisonous, oxidizing, n.o.s. (Inhalation Hazard Zone D)	30 m (100 ft)	0.1 km (0.1 mi)	0.2 km (0.1 mi)	200 m (600 ft)	0.7 km (0.4 mi)	2.0 km (1.3 mi)
3307	124	Liquefied gas, toxic, oxidizing, n.o.s.	60 m (200 ft)	0.4 km (0.3 mi)	2.1 km (1.3 mi)	600 m (2000 ft)	2.6 km (1.7 mi)	8.6 km (5.4 mi)
3307	124	Liquefied gas, toxic, oxidizing, n.o.s. (Inhalation Hazard Zone A)						
3307	124	Liquefied gas, toxic, oxidizing, n.o.s. (Inhalation Hazard Zone B)	60 m (200 ft)	0.3 km (0.2 mi)	1.1 km (0.7 mi)	400 m (1250 ft)	2.5 km (1.5 mi)	6.7 km (4.2 mi)
3307	124	Liquefied gas, toxic, oxidizing, n.o.s. (Inhalation Hazard Zone C)	30 m (100 ft)	0.1 km (0.1 mi)	0.3 km (0.2 mi)	200 m (600 ft)	0.9 km (0.6 mi)	2.8 km (1.7 mi)
3307	124	Liquefied gas, toxic, oxidizing, n.o.s. (Inhalation Hazard Zone D)	30 m (100 ft)	0.1 km (0.1 mi)	0.2 km (0.1 mi)	200 m (600 ft)	0.7 km (0.4 mi)	2.0 km (1.3 mi)
3308	123	Liquefied gas, poisonous, corrosive, n.o.s.	100 m (300 ft)	0.5 km (0.4 mi)	2.6 km (1.6 mi)	600 m (2000 ft)	3.5 km (2.2 mi)	9.4 km (5.9 mi)
3308	123	Liquefied gas, poisonous, corrosive, n.o.s. (Inhalation Hazard Zone A)						

"+" means distance can be larger in certain atmospheric conditions

TABLE 1 - INITIAL ISOLATION AND PROTECTIVE ACTION DISTANCES

ID No.	Guide	NAME OF MATERIAL	SMALL SPILLS (From a small package or small leak from a large package)				LARGE SPILLS (From a large package or from many small packages)			
			First ISOLATE in all Directions	Then PROTECT persons Downwind during-			First ISOLATE in all Directions	Then PROTECT persons Downwind during-		
				DAY		NIGHT		DAY		NIGHT
			Meters (Feet)	Kilometers (Miles)		Kilometers (Miles)	Meters (Feet)	Kilometers (Miles)		Kilometers (Miles)
3308	123	Liquefied gas, poisonous, corrosive, n.o.s. (Inhalation Hazard Zone B)	60 m (200 ft)	0.3 km (0.2 mi)		1.2 km (0.8 mi)	300 m (1000 ft)	1.5 km (0.9 mi)		4.6 km (2.9 mi)
3308	123	Liquefied gas, poisonous, corrosive, n.o.s. (Inhalation Hazard Zone C)	30 m (100 ft)	0.1 km (0.1 mi)		0.3 km (0.2 mi)	150 m (500 ft)	0.9 km (0.6 mi)		2.8 km (1.7 mi)
3308	123	Liquefied gas, poisonous, corrosive, n.o.s. (Inhalation Hazard Zone D)	30 m (100 ft)	0.1 km (0.1 mi)		0.2 km (0.1 mi)	150 m (500 ft)	0.8 km (0.5 mi)		2.0 km (1.3 mi)
3308	123	Liquefied gas, toxic, corrosive, n.o.s.	100 m (300 ft)	0.5 km (0.4 mi)		2.6 km (1.6 mi)	600 m (2000 ft)	3.5 km (2.2 mi)		9.4 km (5.9 mi)
3308	123	Liquefied gas, toxic, corrosive, n.o.s. (Inhalation Hazard Zone A)								
3308	123	Liquefied gas, toxic, corrosive, n.o.s. (Inhalation Hazard Zone B)	60 m (200 ft)	0.3 km (0.2 mi)		1.2 km (0.8 mi)	300 m (1000 ft)	1.5 km (0.9 mi)		4.6 km (2.9 mi)
3308	123	Liquefied gas, toxic, corrosive, n.o.s. (Inhalation Hazard Zone C)	30 m (100 ft)	0.1 km (0.1 mi)		0.3 km (0.2 mi)	150 m (500 ft)	0.9 km (0.6 mi)		2.8 km (1.7 mi)
3308	123	Liquefied gas, toxic, corrosive, n.o.s. (Inhalation Hazard Zone D)	30 m (100 ft)	0.1 km (0.1 mi)		0.2 km (0.1 mi)	150 m (500 ft)	0.8 km (0.5 mi)		2.0 km (1.3 mi)

ID No.	Guide No.	NAME OF MATERIAL	SMALL SPILLS — First ISOLATE in all Directions	SMALL SPILLS — Then PROTECT persons Downwind during DAY	SMALL SPILLS — NIGHT	LARGE SPILLS — First ISOLATE in all Directions	LARGE SPILLS — Then PROTECT persons Downwind during DAY	LARGE SPILLS — NIGHT
3309	**119**	Liquefied gas, poisonous, flammable, corrosive, n.o.s.						
3309	**119**	Liquefied gas, poisonous, flammable, corrosive, n.o.s. (Inhalation Hazard Zone A)	100 m (300 ft)	0.5 km (0.4 mi)	2.6 km (1.6 mi)	600 m (2000 ft)	3.5 km (2.2 mi)	9.4 km (5.9 mi)
3309	**119**	Liquefied gas, poisonous, flammable, corrosive, n.o.s. (Inhalation Hazard Zone B)	60 m (200 ft)	0.3 km (0.2 mi)	1.2 km (0.8 mi)	300 m (1000 ft)	1.5 km (0.9 mi)	4.6 km (2.9 mi)
3309	**119**	Liquefied gas, poisonous, flammable, corrosive, n.o.s. (Inhalation Hazard Zone C)	30 m (100 ft)	0.1 km (0.1 mi)	0.3 km (0.2 mi)	200 m (600 ft)	0.9 km (0.6 mi)	2.8 km (1.7 mi)
3309	**119**	Liquefied gas, poisonous, flammable, corrosive, n.o.s. (Inhalation Hazard Zone D)	30 m (100 ft)	0.1 km (0.1 mi)	0.2 km (0.1 mi)	200 m (600 ft)	0.8 km (0.5 mi)	2.0 km (1.3 mi)
3309	**119**	Liquefied gas, toxic, flammable, corrosive, n.o.s.						
3309	**119**	Liquefied gas, toxic, flammable, corrosive, n.o.s. (Inhalation Hazard Zone A)	100 m (300 ft)	0.5 km (0.4 mi)	2.6 km (1.6 mi)	600 m (2000 ft)	3.5 km (2.2 mi)	9.4 km (5.9 mi)
3309	**119**	Liquefied gas, toxic, flammable, corrosive, n.o.s. (Inhalation Hazard Zone B)	60 m (200 ft)	0.3 km (0.2 mi)	1.2 km (0.8 mi)	300 m (1000 ft)	1.5 km (0.9 mi)	4.6 km (2.9 mi)
3309	**119**	Liquefied gas, toxic, flammable, corrosive, n.o.s. (Inhalation Hazard Zone C)	30 m (100 ft)	0.1 km (0.1 mi)	0.3 km (0.2 mi)	200 m (600 ft)	0.9 km (0.6 mi)	2.8 km (1.7 mi)
3309	**119**	Liquefied gas, toxic, flammable, corrosive, n.o.s. (Inhalation Hazard Zone D)	30 m (100 ft)	0.1 km (0.1 mi)	0.2 km (0.1 mi)	200 m (600 ft)	0.8 km (0.5 mi)	2.0 km (1.3 mi)

"+" means distance can be larger in certain atmospheric conditions

TABLE 1 - INITIAL ISOLATION AND PROTECTIVE ACTION DISTANCES

ID No.	Guide	NAME OF MATERIAL	SMALL SPILLS (From a small package or small leak from a large package)			LARGE SPILLS (From a large package or from many small packages)		
			First ISOLATE in all Directions	Then PROTECT persons Downwind during—		First ISOLATE in all Directions	Then PROTECT persons Downwind during—	
			Meters (Feet)	DAY Kilometers (Miles)	NIGHT Kilometers (Miles)	Meters (Feet)	DAY Kilometers (Miles)	NIGHT Kilometers (Miles)
3310	124	Liquefied gas, poisonous, oxidizing, corrosive, n.o.s. (Inhalation Hazard Zone A)	100 m (300 ft)	0.5 km (0.4 mi)	2.6 km (1.6 mi)	600 m (2000 ft)	3.5 km (2.2 mi)	9.4 km (5.9 mi)
3310	124	Liquefied gas, poisonous, oxidizing, corrosive, n.o.s. (Inhalation Hazard Zone B)	60 m (200 ft)	0.3 km (0.2 mi)	1.1 km (0.7 mi)	400 m (1250 ft)	2.5 km (1.5 mi)	6.7 km (4.2 mi)
3310	124	Liquefied gas, poisonous, oxidizing, corrosive, n.o.s. (Inhalation Hazard Zone C)	30 m (100 ft)	0.1 km (0.1 mi)	0.3 km (0.2 mi)	200 m (600 ft)	0.9 km (0.6 mi)	2.8 km (1.7 mi)
3310	124	Liquefied gas, poisonous, oxidizing, corrosive, n.o.s. (Inhalation Hazard Zone D)	30 m (100 ft)	0.1 km (0.1 mi)	0.2 km (0.1 mi)	200 m (600 ft)	0.8 km (0.5 mi)	2.0 km (1.3 mi)
3310	124	Liquefied gas, toxic, oxidizing, corrosive, n.o.s. (Inhalation Hazard Zone A)	100 m (300 ft)	0.5 km (0.4 mi)	2.6 km (1.6 mi)	600 m (2000 ft)	3.5 km (2.2 mi)	9.4 km (5.9 mi)
3310	124	Liquefied gas, toxic, oxidizing, corrosive, n.o.s. (Inhalation Hazard Zone B)	60 m (200 ft)	0.3 km (0.2 mi)	1.1 km (0.7 mi)	400 m (1250 ft)	2.5 km (1.5 mi)	6.7 km (4.2 mi)

ID No.	Guide No.	Name of Material						
3310	124	Liquefied gas, toxic, oxidizing, corrosive, n.o.s. (Inhalation Hazard Zone C)	30 m (100 ft)	0.1 km (0.1 mi)	0.3 km (0.2 mi)	200 m (600 ft)	0.9 km (0.6 mi)	2.8 km (1.7 mi)
3310	124	Liquefied gas, toxic, oxidizing, corrosive, n.o.s. (Inhalation Hazard Zone D)	30 m (100 ft)	0.1 km (0.1 mi)	0.2 km (0.1 mi)	200 m (600 ft)	0.8 km (0.5 mi)	2.0 km (1.3 mi)
3318	125	Ammonia solution, with more than 50% Ammonia	30 m (100 ft)	0.1 km (0.1 mi)	0.2 km (0.1 mi)	150 m (500 ft)	0.8 km (0.5 mi)	2.0 km (1.3 mi)
3355	119	Insecticide gas, poisonous, flammable, n.o.s.	100 m (300 ft)	0.5 km (0.3 mi)	2.2 km (1.4 mi)	600 m (2000 ft)	2.6 km (1.7 mi)	8.6 km (5.4 mi)
3355	119	Insecticide gas, poisonous, flammable, n.o.s. (Inhalation Hazard Zone A)						
3355	119	Insecticide gas, poisonous, flammable, n.o.s. (Inhalation Hazard Zone B)	30 m (100 ft)	0.1 km (0.1 mi)	0.3 km (0.2 mi)	300 m (1000 ft)	1.3 km (0.8 mi)	3.5 km (2.2 mi)
3355	119	Insecticide gas, poisonous, flammable, n.o.s. (Inhalation Hazard Zone C)	30 m (100 ft)	0.1 km (0.1 mi)	0.3 km (0.2 mi)	200 m (600 ft)	1.0 km (0.7 mi)	3.2 km (2.0 mi)
3355	119	Insecticide gas, poisonous, flammable, n.o.s. (Inhalation Hazard Zone D)	30 m (100 ft)	0.1 km (0.1 mi)	0.2 km (0.1 mi)	200 m (600 ft)	0.8 km (0.5 mi)	2.0 km (1.3 mi)
3355	119	Insecticide gas, toxic, flammable, n.o.s.	100 m (300 ft)	0.5 km (0.3 mi)	2.2 km (1.4 mi)	600 m (2000 ft)	2.6 km (1.7 mi)	8.6 km (5.4 mi)
3355	119	Insecticide gas, toxic, flammable, n.o.s. (Inhalation Hazard Zone A)						
3355	119	Insecticide gas, toxic, flammable, n.o.s. (Inhalation Hazard Zone B)	30 m (100 ft)	0.1 km (0.1 mi)	0.3 km (0.2 mi)	300 m (1000 ft)	1.3 km (0.8 mi)	3.5 km (2.2 mi)

"+" means distance can be larger in certain atmospheric conditions

TABLE 1 - INITIAL ISOLATION AND PROTECTIVE ACTION DISTANCES

ID No.	Guide	NAME OF MATERIAL	SMALL SPILLS (From a small package or small leak from a large package)				LARGE SPILLS (From a large package or from many small packages)				
			First ISOLATE in all Directions	Then PROTECT persons Downwind during-			First ISOLATE in all Directions	Then PROTECT persons Downwind during-			
				DAY		NIGHT		DAY		NIGHT	
			Meters (Feet)	Kilometers (Miles)		Kilometers (Miles)	Meters (Feet)	Kilometers (Miles)		Kilometers (Miles)	
3355	119	Insecticide gas, toxic, flammable, n.o.s. (Inhalation Hazard Zone C)	30 m (100 ft)	0.1 km (0.1 mi)		0.3 km (0.2 mi)	200 m (600 ft)	1.0 km (0.7 mi)		3.2 km (2.0 mi)	
3355	119	Insecticide gas, toxic, flammable, n.o.s. (Inhalation Hazard Zone D)	30 m (100 ft)	0.1 km (0.1 mi)		0.2 km (0.1 mi)	200 m (600 ft)	0.8 km (0.5 mi)		2.0 km (1.3 mi)	
3361	156	Chlorosilanes, poisonous, corrosive, n.o.s. (when spilled in water)	30 m (100 ft)	0.1 km (0.1 mi)		0.2 km (0.1 mi)	60 m (200 ft)	0.5 km (0.3 mi)		1.6 km (1.0 mi)	
3361	156	Chlorosilanes, toxic, corrosive, n.o.s. (when spilled in water)									
3362	155	Chlorosilanes, poisonous, corrosive, flammable, n.o.s. (when spilled in water)	30 m (100 ft)	0.1 km (0.1 mi)		0.2 km (0.1 mi)	60 m (200 ft)	0.5 km (0.3 mi)		1.6 km (1.0 mi)	
3362	155	Chlorosilanes, toxic, corrosive, flammable, n.o.s. (when spilled in water)									
3381	151	Poisonous by inhalation liquid, n.o.s. (Inhalation Hazard Zone A)	60 m (200 ft)	0.4 km (0.3 mi)		1.3 km (0.8 mi)	200 m (600 ft)	2.3 km (1.4 mi)		5.1 km (3.2 mi)	
3381	151	Toxic by inhalation liquid, n.o.s. (Inhalation Hazard Zone A)									

ID No.	Guide No.	Name of Material	SMALL SPILLS First ISOLATE	SMALL SPILLS Then PROTECT Day	SMALL SPILLS Then PROTECT Night	LARGE SPILLS First ISOLATE	LARGE SPILLS Then PROTECT Day	LARGE SPILLS Then PROTECT Night
3382	151	Poisonous by inhalation liquid, n.o.s. (Inhalation Hazard Zone B)	30 m (100 ft)	0.2 km (0.1 mi)	0.2 km (0.1 mi)	60 m (200 ft)	0.5 km (0.3 mi)	0.7 km (0.5 mi)
3382	151	Toxic by inhalation liquid, n.o.s. (Inhalation Hazard Zone B)						
3383	131	Poisonous by inhalation liquid, flammable, n.o.s. (Inhalation Hazard Zone A)	60 m (200 ft)	0.8 km (0.5 mi)	1.7 km (1.1 mi)	300 m (1000 ft)	4.0 km (2.5 mi)	6.5 km (4.1 mi)
3383	131	Toxic by inhalation liquid, flammable, n.o.s. (Inhalation Hazard Zone A)						
3384	131	Poisonous by inhalation liquid, flammable, n.o.s. (Inhalation Hazard Zone B)	30 m (100 ft)	0.1 km (0.1 mi)	0.2 km (0.1 mi)	60 m (200 ft)	0.5 km (0.3 mi)	0.7 km (0.5 mi)
3384	131	Toxic by inhalation liquid, flammable, n.o.s. (Inhalation Hazard Zone B)						
3385	139	Poisonous by inhalation liquid, water-reactive, n.o.s. (Inhalation Hazard Zone A)	60 m (200 ft)	0.4 km (0.3 mi)	1.3 km (0.8 mi)	200 m (600 ft)	2.3 km (1.4 mi)	5.1 km (3.2 mi)
3385	139	Toxic by inhalation liquid, water-reactive, n.o.s. (Inhalation Hazard Zone A)						
3386	139	Poisonous by inhalation liquid, water-reactive, n.o.s. (Inhalation Hazard Zone B)	30 m (100 ft)	0.2 km (0.1 mi)	0.2 km (0.1 mi)	60 m (200 ft)	0.5 km (0.3 mi)	0.7 km (0.5 mi)
3386	139	Toxic by inhalation liquid, water-reactive, n.o.s. (Inhalation Hazard Zone B)						

"+" means distance can be larger in certain atmospheric conditions

TABLE 1 - INITIAL ISOLATION AND PROTECTIVE ACTION DISTANCES

ID No.	Guide	NAME OF MATERIAL	SMALL SPILLS (From a small package or small leak from a large package) First ISOLATE in all Directions		SMALL SPILLS Then PROTECT persons Downwind during- DAY		NIGHT		LARGE SPILLS (From a large package or from many small packages) First ISOLATE in all Directions		LARGE SPILLS Then PROTECT persons Downwind during- DAY		NIGHT	
			Meters	(Feet)	Kilometers	(Miles)	Kilometers	(Miles)	Meters	(Feet)	Kilometers	(Miles)	Kilometers	(Miles)
3387	**142**	Poisonous by inhalation liquid, oxidizing, n.o.s. (Inhalation Hazard Zone A)	30 m	(100 ft)	0.4 km	(0.2 mi)	1.4 km	(0.9 mi)	200 m	(600 ft)	2.3 km	(1.4 mi)	5.1 km	(3.2 mi)
3387	**142**	Toxic by inhalation liquid, oxidizing, n.o.s. (Inhalation Hazard Zone A)												
3388	**142**	Poisonous by inhalation liquid, oxidizing, n.o.s. (Inhalation Hazard Zone B)	30 m	(100 ft)	0.1 km	(0.1 mi)	0.3 km	(0.2 mi)	60 m	(200 ft)	0.5 km	(0.4 mi)	1.0 km	(0.6 mi)
3388	**142**	Toxic by inhalation liquid, oxidizing, n.o.s. (Inhalation Hazard Zone B)												
3389	**154**	Poisonous by inhalation liquid, corrosive, n.o.s. (Inhalation Hazard Zone A)	60 m	(200 ft)	0.4 km	(0.2 mi)	0.9 km	(0.6 mi)	200 m	(600 ft)	1.5 km	(1.0 mi)	3.0 km	(1.9 mi)
3389	**154**	Toxic by inhalation liquid, corrosive, n.o.s. (Inhalation Hazard Zone A)												
3390	**154**	Poisonous by inhalation liquid, corrosive, n.o.s. (Inhalation Hazard Zone B)	30 m	(100 ft)	0.2 km	(0.1 mi)	0.2 km	(0.1 mi)	30 m	(100 ft)	0.4 km	(0.3 mi)	0.7 km	(0.4 mi)
3390	**154**	Toxic by inhalation liquid, corrosive, n.o.s. (Inhalation Hazard Zone B)												

ID No.	Guide No.	Name of Material	SMALL SPILLS — First ISOLATE in all Directions (Meters/Feet)	SMALL SPILLS — Then PROTECT persons Downwind during DAY (Kilometers/Miles)	SMALL SPILLS — Then PROTECT persons Downwind during NIGHT (Kilometers/Miles)	LARGE SPILLS — First ISOLATE in all Directions (Meters/Feet)	LARGE SPILLS — Then PROTECT persons Downwind during DAY (Kilometers/Miles)	LARGE SPILLS — Then PROTECT persons Downwind during NIGHT (Kilometers/Miles)
3456	157	Nitrosylsulfuric acid, solid **(when spilled in water)**	30 m (100 ft)	0.1 km (0.1 mi)	0.5 km (0.3 mi)	200 m (600 ft)	0.7 km (0.5 mi)	2.5 km (1.6 mi)
3456	157	Nitrosylsulphuric acid, solid **(when spilled in water)**	30 m (100 ft)	0.1 km (0.1 mi)	0.5 km (0.3 mi)	200 m (600 ft)	0.7 km (0.5 mi)	2.5 km (1.6 mi)
3461	135	Aluminum alkyl halides, solid **(when spilled in water)**	30 m (100 ft)	0.1 km (0.1 mi)	0.2 km (0.1 mi)	60 m (200 ft)	0.4 km (0.3 mi)	1.3 km (0.8 mi)
3488	131	Poisonous by inhalation liquid, flammable, corrosive, n.o.s. (Inhalation Hazard Zone A)	60 m (200 ft)	0.8 km (0.5 mi)	1.7 km (1.1 mi)	300 m (1000 ft)	4.0 km (2.5 mi)	6.5 km (4.1 mi)
3488	131	Toxic by inhalation liquid, flammable, corrosive, n.o.s. (Inhalation Hazard Zone A)	60 m (200 ft)	0.8 km (0.5 mi)	1.7 km (1.1 mi)	300 m (1000 ft)	4.0 km (2.5 mi)	6.5 km (4.1 mi)
3489	131	Poisonous by inhalation liquid, flammable, corrosive, n.o.s. (Inhalation Hazard Zone B)	30 m (100 ft)	0.1 km (0.1 mi)	0.2 km (0.1 mi)	60 m (200 ft)	0.5 km (0.3 mi)	0.7 km (0.5 mi)
3489	131	Toxic by inhalation liquid, flammable, corrosive, n.o.s. (Inhalation Hazard Zone B)	30 m (100 ft)	0.1 km (0.1 mi)	0.2 km (0.1 mi)	60 m (200 ft)	0.5 km (0.3 mi)	0.7 km (0.5 mi)
3490	155	Poisonous by inhalation liquid, water-reactive, flammable, n.o.s. (Inhalation Hazard Zone A)	60 m (200 ft)	0.8 km (0.5 mi)	1.7 km (1.1 mi)	300 m (1000 ft)	4.0 km (2.5 mi)	6.5 km (4.1 mi)
3490	155	Toxic by inhalation liquid, water-reactive, flammable, n.o.s. (Inhalation Hazard Zone A)	60 m (200 ft)	0.8 km (0.5 mi)	1.7 km (1.1 mi)	300 m (1000 ft)	4.0 km (2.5 mi)	6.5 km (4.1 mi)
3491	155	Poisonous by inhalation liquid, water-reactive, flammable, n.o.s. (Inhalation Hazard Zone B)	30 m (100 ft)	0.1 km (0.1 mi)	0.2 km (0.1 mi)	60 m (200 ft)	0.5 km (0.3 mi)	0.7 km (0.5 mi)
3491	155	Toxic by inhalation liquid, water-reactive, flammable, n.o.s. (Inhalation Hazard Zone B)	30 m (100 ft)	0.1 km (0.1 mi)	0.2 km (0.1 mi)	60 m (200 ft)	0.5 km (0.3 mi)	0.7 km (0.5 mi)

"+" means distance can be larger in certain atmospheric conditions

TABLE 1 - INITIAL ISOLATION AND PROTECTIVE ACTION DISTANCES

ID No.	Guide	NAME OF MATERIAL	SMALL SPILLS (From a small package or small leak from a large package)					LARGE SPILLS (From a large package or from many small packages)				
			First ISOLATE in all Directions		Then PROTECT persons Downwind during-			First ISOLATE in all Directions		Then PROTECT persons Downwind during-		
					DAY		NIGHT			DAY		NIGHT
			Meters	(Feet)	Kilometers (Miles)		Kilometers (Miles)	Meters	(Feet)	Kilometers (Miles)		Kilometers (Miles)
3492	131	Poisonous by inhalation liquid, corrosive, flammable, n.o.s. (Inhalation Hazard Zone A)	60 m	(200 ft)	0.8 km	(0.5 mi)	1.7 km (1.1 mi)	300 m	(1000 ft)	4.0 km	(2.5 mi)	6.5 km (4.1 mi)
3492	131	Toxic by inhalation liquid, corrosive, flammable, n.o.s. (Inhalation Hazard Zone A)										
3493	131	Poisonous by inhalation liquid, corrosive, flammable, n.o.s. (Inhalation Hazard Zone B)	30 m	(100 ft)	0.1 km	(0.1 mi)	0.2 km (0.1 mi)	60 m	(200 ft)	0.5 km	(0.3 mi)	0.7 km (0.5 mi)
3493	131	Toxic by inhalation liquid, corrosive, flammable, n.o.s. (Inhalation Hazard Zone B)										
3494	131	Petroleum sour crude oil, flammable, toxic	30 m	(100 ft)	0.2 km	(0.1 mi)	0.2 km (0.1 mi)	60 m	(200 ft)	0.5 km	(0.3 mi)	0.7 km (0.5 mi)
9191	143	Chlorine dioxide, hydrate, frozen (when spilled in water)	30 m	(100 ft)	0.1 km	(0.1 mi)	0.1 km (0.1 mi)	30 m	(100 ft)	0.2 km	(0.2 mi)	0.6 km (0.4 mi)
9202	168	Carbon monoxide, refrigerated liquid (cryogenic liquid)	30 m	(100 ft)	0.1 km	(0.1 mi)	0.2 km (0.1 mi)	200 m	(600 ft)	1.2 km	(0.8 mi)	4.8 km (3.0 mi)
9206	137	Methyl phosphonic dichloride	30 m	(100 ft)	0.1 km	(0.1 mi)	0.2 km (0.1 mi)	30 m	(100 ft)	0.4 km	(0.3 mi)	0.6 km (0.4 mi)
9263	156	Chloropivaloyl chloride	30 m	(100 ft)	0.1 km	(0.1 mi)	0.1 km (0.1 mi)	30 m	(100 ft)	0.3 km	(0.2 mi)	0.3 km (0.2 mi)
9264	151	3,5-Dichloro-2,4,6-trifluoropyridine	30 m	(100 ft)	0.1 km	(0.1 mi)	0.1 km (0.1 mi)	30 m	(100 ft)	0.3 km	(0.2 mi)	0.3 km (0.2 mi)

ID No.	Guide No.	NAME OF MATERIAL	30 m (100 ft)	0.2 km (0.1 mi)	0.5 km (0.3 mi)	100 m (300 ft)	0.9 km (0.6 mi)	1.9 km (1.2 mi)
9269	**132**	Trimethoxysilane						

See Next Page for Table of Water-Reactive Materials Which Produce Toxic Gases

"+" means distance can be larger in certain atmospheric conditions

HOW TO USE TABLE 2 – WATER-REACTIVE MATERIALS
WHICH PRODUCE TOXIC GASES

Table 2 lists materials which produce large amounts of Toxic Inhalation Hazard (TIH) gases when spilled in water and identifies the TIH gases produced.

The materials are listed by ID number order.

These Water Reactive materials are easily identified in Table 1 as their name is immediately followed by (**when spilled in water**).

Note: Some Water Reactive materials are also TIH materials themselves (e.g., Bromine trifluoride (1746), Thionyl chloride (1836), etc.). In these instances, two entries are provided in **Table 1** for land-based and water-based spills. If the Water Reactive material **is NOT** a TIH and this material **is NOT** spilled in water, **Table 1** and **Table 2** do not apply and safety distances will be found within the appropriate orange guide.

TABLE 2 - WATER-REACTIVE MATERIALS WHICH PRODUCE TOXIC GASES

Materials Which Produce Large Amounts of Toxic-by-Inhalation (TIH) Gas(es)
When Spilled in Water

ID No.	Guide No.	Name of Material	TIH Gas(es) Produced
1162	155	Dimethyldichlorosilane	HCl
1183	139	Ethyldichlorosilane	HCl
1196	155	Ethyltrichlorosilane	HCl
1242	139	Methyldichlorosilane	HCl
1250	155	Methyltrichlorosilane	HCl
1295	139	Trichlorosilane	HCl
1298	155	Trimethylchlorosilane	HCl
1305	155P	Vinyltrichlorosilane	HCl
1305	155P	Vinyltrichlorosilane, stabilized	HCl
1340	139	Phosphorus pentasulfide, free from yellow and white Phosphorus	H_2S
1340	139	Phosphorus pentasulphide, free from yellow and white Phosphorus	H_2S
1360	139	Calcium phosphide	PH_3
1384	135	Sodium dithionite	H_2S SO_2
1384	135	Sodium hydrosulfite	H_2S SO_2
1384	135	Sodium hydrosulphite	H_2S SO_2
1397	139	Aluminum phosphide	PH_3
1419	139	Magnesium aluminum phosphide	PH_3
1432	139	Sodium phosphide	PH_3
1541	155	Acetone cyanohydrin, stabilized	HCN
1680	157	Potassium cyanide	HCN
1680	157	Potassium cyanide, solid	HCN
1689	157	Sodium cyanide	HCN
1689	157	Sodium cyanide, solid	HCN

Chemical Symbols for TIH Gases:

Br_2	Bromine	HF	Hydrogen fluoride	NO_2	Nitrogen dioxide
Cl_2	Chlorine	HI	Hydrogen iodide	PH_3	Phosphine
HBr	Hydrogen bromide	H_2S	Hydrogen sulfide	SO_2	Sulfur dioxide
HCl	Hydrogen chloride	H_2S	Hydrogen sulphide	SO_2	Sulphur dioxide
HCN	Hydrogen cyanide	NH_3	Ammonia		

Use this list only when material is spilled in water.

TABLE 2 - WATER-REACTIVE MATERIALS WHICH PRODUCE TOXIC GASES

Materials Which Produce Large Amounts of Toxic-by-Inhalation (TIH) Gas(es)
When Spilled in Water

ID No.	Guide No.	Name of Material	TIH Gas(es) Produced	
1716	156	Acetyl bromide	HBr	
1717	155	Acetyl chloride	HCl	
1724	155	Allyltrichlorosilane, stabilized	HCl	
1725	137	Aluminum bromide, anhydrous	HBr	
1726	137	Aluminum chloride, anhydrous	HCl	
1728	155	Amyltrichlorosilane	HCl	
1732	157	Antimony pentafluoride	HF	
1741	125	Boron trichloride	HCl	
1745	144	Bromine pentafluoride	HF	Br_2
1746	144	Bromine trifluoride	HF	Br_2
1747	155	Butyltrichlorosilane	HCl	
1752	156	Chloroacetyl chloride	HCl	
1753	156	Chlorophenyltrichlorosilane	HCl	
1754	137	Chlorosulfonic acid	HCl	
1754	137	Chlorosulfonic acid and Sulfur trioxide mixture	HCl	
1754	137	Chlorosulphonic acid	HCl	
1754	137	Chlorosulphonic acid and Sulphur trioxide mixture	HCl	
1754	137	Sulfur trioxide and Chlorosulfonic acid	HCl	
1754	137	Sulphur trioxide and Chlorosulphonic acid	HCl	
1758	137	Chromium oxychloride	HCl	
1762	156	Cyclohexenyltrichlorosilane	HCl	
1763	156	Cyclohexyltrichlorosilane	HCl	
1765	156	Dichloroacetyl chloride	HCl	

Chemical Symbols for TIH Gases:

Br_2	Bromine	HF	Hydrogen fluoride	NO_2	Nitrogen dioxide
Cl_2	Chlorine	HI	Hydrogen iodide	PH_3	Phosphine
HBr	Hydrogen bromide	H_2S	Hydrogen sulfide	SO_2	Sulfur dioxide
HCl	Hydrogen chloride	H_2S	Hydrogen sulphide	SO_2	Sulphur dioxide
HCN	Hydrogen cyanide	NH_3	Ammonia		

TABLE 2 - WATER-REACTIVE MATERIALS WHICH PRODUCE TOXIC GASES

Materials Which Produce Large Amounts of Toxic-by-Inhalation (TIH) Gas(es)
When Spilled in Water

ID No.	Guide No.	Name of Material	TIH Gas(es) Produced
1766	156	Dichlorophenyltrichlorosilane	HCl
1767	155	Diethyldichlorosilane	HCl
1769	156	Diphenyldichlorosilane	HCl
1771	156	Dodecyltrichlorosilane	HCl
1777	137	Fluorosulfonic acid	HF
1777	137	Fluorosulphonic acid	HF
1781	156	Hexadecyltrichlorosilane	HCl
1784	156	Hexyltrichlorosilane	HCl
1799	156	Nonyltrichlorosilane	HCl
1800	156	Octadecyltrichlorosilane	HCl
1801	156	Octyltrichlorosilane	HCl
1804	156	Phenyltrichlorosilane	HCl
1806	137	Phosphorus pentachloride	HCl
1808	137	Phosphorus tribromide	HBr
1809	137	Phosphorus trichloride	HCl
1810	137	Phosphorus oxychloride	HCl
1815	132	Propionyl chloride	HCl
1816	155	Propyltrichlorosilane	HCl
1818	157	Silicon tetrachloride	HCl
1828	137	Sulfur chlorides	HCl SO_2 H_2S
1828	137	Sulphur chlorides	HCl SO_2 H_2S
1834	137	Sulfuryl chloride	HCl
1834	137	Sulphuryl chloride	HCl

Chemical Symbols for TIH Gases:

Br_2	Bromine	HF	Hydrogen fluoride	NO_2	Nitrogen dioxide
Cl_2	Chlorine	HI	Hydrogen iodide	PH_3	Phosphine
HBr	Hydrogen bromide	H_2S	Hydrogen sulfide	SO_2	Sulfur dioxide
HCl	Hydrogen chloride	H_2S	Hydrogen sulphide	SO_2	Sulphur dioxide
HCN	Hydrogen cyanide	NH_3	Ammonia		

TABLE2 - WATER-REACTIVE MATERIALS WHICH PRODUCE TOXIC GASES

Materials Which Produce Large Amounts of Toxic-by-Inhalation (TIH) Gas(es)
When Spilled in Water

ID No.	Guide No.	Name of Material	TIH Gas(es) Produced
1836	137	Thionyl chloride	HCl SO_2
1838	137	Titanium tetrachloride	HCl
1898	156	Acetyl iodide	HI
1923	135	Calcium dithionite	H_2S SO_2
1923	135	Calcium hydrosulfite	H_2S SO_2
1923	135	Calcium hydrosulphite	H_2S SO_2
1929	135	Potassium dithionite	H_2S SO_2
1929	135	Potassium hydrosulfite	H_2S SO_2
1929	135	Potassium hydrosulphite	H_2S SO_2
1931	171	Zinc dithionite	H_2S SO_2
1931	171	Zinc hydrosulfite	H_2S SO_2
1931	171	Zinc hydrosulphite	H_2S SO_2
2004	135	Magnesium diamide	NH_3
2011	139	Magnesium phosphide	PH_3
2012	139	Potassium phosphide	PH_3
2013	139	Strontium phosphide	PH_3
2308	157	Nitrosylsulfuric acid	NO_2
2308	157	Nitrosylsulfuric acid, liquid	NO_2
2308	157	Nitrosylsulfuric acid, solid	NO_2
2308	157	Nitrosylsulphuric acid	NO_2
2308	157	Nitrosylsulphuric acid, liquid	NO_2
2308	157	Nitrosylsulphuric acid, solid	NO_2
2353	132	Butyryl chloride	HCl

Chemical Symbols for TIH Gases:

Br_2	Bromine	HF	Hydrogen fluoride	NO_2	Nitrogen dioxide
Cl_2	Chlorine	HI	Hydrogen iodide	PH_3	Phosphine
HBr	Hydrogen bromide	H_2S	Hydrogen sulfide	SO_2	Sulfur dioxide
HCl	Hydrogen chloride	H_2S	Hydrogen sulphide	SO_2	Sulphur dioxide
HCN	Hydrogen cyanide	NH_3	Ammonia		

Use this list only when material is spilled in water.

TABLE 2 - WATER-REACTIVE MATERIALS WHICH PRODUCE TOXIC GASES

Materials Which Produce Large Amounts of Toxic-by-Inhalation (TIH) Gas(es) *When Spilled in Water*

ID No.	Guide No.	Name of Material	TIH Gas(es) Produced
2395	132	Isobutyryl chloride	HCl
2434	156	Dibenzyldichlorosilane	HCl
2435	156	Ethylphenyldichlorosilane	HCl
2437	156	Methylphenyldichlorosilane	HCl
2495	144	Iodine pentafluoride	HF
2691	137	Phosphorus pentabromide	HBr
2692	157	Boron tribromide	HBr
2806	138	Lithium nitride	NH_3
2977	166	Radioactive material, Uranium hexafluoride, fissile	HF
2977	166	Uranium hexafluoride, fissile containing more than 1% Uranium-235	HF
2978	166	Radioactive material, Uranium hexafluoride	HF
2978	166	Uranium hexafluoride	HF
2978	166	Uranium hexafluoride, non fissile or fissile-excepted	HF
2985	155	Chlorosilanes, flammable, corrosive, n.o.s	HCl
2985	155	Chlorosilanes, n.o.s	HCl
2986	155	Chlorosilanes, corrosive, flammable, n.o.s	HCl
2986	155	Chlorosilanes, n.o.s	HCl
2987	156	Chlorosilanes, corrosive, n.o.s	HCl
2987	156	Chlorosilanes, n.o.s	HCl
2988	139	Chlorosilanes, n.o.s	HCl
2988	139	Chlorosilanes, water-reactive, flammable, corrosive, n.o.s.	HCl
3048	157	Aluminum phosphide pesticide	PH_3

Chemical Symbols for TIH Gases:

Br_2	Bromine	HF	Hydrogen fluoride	NO_2	Nitrogen dioxide
Cl_2	Chlorine	HI	Hydrogen iodide	PH_3	Phosphine
HBr	Hydrogen bromide	H_2S	Hydrogen sulfide	SO_2	Sulfur dioxide
HCl	Hydrogen chloride	H_2S	Hydrogen sulphide	SO_2	Sulphur dioxide
HCN	Hydrogen cyanide	NH_3	Ammonia		

TABLE 2 - WATER-REACTIVE MATERIALS WHICH PRODUCE TOXIC GASES

Materials Which Produce Large Amounts of Toxic-by-Inhalation (TIH) Gas(es)
When Spilled in Water

ID No.	Guide No.	Name of Material	TIH Gas(es) Produced
3049	138	Metal alkyl halides, water-reactive, n.o.s	HCl
3049	138	Metal aryl halides, water-reactive, n.o.s	HCl
3052	135	Aluminum alkyl halide	HCl
3052	135	Aluminum alkyl halides, liquid	HCl
3052	135	Aluminum alkyl halides, solid	HCl
3361	156	Chlorosilanes, poisonous, corrosive, n.o.s.	HCl
3361	156	Chlorosilanes, toxic, corrosive, n.o.s.	HCl
3362	155	Chlorosilanes, poisonous, corrosive, flammable, n.o.s.	HCl
3362	155	Chlorosilanes, toxic, corrosive, flammable, n.o.s.	HCl
3456	157	Nitrosylsulfuric acid, solid	NO_2
3456	157	Nitrosylsulphuric acid, solid	NO_2
3461	135	Aluminum alkyl halides, solid	HCl
9191	143	Chlorine dioxide, hydrate, frozen	Cl_2

Chemical Symbols for TIH Gases:

Br_2	Bromine	HF	Hydrogen fluoride	NO_2	Nitrogen dioxide
Cl_2	Chlorine	HI	Hydrogen iodide	PH_3	Phosphine
HBr	Hydrogen bromide	H_2S	Hydrogen sulfide	SO_3	Sulfur dioxide
HCl	Hydrogen chloride	H_2S	Hydrogen sulphide	SO_2	Sulphur dioxide
HCN	Hydrogen cyanide	NH_3	Ammonia		

Use this list only when material is spilled in water.

NOTES

HOW TO USE TABLE 3 – INITIAL ISOLATION AND PROTECTIVE ACTION DISTANCES FOR DIFFERENT QUANTITIES OF SIX COMMON TIH GASES

Table 3 lists Toxic Inhalation Hazard materials that may be more commonly encountered.

The selected materials are:

- Ammonia (UN1005)
- Chlorine (UN1017)
- Ethylene oxide (UN1040)
- Hydrogen chloride (UN1050) and Hydrogen chloride, refrigerated liquid (UN2186)
- Hydrogen fluoride (UN1052)
- Sulfur dioxide/Sulphur dioxide (UN1079)

The materials are presented in alphabetical order and provide Initial Isolation and Protective Action Distances for large spills (more than 208 liters or 55 US gallons) involving different container types (therefore different volume capacities) for day time and night time situations and different wind speeds.

TABLE 3 - INITIAL ISOLATION AND PROTECTIVE ACTION DISTANCES FOR DIFFERENT QUANTITIES OF SIX COMMON TIH GASES

UN1005 Ammonia, anhydrous: Large Spills

Then **PROTECT** persons Downwind during

TRANSPORT CONTAINER	First ISOLATE in all Directions		DAY						NIGHT					
			Low wind (< 6 mph = < 10 km/h)		Moderate wind (6-12 mph = 10 - 20 km/h)		High wind (> 12 mph = > 20 km/h)		Low wind (< 6 mph = < 10 km/h)		Moderate wind (6-12 mph = 10 - 20 km/h)		High wind (> 12 mph = > 20 km/h)	
	Meters	(Feet)	Km	(Miles)	Km	(Miles)	Km	(Miles)	Km	(Miles)	Km	(Miles)	Km	(Miles)
Rail tank car	300	(1000)	2.3	(1.4)	1.3	(0.8)	1.0	(0.6)	6.3	(3.9)	2.6	(1.6)	1.3	(0.8)
Highway tank truck or trailer	125	(400)	1.0	(0.6)	0.5	(0.3)	0.3	(0.2)	2.6	(1.6)	0.8	(0.5)	0.5	(0.3)
Agricultural nurse tank	60	(200)	0.6	(0.4)	0.3	(0.2)	0.3	(0.2)	1.5	(0.9)	0.5	(0.3)	0.3	(0.2)
Multiple small cylinders	30	(100)	0.3	(0.2)	0.2	(0.1)	0.2	(0.1)	0.8	(0.5)	0.3	(0.2)	0.2	(0.1)

UN1017 Chlorine: Large Spills

TRANSPORT CONTAINER	First ISOLATE in all Directions		DAY						NIGHT					
	Meters	(Feet)	Km	(Miles)	Km	(Miles)	Km	(Miles)	Km	(Miles)	Km	(Miles)	Km	(Miles)
Rail tank car	1000	(3000)	11+	(7+)	9.0	(5.6)	5.5	(3.4)	11+	(7+)	11+	(7+)	7.1	(4.4)
Highway tank truck or trailer	1000	(3000)	10.6	(6.6)	3.5	(2.2)	2.9	(1.8)	11+	(7+)	5.5	(3.4)	4.2	(2.6)
Multiple ton cylinders	400	(1250)	4.0	(2.5)	1.5	(0.9)	1.1	(0.7)	7.9	(4.9)	2.7	(1.7)	1.5	(0.9)
Multiple small cylinders or single ton cylinder	250	(800)	2.6	(1.6)	1.0	(0.6)	0.8	(0.5)	5.6	(3.5)	1.8	(1.1)	0.8	(0.5)

"+" means distance can be larger in certain atmospheric conditions

UN1040 Ethylene oxide: Large Spills

TRANSPORT CONTAINER	First ISOLATE in all Directions		Then PROTECT persons Downwind during					
			DAY			NIGHT		
			Low wind (< 6 mph = < 10 km/h)	Moderate wind (6-12 mph = 10 - 20 km/h)	High wind (> 12 mph = > 20 km/h)	Low wind (< 6 mph = < 10 km/h)	Moderate wind (6-12 mph = 10 - 20 km/h)	High wind (> 12 mph = > 20 km/h)
	Meters (Feet)		Km (Miles)	Km (Miles)	Km (Miles)	Km (Miles)	Km (Miles)	Km (Miles)
Rail tank car	200	(600)	1.4 (0.9)	0.8 (0.5)	0.6 (0.4)	4.0 (2.5)	1.4 (0.9)	0.8 (0.5)
Highway tank truck or trailer	100	(300)	0.8 (0.5)	0.5 (0.3)	0.3 (0.2)	2.1 (1.3)	0.6 (0.4)	0.5 (0.3)
Multiple small cylinders or single ton cylinder	30	(100)	0.3 (0.2)	0.2 (0.1)	0.2 (0.1)	0.8 (0.5)	0.3 (0.2)	0.2 (0.1)

UN1050 Hydrogen chloride: Large Spills
UN2186 Hydrogen chloride, refrigerated liquid: Large Spills

TRANSPORT CONTAINER			Low wind (< 6 mph = < 10 km/h)	Moderate wind (6-12 mph = 10 - 20 km/h)	High wind (> 12 mph = > 20 km/h)	Low wind (< 6 mph = < 10 km/h)	Moderate wind (6-12 mph = 10 - 20 km/h)	High wind (> 12 mph = > 20 km/h)
Rail tank car	600	(2000)	6.1 (3.8)	2.3 (1.4)	1.8 (1.1)	11+ (7+)	4.0 (2.5)	2.6 (1.6)
Highway tank truck or trailer	300	(1000)	3.1 (1.9)	1.1 (0.7)	0.8 (0.5)	7.4 (4.6)	2.1 (1.3)	1.0 (0.6)
Multiple ton cylinders	60	(200)	0.6 (0.4)	0.3 (0.2)	0.2 (0.1)	1.8 (1.1)	0.3 (0.2)	0.2 (0.1)
Multiple small cylinders or single ton cylinder	45	(150)	0.5 (0.3)	0.2 (0.1)	0.2 (0.1)	1.5 (0.9)	0.3 (0.2)	0.2 (0.1)

UN1052 Hydrogen fluoride: Large Spills

Then **PROTECT** persons Downwind during

TRANSPORT CONTAINER	First ISOLATE in all Directions		DAY						NIGHT					
			Low wind (< 6 mph = < 10 km/h)		Moderate wind (6-12 mph = 10 - 20 km/h)		High wind (> 12 mph = > 20 km/h)		Low wind (< 6 mph = < 10 km/h)		Moderate wind (6-12 mph = 10 - 20 km/h)		High wind (> 12 mph = > 20 km/h)	
	Meters	(Feet)	Km	(Miles)	Km	(Miles)	Km	(Miles)	Km	(Miles)	Km	(Miles)	Km	(Miles)
Rail tank car	400	(1250)	3.2	(2.0)	1.9	(1.2)	1.6	(1.0)	7.9	(4.9)	3.1	(1.9)	1.9	(1.2)
Highway tank truck or trailer	210	(700)	1.9	(1.2)	1.0	(0.6)	0.8	(0.5)	3.9	(2.4)	1.6	(1.0)	1.0	(0.6)
Multiple small cylinders or single ton cylinder	100	(300)	0.8	(0.5)	0.3	(0.2)	0.3	(0.2)	1.6	(1.0)	0.5	(0.3)	0.3	(0.2)

UN1079 Sulfur dioxide/Sulphur dioxide: Large Spills

TRANSPORT CONTAINER	First ISOLATE in all Directions		DAY						NIGHT					
	Meters	(Feet)	Km	(Miles)	Km	(Miles)	Km	(Miles)	Km	(Miles)	Km	(Miles)	Km	(Miles)
Rail tank car	1000	(3000)	11+	(7+)	11+	(7+)	7.6	(4.7)	11+	(7+)	11+	(7+)	10.8	(6.7)
Highway tank truck or trailer	1000	(3000)	11+	(7+)	7.6	(4.7)	5.1	(3.2)	11+	(7+)	10	(6.2)	6.1	(3.8)
Multiple ton cylinders	600	(2000)	7.1	(4.4)	2.7	(1.7)	1.9	(1.2)	10.5	(6.5)	4.7	(2.9)	2.9	(1.8)
Multiple small cylinders or single ton cylinder	300	(1000)	5.3	(3.3)	1.6	(1.0)	1.1	(0.7)	7.9	(4.9)	2.7	(1.7)	1.5	(0.9)

"+" means distance can be larger in certain atmospheric conditions

ERG2012 USER'S GUIDE

The 2012 Emergency Response Guidebook (ERG2012) was developed jointly by Transport Canada (TC), the U.S. Department of Transportation (DOT), the Secretariat of Transport and Communications of Mexico (SCT) and with the collaboration of CIQUIME (Centro de Información Química para Emergencias) of Argentina, for use by fire fighters, police, and other emergency services personnel who may be the first to arrive at the scene of a transportation incident involving dangerous goods. **It is primarily a guide to aid first responders in quickly identifying the specific or generic hazards of the material(s) involved in the incident, and protecting themselves and the general public during the initial response phase of the incident.** For the purposes of this guidebook, the "initial response phase" is that period following arrival at the scene of an incident during which the presence and/or identification of dangerous goods is confirmed, protective actions and area securement are initiated, and assistance of qualified personnel is requested. It is not intended to provide information on the physical or chemical properties of dangerous goods.

This guidebook will assist responders in making initial decisions upon arriving at the scene of a dangerous goods incident. It should not be considered as a substitute for emergency response training, knowledge or sound judgment. ERG2012 does not address all possible circumstances that may be associated with a dangerous goods incident. It is primarily designed for use at a dangerous goods incident occurring on a highway or railroad. Be mindful that there may be limited value in its application at fixed facility locations.

ERG2012 incorporates dangerous goods lists from the most recent United Nations Recommendations as well as from other international and national regulations. Explosives are not listed individually by either proper shipping name or ID Number. They do, however, appear under the general heading "Explosives" on the first page of the ID Number index (yellow-bordered pages) and alphabetically in the Name of Material index (blue-bordered pages). Also, the letter **(P)** following the guide number in the yellow-bordered and blue-bordered pages identifies those materials which present a polymerization hazard under certain conditions, for example: Acrolein, stabilized **131P**.

First responders at the scene of a dangerous goods incident should seek additional specific information about any material in question as soon as possible. The information received by contacting the appropriate emergency response agency, by calling the emergency response telephone number on the shipping document, or by consulting the information on or accompanying the shipping document, may be more specific and accurate than this guidebook in providing guidance for the materials involved.

BEFORE AN EMERGENCY – BECOME FAMILIAR WITH THIS GUIDEBOOK! In the U.S., according to the requirements of the U.S. Department of Labor's Occupational Safety and Health Administration (OSHA, 29 CFR 1910.120), and regulations issued by the U.S. Environmental Protection Agency (EPA, 40 CFR Part 311), first responders must be trained regarding the use of this guidebook.

GUIDEBOOK CONTENTS

1-Yellow-bordered pages: Index list of dangerous goods in numerical order of ID number. This section quickly identifies the guide to be consulted from the ID Number of the material involved. This list displays the 4-digit ID number of the material followed by its assigned emergency response guide and the material name.

For example:	ID No.	GUIDE No.	Name of Material
	1090	127	Acetone

2-Blue-bordered pages: Index list of dangerous goods in alphabetical order of material name. This section quickly identifies the guide to be consulted from the name of the material involved. This list displays the name of the material followed by its assigned emergency response guide and 4-digit ID number.

For example:	Name of Material	GUIDE No.	ID No.
	Sulfuric acid	137	1830

3-Orange-bordered pages: This section is the most important section of the guidebook because it is where all safety recommendations are provided. It comprises a total of 62 individual guides, presented in a two-page format. Each guide provides safety recommendations and emergency response information to protect yourself and the public. The left hand page provides safety related information whereas the right hand page provides emergency response guidance and activities for fire situations, spill or leak incidents and first aid. Each guide is designed to cover a group of materials which possess similar chemical and toxicological characteristics.

The guide title identifies the general hazards of the dangerous goods covered.

For example: GUIDE 124 - Gases-Toxic and/or Corrosive-Oxidizing.

Each guide is divided into three main sections: the first section describes **potential hazards** that the material may display in terms of fire/explosion and health effects upon exposure. The highest potential is listed first. The emergency responder should consult this section first. This allows the responder to make decisions regarding the protection of the emergency response team as well as the surrounding population.

The second section outlines suggested **public safety** measures based on the situation at hand. It provides general information regarding immediate isolation of the incident site, recommended type of protective clothing and respiratory protection. Suggested evacuation distances are listed for small and large spills and for fire situations (fragmentation hazard). It also directs the reader to consult the tables listing Toxic Inhalation Hazard (TIH) materials, chemical warfare agents and water-reactive materials (green-bordered pages) when the material is highlighted in the yellow-bordered and blue-bordered pages.

The third section covers **emergency response** actions, including first aid. It outlines special precautions for incidents which involve fire, spill or chemical exposure. Several recommendations are listed under each part which will further assist in the decision making process. The information on first aid is general guidance prior to seeking medical care.

4-Green-bordered pages: This section contains three tables.

Table 1 lists, by ID number order, TIH materials, including certain chemical warfare agents, and water-reactive materials which produce toxic gases upon contact with water. This table provides two different types of recommended safe distances which are "Initial isolation distances" and "Protective action distances". The materials are highlighted in green for easy identification in both numeric (yellow-bordered pages) and alphabetic (blue-bordered pages) lists of the guidebook. This table provides distances for both small (approximately 208 liters (55 US gallons) or less for liquids and 300 kilograms (660 pounds) or less for solids when spilled in water) and large spills (more than 208 liters (55 US gallons) for liquids and more than 300 kilograms (660 pounds) for solids when spilled in water) for all highlighted materials. The list is further subdivided into daytime and nighttime situations. This is necessary due to varying atmospheric conditions which greatly affect the size of the hazardous area. The distances change from daytime to nighttime due to different mixing and dispersion conditions in the air. During the night, the air is generally calmer and this causes the material to disperse less and therefore create a toxic zone which is greater than would usually occur during the day. During the day, a more active atmosphere will cause a greater dispersion of the material resulting in a lower concentration of the material in the surrounding air. The actual area where toxic levels are reached will be smaller (due to increased dispersion). In fact, it is the quantity or concentration of the material vapor that poses problems not its mere presence.

The "Initial Isolation Distance" is a distance within which all persons should be considered for evacuation <u>in all directions</u> from the actual spill/leak source. It is a distance (radius) which defines a circle (Initial Isolation Zone) within which persons may be exposed to dangerous concentrations upwind of the source and may be exposed to life threatening concentrations downwind of the source. For example, in the case of Compressed gas, toxic, n.o.s., ID No. 1955, Inhalation Hazard Zone A, the isolation distance for small spills is 100 meters (300 feet), therefore, representing an evacuation circle of 200 meters (600 feet) in diameter.

For the same material, the "Protective Action Distance" for a small spill is 0.5 kilometers (0.3 mile) for a daytime incident and 2.2 kilometers (1.4 miles) for a nighttime incident, these distances represent a downwind distance from the spill/leak source within which Protective Actions could be implemented. Protective Actions are those steps taken to preserve the health and safety of emergency responders and the public. People in this area could be evacuated and/or sheltered in-place. For more information, consult pages 285 to 291.

What is a TIH? It is a gas or volatile liquid which is known to be so toxic to humans as to pose a hazard to health during transportation, or in the absence of adequate data on human toxicity, is presumed to be toxic to humans because when tested on laboratory animals it has a Lethal Concentration 50 (LC50) value of not more than 5000 ppm.

It is important to note that even though the term zone is used, the hazard zones do not represent any actual area or distance. The assignment of the zones is strictly a function of their Lethal Concentration 50 (LC50); for example, TIH Zone A is more toxic than Zone D. All distances which are listed in the green-bordered pages are calculated by the use of mathematical models for each TIH material. For the assignment of hazard zones refer to the glossary.

Page 358

Table 2 lists, by ID number order, materials that produce large amounts of Toxic Inhalation Hazard (TIH) gases when spilled in water and identifies the TIH gases produced. These Water Reactive materials are easily identified in **Table 1** as their name is immediately followed by **(when spilled in water)**. Some Water Reactive materials are also TIH materials themselves (e.g., Bromine trifluoride (1746), Thionyl chloride (1836), etc.). In these instances, two entries are provided in **Table 1** for land-based and water-based spills. If the Water Reactive material is NOT a TIH and this material is NOT spilled in water, **Table 1** and **Table 2** do not apply and safety distances will be found within the appropriate orange-bordered guide.

Table 3 provides, by alphabetical order of material name, initial isolation and protective action distances for six Toxic Inhalation Hazard materials that may be more commonly encountered. The selected materials are:

- Ammonia, anhydrous (UN1005)
- Chlorine (UN1017)
- Ethylene oxide (UN1040)
- Hydrogen chloride (UN1050) and Hydrogen chloride, refrigerated liquid (UN2186)
- Hydrogen fluoride (UN1052)
- Sulfur dioxide/Sulphur dioxide (UN1079)

The table provides Initial Isolation and Protective Action Distances for large spills (more than 208 liters or 55 US gallons) involving different container types (therefore different volume capacities) for day time and night time situations and different wind speeds.

ISOLATION AND EVACUATION DISTANCES

Isolation or evacuation distances are shown in the guides (orange-bordered pages) and in the Table 1 - Initial Isolation and Protective Action Distances (green-bordered pages). This may confuse users not thoroughly familiar with ERG2012.

It is important to note that some guides refer only to non-TIH materials (36 guides), some refer to both TIH and non-TIH materials (21 guides) and some (5 guides) refer only to TIH or Water-reactive materials (WRM). A guide refers to both TIH and non-TIH materials (for example see GUIDE 131) when the following sentence appears under the title EVACUATION-Spill: "See Table 1 - Initial Isolation and Protective Action Distances for highlighted materials. For non-highlighted materials, increase, in the downwind direction, as necessary, the isolation distance shown under 'PUBLIC SAFETY.'" A guide refers only to TIH or WRM materials (for example see GUIDE 124) when the following sentence appears under the title EVACUATION-Spill: "See Table 1 - Initial Isolation and Protective Action Distances". If the previous sentences do not appear in a guide, then this particular guide refers only to non-TIH materials (for example see GUIDE 128).

In order to identify appropriate isolation and protective action distances, use the following:

If you are dealing with a **TIH/WRM/Chemical warfare** material (highlighted entries in the index lists), the isolation and evacuation distances are found directly in the green-bordered pages. The guides (orange-bordered pages) also remind the user to refer to the green-bordered pages for evacuation specific information involving highlighted materials.

If you are dealing with a **non-TIH material but the guide refers to both TIH and non-TIH materials,** an immediate isolation distance is provided under the heading PUBLIC SAFETY as a precautionary measure to prevent injuries. It applies to the non-TIH materials only. In addition, for evacuation purposes, the guide informs the user under the title EVACUATION-Spill to increase, for non-highlighted materials, in the downwind direction, if necessary, the immediate isolation distance listed under "PUBLIC SAFETY". For example, GUIDE 131 – Flammable Liquids-Toxic, instructs the user to: "As an immediate precautionary measure, isolate spill or leak area for at least 50 meters (150 feet) in all directions." In case of a large spill, the isolation area could be expanded from 50 meters (150 feet) to a distance deemed as safe by the On-scene commander and emergency responders.

If you are dealing with a **non-TIH material and the guide refers only to non-TIH materials,** the immediate isolation and evacuation distances are specified as actual distances in the guide (orange-bordered pages) and are not referenced in the green-bordered pages.

Note 1: If an entry is highlighted in green in either the yellow-bordered or blue-bordered pages AND THERE IS NO FIRE, go directly to Table 1 - Initial Isolation and Protective Action Distances (green-bordered pages) and look up the ID number and name of material to obtain initial isolation and protective action distances. IF THERE IS A FIRE, or IF A FIRE IS INVOLVED, ALSO CONSULT the assigned guide (orange-bordered pages) and apply as appropriate the evacuation information shown under PUBLIC SAFETY.

Note 2: If the name in **Table 1** is shown with "*When Spilled In Water*", these materials produce large amounts of Toxic Inhalation Hazard (TIH) gases when spilled in water. Some Water Reactive materials are also TIH materials themselves (e.g., Bromine trifluoride (1746), Thionyl chloride (1836), etc.). In these instances, two entries are provided in **Table 1** for land-based and water-based spills. If the Water Reactive material **is NOT** a TIH and this material **is NOT** spilled in water, **Table 1** and **Table 2** do not apply and safety distances will be found within the appropriate orange-bordered guide.

PROTECTIVE CLOTHING

Street Clothing and Work Uniforms. These garments, such as uniforms worn by police and emergency medical services personnel, provide almost no protection from the harmful effects of dangerous goods.

Structural Fire Fighters' Protective Clothing (SFPC). This category of clothing, often called turnout or bunker gear, means the protective clothing normally worn by fire fighters during structural fire fighting operations. It includes a helmet, coat, pants, boots, gloves and a hood to cover parts of the head not protected by the helmet and facepiece. This clothing must be used with full-facepiece positive pressure self-contained breathing apparatus (SCBA). This protective clothing should, at a minimum, meet the OSHA Fire Brigades Standard (29 CFR 1910.156). Structural fire fighters' protective clothing provides limited protection from heat and cold, but may not provide adequate protection from the harmful vapors or liquids that are encountered during dangerous goods incidents. Each guide includes a statement about the use of SFPC in incidents involving those materials referenced by that guide. Some guides state that SFPC provides limited protection. In those cases, the responder wearing SFPC and SCBA may be able to perform an expedient, that is quick "in-and-out", operation. However, this type of operation can place the responder at risk of exposure, injury or death. The incident commander makes the decision to perform this operation only if an overriding benefit can be gained (i.e., perform an immediate rescue, turn off a valve to control a leak, etc.). The coverall-type protective clothing customarily worn to fight fires in forests or wildlands is not SFPC and **is not** recommended nor referred to elsewhere in this guidebook.

Positive Pressure Self-Contained Breathing Apparatus (SCBA). This apparatus provides a constant, positive pressure flow of air within the facepiece, even if one inhales deeply while doing heavy work. Use apparatus certified by NIOSH and the Department of Labor/Mine Safety and Health Administration in accordance with 42 CFR Part 84. Use it in accordance with the requirements for respiratory protection specified in OSHA 29 CFR 1910.134 (Respiratory Protection) and/or 29 CFR 1910.156 (f) (Fire Brigades Standard). Chemical-cartridge respirators or other filtering masks are not acceptable substitutes for positive pressure self-contained breathing apparatus. Demand-type SCBA does not meet the OSHA 29 CFR 1910.156 (f)(1)(i) of the Fire Brigades Standard. If it is suspected that a Chemical Warfare Agent (CW) is involved, the use of NIOSH-certified respirators with CBRN protection are highly recommended.

Chemical Protective Clothing and Equipment. Safe use of this type of protective clothing and equipment requires specific skills developed through training and experience. It is generally not available to, or used by, first responders. This type of special clothing may protect against one chemical, yet be readily permeated by chemicals for which it was not designed. Therefore, protective clothing should not be used unless it is compatible with the released material. This type of special clothing offers little or no protection against heat and/or cold. Examples of this type of equipment have been described as (1) Vapor Protective Suits (NFPA 1991), also known as Totally-Encapsulating Chemical Protective (TECP) Suits or Level A* protection (OSHA 29 CFR 1910.120, Appendix A & B), and (2) Liquid-Splash

Protective Suits (NFPA 1992 & 1993), also known as Level B* or C* protection (OSHA 29 CFR 1910.120, Appendix A & B) or suits for chemical/biological terrorism incidents (NFPA 1994), class 1, 2 or 3 Ensembles and Standard CAN/CGSB/CSA-Z1610-11 – Protection of first responders from chemical, biological, radiological, and nuclear (CBRN) events (2011). No single protective clothing material will protect you from all dangerous goods. Do not assume any protective clothing is resistant to cold and/or heat or flame exposure unless it is so certified by the manufacturer (NFPA 1991 5-3 Flammability Resistance Test and 5-6 Cold Temperature Performance Test).

* Consult glossary for additional protection levels under the heading "Protective Clothing".

FIRE AND SPILL CONTROL

FIRE CONTROL

Water is the most common and generally most available fire extinguishing agent. Exercise caution in selecting a fire extinguishing method since there are many factors to be considered in an incident. Water may be ineffective in fighting fires involving some materials; its effectiveness depends greatly on the method of application.

Fires involving a spill of flammable liquids are generally controlled by applying a fire fighting foam to the surface of the burning material. Fighting flammable liquid fires requires foam concentrate which is <u>chemically compatible</u> with the burning material, <u>correct mixing</u> of the foam concentrate with water and air, and <u>careful application and maintenance</u> of the foam blanket. There are two general types of fire fighting foam: regular and alcohol-resistant. Examples of regular foam are protein-base, fluoroprotein, and aqueous film forming foam (AFFF). Some flammable liquids, including many petroleum products, can be controlled by applying regular foam. Other flammable liquids, including polar solvents (flammable liquids which are water soluble) such as alcohols and ketones, have different chemical properties. A fire involving these materials cannot be easily controlled with regular foam and requires application of alcohol-resistant foam. Polar-solvent fires may be difficult to control and require a higher foam application rate than other flammable liquid fires (see NFPA/ANSI Standards 11 and 11A for further information). Refer to the appropriate guide to determine which type of foam is recommended. Although it is impossible to make specific recommendations for flammable liquids which have subsidiary corrosive or toxic hazards, alcohol-resistant foam may be effective for many of these materials. The emergency response telephone number on the shipping document, or the appropriate emergency response agency, should be contacted as soon as possible for guidance on the proper fire extinguishing agent to use. The final selection of the agent and method depends on many factors such as incident location, exposure hazards, size of the fire, environmental concerns, as well as the availability of extinguishing agents and equipment at the scene.

WATER REACTIVE MATERIALS

Water is sometimes used to flush spills and to reduce or direct vapors in spill situations. Some of the materials covered by the guidebook can react violently or even explosively with water. In these cases, consider letting the fire burn or leaving the spill alone (except to prevent its spreading by diking) until additional technical advice can be obtained. The applicable guides clearly warn you of these potentially dangerous reactions. These materials require technical advice since

(1) water getting inside a ruptured or leaking container may cause an explosion;

(2) water may be needed to cool adjoining containers to prevent their rupturing (exploding) or further spread of the fires;

(3)   water may be effective in mitigating an incident involving a water-reactive material only if it can be applied at a sufficient flooding rate for an extended period; and

(4)   the products from the reaction with water may be more toxic, corrosive, or otherwise more undesirable than the product of the fire without water applied.

When responding to an incident involving water-reactive materials, take into account the existing conditions such as wind, precipitation, location and accessibility to the incident, as well as the availability of the agents to control the fire or spill. Because there are variables to consider, the decision to use water on fires or spills involving water-reactive materials should be based on information from an authoritative source; for example, a producer of the material, who can be contacted through the emergency response telephone number or the appropriate emergency response agency.

VAPOR CONTROL

Limiting the amount of vapor released from a pool of flammable or corrosive liquids is an operational concern. It requires the use of proper protective clothing, specialized equipment, appropriate chemical agents, and skilled personnel. Before engaging in vapor control, get advice from an authoritative source as to the proper tactics.

There are several ways to minimize the amount of vapors escaping from pools of spilled liquids, such as special foams, adsorbing agents, absorbing agents, and neutralizing agents. To be effective, these vapor control methods must be selected for the specific material involved and performed in a manner that will mitigate, not worsen, the incident.

Where specific materials are known, such as at manufacturing or storage facilities, it is desirable for the dangerous goods response team to prearrange with the facility operators to select and stockpile these control agents in advance of a spill. In the field, first responders may not have the most effective vapor control agent for the material available. They are likely to have only water and only one type of fire fighting foam on their vehicles. If the available foam is inappropriate for use, they are likely to use water spray. Because the water is being used to form a vapor seal, care must be taken not to churn or further spread the spill during application. Vapors that do not react with water may be directed away from the site using the air currents surrounding the water spray. Before using water spray or other methods to safely control vapor emission or to suppress ignition, obtain technical advice, based on specific chemical name identification.

BLEVE (Boiling Liquid Expanding Vapor Explosion)

The following section presents, in a two-page format, background information on BLEVEs and includes a chart that provides important safety-related information to consider when confronted with this type of situation involving Liquefied Petroleum Gases (LPG), UN1075. LPGs include the following flammable gases; Butane, UN1011; Butylene, UN1012; Isobutylene, UN1055; Propylene, UN2077; Isobutane, UN1969; and Propane, UN1978.

What are the main hazards from a BLEVE?

The main hazards from a propane or LPG BLEVE are:
- fire
- thermal radiation from the fire
- blast
- projectiles

The danger from these decreases as you move away from the BLEVE centre. The furthest reaching hazard is projectiles.

This information was prepared for Transport Canada, the Canadian Association of Fire Chiefs and the Propane Gas Association of Canada Inc. by Dr. A. M. Birk, Queen's University, Kingston (Ontario) Canada.

For a free download or to order a DVD of the video *BLEVE Response and Prevention*, please visit <http://www.tc.gc.ca/eng/tdg/bleve-1119.htm> or contact us at 1-888-830-4911, or by Email: MPS@tc.gc.ca.

To download a free copy, first click on the green "View/Download" button and then left-click the video link to view the video or right-click to download a copy by selecting "Save target as" to save to your computer.

BLEVE – SAFETY PRECAUTIONS

Use with caution. The following table gives a summary of tank properties, critical times, critical distances and cooling water flow rates for various tank sizes. This table is provided to give responders some guidance but it should be used with caution.

Tank dimensions are approximate and can vary depending on the tank design and application.

Minimum time to failure is based on *severe torch fire impingement* on the vapour space of a tank in good condition, and is approximate. Tanks may fail earlier if they are damaged or corroded. Tanks may fail minutes or hours later than these minimum times depending on the conditions. It has been assumed here that the tanks are not equipped with thermal barriers or water spray cooling.

Minimum time to empty is based on an engulfing fire with a properly sized pressure relief valve. If the tank is only partially engulfed then time to empty will increase (i.e., if tank is 50% engulfed then the tanks will take twice as long to empty). Once again, it has been assumed that the tank is not equipped with a thermal barrier or water spray.

Tanks equipped with thermal barriers or water spray cooling significantly increase the times to failure and the times to empty. A thermal barrier can reduce the heat input to a tank by a factor of ten or more. This means it could take ten times as long to empty the tank through the Pressure Relief Valve (PRV).

Fireball radius and emergency response distance is based on mathematical equations and is approximate. They assume spherical fireballs and this is not always the case.

Two safety distances for public evacuation. The minimum distance is based on tanks that are launched with a small elevation angle (i.e., a few degrees above horizontal). This is most common for horizontal cylinders. The preferred evacuation distance has more margin of safety since it assumes the tanks are launched at a 45 degree angle to the horizontal. This might be more appropriate if a vertical cylinder is involved.

It is understood that these distances are very large and may not be practical in a highly populated area. However, it should be understood that the risks increase rapidly the closer you are to a BLEVE. Keep in mind that the furthest reaching projectiles tend to come off in the zones 45 degrees on each side of the tank ends.

Water flow rate is based on $\sqrt[5]{\text{capacity (USgal)}}$ **= usgal/min needed to cool tank metal.**

Warning: the data given are approximate and should only be used with extreme caution. For example, where times are given for tank failure or tank emptying through the pressure relief valve – these times are typical but they can vary from situation to situation. Therefore, never risk life based on these times.

BLEVE
(USE WITH CAUTION)

Capacity Litres (Gallons)	Diameter Meters (Feet)	Length Meters (Feet)	Propane Mass Kilograms (Lbs)	Minimum time to failure for severe torch Minutes	Approximate time to empty for engulfing fire Minutes	Fireball radius Meters (Feet)	Emergency response distance Meters (Feet)	Minimum evacuation distance Meters (Feet)	Preferred evacuation distance Meters (Feet)	Cooling water flow rate Litres/min	USgal/min
100 (38.6)	0.3 (1)	1.5 (4.9)	40 (88)	4	8	10 (33)	90 (295)	154 (505)	307 (1007)	94.6	25
400 (154.4)	0.61 (2)	1.5 (4.9)	160 (353)	4	12	16 (53)	90 (295)	244 (801)	488 (1601)	189.3	50
2000 (772)	0.96 (3.2)	3 (9.8)	800 (1764)	5	18	28 (92)	111 (364)	417 (1368)	834 (2736)	424	112
4000 (1544)	1 (3.3)	4.9 (16.1)	1600 (3527)	5	20	35 (115)	140 (459)	525 (1722)	1050 (3445)	598	158
8000 (3088)	1.25 (4.1)	6.5 (21.3)	3200 (7055)	6	22	44 (144)	176 (577)	661 (2169)	1323 (4341)	848	224
22000 (8492)	2.1 (6.9)	6.7 (22)	8800 (19400)	7	28	62 (203)	247 (810)	926 (3038)	1852 (6076)	1404	371
42000 (16212)	2.1 (6.9)	11.8 (38.7)	16800 (37037)	7	32	77 (253)	306 (1004)	1149 (3770)	2200 (7218)	1938	512
82000 (31652)	2.75 (9)	13.7 (45)	32800 (72310)	8	40	96 (315)	383 (1257)	1435 (4708)	2200 (7218)	2710	716
140000 (54040)	3.3 (10.8)	17.2 (56.4)	56000 (123457)	9	45	114 (374)	457 (1499)	1715 (5627)	2200 (7218)	3539	935

CRIMINAL/TERRORIST USE OF CHEMICAL/BIOLOGICAL/RADIOLOGICAL AGENTS

The following is intended to supply information to first responders for use in making a preliminary assessment of a situation that they suspect involves criminal/terrorist use of chemical, biological agents and/or radioactive materials (CBRN). To aid in the assessment, a list of observable indicators of the use and/or presence of a CB agent or radioactive material is provided in the following paragraphs. This section ends with a Safe Standoff Distance Chart for various threats when Improvised Explosive Devices are involved.

DIFFERENCES BETWEEN A CHEMICAL, BIOLOGICAL AND RADIOLOGICAL AGENT

Chemical and biological agents as well as radioactive materials can be dispersed in the air we breathe, the water we drink, or on surfaces we physically contact. Dispersion methods may be as simple as opening a container, using conventional (garden) spray devices, or as elaborate as detonating an improvised explosive device.

Chemical Incidents are characterized by the rapid onset of medical symptoms (minutes to hours) and easily observed signatures (colored residue, dead foliage, pungent odor, dead insects and animals).

Biological Incidents are characterized by the onset of symptoms in hours to days. Typically, there will be no characteristic signatures because biological agents are usually odorless and colorless. Because of the delayed onset of symptoms in a biological incident, the area affected may be greater due to the movement of infected individuals.

Radiological Incidents are characterized by the onset of symptoms, if any, in days to weeks or longer. Typically, there will be no characteristic signatures because radioactive materials are usually odorless and colorless. Specialized equipment is required to determine the size of the affected area, and whether the level of radioactivity presents an immediate or long-term health hazard. Because radioactivity is not detectable without special equipment, the affected area may be greater due to the migration of contaminated individuals.

At the levels created by most probable sources, not enough radiation would be generated to kill people or cause severe illness. In a radiological incident generated by a "dirty bomb", or Radiological Dispersal Device (RDD), in which a conventional explosive is detonated to spread radioactive contamination, the primary hazard is from the explosion. However, certain radioactive materials dispersed in the air could contaminate up to several city blocks, creating fear and possibly panic, and requiring potentially costly cleanup.

INDICATORS OF A POSSIBLE CHEMICAL INCIDENT

Dead animals/birds/fish

Not just an occasional road kill, but numerous animals (wild and domestic, small and large), birds, and fish in the same area.

Lack of insect life

If normal insect activity (ground, air, and/or water) is missing, check the ground/water surface/shore line for dead insects. If near water, check for dead fish/aquatic birds.

INDICATORS OF A POSSIBLE CHEMICAL INCIDENT (Continued)

Unexplained odors
Smells may range from fruity to flowery to sharp/pungent to garlic/ horseradish-like to bitter almonds/peach kernels to new mown hay. It is important to note that the particular odor is completely out of character with its surroundings.

Unusual numbers of dying or sick people (mass casualties)
Health problems including nausea, disorientation, difficulty in breathing, convulsions, localized sweating, conjunctivitis (reddening of eyes/nerve agent symptoms), erythema (reddening of skin/vesicant symptoms) and death.

Pattern of casualties
Casualties will likely be distributed downwind, or if indoors, by the air ventilation system.

Blisters/rashes
Numerous individuals experiencing unexplained water-like blisters, weals (like bee stings), and/or rashes.

Illness in confined area
Different casualty rates for people working indoors versus outdoors dependent on where the agent was released.

Unusual liquid droplets
Numerous surfaces exhibit oily droplets/film; numerous water surfaces have an oily film. (No recent rain.)

Different looking areas
Not just a patch of dead weeds, but trees, shrubs, bushes, food crops, and/or lawns that are dead, discolored, or withered. (No current drought.)

Low-lying clouds
Low-lying cloud/fog-like condition that is not consistent with its surroundings.

Unusual metal debris
Unexplained bomb/munitions-like material, especially if it contains a liquid.

INDICATORS OF A POSSIBLE BIOLOGICAL INCIDENT

Unusual numbers of sick or dying people or animals
Any number of symptoms may occur. Casualties may occur hours to days after an incident has occurred. The time required before symptoms are observed is dependent on the agent used.

Unscheduled and unusual spray being disseminated
Especially if outdoors during periods of darkness.

Abandoned spray devices
Devices may not have distinct odors.

INDICATORS OF A POSSIBLE RADIOLOGICAL INCIDENT

Radiation Symbols
Containers may display a "propeller" radiation symbol.

Unusual metal debris
Unexplained bomb/munitions-like material.

INDICATORS OF A POSSIBLE RADIOLOGICAL INCIDENT (continued)

Heat-emitting material   Material that is hot or seems to emit heat without any sign of an external heat source.

Glowing material   Strongly radioactive material may emit or cause radioluminescence.

Sick people/animals   In very improbable scenarios there may be unusual numbers of sick or dying people or animals. Casualties may occur hours to days or weeks after an incident has occurred. The time required before symptoms are observed is dependent on the radioactive material used, and the dose received. Possible symptoms include skin reddening or vomiting.

PERSONAL SAFETY CONSIDERATIONS

When approaching a scene that may involve CB agents or radioactive materials, the most critical consideration is the safety of oneself and other responders. Protective clothing and respiratory protection of appropriate level of safety must be used. In incidents where it is suspected that CBRN materials have been used as weapons, NIOSH-certified respirators with CBRN protection are highly recommended. Be aware that the presence and identification of CB agents or radioactive materials may not be verifiable, especially in the case of biological or radiological agents. The following actions/measures to be considered are applicable to either a chemical, biological or radiological incident. The guidance is general in nature, not all encompassing, and its applicability should be evaluated on a case-by-case basis.

Approach and response strategies. Protect yourself and use a safe approach (minimize any exposure time, maximize the distance between you and the item that is likely to harm you, use cover as protection and wear appropriate personal protective equipment and respiratory protection). Identify and estimate the hazard by using indicators as provided above. Isolate the area and secure the scene; potentially contaminated people should be isolated and decontaminated as soon as possible. To the extent possible, take measures to limit the spread of contamination. In the event of a chemical incident, the fading of chemical odors is not necessarily an indication of reduced vapor concentrations. Some chemicals deaden the senses giving the false perception that the chemical is no longer present.

If there is any indication that an area may be contaminated with radioactive materials, including the site of any non-accidental explosion, responder personnel should be equipped with radiation detection equipment that would alert them if they are entering a radiologically compromised environment, and should have received adequate training in its use. This equipment should be designed in such a way that it can also alert the responders when an unacceptable ambient dose rate or ambient dose has been reached.

Initial actions to consider in a potential CBRN/Hazmat Terrorism Event:

- Avoid using cell phones, radios, etc. within 100 meters (300 feet) of a suspect device
- NOTIFY your local police by calling 911.
- Set up Incident command upwind and uphill of the area.
- Do NOT touch or move suspicious packages/containers.
- Be cautious regarding potential presence of secondary devices (e.g. Improvised Explosive Devices, IEDs).
- Avoid contamination.
- Limit access to only those responsible for rescue of victims or assessment of unknown materials or devices.
- Evacuate and isolate individuals potentially exposed to dangerous goods/hazardous materials.
- Isolate contaminated areas and secure the scene for analysis of material.

Decontamination measures. Emergency responders should follow standard decontamination procedures (flush-strip-flush). Mass casualty decontamination should begin as soon as possible by stripping (all clothing) and flushing (soap and water). If biological agents are involved or suspected, careful washing and use of a brush are more effective. If chemical agents are suspected, the most important and effective decontamination will be the one done within the first one or two minutes. If possible, further decontamination should be performed using a 0.5% hypochlorite solution (1 part household bleach mixed with 9 parts water). If biological agents are suspected, a contact time of 10 to 15 minutes should be allowed before rinsing. The solution can be used on soft tissue wounds, but must not be used in eyes or open wounds of the abdomen, chest, head, or spine. For further information contact the agencies listed in this guidebook.

For persons contaminated with radioactive material, remove them to a low radiation area if necessary. Remove their clothing and place it in a clearly marked sealed receptacle, such as a plastic bag, for later testing. Use decontamination methods described above, but avoid breaking the skin, e.g., from shaving, or overly vigorous brushing. External radiological contamination on intact skin surface rarely causes a high enough dose to be a hazard to either the contaminated person or the first responders. For this reason, except in very unusual circumstances, an injured person who is also radiologically contaminated should be medically stabilized, taking care to minimize the spread of the contamination to the extent possible, before decontamination measures are initiated.

Note: The above information was developed in part by the Department of National Defence (Canada), the U.S. Department of the Army, Aberdeen Proving Ground and the Federal Bureau of Investigation (FBI).

Improvised Explosive Device (IED)
SAFE STAND OFF DISTANCE

	Threat Description	Explosives Mass (TNT equivalent)[1]		Building Evacuation Distance[2]		Outdoor Evacuation Distance[3]	
High Explosives (TNT Equivalent)	Pipe Bomb	5 lbs	2.3 kg	70 ft	21 m	850 ft	259 m
	Suicide Belt	10 lbs	4.5 kg	90 ft	27 m	1,080 ft	330 m
	Suicide Vest	20 lbs	9 kg	110 ft	34 m	1,360 ft	415 m
	Briefcase/Suitcase Bomb	50 lbs	23 kg	150 ft	46 m	1,850 ft	564 m
	Compact Sedan	500 lbs	227 kg	320 ft	98 m	1,500 ft	457 m
	Sedan	1,000 lbs	454 kg	400 ft	122 m	1,750 ft	534 m
	Passenger/Cargo Van	4,000 lbs	1 814 kg	640 ft	195 m	2,750 ft	838 m
	Small Moving Van/ Delivery Truck	10,000 lbs	4 536 kg	860 ft	263 m	3,750 ft	1 143 m
	Moving Van/Water Truck	30,000 lbs	13 608 kg	1,240 ft	375 m	6,500 ft	1 982 m
	Semitrailer	60,000 lbs	27 216 kg	1,570 ft	475 m	7,000 ft	2 134 m

	Threat Description	LPG Mass/ Volume[1]		Fireball Diameter[4]		Safe Distance[5]	
Liquefied Petroleum Gas (LPG - Butane or Propane)	Small LPG Tank	20 lbs/5 gal	9 kg/19 L	40 ft	12 m	160 ft	48 m
	Large LPG Tank	100 lbs/25 gal	45 kg/95 L	69 ft	21 m	276 ft	84 m
	Commercial/ Residential LPG Tank	2,000 lbs/500 gal	907 kg/1 893 L	184 ft	56 m	736 ft	224 m
	Small LPG Truck	8,000 lbs/2,000 gal	3 630 kg/7 570 L	292 ft	89 m	1,168 ft	356 m
	Semitanker LPG	40,000 lbs/10,000 gal	18 144 kg/37 850 L	499 ft	152 m	1,996 ft	608 m

[1] Based on the maximum amount of material that could reasonably fit into a container or vehicle. Variations possible.

[2] Governed by the ability of an unreinforced building to withstand severe damage or collapse.

[3] Governed by the greater of fragment throw distance or glass breakage/falling glass hazard distance. These distances can be reduced for personnel wearing ballistic protection. Note that the pipe bomb, suicide belt/vest, and briefcase/ suitcase bomb are assumed to have a fragmentation characteristic that requires greater standoff distances than an equal amount of explosives in a vehicle.

[4] Assuming efficient mixing of the flammable gas with ambient air.

[5] Determined by U.S. firefighting practices wherein safe distances are approximately 4 times the flame height. Note that an LPG tank filled with high explosives would require a significantly greater standoff distance than if it were filled with LPG.

NOTES

Glossary

AEGL(s) Acute Exposure Guideline Level(s), AEGLs represent threshold exposure limits for the general public after a once-in-a-lifetime, or rare, exposure and are applicable to emergency exposure periods ranging from 10 minutes to 8 hours. Three levels AEGL-1, AEGL-2 and AEGL-3 are developed for each of five exposure periods (10 and 30 minutes, 1 hour, 4 hours, and 8 hours) and are distinguished by varying degrees of severity of toxic effects; see AEGL-1, AEGL-2 and AEGL-3.

AEGL-1 AEGL-1 is the airborne concentration (expressed as parts per million or milligrams per cubic meter [ppm or mg/m^3]) of a substance above which it is predicted that the general population, including susceptible individuals, could experience notable discomfort, irritation, or certain asymptomatic, non-sensory effects. However, the effects are not disabling and are transient and reversible upon cessation of exposure.

AEGL-2 AEGL-2 is the airborne concentration (expressed as ppm or mg/m^3) of a substance above which it is predicted that the general population, including susceptible individuals, could experience irreversible or other serious, long-lasting adverse health effects or an impaired ability to escape.

AEGL-3 AEGL-3 is the airborne concentration (expressed as ppm or mg/m^3) of a substance above which it is predicted that the general population, including susceptible individuals, could experience life-threatening health effects or death.

Alcohol resistant foam A foam that is resistant to "polar" chemicals such as ketones and esters which may break down other types of foam.

Biological agents Living organisms that cause disease, sickness and mortality in humans. Anthrax and Ebola are examples of biological agents. **Refer to GUIDE 158.**

Blister agents (vesicants) Substances that cause blistering of the skin. Exposure is through liquid or vapor contact with any exposed tissue (eyes, skin, lungs). Mustard (H), Distilled Mustard (HD), Nitrogen Mustard (HN) and Lewisite (L) are blister agents.

Symptoms: Red eyes, skin irritation, burning of skin, blisters, upper respiratory damage, cough, hoarseness.

Glossary

Blood agents

Substances that injure a person by interfering with cell respiration (the exchange of oxygen and carbon dioxide between blood and tissues). Hydrogen cyanide (AC) and Cyanogen chloride (CK) are blood agents.

Symptoms: Respiratory distress, headache, unresponsiveness, seizures, coma.

Burn

Refers to either a chemical or thermal burn, the former may be caused by corrosive substances and the latter by liquefied cryogenic gases, hot molten substances, or flames.

CBRN

Chemical, biological, radiological or nuclear warfare agent.

Choking agents

Substances that cause physical injury to the lungs. Exposure is through inhalation. In extreme cases, membranes swell and lungs become filled with liquid (pulmonary edema). Death results from lack of oxygen; hence, the victim is "choked". Phosgene (CG) is a choking agent.

Symptoms: Irritation to eyes/nose/throat, respiratory distress, nausea and vomiting, burning of exposed skin.

CO_2

Carbon dioxide gas.

Cold zone

Area where the command post and support functions that are necessary to control the incident are located. This is also referred to as the clean zone, green zone or support zone in other documents. (EPA Standard Operating Safety Guidelines, OSHA 29 CFR 1910.120, NFPA 472)

Combustible liquid

Liquids which have a flash point greater than 60°C (140°F) and below 93°C (200°F). U.S. regulations permit a flammable liquid with a flash point between 38°C (100°F) and 60°C (140°F) to be reclassed as a combustible liquid.

Compatibility Group

Letters identify explosives that are deemed to be compatible. The definition of these Compatibility Groups in this Glossary are intended to be descriptive. Please consult the transportation of dangerous goods/hazardous materials or explosives regulations of your jurisdiction for the exact wording of the definitions. Class 1 materials are considered to be "compatible" if they can be transported together without significantly increasing either the probability of an incident or, for a given quantity, the magnitude of the effects of such an incident.

A   Substances which are expected to mass detonate very soon after fire reaches them.

Glossary

B   Articles which are expected to mass detonate very soon after fire reaches them.

C   Substances or articles which may be readily ignited and burn violently without necessarily exploding.

D   Substances or articles which may mass detonate (with blast and/or fragment hazard) when exposed to fire.

E&F Articles which may mass detonate in a fire.

G   Substances and articles which may mass explode and give off smoke or toxic gases.

H   Articles which in a fire may eject hazardous projectiles and dense white smoke.

J   Articles which may mass explode.

K   Articles which in a fire may eject hazardous projectiles and toxic gases.

L   Substances and articles which present a special risk and could be activated by exposure to air or water.

N   Articles which contain only extremely insensitive detonating substances and demonstrate a negligible probability of accidental ignition or propagation.

S   Packaged substances or articles which, if accidentally initiated, produce effects that are usually confined to the immediate vicinity.

Control zones   Designated areas at dangerous goods incidents, based on safety and the degree of hazard. Many terms are used to describe control zones; however, in this guidebook, these zones are defined as the hot/exclusion/red/restricted zone, warm/contamination reduction/yellow/limited access zone, and cold/support/green/clean zone. (EPA Standard Operating Safety Guidelines, OSHA 29 CFR 1910.120, NFPA 472)

Cryogenic liquid   A refrigerated, liquefied gas that has a boiling point colder than -90°C (-130°F) at atmospheric pressure.

Dangerous Water Reactive Material   Produces significant toxic gas when it comes in contact with water.

Decomposition products Products of a chemical or thermal break-down of a substance.

Glossary

Decontamination

The removal of dangerous goods from personnel and equipment to the extent necessary to prevent potential adverse health effects. Always avoid direct or indirect contact with dangerous goods; however, if contact occurs, personnel should be decontaminated as soon as possible. Since the methods used to decontaminate personnel and equipment differ from one chemical to another, contact the chemical manufacturer, through the agencies listed on the inside back cover, to determine the appropriate procedure. Contaminated clothing and equipment should be removed after use and stored in a controlled area (warm/contamination reduction/yellow/limited access zone) until cleanup procedures can be initiated. In some cases, protective clothing and equipment cannot be decontaminated and must be disposed of in a proper manner.

Dry chemical

A preparation designed for fighting fires involving flammable liquids, pyrophoric substances and electrical equipment. Common types contain sodium bicarbonate or potassium bicarbonate.

Edema

The accumulation of an excessive amount of watery fluid in cells and tissues. Pulmonary edema is an excessive buildup of water in the lungs, for instance, after inhalation of a gas that is corrosive to lung tissue.

ERPG(s)

Emergency Response Planning Guideline(s). Values intended to provide estimates of concentration ranges above which one could reasonably anticipate observing adverse health effects; see ERPG-1, ERPG-2 and ERPG-3.

ERPG-1

The maximum airborne concentration below which it is believed nearly all individuals could be exposed for up to 1 hour without experiencing more than mild, transient adverse health effects or without perceiving a clearly defined objectionable odor.

ERPG-2

The maximum airborne concentration below which it is believed nearly all individuals could be exposed for up to 1 hour without experiencing or developing irreversible or other serious health effects or symptoms that could impair an individual's ability to take protective action.

ERPG-3

The maximum airborne concentration below which it is believed nearly all individuals could be exposed for up to 1 hour without experiencing or developing life-threatening health effects.

Flammable liquid

A liquid that has a flash point of 60°C (140°F) or lower.

Glossary

Flash point

Lowest temperature at which a liquid or solid gives off vapor in such a concentration that, when the vapor combines with air near the surface of the liquid or solid, a flammable mixture is formed. Hence, the lower the flash point, the more flammable the material.

Hazard zones (Inhalation Hazard Zones)

HAZARD ZONE A: Gases: LC50 of less than or equal to 200 ppm,
Liquids: V equal to or greater than 500 LC50 and LC50 less than or equal to 200 ppm,

HAZARD ZONE B: Gases: LC50 greater than 200 ppm and less than or equal to 1000 ppm, Liquids: V equal to or greater than 10 LC50; LC50 less than or equal to 1000 ppm and criteria for Hazard Zone A are not met.

HAZARD ZONE C: LC50 greater than 1000 ppm and less than or equal to 3000 ppm,

HAZARD ZONE D: LC50 greater than 3000 ppm and less than or equal to 5000 ppm.

Hot zone

Area immediately surrounding a dangerous goods incident which extends far enough to prevent adverse effects from released dangerous goods to personnel outside the zone. This zone is also referred to as exclusion zone, red zone or restricted zone in other documents. (EPA Standard Operating Safety Guidelines, OSHA 29 CFR 1910.120, NFPA 472)

IED

See "Improvised Explosive Device".

Immiscible

In this guidebook, means that a material does not mix readily with water.

Improvised Explosive Device

A bomb that is manufactured from commercial, military or homemade explosives.

Large spill

A spill that involves quantities that are greater than 208 liters (55 US gallons) for liquids and greater than 300 kilograms (660 pounds) for solids.

LC50

Lethal concentration 50. The concentration of a material administered by inhalation that is expected to cause the death of 50% of an experimental animal population within a specified time. (Concentration is reported in either ppm or mg/m^3)

Glossary

Mass explosion	Explosion which affects almost the entire load virtually instantaneously.
mg/m³	Milligrams of a material per cubic meter of air.
Miscible	In this guidebook, means that a material mixes readily with water.
mL/m³	Milliliters of a material per cubic meter of air. (1 mL/m³ equals 1 ppm)
Nerve agents	Substances that interfere with the central nervous system. Exposure is primarily through contact with the liquid (via skin and eyes) and secondarily through inhalation of the vapor. Tabun (GA), Sarin (GB), Soman (GD) and VX are nerve agents.
	Symptoms: Pinpoint pupils, extreme headache, severe tightness in the chest, dyspnea, runny nose, coughing, salivation, unresponsiveness, seizures.
Non-polar	See "Immiscible".
n.o.s.	These letters refer to "not otherwise specified". The entries which use this description are generic names such as "Corrosive liquid, n.o.s." This means that the actual chemical name for that corrosive liquid is not listed in the regulations; therefore, a generic name must be used to describe it on shipping papers.
Noxious	In this guidebook, means that a material may be harmful or injurious to health or physical well-being.
Oxidizer	A chemical which supplies its own oxygen and which helps other combustible material burn more readily.
P	The letter (**P**) following a guide number in the yellow-bordered and blue-bordered pages identifies a material which may polymerize violently under high temperature conditions or contamination with other products. It is used to identify materials that have a strong potential for polymerization in the absence of an inhibitor or due to the inhibitor depletion caused by the accident conditions. This polymerization will produce heat and high pressure buildup in containers which may explode or rupture. (See polymerization below)
Packing Group	The Packing Group (PG) is assigned based on the degree of danger presented by the hazardous material:
	PG I : Great danger
	PG II : Medium danger
	PG III : Minor danger

Glossary

PG   See Packing Group

pH   pH is a value that represents the acidity or alkalinity of a water solution. Pure water has a pH of 7. A pH value below 7 indicates an acid solution (a pH of 1 is extremely acidic). A pH above 7 indicates an alkaline solution (a pH of 14 is extremely alkaline). Acids and alkalies (bases) are commonly referred to as corrosive materials.

PIH   Poison Inhalation Hazard. Term used to describe gases and volatile liquids that are toxic when inhaled. (Same as TIH)

Polar   See "Miscible".

Polymerization   This term describes a chemical reaction which is generally associated with the production of plastic substances. Basically, the individual molecules of the chemical (liquid or gas) react with each other to produce what can be described as a long chain. These chains can be formed in many useful applications. A well known example is the styrofoam (polystyrene) coffee cup which is formed when liquid molecules of styrene react with each other or polymerize forming a solid, therefore changing the name from styrene to polystyrene (poly means many).

ppm   Parts per million. (1 ppm equals 1 mL/m^3)

Protective clothing   Includes both respiratory and physical protection. One cannot assign a level of protection to clothing or respiratory devices separately. These levels were accepted and defined by response organizations such as U.S. Coast Guard, NIOSH, and U.S. EPA.

Level A: SCBA plus totally encapsulating chemical resistant clothing (permeation resistant).

Level B: SCBA plus hooded chemical resistant clothing (splash suit).

Level C: Full or half-face respirator plus hooded chemical resistant clothing (splash suit).

Level D: Coverall with no respiratory protection.

Pyrophoric   A material which ignites spontaneously upon exposure to air (or oxygen).

Glossary

Radiation Authority As referred to in GUIDES 161 through 166 for radioactive materials, the Radiation Authority is either a Federal, state/provincial agency or state/province designated official. The responsibilities of this authority include evaluating radiological hazard conditions during normal operations and during emergencies. If the identity and telephone number of the authority are not known by emergency responders, or included in the local response plan, the information can be obtained from the agencies listed on the inside back cover. They maintain a periodically updated list of radiation authorities.

Radioactivity The property of some substances to emit invisible and potentially harmful radiation.

Refrigerated liquid See "Cryogenic liquid".

Small spill A spill that involves quantities that are less than 208 liters (55 U.S. Gallons) for liquids and less than 300 kilograms (660 pounds) for solids.

Straight (solid) stream Method used to apply or distribute water from the end of a hose. The water is delivered under pressure for penetration. In an efficient straight (solid) stream, approximately 90% of the water passes through an imaginary circle 38 cm (15 inches) in diameter at the breaking point. Hose (solid or straight) streams are frequently used to cool tanks and other equipment exposed to flammable liquid fires, or for washing burning spills away from danger points. However, straight streams will cause a spill fire to spread if improperly used or when directed into open containers of flammable and combustible liquids.

TIH Toxic Inhalation Hazard. Term used to describe gases and volatile liquids that are toxic when inhaled. (Same as PIH)

V Saturated vapor concentration in air of a material in mL/m^3 (volatility) at 20°C and standard atmospheric pressure.

Vapor density Weight of a volume of pure vapor or gas (with no air present) compared to the weight of an equal volume of dry air at the same temperature and pressure. A vapor density less than 1 (one) indicates that the vapor is lighter than air and will tend to rise. A vapor density greater than 1 (one) indicates that the vapor is heavier than air and may travel along the ground.

Vapor pressure Pressure at which a liquid and its vapor are in equilibrium at a given temperature. Liquids with high vapor pressures evaporate rapidly.

Glossary

Viscosity

Measure of a liquid's internal resistance to flow. This property is important because it indicates how fast a material will leak out through holes in containers or tanks.

Warm zone

Area between Hot and Cold zones where personnel and equipment decontamination and hot zone support take place. It includes control points for the access corridor and thus assists in reducing the spread of contamination. Also referred to as the contamination reduction corridor (CRC), contamination reduction zone (CRZ), yellow zone or limited access zone in other documents. (EPA Standard Operating Safety Guidelines, OSHA 29 CFR 1910.120, NFPA 472)

Water-sensitive

Substances which may produce flammable and/or toxic decomposition products upon contact with water.

Water spray (fog)

Method or way to apply or distribute water. The water is finely divided to provide for high heat absorption. Water spray patterns can range from about 10 to 90 degrees. Water spray streams can be used to extinguish or control the burning of a fire or to provide exposure protection for personnel, equipment, buildings, etc. **(This method can be used to absorb vapors, knock-down vapors or disperse vapors. Direct a water spray (fog), rather than a straight (solid) stream, into the vapor cloud to accomplish any of the above).**

Water spray is particularly effective on fires of flammable liquids and volatile solids having flash points above 37.8°C (100°F).

Regardless of the above, water spray can be used successfully on flammable liquids with low flash points. The effectiveness depends particularly on the method of application. With proper nozzles, even gasoline spill fires of some types have been extinguished when coordinated hose lines were used to sweep the flames off the surface of the liquid. Furthermore, water spray carefully applied has frequently been used with success in extinguishing fires involving flammable liquids with high flash points (or any viscous liquids) by causing frothing to occur only on the surface, and this foaming action blankets and extinguishes the fire.

PUBLICATION DATA

The 2012 Emergency Response Guidebook (ERG2012) was prepared by the staff of Transport Canada, the U.S. Department of Transportation, and the Secretariat of Communications and Transport of Mexico with the assistance of many interested parties from government and industry including the collaboration of CIQUIME of Argentina. The principal authors of the ERG are Transport Canada's Michel Cloutier and U.S. DOT's George Cushmac. Printing and publication services are provided through U.S. DOT's Pipeline and Hazardous Materials Safety Administration, (PHMSA) Outreach, Training, and Grants Division.

ERG2012 is based on earlier Transport Canada, U.S. DOT, and Secretariat of Communications and Transport emergency response guidebooks. ERG2012 is published in three languages: English, French and Spanish. The Emergency Response Guidebook has been translated and printed in other languages, including Chinese, German, Hebrew, Japanese, Portuguese, Korean, Hungarian, Polish, Turkish and Thai.

We encourage countries that wish to translate this Guidebook to please contact any of the websites or telephone numbers in the next paragraph.

DISTRIBUTION OF THIS GUIDEBOOK

The primary objective is to place one copy of the ERG2012 in each publicly owned emergency service vehicle through distribution to Federal, state, provincial and local public safety authorities. The distribution of this guidebook is being accomplished through the voluntary cooperation of a network of key agencies. Emergency service organizations that have not yet received copies of ERG2012 should contact the respective distribution center in their country, state or province. In the U.S., information about the distribution center for your location may be obtained from the Office of Hazardous Materials Safety web site at http://hazmat.dot.gov or call 202-366-4900. In Canada, contact CANUTEC at 613-992-4624 or via the web site at < http://www.canutec.gc.ca for information >. In Mexico, call SCT at 52-55-5684-1275 or 684-0188 or via email at iflores@sct.gob.mx. In Argentina, call CIQUIME at 011-4613-1100, or via the web site at http://www.ciquime.org.ar, or via email at gre2012@ciquime.org.ar

REPRODUCTION AND RESALE

Copies of this document which are provided free of charge to fire, police and other emergency services may not be resold. ERG2012 (PHH50-ERG2012) may be reproduced without further permission subject to the following:

The names and the seals of the participating governments may not be reproduced on a copy of this document unless that copy accurately reproduces the entire content (text, format, and coloration) of this document without modification. In addition, the publisher's full name and address must be displayed on the outside back cover of each copy, replacing the wording placed on the center of the back cover.

Constructive comments concerning ERG2012 are solicited; in particular, comments concerning its use in handling incidents involving dangerous goods. Comments should be addressed to:

In Canada:

Director, CANUTEC
Transport Dangerous Goods
Transport Canada
Ottawa, Ontario
Canada K1A 0N5

Phone: 613-992-4624 (information)
Fax: 613-954-5101
Email: canutec@tc.gc.ca

In the U.S.:

U. S. Department of Transportation
Pipeline and Hazardous Materials Safety Administration
Outreach, Training, and Grants Division (PHH-50)
Washington, DC 20590-0001

Phone: 202-366-4900
Fax: 202-366-7342
Email: ERG2012@dot.gov

In Mexico:

Secretariat for Communications and Transport
Land Transport Directorate
Hazardous Materials and Wastes Directorate
Calz. de las Bombas No. 411-9 piso
Col. San Bartolo Coapa
Coyoacan 04800, D.F.
Mexico

Phone and Fax: +52-55-5684-1275 and 684-0188

In Argentina:

Chemistry Information Center for Emergencies (CIQUIME)
Juan Bautista Alberdi 2986
C1406GSS Buenos Aires, Argentina
Tel. +54-11-4613-1100   Fax (011) 4613-3707
Email: gre2012@ciquime.org.ar

The Emergency Response Guidebook is normally revised and reissued every four years. However, in the event of a significant mistake, omission or change in the state of knowledge, special instructions to change the guidebook (in pen-and-ink, with paste-over stickers, or with a supplement) may be issued.

Users of this guidebook should check periodically (about every 6 months) to make sure their version is current. Changes should be annotated below. Contact:

DOT/PHMSA
http://hazmat.dot.gov/pubs/erg/guidebook.htm

TRANSPORT CANADA
http://www.tc.gc.ca/eng/canutec/guide-guide-338.htm

CIQUIME
http://www.ciquime.org.ar

This guidebook incorporates changes dated:

_____

_____

_____

CANADA AND UNITED STATES NATIONAL RESPONSE CENTERS

CANADA

1. CANUTEC

CANUTEC is the **Canadian Transport Emergency Centre** operated by the Transport Dangerous Goods Directorate of Transport Canada.

CANUTEC provides a national bilingual (French and English) advisory service and is staffed by professional scientists experienced and trained in interpreting technical information and providing emergency response advice.

In an emergency, CANUTEC may be called collect at 613-996-6666 (24 hours)
*666 cellular (Press Star 666, Canada only)

In a non-emergency situation, please call the information line at 613-992-4624 (24 hours).

2. PROVINCIAL/TERRITORIAL AGENCIES

Although technical information and emergency response assistance can be obtained from **CANUTEC**, there are federal, provincial and territorial regulations requiring the reporting of dangerous goods incidents to certain authorities.

The following list of provincial/territorial agencies is supplied for your convenience.

Province	Emergency Authority and/or Telephone Number
Alberta	Local Police and Provincial Authorities 1-800-272-9600 or 780-422-9600
British Columbia	Local Police and Provincial Authorities 1-800-663-3456
Manitoba	Provincial Authority 204-945-4888 and Local Police or fire brigade, as appropriate
New Brunswick	Local Police or 1-800-565-1633 or 902-426-6030
Newfoundland and Labrador	Local Police and 709-772-2083
Northwest Territories	867-920-8130
Nova Scotia	Local Police or 1-800-565-1633 or 902-426-6030
Nunavut	Local Police and 867-920-8130 or 1-800-693-1666
Ontario	Local Police
Prince Edward Island	Local Police or 1-800-565-1633 or 902-426-6030
Quebec	Local Police
Saskatchewan	Local Police or 1-800-667-7525
Yukon Territory	867-667-7244

NOTE:

1. The appropriate federal agency must be notified in the case of rail, air or marine incidents.
2. The nearest police department must be notified in the case of lost, stolen or misplaced explosives, radioactive materials or infectious substances.
3. **CANUTEC must** be notified in the case of:
   a. lost, stolen or unlawfully interfered with dangerous goods (except Class 9);
   b. an incident involving infectious substances;
   c. an accidental release from a cylinder that has suffered a catastrophic failure;
   d. an incident where the shipping documents display **CANUTEC's** telephone number 613-996-6666 as the emergency telephone number; or
   e. a dangerous goods incident in which a railway vehicle, a ship, an aircraft, an aerodrome or an air cargo facility is involved.

UNITED STATES

NATIONAL RESPONSE CENTER (NRC)

The NRC, which is operated by the U.S. Coast Guard, receives reports required when dangerous goods and hazardous substances are spilled. After receiving notification of an incident, the NRC will immediately notify the appropriate Federal On-Scene Coordinator and concerned Federal agencies. Federal law requires that anyone who releases into the environment a reportable quantity of a hazardous substance (including oil when water is, or may be affected) or a material identified as a marine pollutant, must **immediately** notify the NRC. When in doubt as to whether the amount released equals the required reporting levels for these materials, the NRC should be notified.

CALL **NRC** (24 hours)

1-800-424-8802

(Toll-free in the U.S., Canada, and the U.S. Virgin Islands)

202-267-2675 in the District of Columbia

Calling the emergency response telephone number, CHEMTREC®, CHEMTEL, INC., INFOTRAC or 3E COMPANY, does not constitute compliance with regulatory requirements to call the NRC.

EMERGENCY RESPONSE TELEPHONE NUMBERS

MEXICO
1. **SETIQ**

01-800-00-214-00 in the Mexican Republic
For calls originating in Mexico City and the Metropolitan Area
5559-1588
For calls originating elsewhere, call
+52-55-5559-1588

2. **CENACOM**

01-800-00-413-00 in the Mexican Republic
For calls originating in Mexico City and the Metropolitan Area
5128-0000 exts. 11470, 11471, 11472, 11473, 11474, 11475 and 11476
For calls originating elsewhere, call
+52-55-5128-0000 exts. 11470, 11471, 11472, 11474, 11475 and 11476

ARGENTINA
1. **CIQUIME**

0-800-222-2933 in the Republic of Argentina
For calls originating elsewhere, call
+54-11-4613-1100

BRAZIL
1. **PRÓ-QUÍMICA**

0-800-118270
(Toll-free in Brazil)
For calls originating elsewhere, call
+55-11-232-1144
(Collect calls are accepted)

COLOMBIA
1. **CISPROQUIM**

01-800-091-6012 in Colombia
For calls originating in Bogotá, Colombia call
288-6012

For calls originating elsewhere call
+57-1-288-6012

EMERGENCY RESPONSE TELEPHONE NUMBERS

CANADA

1. CANUTEC, provides a 24 hour national bilingual (French and English) emergency response advisory service:

613-996-6666 *

***666 (STAR 666) cellular** (in Canada only)

UNITED STATES

1. CHEMTREC®, a 24 hour emergency response communication service:
1-800-424-9300 *
(Toll-free in the U.S., Canada and the U.S. Virgin Islands)
703-527-3887 For calls originating elsewhere

2. CHEMTEL, INC., a 24 hour emergency response communication service:
1-888-255-3924 *
(Toll-free in the U.S., Canada, Puerto Rico and the U.S. Virgin Islands)
813-248-0585 For calls originating elsewhere

3. INFOTRAC, a 24 hour emergency response communication service:
1-800-535-5053 *
(Toll-free in the U.S., Canada and the U.S. Virgin Islands)
352-323-3500 For calls originating elsewhere

4. 3E COMPANY, a 24 hour emergency response communication service:
1-800-451-8346 *
(Toll-free in the U.S., Canada and the U.S. Virgin Islands)
760-602-8703 For calls originating elsewhere

The emergency response information services shown above have requested to be listed as providers of emergency response information and have agreed to provide emergency response information to all callers. They maintain periodically updated lists of state and Federal radiation authorities who provide information and technical assistance on handling incidents involving radioactive materials.

5. MILITARY SHIPMENTS, for assistance at incidents involving materials being shipped by, for, or to the Department of Defense (DOD), call one of the following numbers (24 hours):
703-697-0218 * - Explosives/ammunition incidents
(U.S. Army Operations Center)
1-800-851-8061 (Toll-free in the U.S.) - All other dangerous goods incidents
(Defense Logistics Agency)

6. NATIONWIDE POISON CONTROL CENTER (United States only)
1-800-222-1222 (Toll-free in the U.S.)

* Collect calls are accepted

NOTES

NOTES

NOTES

NOTES